NX 2022 Tutorial

Online Instructor

Download the resource files by sending us an email to:

Online.books999@gmail.com

Contents

Introduction

NX as a topic of learning is vast and has a broad scope. It is one of the world's most advanced and highly integrated CAD/CAM/CAE product. NX delivers excellent value to enterprises of all sizes by covering the entire range of product development. It speeds up the design process by simplifying intricate product designs.

This tutorial book provides a systematic approach for users to learn NX. It is aimed at those with no previous experience with NX. However, users of previous versions of NX may also find this book useful for them to learn the new enhancements. The user will be guided from starting an NX session to constructing parts, assemblies, and drawings. Each chapter has components explained with the help of various dialogs and screen images.

Scope of this Book

This book is written for students and engineers who are interested to learn NX for designing mechanical components and assemblies, and then generate drawings.

This book provides a systematic approach to learning NX. The topics include Getting Started with NX, Basic Part Modeling, Constructing Assemblies, Constructing Drawings, Additional Modeling Tools, and Sheet Metal Modeling.

Chapter 1: Introduces NX. The user interface, terminology, mouse functions, and shortcut keys are discussed in this chapter.

Chapter 2: Takes you through the creation of your first NX model. You construct simple parts.

Chapter 3: Teaches you to construct assemblies. It explains the Top-down and Bottom-up approaches for designing an assembly. You construct an assembly using the Bottom-up approach.

Chapter 4 teaches you to generate drawings of the models constructed in the earlier chapters. You will also learn to generate exploded views and part list of an assembly.

Chapter 5: In this chapter, you will learn the tools needed to create 2D sketches.

Chapter 6: In this chapter, you will learn additional modeling tools to construct complex models.

Chapter 7: This chapter helps you to create, edit, and use expressions in your designs.

Chapter 8: introduces you to NX Sheet Metal design. You will construct a sheet metal part using the tools available in the NX Sheet Metal environment.

Chapter 9: teaches you to create an assembly using Top-down design approach.

Chapter 10: teaches you to add dimensions and annotations to your drawings.

Chapter 11: introduces you to Finite Element Analysis.

Chapter 12: teaches you to add Product and Manufacturing Information to 3D models

Chapter 13: teaches you to add materials and scene to models. Also, it helps you to render photorealistic images.

Chapter 1: Getting Started

In this chapter, you learn some of the most commonly used features of NX. Also, you learn about the user interface.

In NX, you construct 3D parts and use them to generate 2D drawings and 3D assemblies.

NX is Feature Based. Features are shapes that are combined to build a part. You can modify these shapes individually. For example, the following figure shows a part built using the Extrude and Hole features.

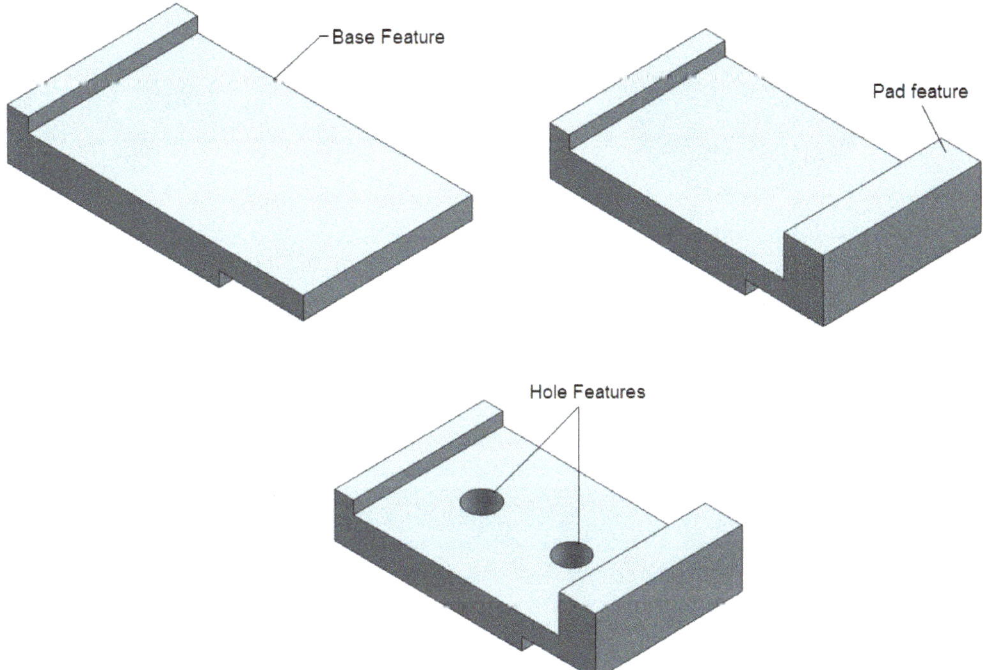

Most of the features are sketch-based. A sketch is a 2D profile and can be extruded, revolved, or swept along a path to construct features.

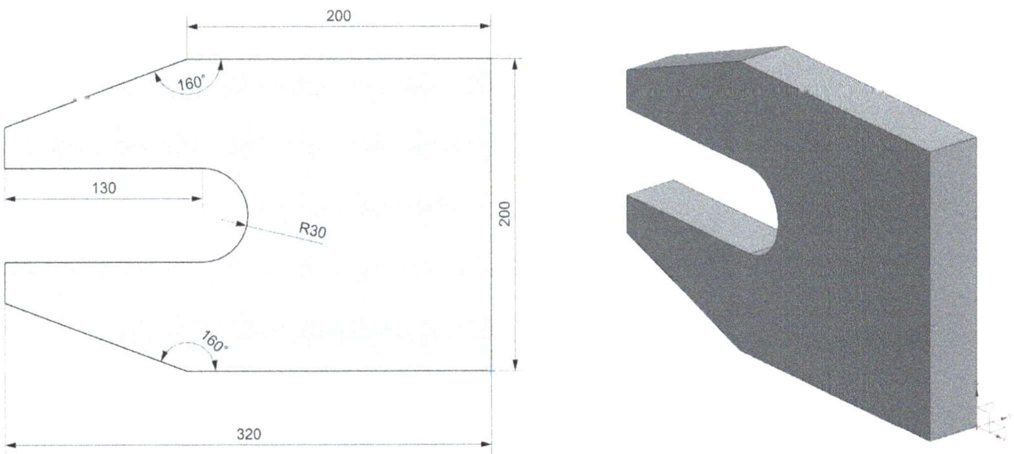

NX is parametric. You can specify standard parameters between the elements of a part. Changing these parameters changes the size and shape of the part. For example, see the design of the body of a flange before and after modifying the parameters of its features.

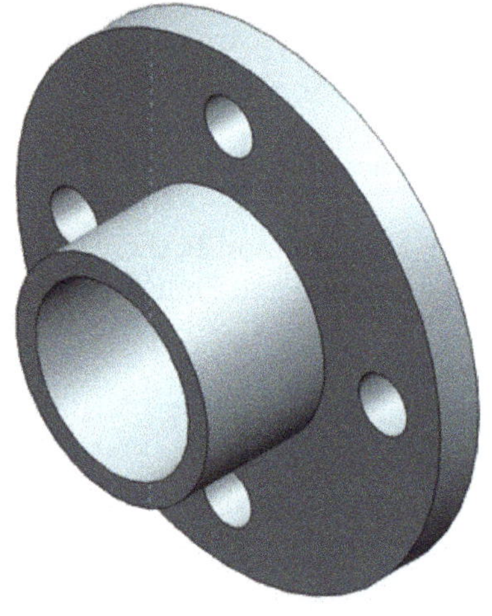

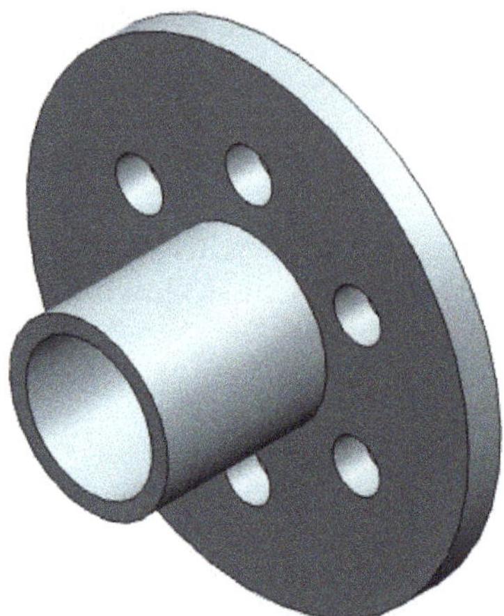

Starting NX

1. Click the Windows button on the taskbar.
2. Scroll down to the **S** section.
3. Click **Siemens NX > NX**.
4. Click **Home** tab > **New** button on the ribbon.
5. On the **New** dialog, click **Templates > Model**.
6. Click the **OK** button.

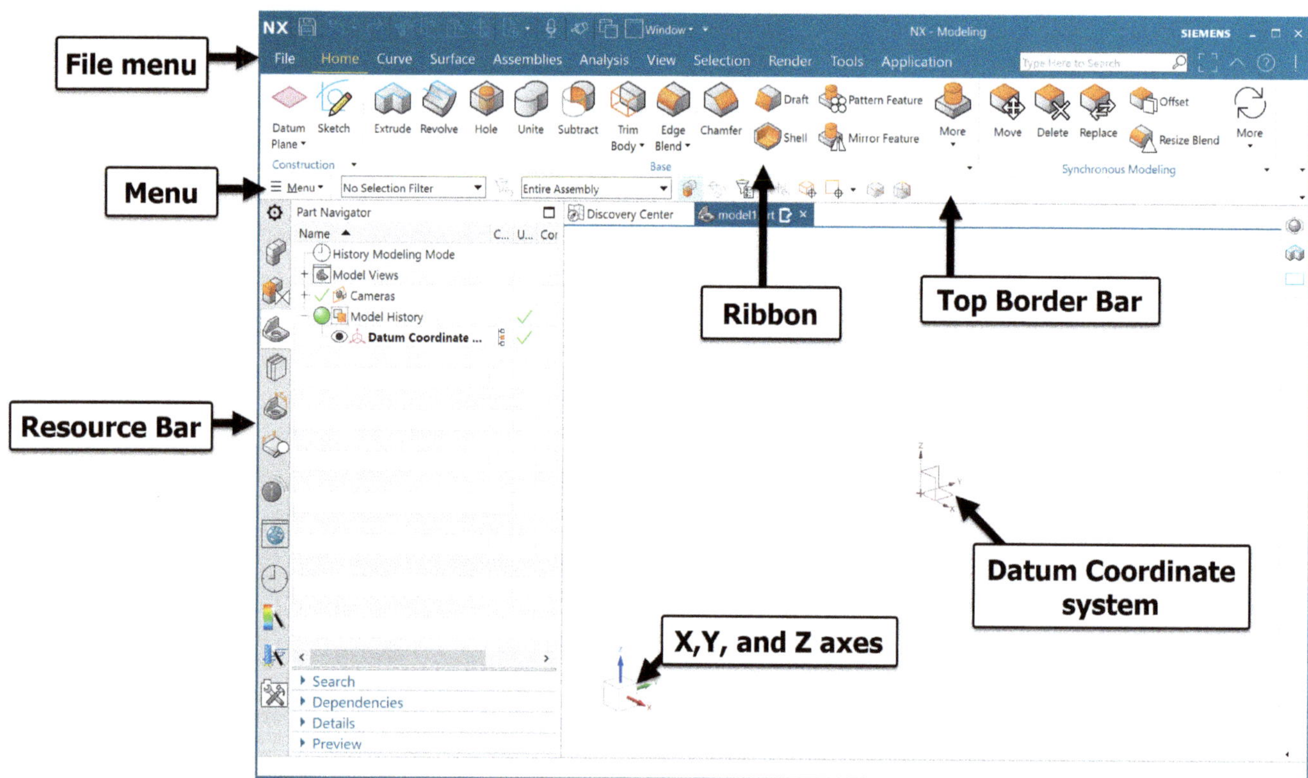

Notice these essential features of the NX window.

User Interface

Various components of the user interface are discussed next.

Quick Access Toolbar

The Quick Access Toolbar is located at the top left corner of the window. It consists of the commonly used commands such as **Save**, **Undo, Redo,** and **Copy**.

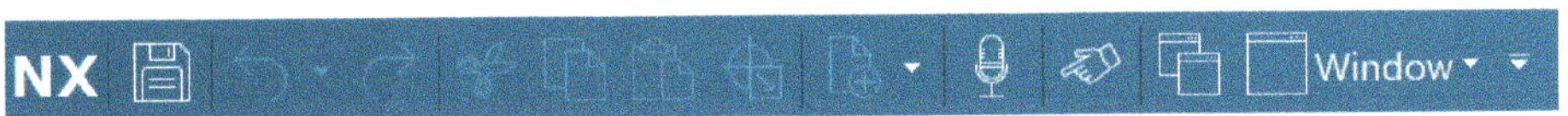

File Menu

The **File Menu** appears when you click on the **File** icon located at the top left corner of the window. The **File Menu** consists of a list of open menus. You can see a list of recently opened documents under the **Recently Opened Parts** section. You can also switch to different applications of NX.

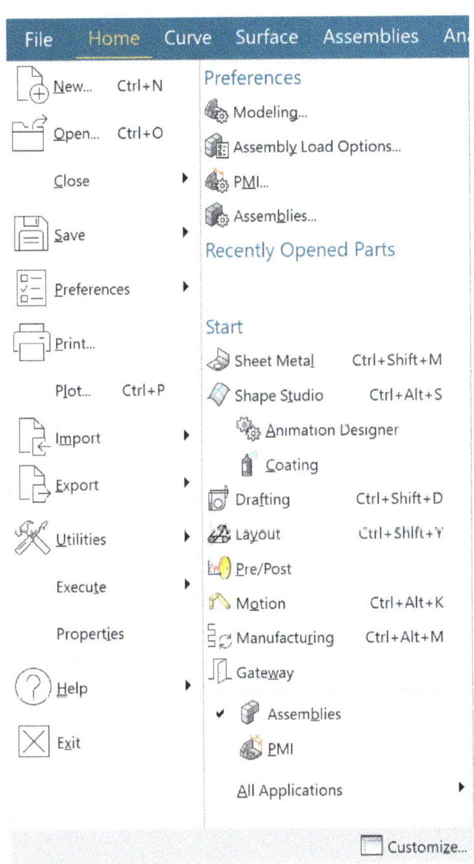

Ribbon

A ribbon is a set of tools, which are used to perform various operations. It is divided into tabs and groups. Various tabs of the ribbon are discussed next.

Home tab

This ribbon tab contains tools such as **New**, **Open**, and **Help**.

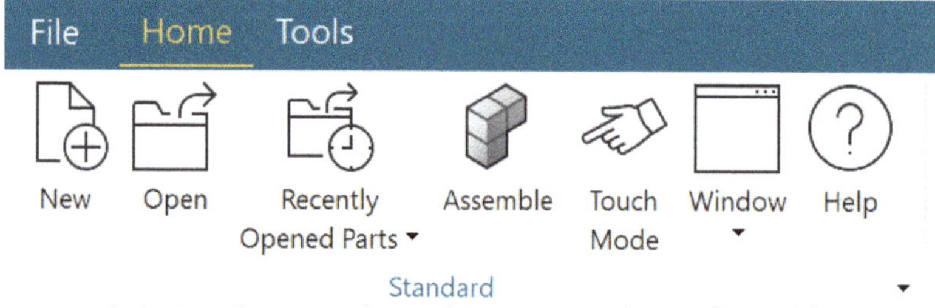

Home tab in the Model template

This ribbon tab contains the tools to construct 3D features.

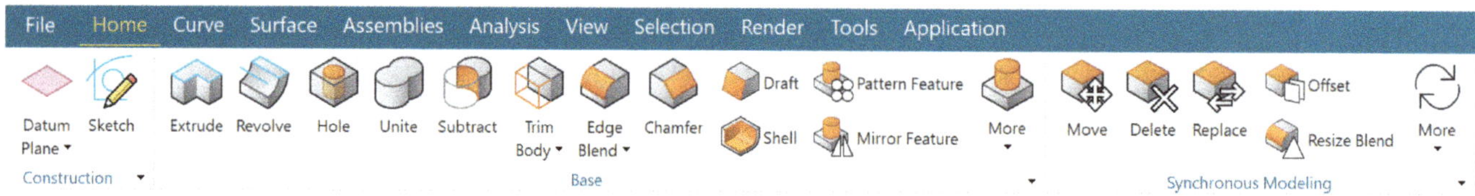

View tab

This ribbon tab contains the tools to modify the display of the model and user interface.

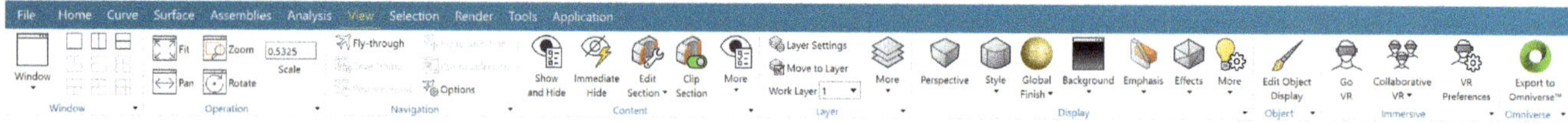

Analysis tab

This ribbon tab has the tools to measure the objects. It also has tools to analyze the draft, curvature, and surface.

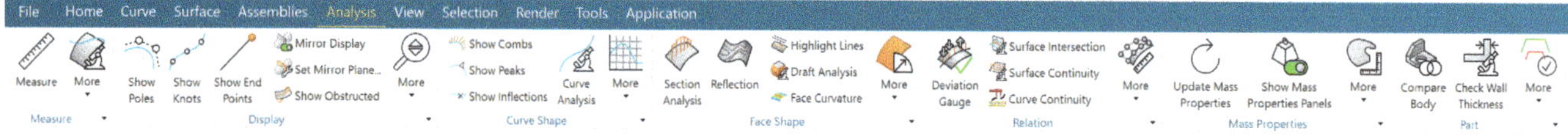

Home tab in Sketch Task environment

This ribbon tab contains all the sketch tools. It is available in a separate environment called the Sketch Task environment. The Sketch Task environment is activated when you activate a Feature modeling tool and click on a planar face or Datum plane.

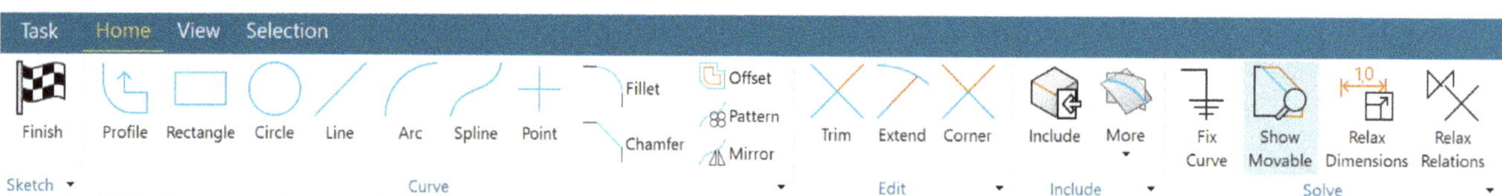

Tools tab

This ribbon tab contains the tools to create expressions, part families, movies, fasteners.

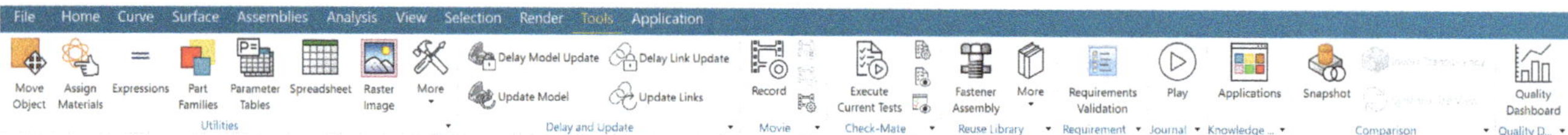

Render tab

This ribbon tab contains the tools to generate photorealistic images.

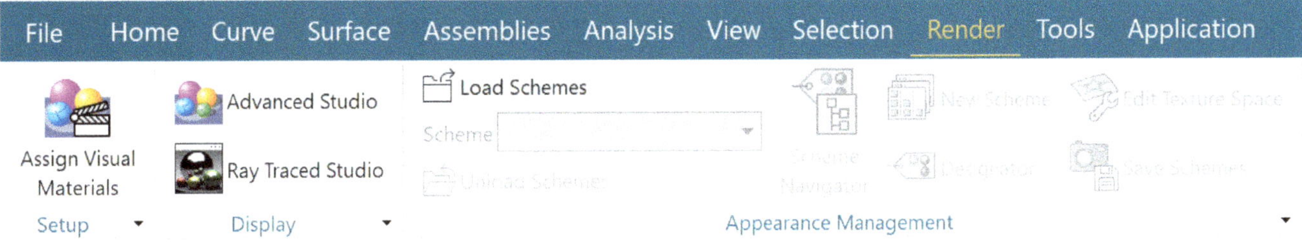

Application tab

This ribbon tab contains the tools to start different applications such as Assemblies, Sheet Metal, and Drafting.

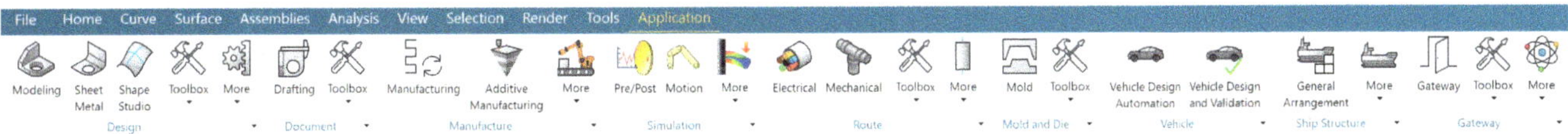

Assemblies tab

This tab contains the tools to construct an assembly. It is available in the **Assembly** and **Model** template.

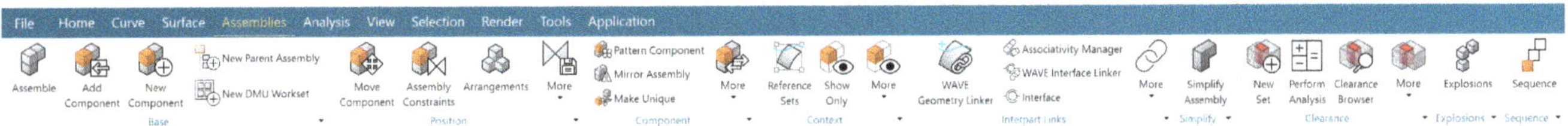

Drafting environment ribbon

In the Drafting Environment, you can generate orthographic views of the 3D model. The ribbon tabs in this environment contain tools to generate 2D drawings.

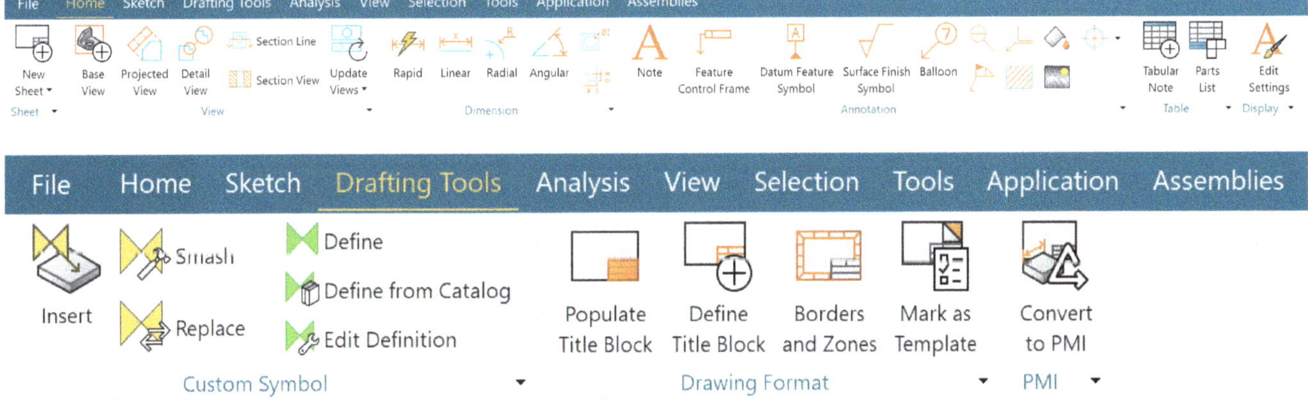

Sheet Metal ribbon

The tools in this ribbon are used to construct sheet metal components.

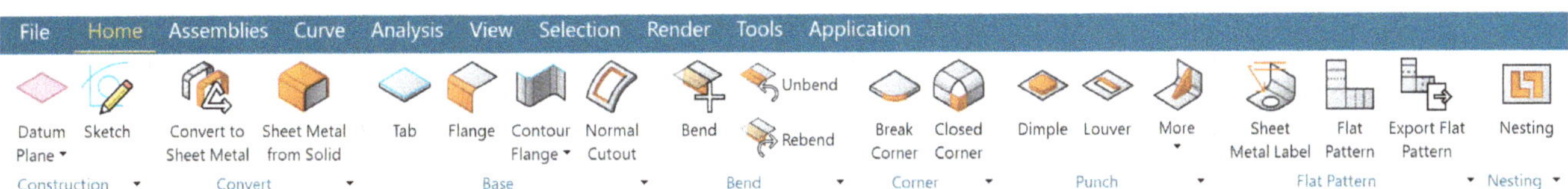

Some tabs are not visible by default. To display a particular tab, right-click on the ribbon and select it from the list displayed.

You can also add a ribbon tab by opening the **Customize** dialog. Click the down arrow located at the bottom right corner of the ribbon and select **Customize**. On the **Customize** dialog, click on different tabs and select/deselect the options.

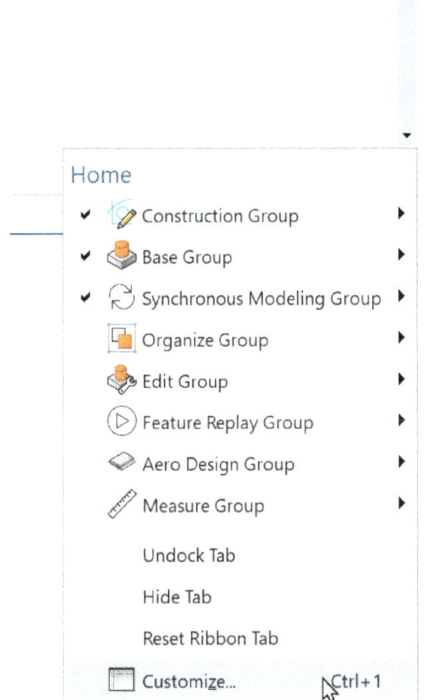

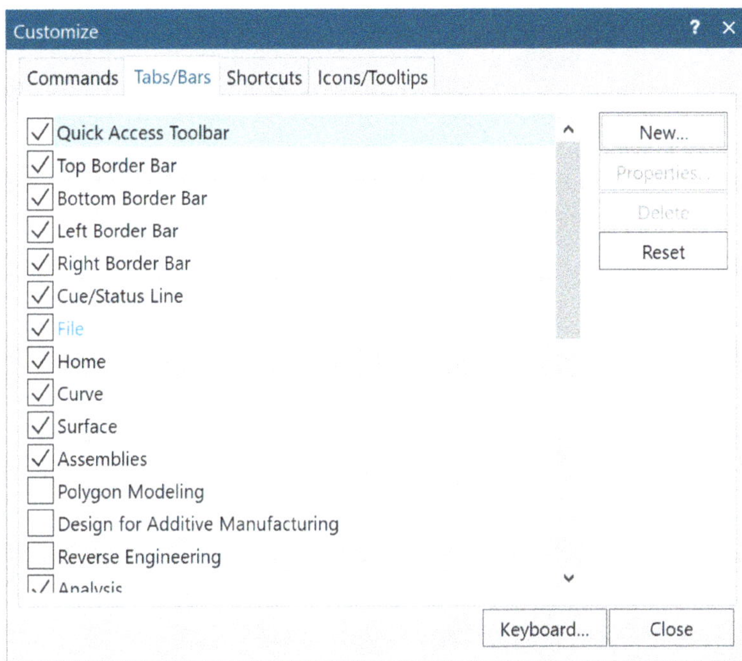

Ribbon Groups and More Galleries

The tools on a ribbon are arranged in various groups depending upon their use. Each group has a **More Gallery**, which contains additional tools.

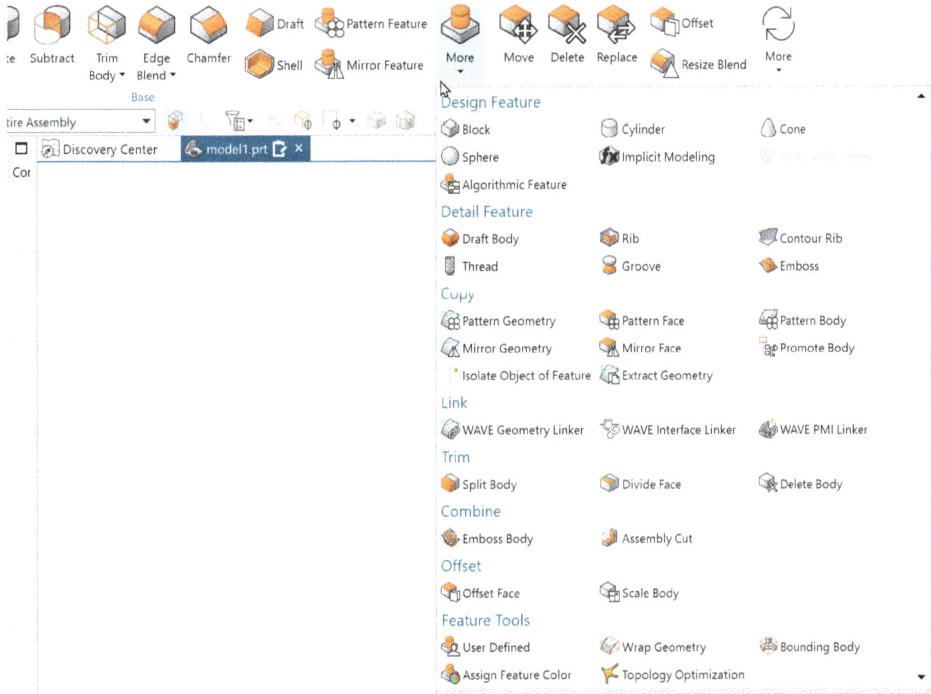

You can add more tools to a ribbon group by clicking the arrow located at the bottom right corner of a group.

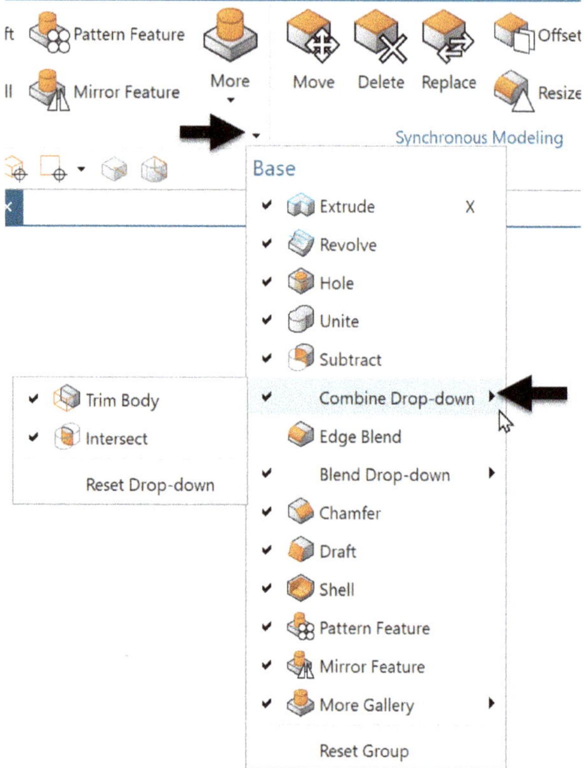

Top Border Bar

The Top Border Bar is available below the ribbon. It consists of all the options to filter the objects that can be selected from the graphics window.

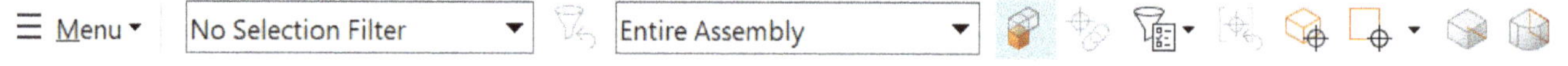

Menu

The menu is located on the Top Border Bar. It consists of various options (menu titles). When you click on a menu title, a drop-down appears. You can select the required option from this drop-down.

Status bar

The Status bar is available below the graphics window. It displays the prompts and the action taken while using the tools.

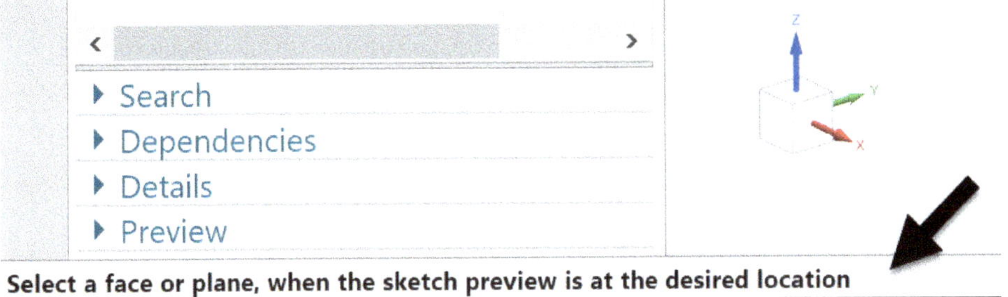

Resource Bar

The Resource Bar is located on the left side of the window. It contains all the navigator windows such as Assembly Navigator, Constraint Navigator, and Part Navigator.

Part Navigator

It contains the list of operations carried while constructing a part.

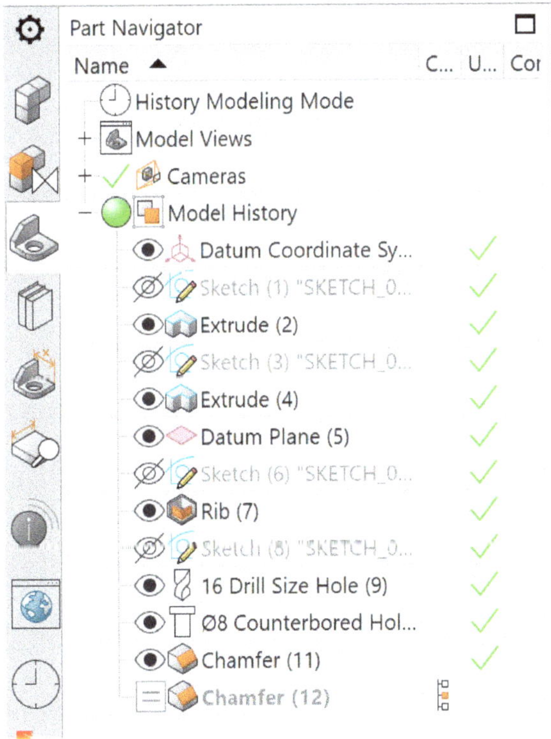

Roles Navigator

The Roles Navigator (click the **Roles** tab on the **Resource Bar**) contains a list of system default and industry-specific roles. A role is a set of tools and ribbon tabs customized for a specific application. For example, the **CAM Essentials** role can be used for performing manufacturing operations. This textbook uses the **Advanced** role.

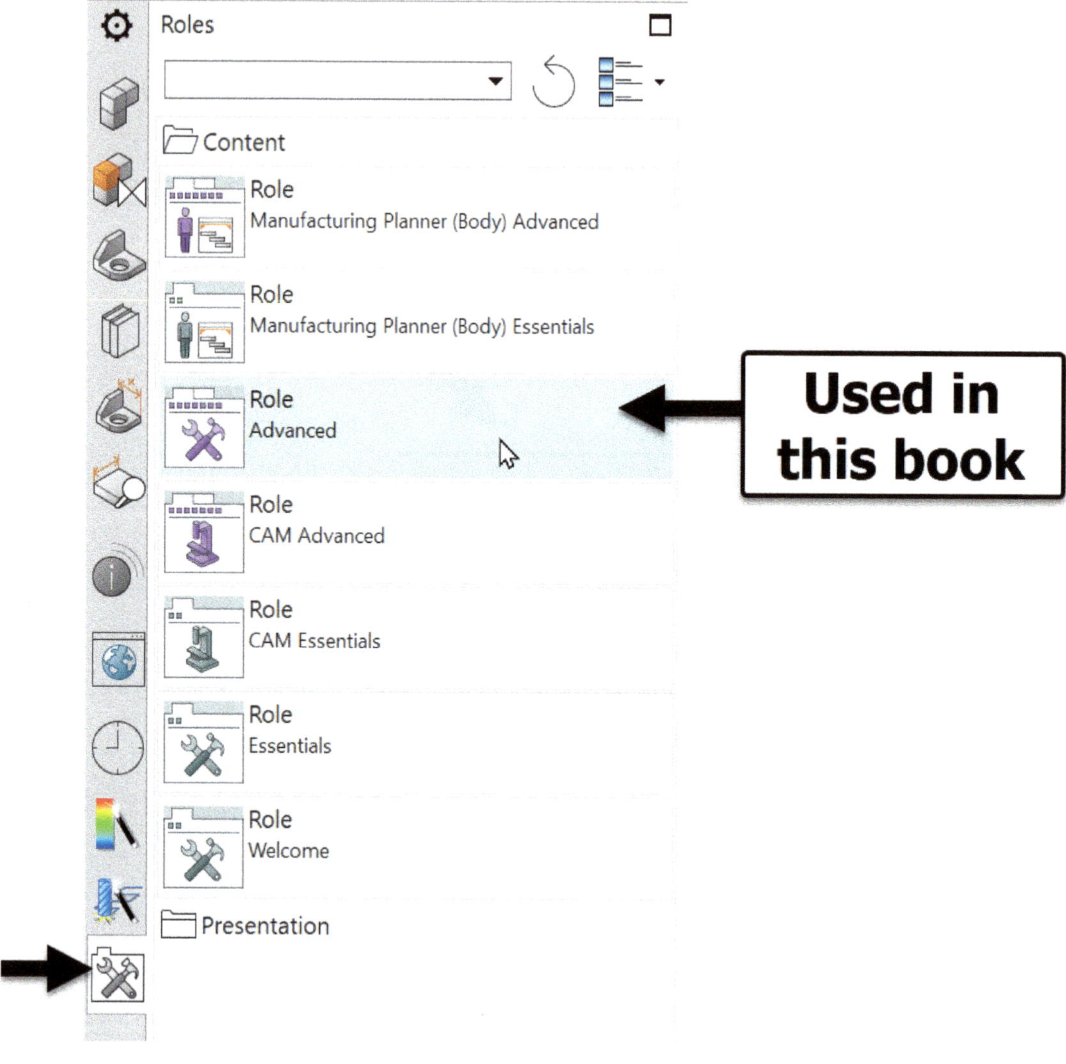

High Definition

The High Definition role displays extra-large icons on the screen. It is suitable for 4K high definition monitors.

The Touch Panel and Touch Tablet roles help you to work with a Multi-touch screen.

Touch Panel

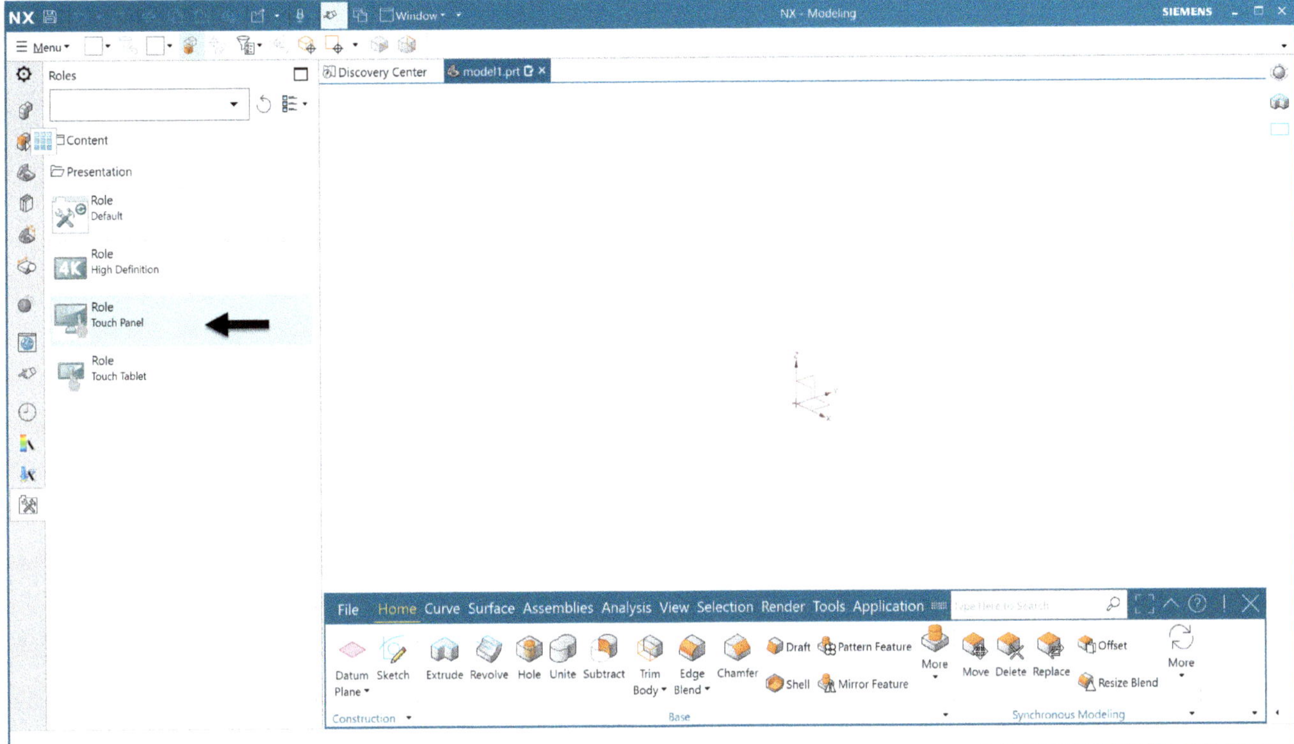

Touch Tablet

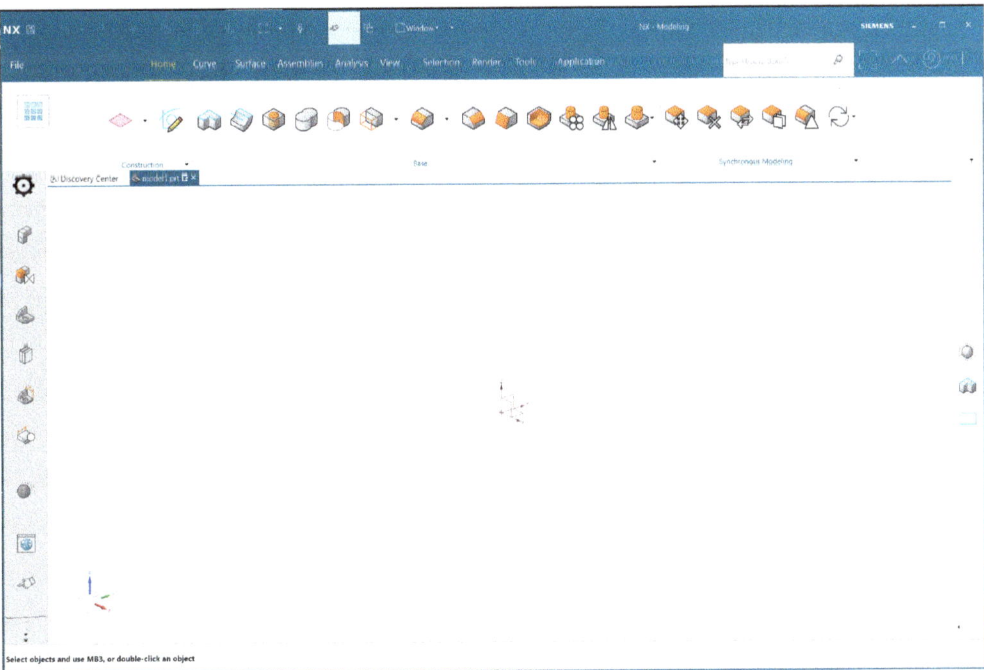

Predict Commands Toolbar

The **Predict Commands** Toolbar is located at the right side of the graphics window and displays the most commonly used commands.

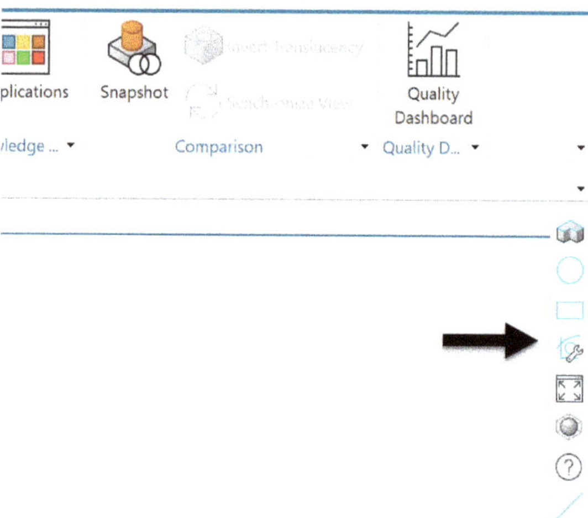

Dialogs

When you execute any command in NX, the dialog related to it appears. The dialog consists of various options. The following figure shows various components of the dialog.

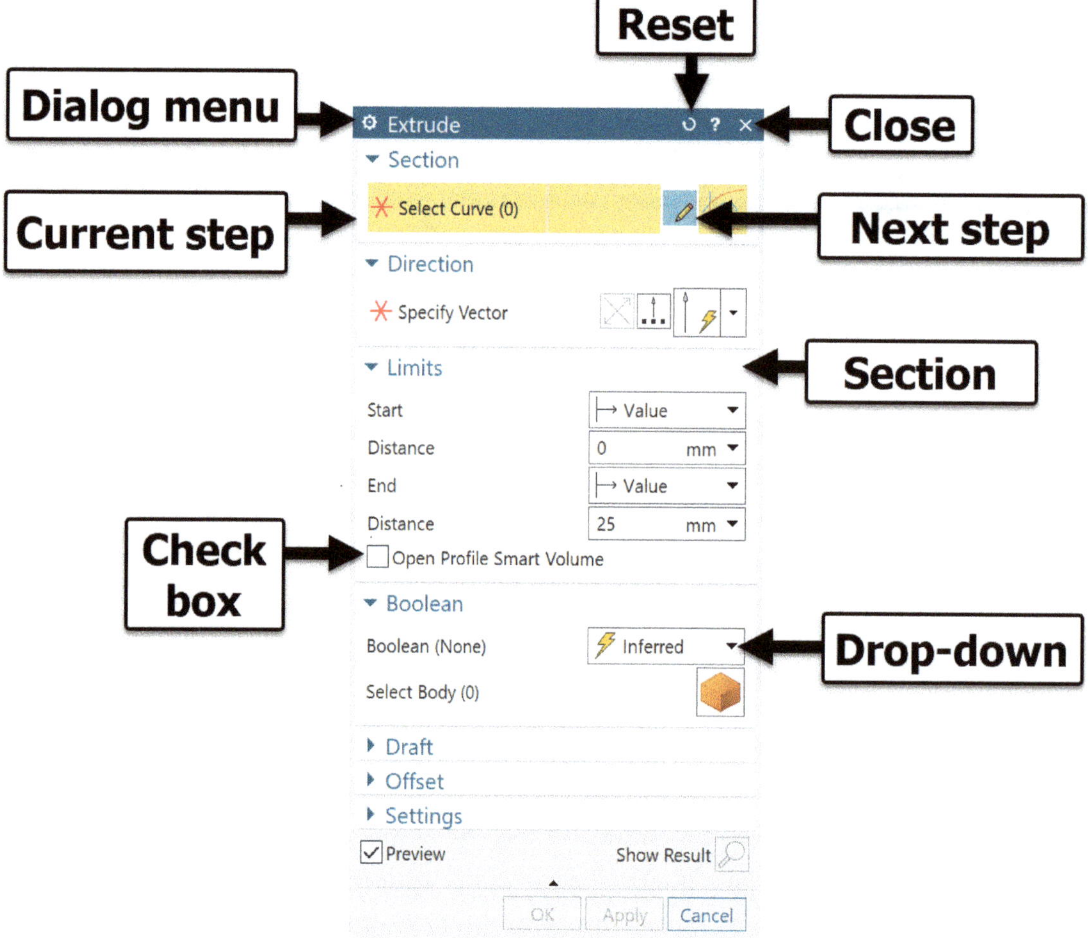

This textbook uses the default options in the dialog. If you have made any changes to the dialog, click the **Reset** button to display the default options.

Mouse Functions

Various functions of the mouse buttons are discussed next.

Left Mouse button (MB1)

When you double-click the left mouse button (MB1) on an object, the dialog related to the object appears. Using this dialog, you can edit the parameters of the objects.

Middle Mouse button (MB2)

Click this button to execute the **OK** command.

Right Mouse button (MB3)

Click this button to display the shortcut menu.

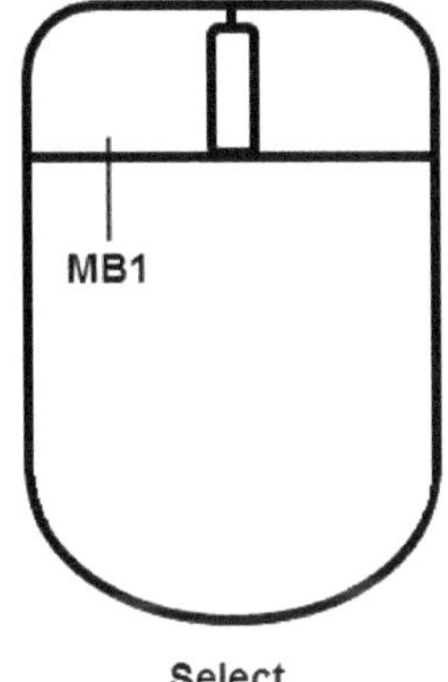

Select

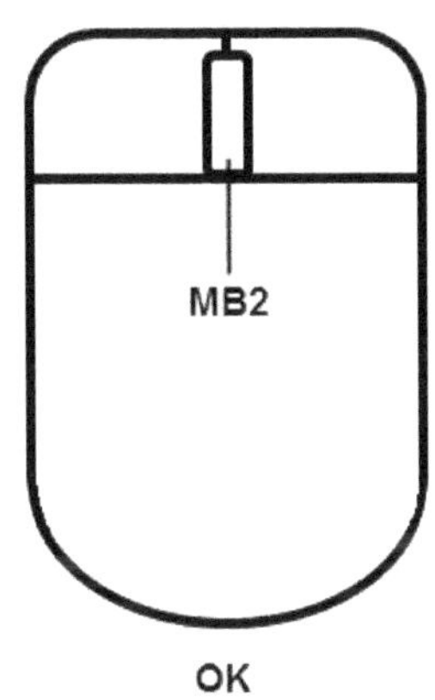

OK

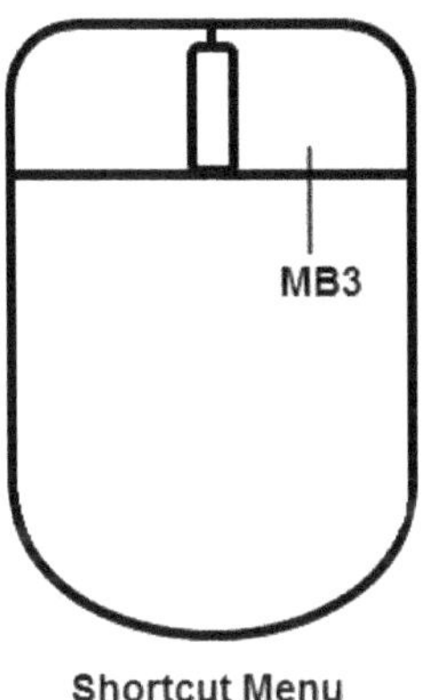

Shortcut Menu

The other functions with a combination of the three mouse buttons are given next.

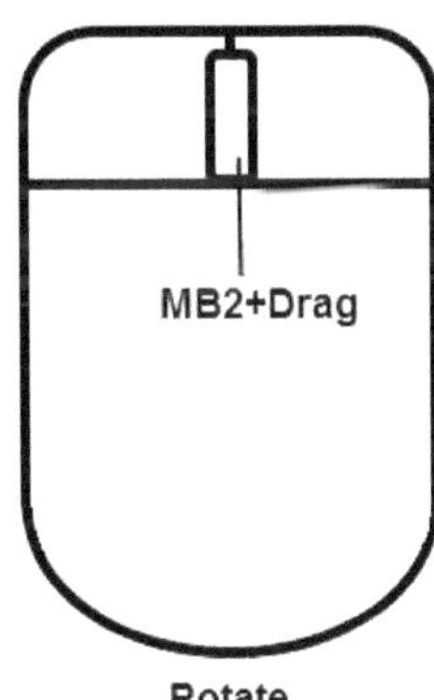

Rotate

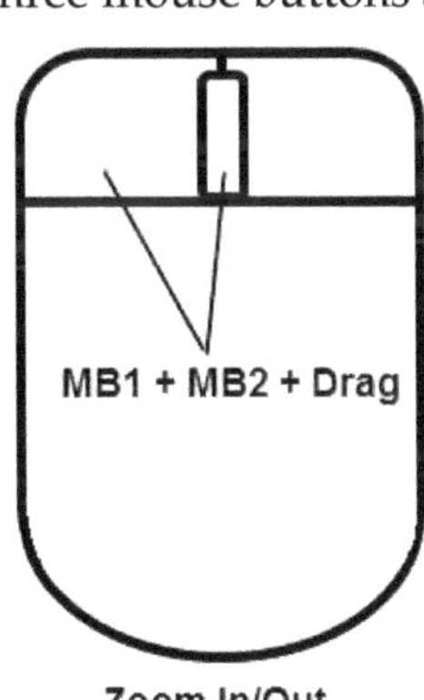

Zoom In/Out

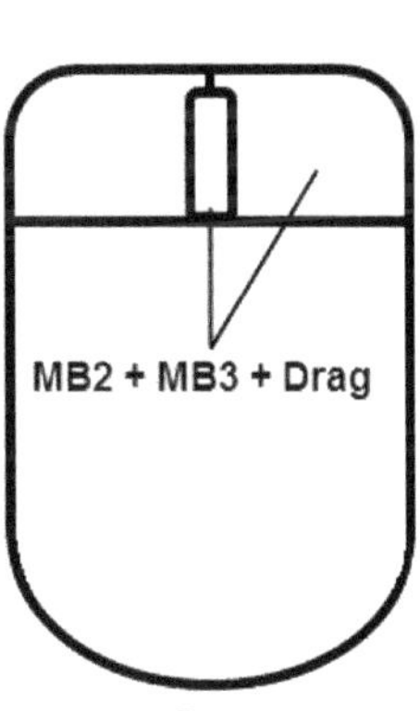

Pan

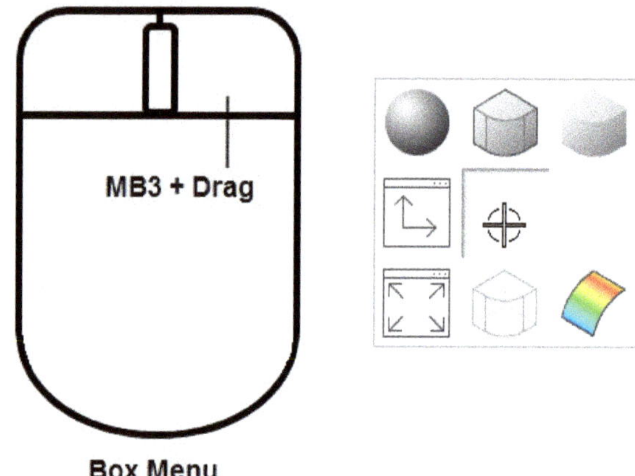

Changing the Background

To change the background color of the window, select an option from the **Background** drop-down located on the **Display** group of the **View** tab of the ribbon.

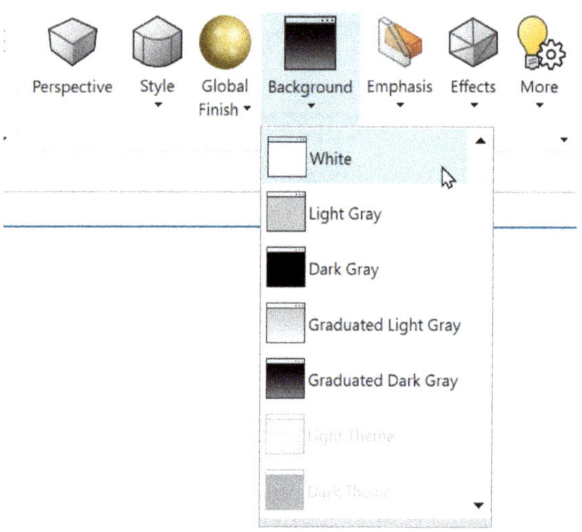

Shortcut Keys

CTRL+Z	(Undo)
CTRL+Y	(Repeat)
CTRL+S	(Save)
F5	(Refresh)
F1	(NX Help)
CTRL+M	(Starts the Modeling environment)
CTRL+SHIFT+D	(Starts the Drafting environment)
CTRL+SHIFT+M	(Starts the NX Sheet Metal environment)
CTRL+ALT+M	(Starts the Manufacturing environment)
X	(Extrude)
CTRL+1	(Customize)
CTRL+D	(Delete)
CTRL+N	(New File)
CTRL+O	(Open File)
CTRL+P	(Plot)

Chapter 2: Modeling Basics

This chapter takes you through the creation of your first NX model. You construct simple parts using NX modeling commands:

In this chapter, you will:

- Construct Sketches
- Construct a base feature
- Add another feature to it
- Construct revolved features
- Apply draft

TUTORIAL 1

This tutorial takes you through the creation of your first NX model. You construct the Disc of an Old ham coupling:

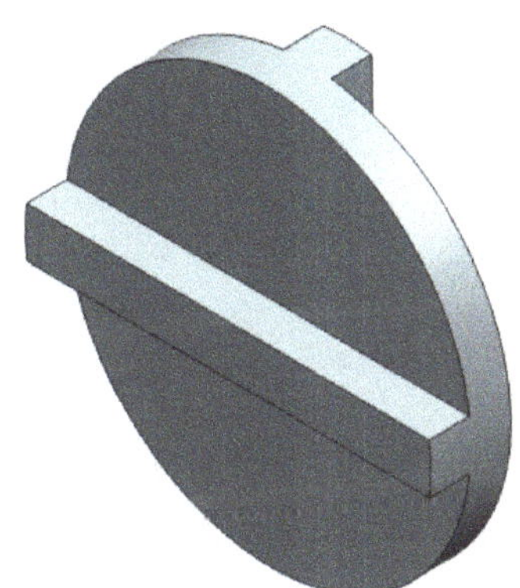

Starting a New Part File

1. To start a new part, click the **New** button on the ribbon; the **New** dialog appears.
2. The **Model** template is the default selection, so click **OK**; a new model window appears.

Starting a Sketch

1. To start a new sketch, click the **Sketch** button on the **Construction** group; the **Create Sketch** dialog appears.

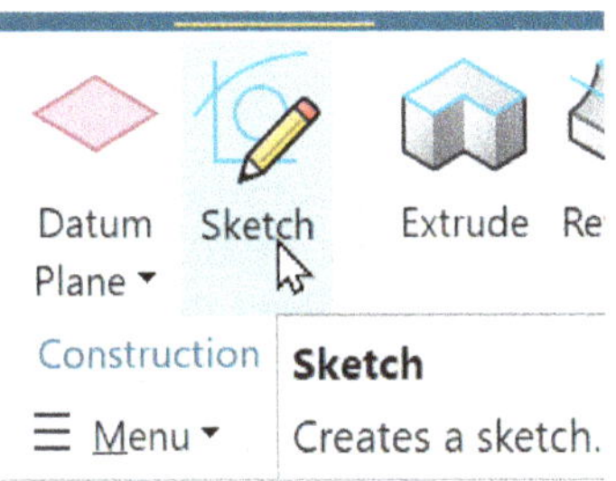

2. Select the Front plane.

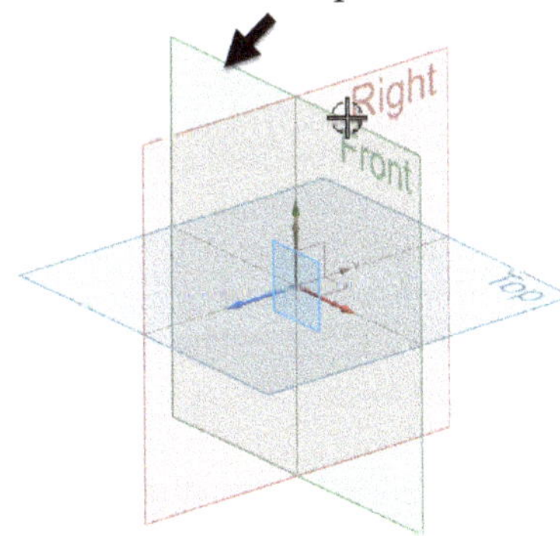

3. Click the **OK** button on the **Create Sketch** dialog; the sketch starts.

The first feature is an extruded feature created from a sketched circular profile. You will begin by sketching the circle.

4. Click **Circle** on the **Curve** group.
5. Select the sketch origin.
6. Drag the pointer and click to draw a circle.

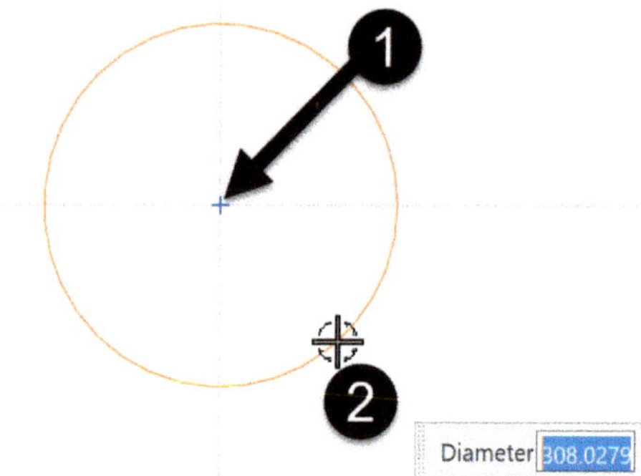

7. Press **ESC** to quit the tool.

Adding Dimensions

In this section, you will specify the size of the sketched circle by adding dimensions.

As you add dimensions, the sketch can attain any one of the following three states:

Fully Constrained sketch: In a fully constrained sketch, the positions of all the entities are fully described by dimensions or constraints or both. In a fully constrained sketch, all the entities are in dark green.

Under Constrained sketch: Additional dimensions or constraints or both are needed to define the geometry completely. In this state, you can drag the sketch elements to modify the sketch. An under constrained sketch element is in maroon color.

Over Constrained sketch: In this state, an object has conflicting dimensions or constraints or both. An over constrained sketch entity is grey. The over constraining dimensions are in red.

1. Select the circle; a dimension is displayed.

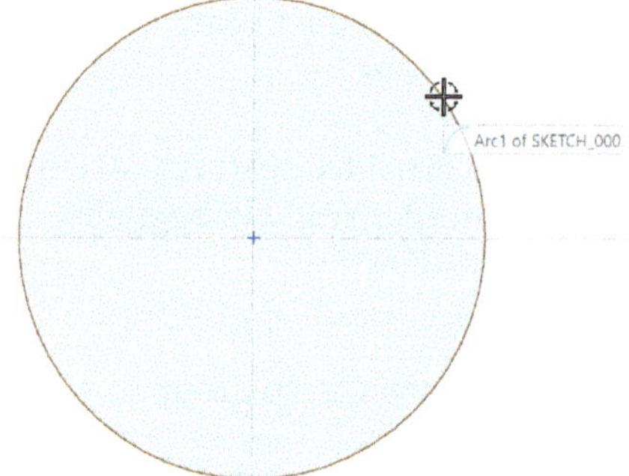

2. Double-click on the dimension displayed on the sketch; the **Dimension** edit box appears.
3. To change the dimension to 100 mm, type the value in the **Dimension** edit box, and then press Enter.
4. Click **Yes** on the message box displayed.

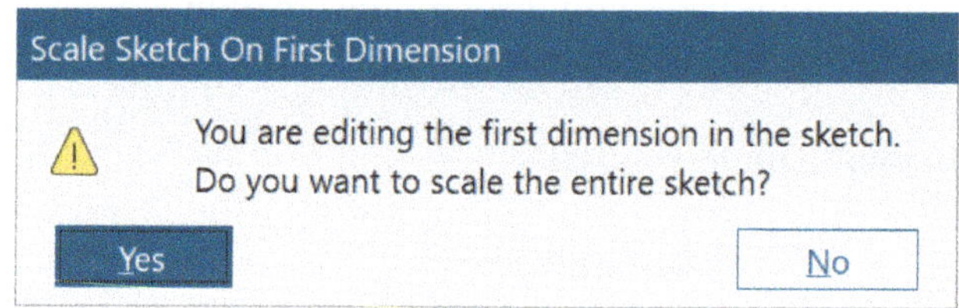

5. On the ribbon, click **Home > Sketch > Finish** .
6. To display the entire circle at full size and to center it in the graphics area, click **Fit** on the **Operation** group of the **View** ribbon tab.

Constructing the Base Feature

The first feature in any part is called the base feature. In this example, you construct this feature by extruding the sketched circle.

1. On the ribbon, **Home > Base > Extrude** ; the **Extrude** dialog appears.
2. Click on the sketch.
3. Type-in **10** in the **End** box attached to the preview.
4. To see how the model would look if you have extruded the sketch in the opposite direction, click the **Reverse Direction** button in the **Direction** section. Again, click on it to extrude the sketch in the front direction.
5. Ensure that **Body Type** in the **Settings** group is set to **Solid**.

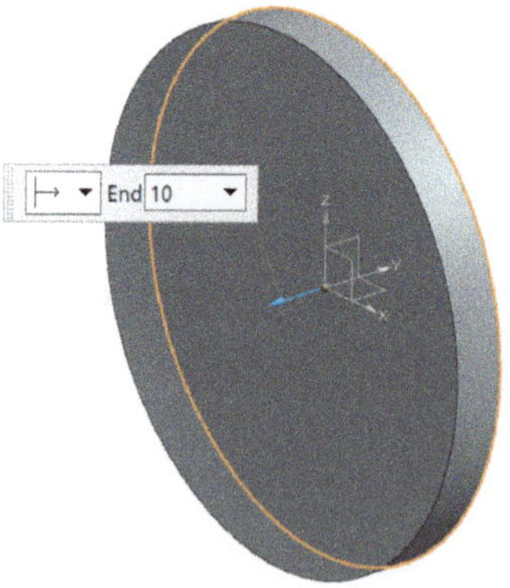

6. Click **OK** to construct the extrusion.

Notice the new feature, Extrude, in the **Part Navigator**.

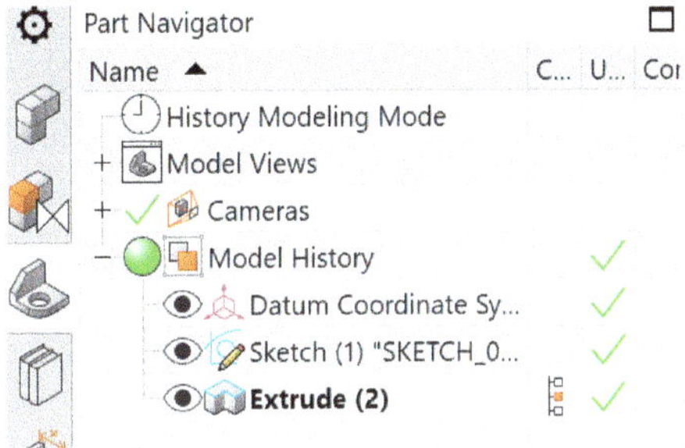

To magnify a model in the graphics area, you can use the tools on the **Operation** group of the **View** tab of the ribbon.

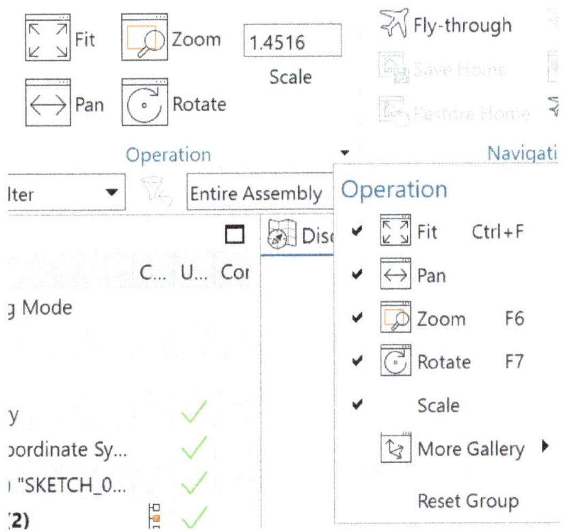

Click **Zoom**, and then drag the pointer to draw a rectangle; the area in the rectangle zooms to fill the window.

Click **Zoom In/Out**, and then drag the pointer. Dragging up zooms out, dragging down zooms in. Note that this command is available on the **More** gallery.

Type in a value in the **Zoom Scale** box located on the **Zoom** group; the model in the graphics window is zoomed based on the value that you enter.

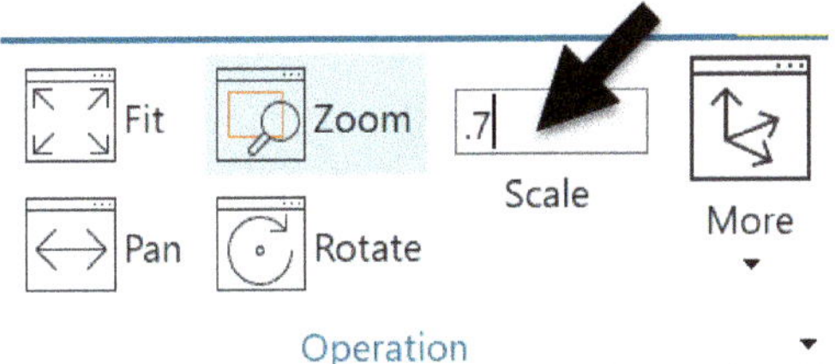

Click **Fit** to display the full part size in the current window.

Click a vertex, an edge, or a feature, and then click **Fit View to Selection**; the selected item zooms to fill the window.

To display the part in different modes, select the an option from the **Style** drop-down on the **Display** group of the **View** tab of the ribbon.

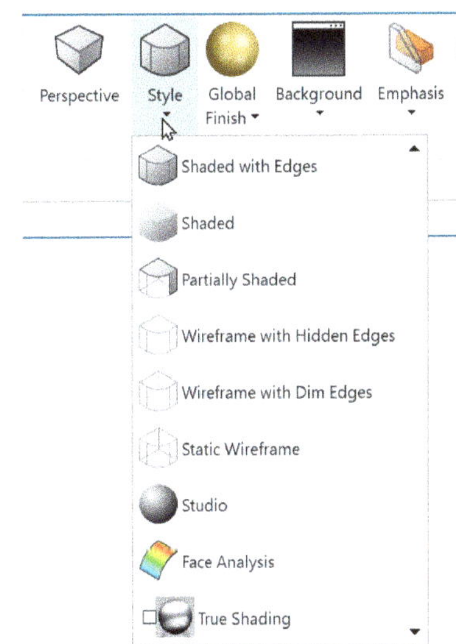

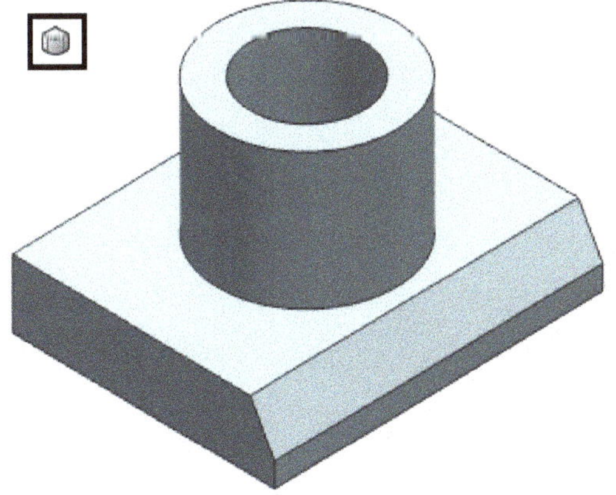

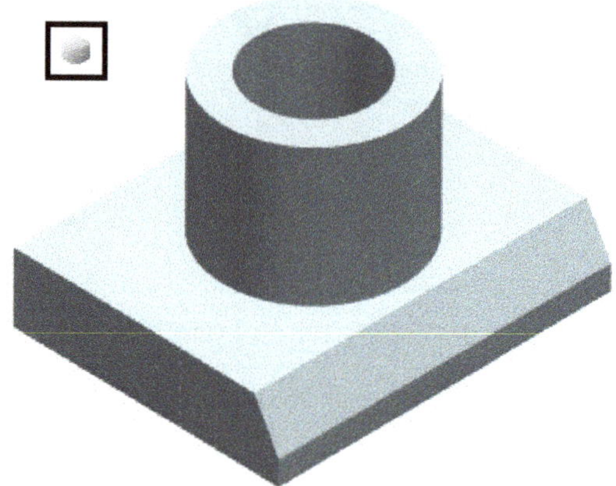

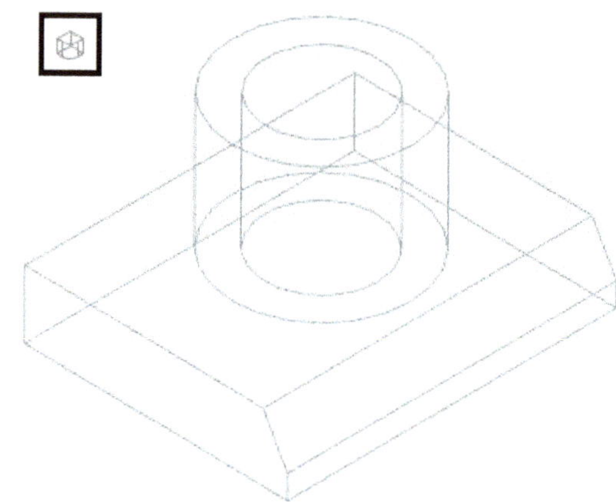

The default display mode for parts and assemblies is **Shaded with Edges**. You may change the display mode whenever you want.

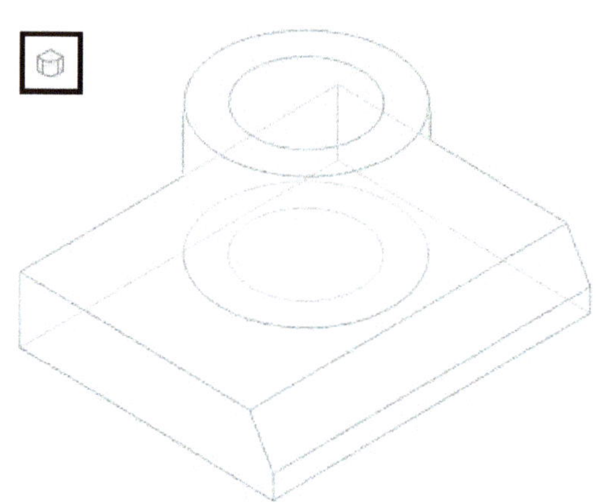

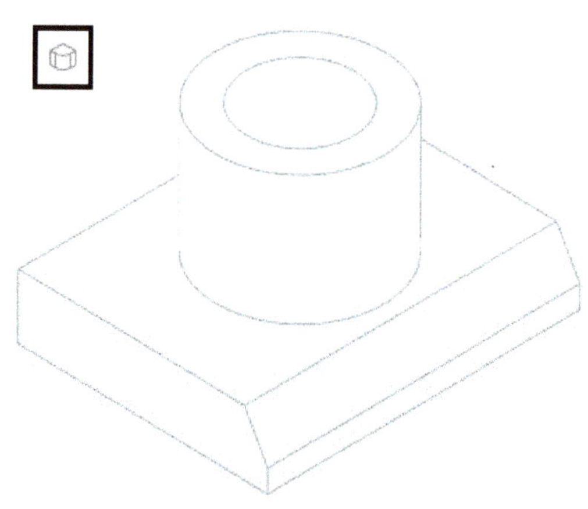

Adding an Extruded Feature

To construct additional features on the part, you need to sketch on the model faces or planes, and then convert them into features.

1. Select **Static Wireframe** from the **Style** drop-down on the **Display** group of the **View** tab of the ribbon.
2. Click **Sketch** on the **Construction** group of the **Home** ribbon tab.
3. Click on the front face of the part to select it, and then click **OK**.
4. Click **Home > Include > More > Project Curve** on the ribbon; the **Project Curve** dialog appears.
5. Click on the circular edge.

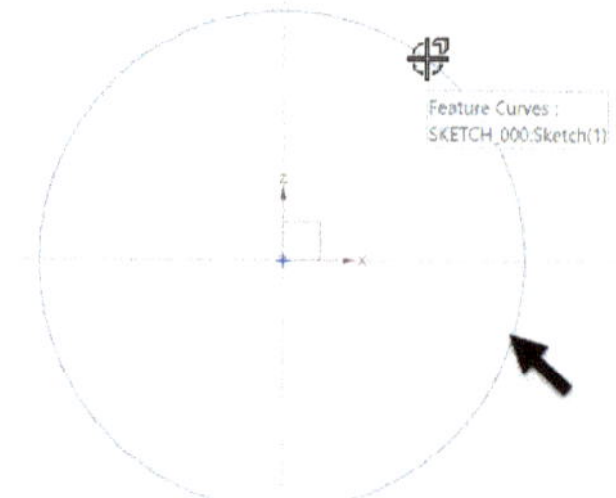

6. Click **OK** on the **Project Curve** dialog; the circular edge projects onto the sketch plane.
7. Click **Line** on the **Curve** group.
8. Click on the circle to specify the first point of the line.

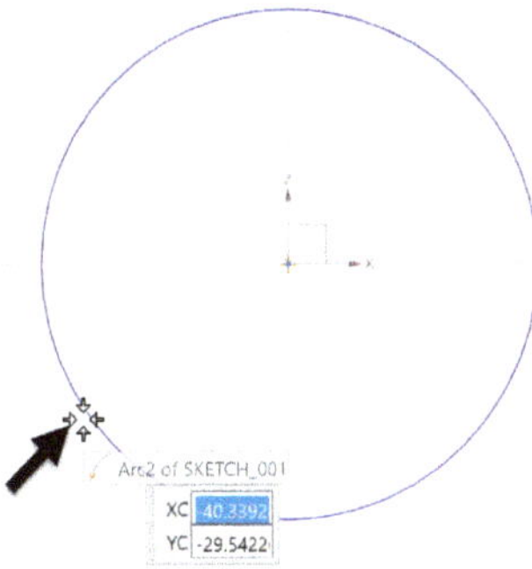

9. Move the pointer towards the right.
10. Click on the circle; a line is drawn.

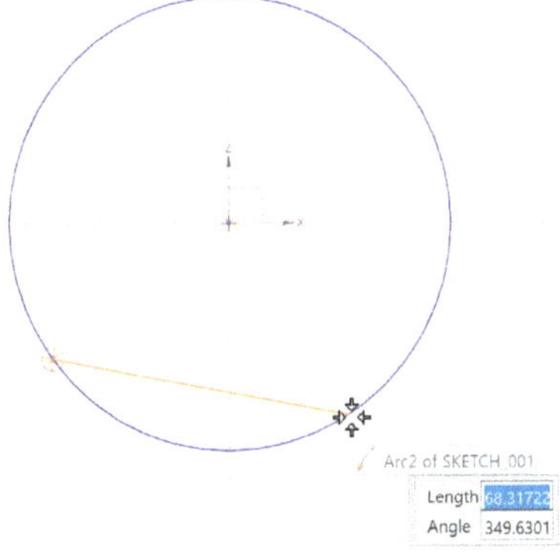

11. Draw another line above the previous line.
12. Press **Esc**.

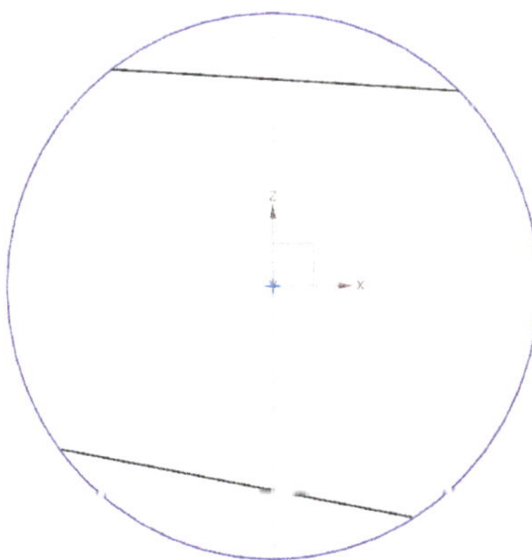

Adding Constraints and Dimensions to the Sketch

To establish the location and size of the sketch, you have to add the necessary constraints and dimensions.

1. Select the two lines.
2. On the **Sketch Scene bar**, click **Horizontal**.

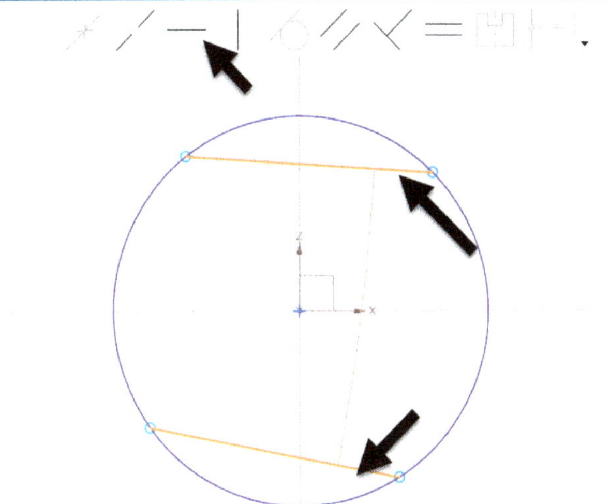

3. On the **Sketch Scene bar**, click **Make Symmetric**  .
4. Select the first and second lines.
5. Select the Horizontal axis as the symmetry line.

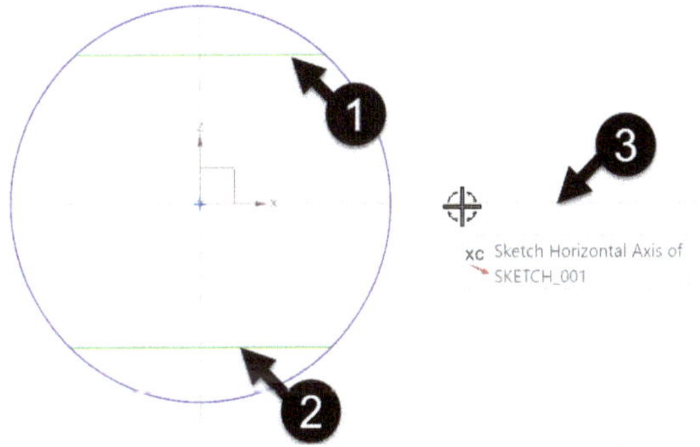

6. Click **OK** on the **Make Symmetric** dialog; the two lines become symmetric about the X-axis.

Adding Dimension

1. Select the two horizontal lines.
2. Double-click on the dimension displayed in the sketch.

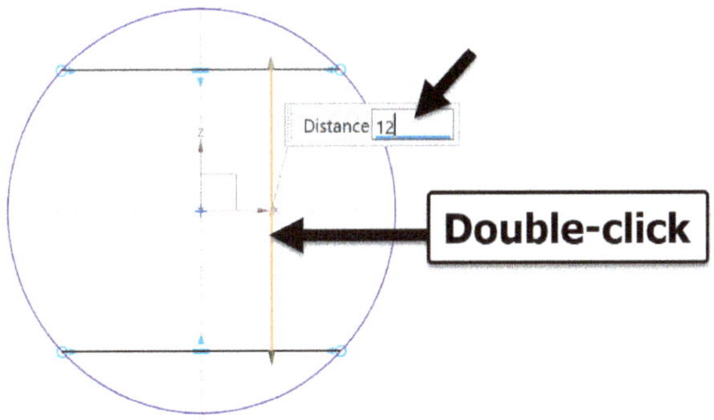

3. Type-in **12** in the box displayed.
4. Press ENTER and then ESC.

Trimming Sketch Entities

1. Click **Trim** on the **Edit** group.
2. Click on the portion of the projected element, as shown.

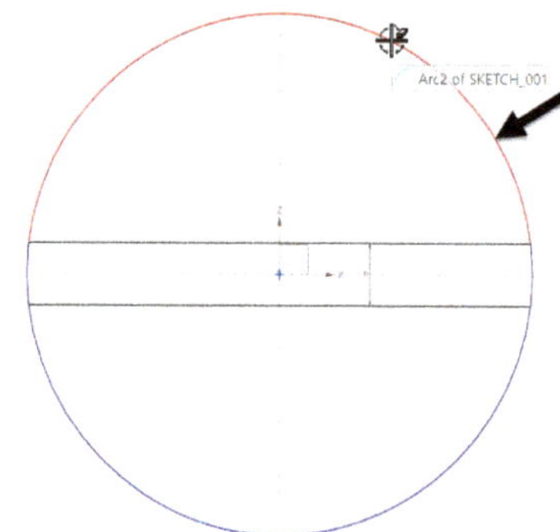

3. Click **OK** to trim the projected element.
4. Select the lower portion of the projected element.
5. Click **Close** on the **Trim** dialog.

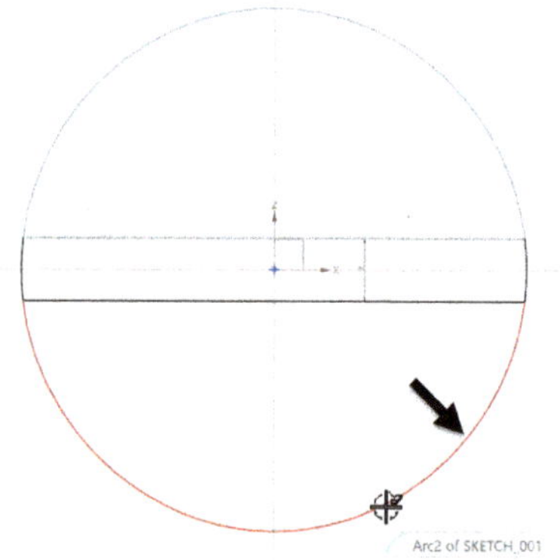

6. Select the left arc of the drawing.
7. Double-click on the radial dimension displayed.
8. Type 50 and press ENTER.

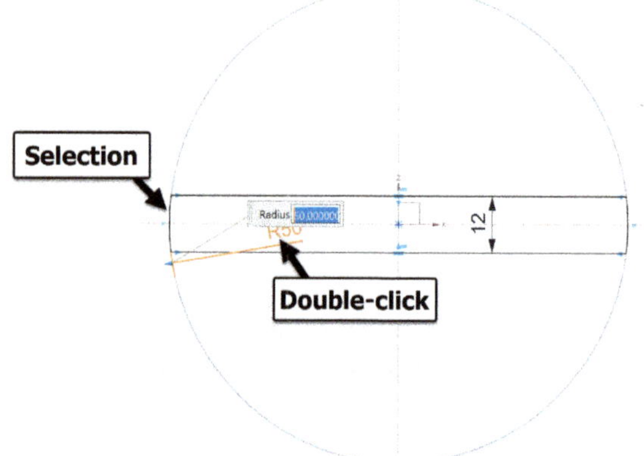

9. Click **Finish** on the **Sketch** group.

Extruding the Sketch

1. Click on the sketch, and then click **Extrude** on the **Shortcuts** toolbar; the **Extrude** dialog appears.

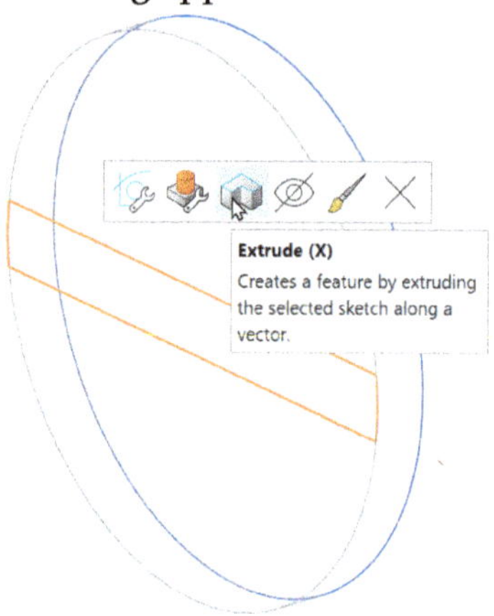

2. Type-in **10** in the **End** box attached to the preview.

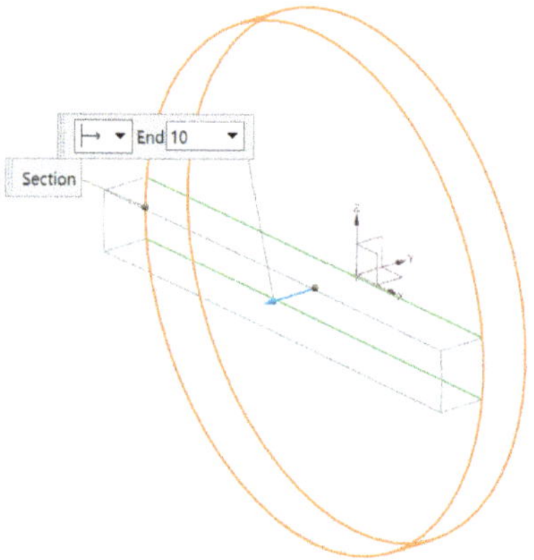

3. Click **OK** to construct the extrusion.
4. To hide the sketch, click **View> Show and Hide**  .
5. On the **Show and Hide** dialog, click **Hide** in the **Sketches** row; the sketches are hidden.
6. Click **Close** on the **Show and Hide** dialog.

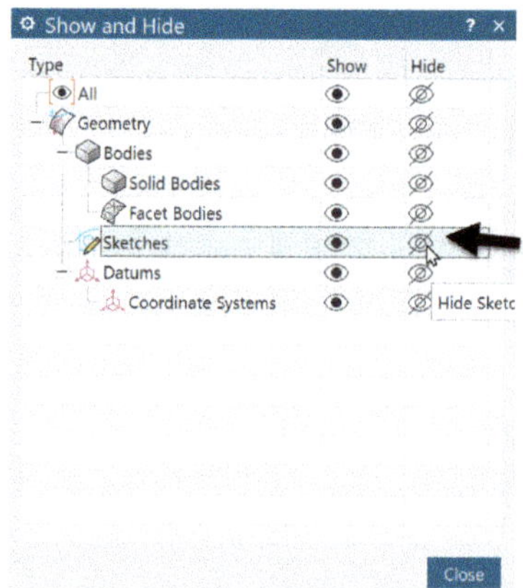

Adding another Extruded Feature

1. Create a sketch on the back face of the base feature:
   - On the ribbon, click **Home > Construction > Sketch.**
   - Select the back face of the model, as shown.

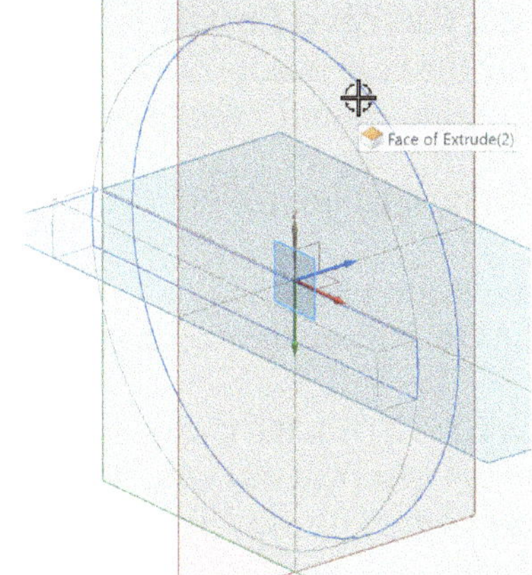

   - Click **OK.**
   - Click **Home > Include > More > Project Curve** on the ribbon; the **Project Curve** dialog appears.
   - Click on the circular edge.
   - Click **OK.**
   - Use the **Line** command to create the lines, as shown.

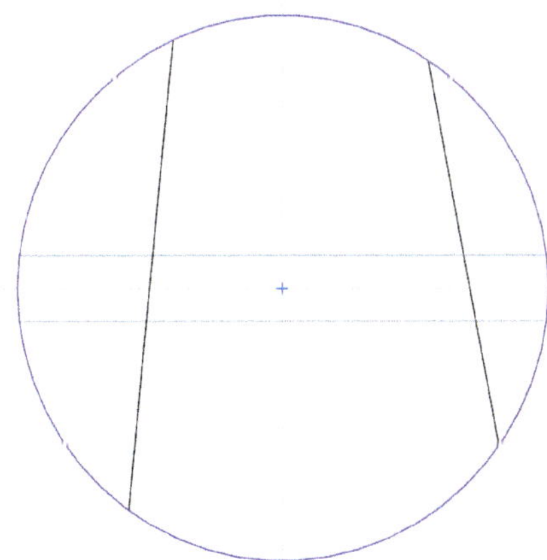

   - Select the two lines and then click the **Vertical** icon on the **Sketch Scene bar**; the selected lines made vertical.
   - Select the two lines and the vertical axis.
   - Click the **Make Symmetric** icon on the **Sketch Scene bar**; the lines are made symmetric about the Vertical axis.

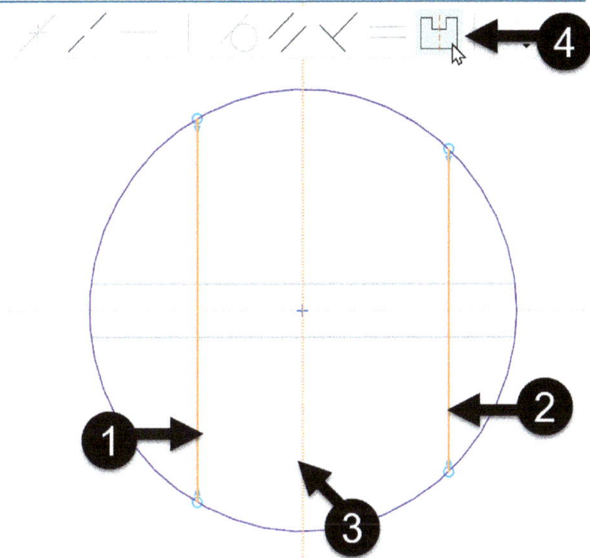

   - Select the two lines and double-click on the dimension displayed between them.
   - Type 12 and press ENTER.
   - Use the **Trim** command to trim the projected curve.

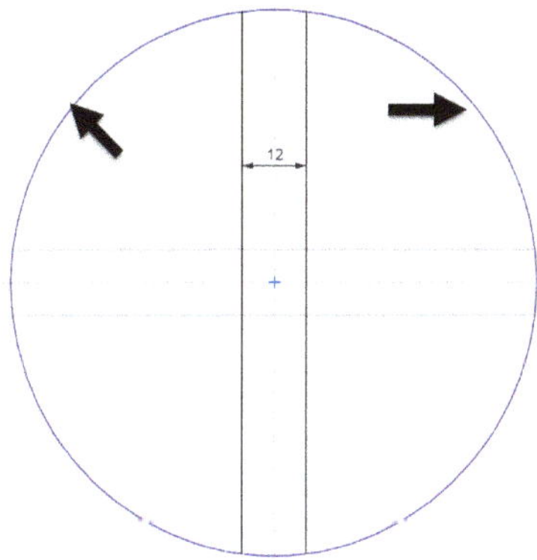

You can use the **Rotate** button from the **View** tab to rotate the model.

2. Select the arc located in the top portion.
3. Double-click on the radial dimension attached to the arc.
4. Type **50** in the **Radius** box and press ENTER.
5. Click **Finish** on the **Sketch** group.
6. Extrude the sketch up to **10** mm thickness.

To move the part view, click **View > Operation > Pan**, then drag the part to move it around in the graphics area.

7. Click **View > Display > Style > Shaded with Edges** on the ribbon.

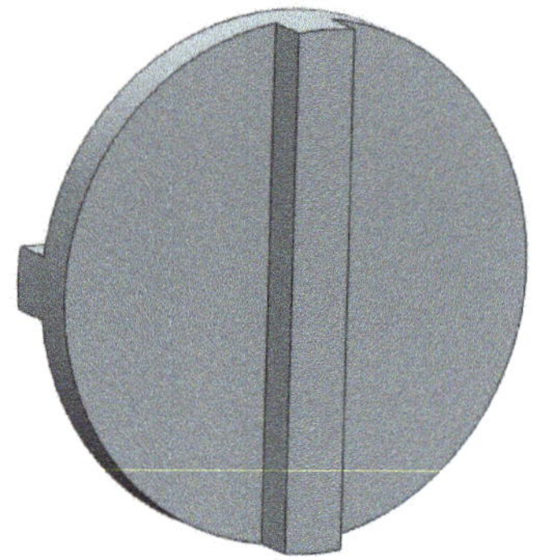

Replaying the Features of the model

1. On the **Top Border Bar**, click **Menu > Tools > Update > Feature Replay**.
2. On the **Feature Replay** dialog, expand the **Settings** section.
3. Type **2** in the **Seconds between Steps** box.
4. Click the **Start** icon in the **Replay Control** section of the **Feature Replay** dialog.
5. Click the **Play** icon to replay the features created in the step-by-step order.
6. Click **Close** on the **Replay Feature** dialog.

Saving and closing the Part

1. Create a new folder **NX** and a sub-folder *C2* inside it.
2. Click **Save** on the **Quick Access Toolbar**; the **Name Parts** dialog appears.
3. Type-in **Disc** in the **Name** box and click the **Folder** button.
4. Browse to the **NX/C2** folder and then click the **OK** button twice.
5. Click **File** tab **> Close > All Parts** to close the opened file.

Note:
*.prt is the file extension for all the files constructed in the Modeling, Assembly, and Drafting environments of NX.

TUTORIAL 2

In this tutorial, you construct a flange by performing the following actions:

- Constructing a revolved feature
- Constructing a cut feature
- Adding fillets

Open a New Part File

1. To open a new part, click **File > New** on the ribbon; the **New** dialog appears.
2. The **Model** is the default selection, so click **OK**; a new model window appears.

Sketching a Revolve Profile

You construct the base feature of the flange by revolving a profile around a centerline.

1. Click the **Sketch** button on the **Construction** group.
2. Select the **Right** plane.
3. Click the **OK** button; the sketch starts.
4. Click **Profile** on the **Curve** group.
5. Click on the vertical axis of the sketch.
6. Move the pointer upward and click on the vertical axis.

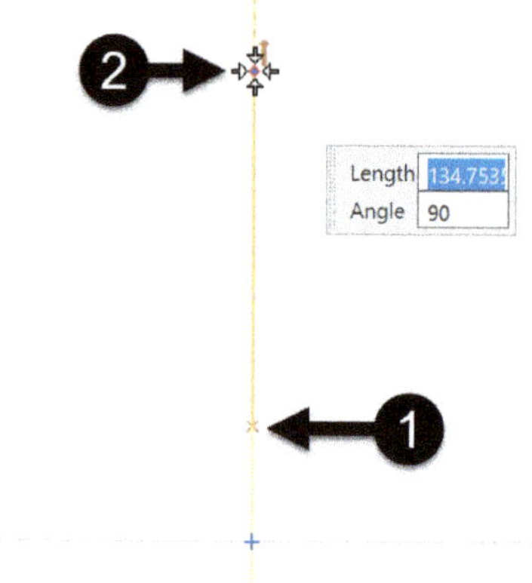

7. Move the pointer horizontally toward left and click.

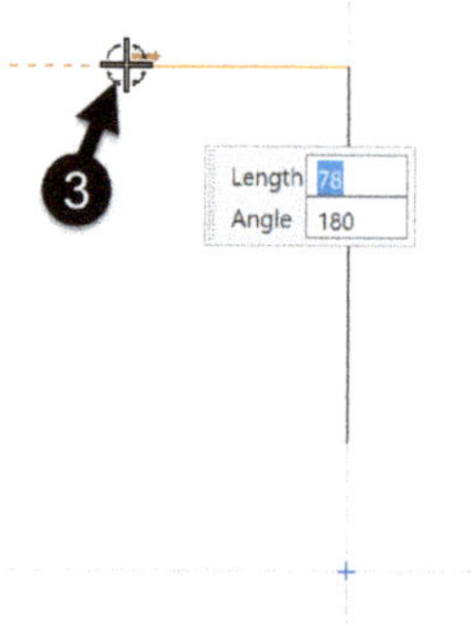

8. Move the pointer vertically downward and click.

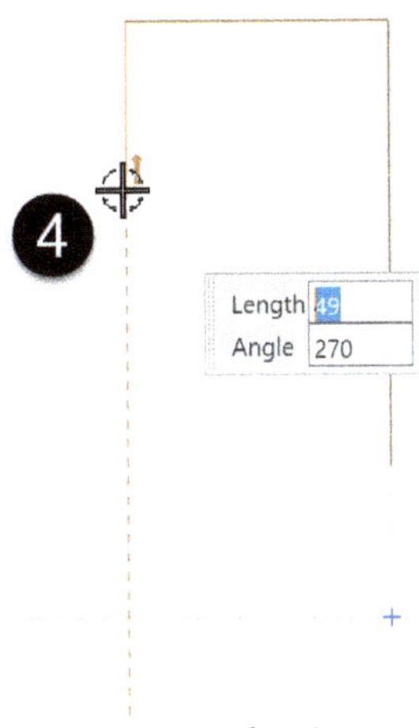

9. Move the pointer horizontally toward left and click.

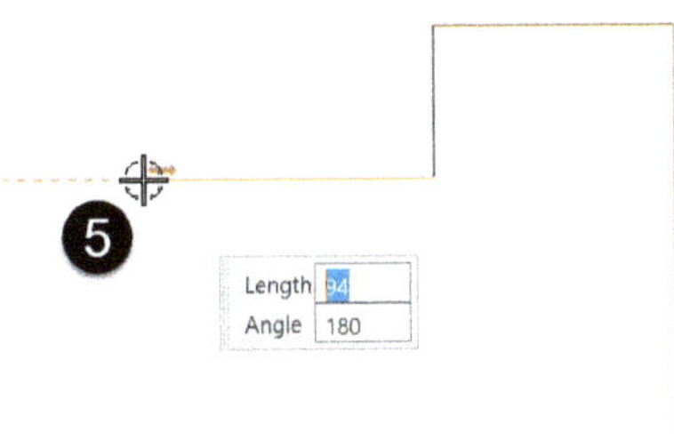

10. Likewise, create two more lines, as shown.

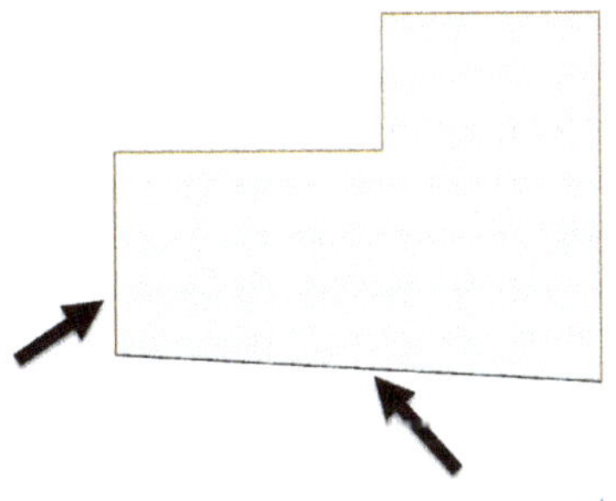

11. Select the lower inclined line.
12. Click the **Make Horizontal** icon on the Sketch Screen bar.

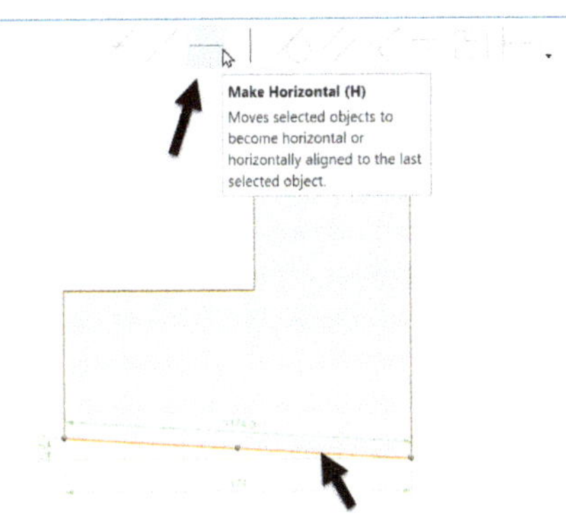

13. Select the Horizontal axis and lower horizontal line; a dimension appears.
14. Double-click on the dimension and type-in **15** in the dimension box.
15. Press **Enter** key. Next, Click in the graphics window.
16. Click **Yes** on the **Scale Sketch On First Dimension** message box; the first dimension of a sketch defines its size. It makes the sketch larger or smaller.

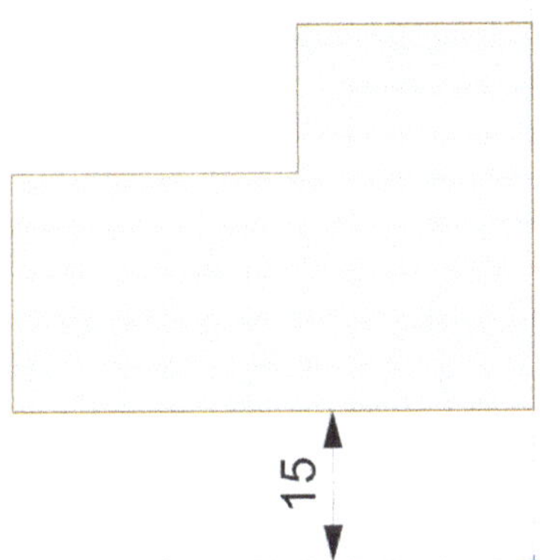

17. Select the **Horizontal axis** and horizontal line, as shown; a dimension appears.

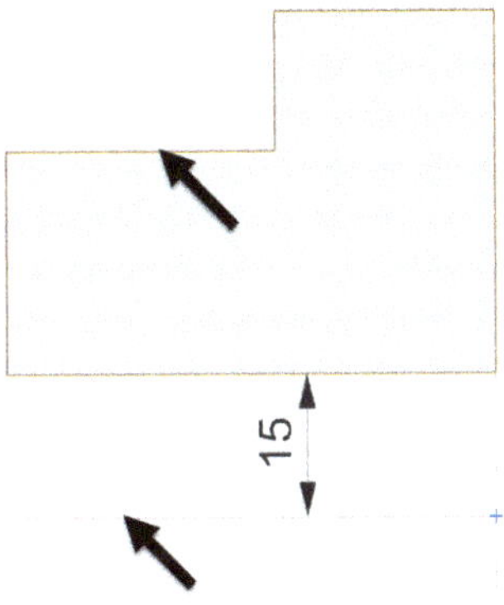

18. Double-click on the dimension, type **30**, and then press ENTER.

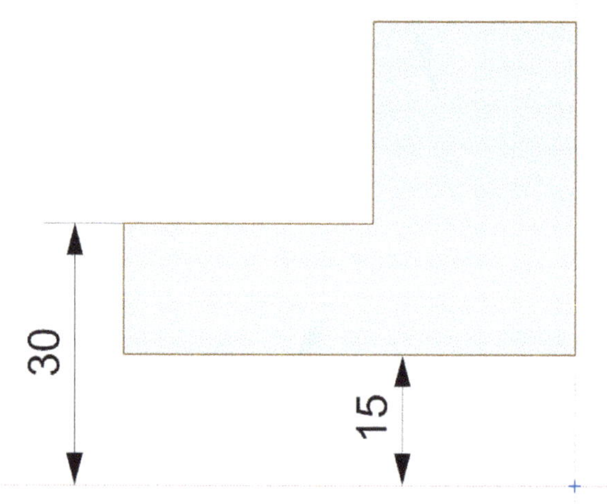

19. Select the **Horizontal axis** and the top horizontal line; a dimension appears.
20. Double-click on the dimension, type **50**, and then press ENTER.
21. Click in the graphics window.

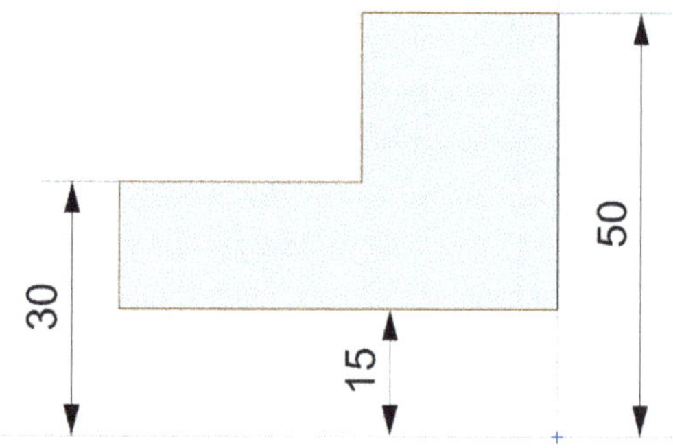

22. Apply the dimension of **20** mm to the top horizontal line, as shown.
23. Apply the dimension of **50** mm to the lower horizontal line.

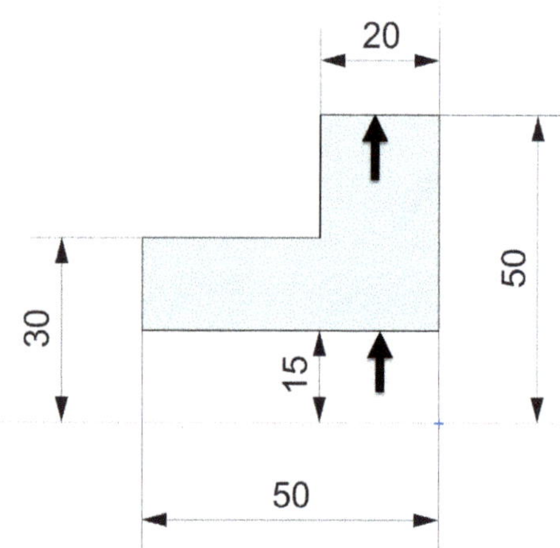

24. Click **Finish** on the **Sketch** group.

Constructing the Revolved Feature

1. On the ribbon, click **Home > Base > Revolve**; the **Revolve** dialog appears.
2. Click on the sketch.
3. Click on **Specify Vector** in the **Axis** group; a vector triad appears.
4. Click on the **Y-axis** of the triad.

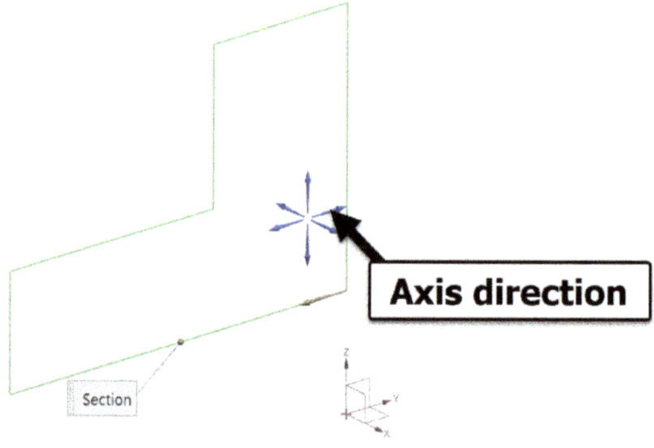

5. Click on the origin point of the **Coordinate** system; the preview of the revolved feature appears.

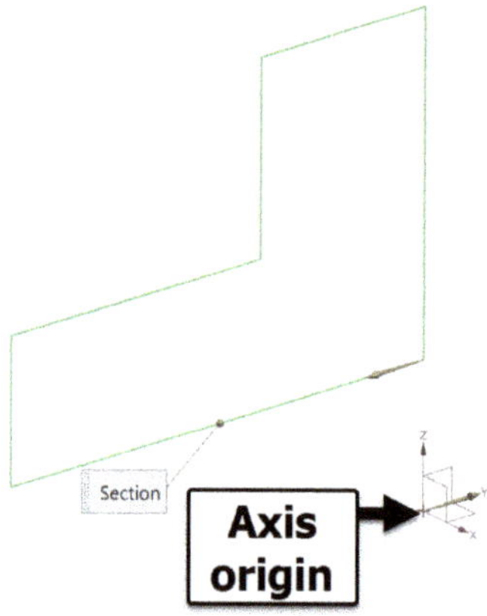

6. Type-in **360** in the **End** box attached to the preview.
7. Click **OK** to construct the revolved feature.

Constructing the Cut feature

1. Click **Extrude** on the **Base** group.
2. Rotate the model geometry and click the back face of the part; the sketch starts.
3. On the ribbon, click **Home** tab **> Curve** group **> Rectangle** .
4. On the **Rectangle** dialog, click the **From Center** icon.
5. Select the sketch origin.
6. Move the pointer horizontally toward the right, and then click outside the model.

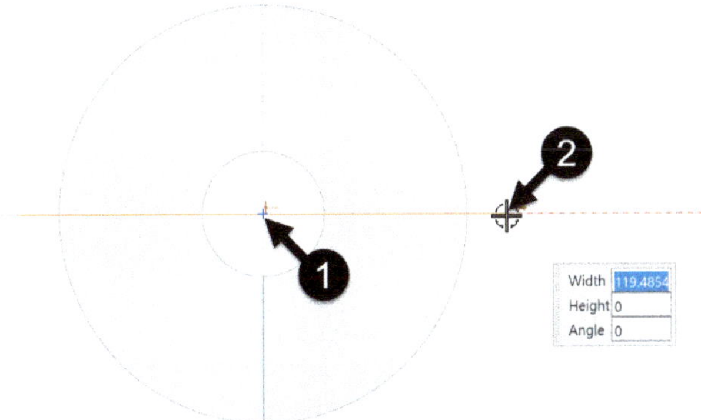

7. Move the pointer upward and click.

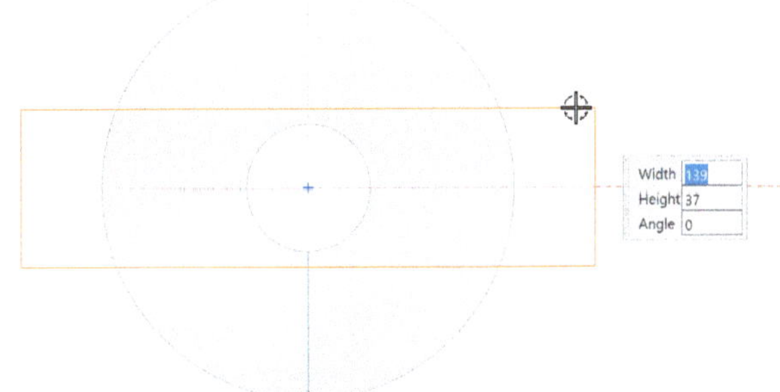

8. Press ESC.
9. Select the right vertical line of the rectangle.
10. Select the dimension displayed.
11. Type 12 and press ENTER.
12. Click No on the on the **Scale Sketch On First Dimension** message box.
13. Click in the graphics window.

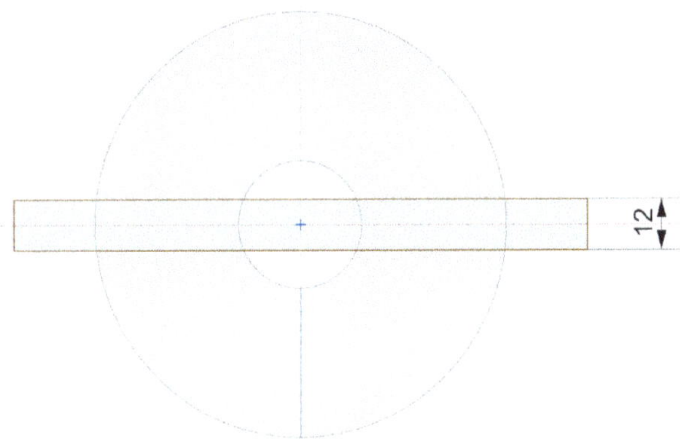

14. Click **Finish** on the **Sketch** group.
15. Enter **10** in the **End** box attached to the preview.
16. Click **Reverse Direction** in the **Direction** section.
17. Select **Subtract** in the **Boolean** section.

18. Click **OK** to construct the cut feature.

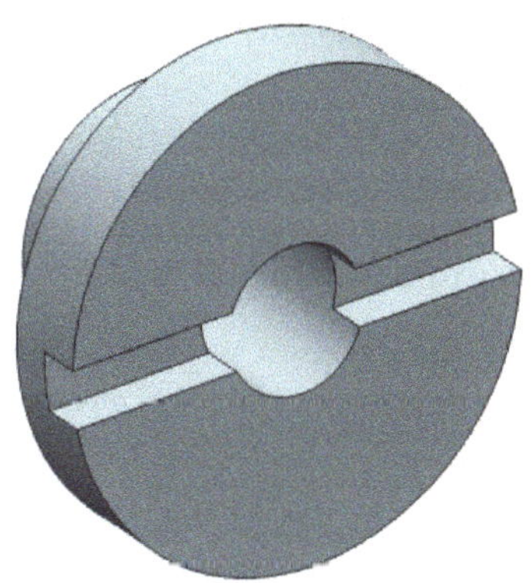

19. Right-click and select **Orient View > Isometric**.

Adding another Cut-out

1. Click **Extrude** on the **Feature** group.
2. Select the front face of the model geometry.
3. On the ribbon, click **Home** tab **> Curve** group **> Rectangle** .
4. On the **Rectangle** dialog, click the **From Center** icon.
5. Click on the horizontal axis at the location, as shown.

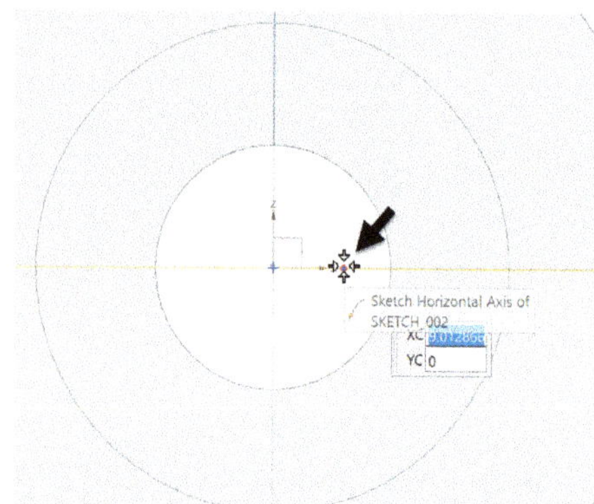

6. Move the pointer horizontally toward the right, and then click at the location, as shown.

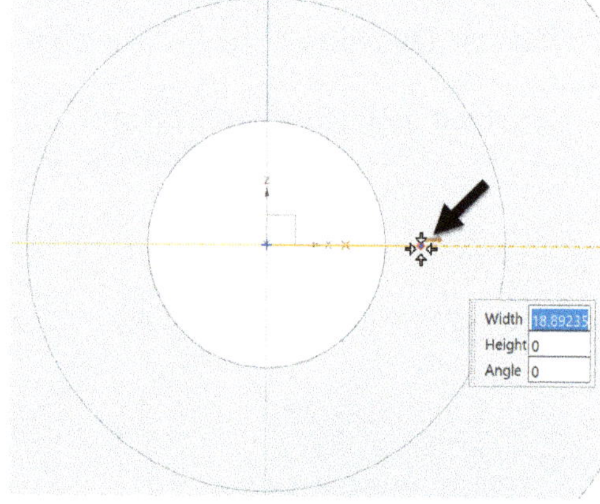

7.
8. Move the pointer upward and click.

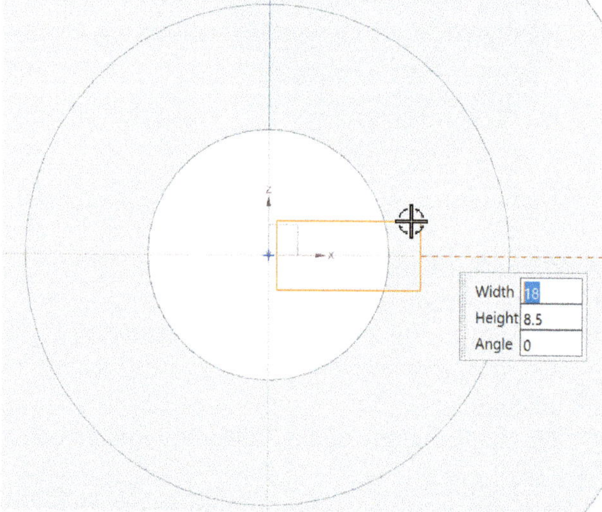

9. Press ESC.
10. Select the right vertical line of the rectangle and the vertical axis of the sketch.
11. Double-click on the dimension displayed.
12. Type 18 and press ENTER.
13. Click **No** on the **Scale Sketch On First Dimension** message box.
14. Click in the graphics window.
15. Add dimensions to the vertical and horizontal lines of the rectangle, as shown.

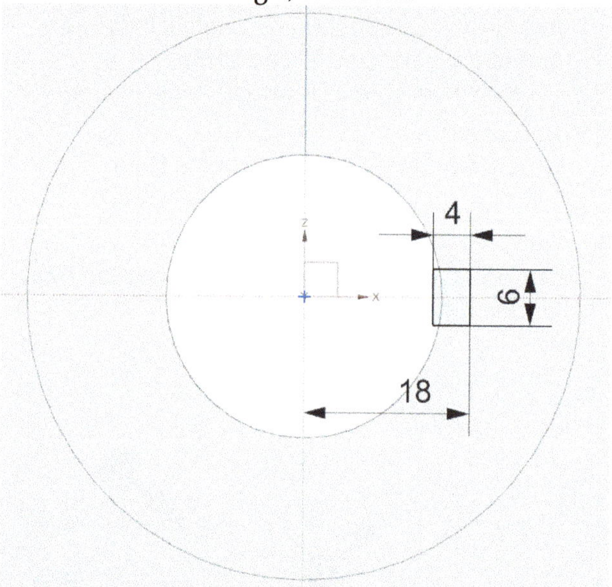

16. Click **Finish** on the **Sketch** group.
17. On the **Extrude** dialog, select **End > Through All** under the **Limits** section.
18. Click **Reverse Direction** in the **Direction** section.
19. Select **Subtract** in the **Boolean** group.
20. Click **OK** to construct the cut-out feature.
21. To change the view to isometric, click **Isometric** on the **View** tab.

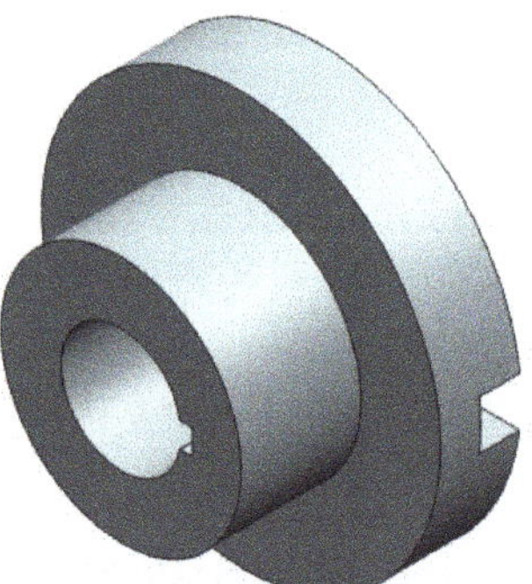

Adding Edge blends

1. Click **Home > Base > Edge Blend** ; the **Edge Blend** dialog appears.
2. Click on the inner circular edge and set **Radius 1** to 5.
3. Click **OK** to add the blend.

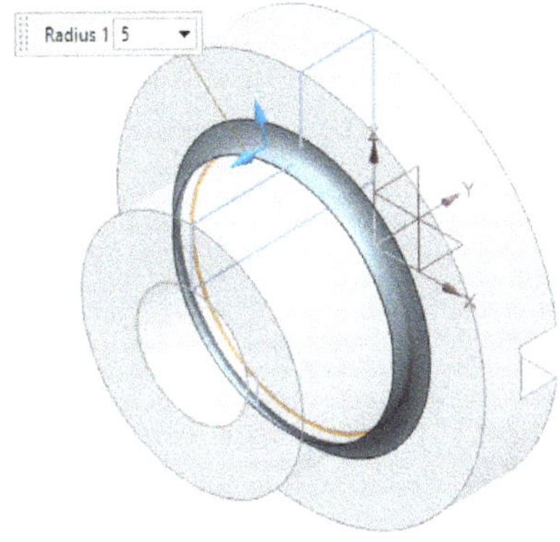

Saving and Closing the Part

1. Click **File > Save > Save**; the **Name Parts** dialog appears.
2. Type **Flange** in the **Name** box, and then click the **Folder** button next to it.
3. Browse to the **NX/C2** folder and then click the **OK** button twice.
4. Click **File > Close > All Parts**.

TUTORIAL 3

In this tutorial, you construct a Shaft by performing the following:

- Constructing a revolved feature
- Constructing a cut feature

Opening a New Part File

1. To open a new part, click the **New** button on the **Standard** group.
2. Select the **Model** template and click **OK**; a new model window appears.

Constructing the Revolved Feature

1. Click **Revolve** on the **Feature** group.
2. Click on the **YZ plane** to select it, and then click **OK**; the sketch starts.

3. On the ribbon, click **Home > Curve > Rectangle** .
4. On the **Rectangle** dialog, click the **By 2 Points** icon.
5. Select the origin point of the sketch.
6. Move the pointer toward the top left corner and click.
7. Add dimensions to the sketch, as shown in the figure.

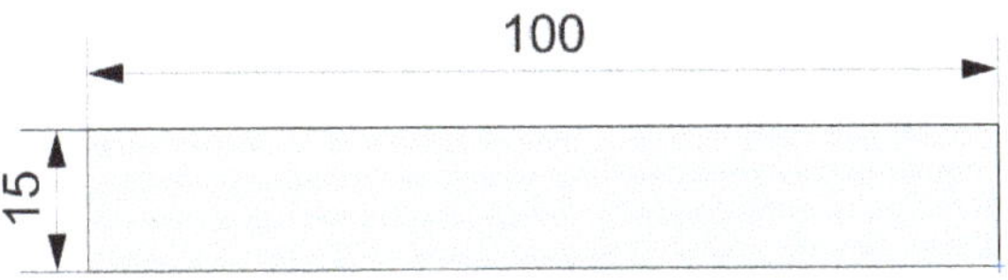

8. Click **Finish** on the **Sketch** group.
9. Click on the **Y-axis** of the triad.
10. Click on the origin point of the coordinate system; the preview appears.
11. Click **OK** to construct the revolved feature.

Creating Cut feature

1. Click **Home > Construction > Sketch** on the ribbon.
2. Click on the front face of the model, and then click **OK**.
3. On the ribbon, click **Home > Curve > Rectangle**.
4. On the **Rectangle** dialog, click the **By 2 Points** icon.
5. Create a rectangle, as shown.

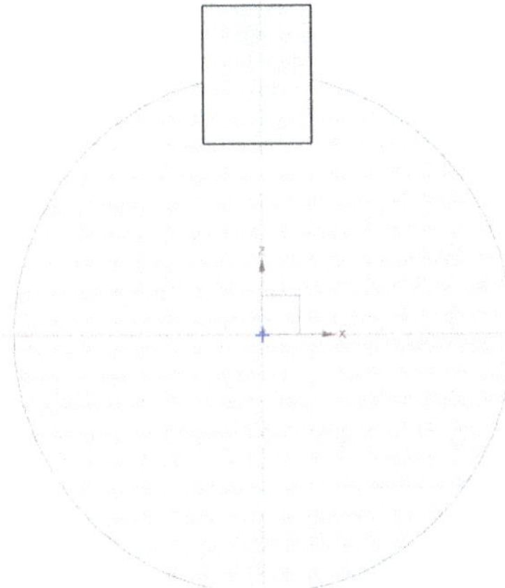

6. On the ribbon, click **Home > Include > More > Project Curve** .
7. Click on the circular edge of the model.
8. Click **OK**.
9. On the ribbon, click **Home > Edit > Trim**.
10. Click on the portion of the projected curve outside the rectangle.

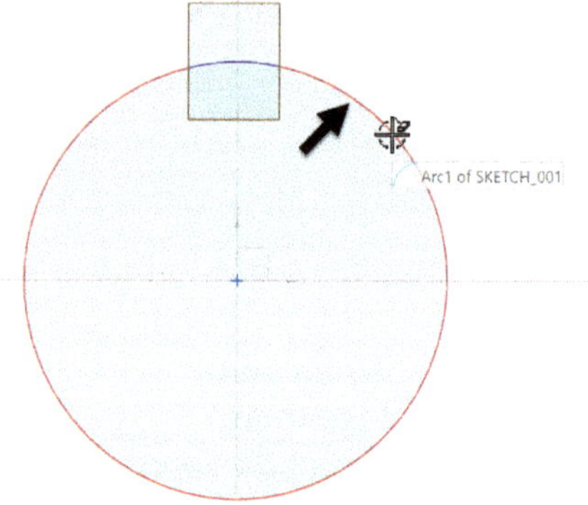

11. Click **OK** to trim the selected portion of the projected curve.
12. Select the entities of the rectangle outside the model.

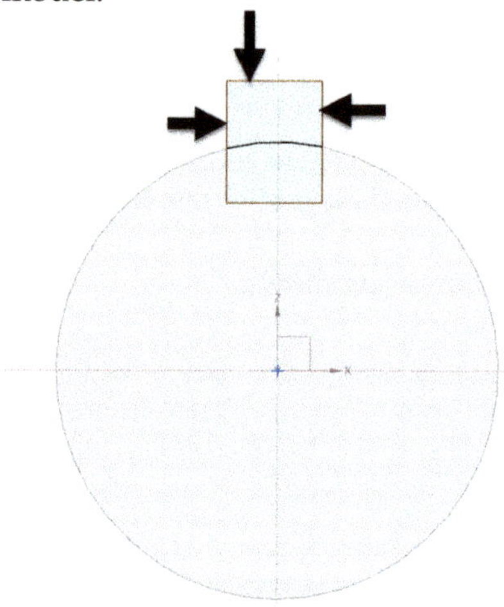

13. Click **Close** on the **Trim** dialog.
14. Use the **Make Symmetric** command to make the vertical lines of the sketch symmetric about the Vertical axis of the sketch.
15. Add dimensions to the sketch.

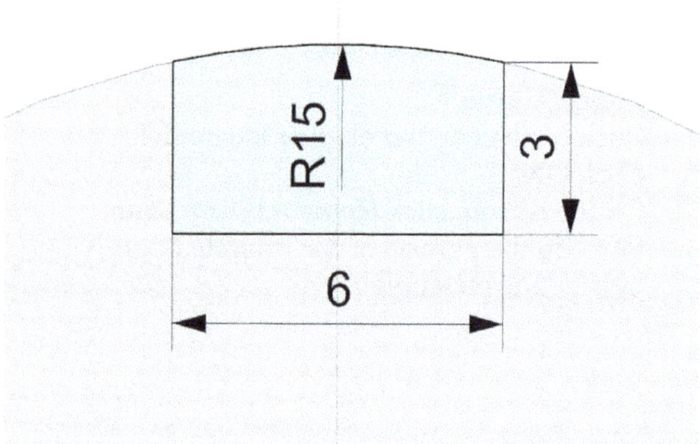

16. Finish the sketch.
17. Click **Extrude** on the **Feature** group.
18. Click on the sketch.
19. Type-in **55** in the **End** box.
20. Click **Reverse Direction** in the **Direction** section.
21. Select **Subtract** from the **Boolean** group.

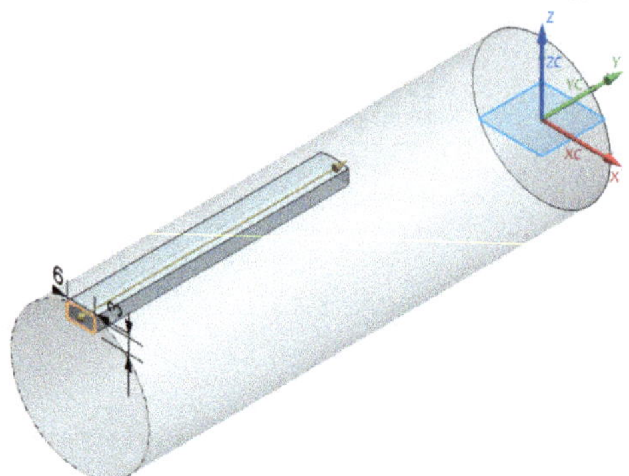

22. Click **OK** to construct the cut feature.

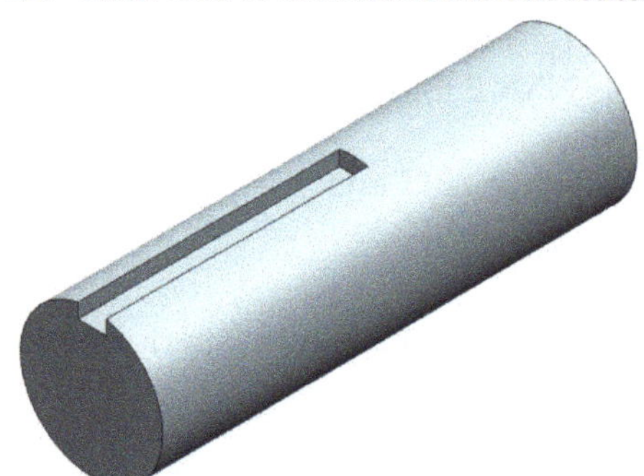

Saving the Part

1. Click **File > Save > Save**; the **Name Parts** dialog appears.
2. Type **Shaft** in the **Name** box and click the **Folder** button.
3. Browse to the **NX/C2** folder and then click the **OK** button twice.
4. Click **File > Close > All Parts**.

TUTORIAL 4

In this tutorial, you construct a Key by performing the following:

- Constructing a Block
- Applying draft

Constructing Extruded feature

1. Open a new part file.
2. On the ribbon, click **Home > Base > More > Design Feature > Block**.
3. On the **Block** dialog, select **Type > Origin and Edge Lengths**.
4. Type-in **6**, **50**, and **6** in the **Length (XC)**, **Width (YC)**, and **Height (ZC)** boxes, respectively.

5. Click on the origin point of the datum coordinate system.

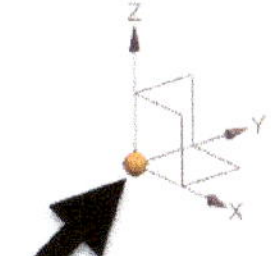

6. Click **OK** to construct the block.

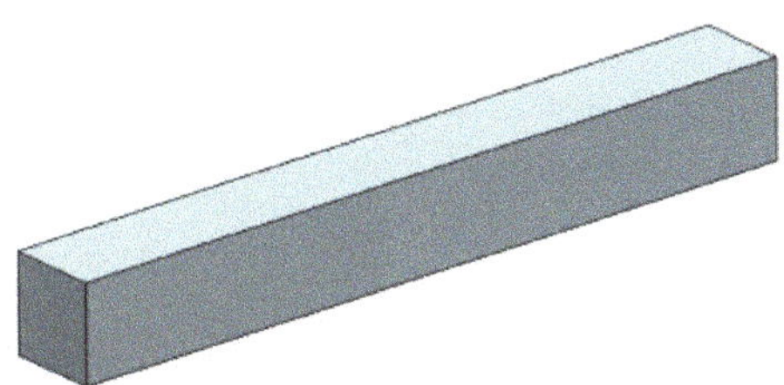

Applying Draft

1. Click **Draft** on the **Feature** group.
2. On the **Draft** dialog, select **Type > Face**.
3. Click on **Y-axis** to specify vector.

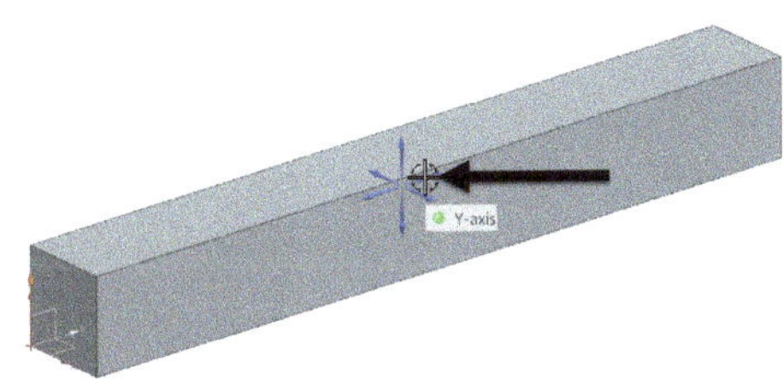

4. Select the front face as the stationary face.

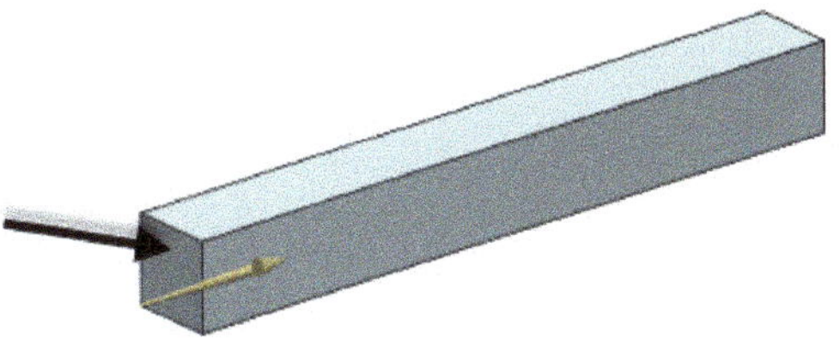

5. Click **Select Face** in the **Faces to Draft** section.
6. Select the top face.

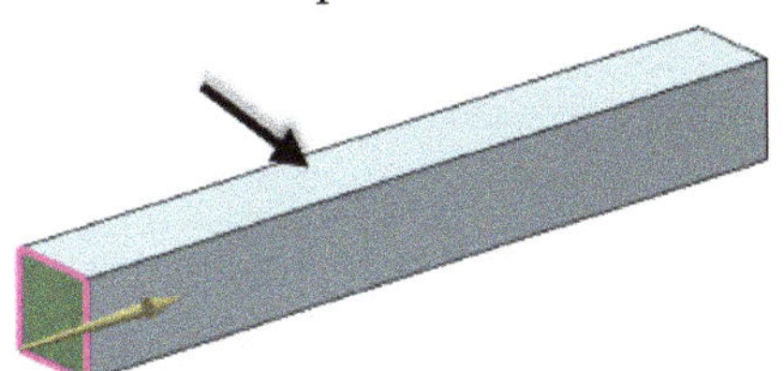

7. Type-in **1** in the **Angle 1** box.
8. Click **OK** to add the draft.

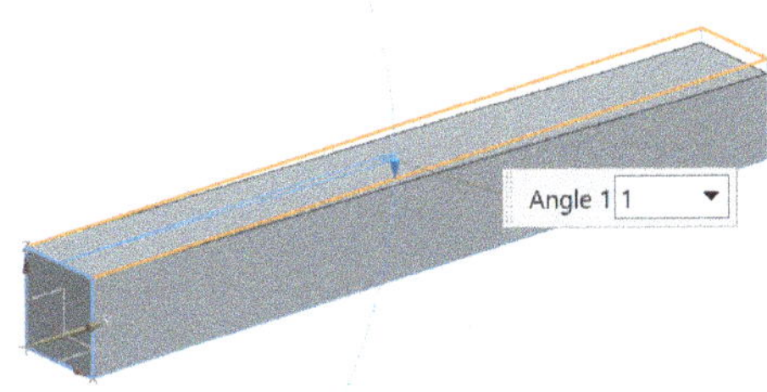

Saving the Part

1. Click **File > Save > Save**; the **Name Parts** dialog appears.
2. Type **Key** in the **Name** box and click the **Folder** button.
3. Browse to the **NX/C2** folder and then click the **OK** button twice.
4. Click **File > Close > All Parts**.

Chapter 3: Constructing Assembly

In this chapter, you will:

- Add Components to an assembly
- Apply constraints between components
- Produce exploded view of the assembly

TUTORIAL 1

This tutorial takes you through the creation of your first assembly. You construct the Oldham coupling assembly:

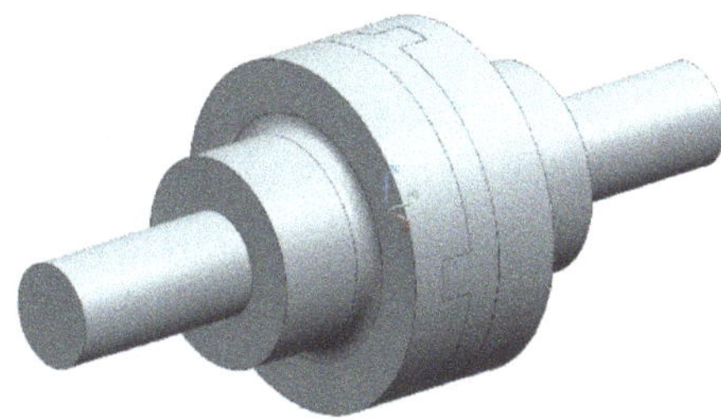

Copying the Part files into a new folder

1. Create a folder named **Oldham_Coupling** at the location NX/C3.
2. Copy all the part files constructed in the previous chapter to this folder.

Opening a New Assembly File

1. To open a new assembly, click **File > New**; the **New** dialog appears.
2. Click **Assembly** in the **Templates** group.
3. Click **OK**; a new assembly window appears. Also, the **Assemble** dialog appears.
4. Click **Cancel** on the **Assemble** dialog.

Inserting the Base Component

1. On the ribbon, click **Assemblies > Base > Add Component** .
2. To insert the base component, click the **Open** button in the **Part To Place** section of the **Add Component** dialog.
3. Browse to the location NX/C3/Oldham_Coupling and double-click on **Flange.prt**.
4. On the **Add Component** dialog, select **Component Anchor** > **Absolute** in the **Location** section.
5. Select **Assembly Location > WCS**.
6. Under the **Settings** section, select **Reference Set** > **Entire Part**. The **Entire Part** option displays all the datum planes, sketches, and features of the part.
7. Click **OK** to place the Flange at the origin.

The **Create Fix Constraint** message box appears on the screen.

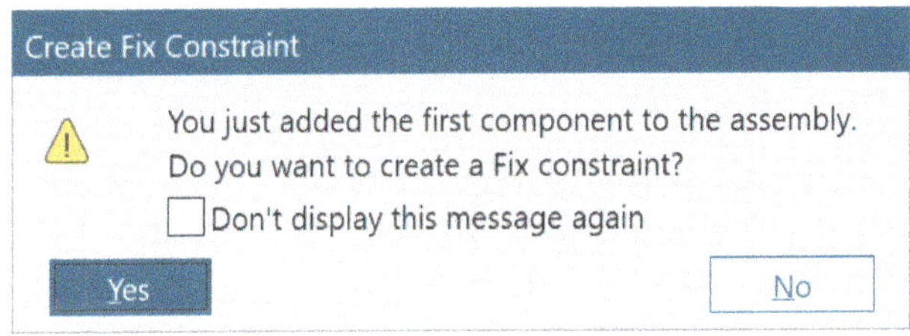

8. Click **No** on the **Create Fix Constraint** message box.

There are two ways of constructing any assembly model.

- Top-Down Approach
- Bottom-Up Approach

Top-Down Approach
You open the assembly file and then construct components files in it.

Bottom-Up Approach
You construct the components first, and then add them to the assembly file. In this tutorial, you construct the assembly using this approach.

Adding the second component

1. To insert the second component, click **Assemblies > Base > Add Component** on the ribbon; the **Add Component** dialog appears.
2. On the **Add Component** dialog, click the **Open** button in the **Part To Place** section.
3. Browse to the location

NX/C3/Oldham_Coupling and double-click on **Shaft.prt**.

4. Under the **Placement** section, select the **Constrain** option.
5. Under the **Settings** section, select **Reference Set > Entire Part**.

After adding the components to the assembly environment, you have to apply constraints between them. By applying constraints, you establish relationships between components. You can apply the following types of constraints between components.

Touch Align: Using this constraint, you can make two faces coplanar to each other. Note that if you set the **Orientation** to **Align**, the faces will point in the same direction. You can also align the centerlines of the round faces.

Concentric: This constraint makes the centers of circular edges coincident. Also, the circular edges will be on the same plane.

Distance: This constraint provides an offset distance between two objects.

Fix: This constraint fixes a component at its current position.

Parallel: This constraint makes two objects parallel to each other.

Perpendicular: This constraint makes two objects perpendicular to each other.

Fit: This constraint brings two cylindrical faces together. Note that they should have the same radius.

Bond: This constraint makes the selected components rigid so that they move together.

Center: This constraint positions the selected component at a center plane between two components.

Angle: Applies angle between two components.

Align/Lock: Aligns the axes of two cylindrical faces and locks the rotation.

6. On the **Add Components** dialog, select **Constraint Type > Touch Align**.
7. Under the **Geometry to Constrain** section, select **Orientation > Infer Center/Axis**.
8. Under the **Settings** section, expand the **Interaction Options** sub-section, and then uncheck the **Preview** option.
9. Check the **Preview Window** option; the **Component Preview** window appears.

10. Click on the circular face of the Shaft.

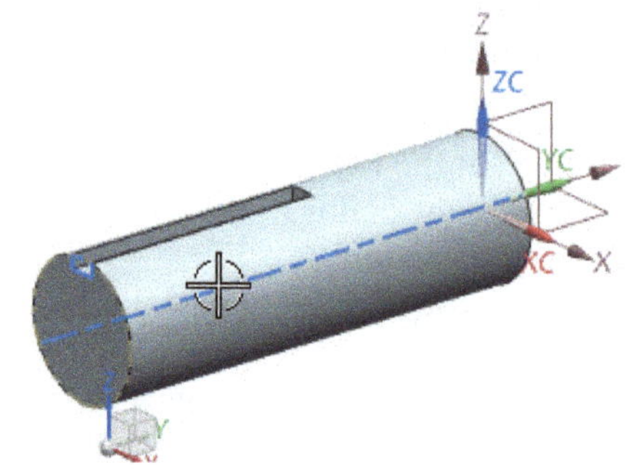

11. Click on any round face of the Flange.

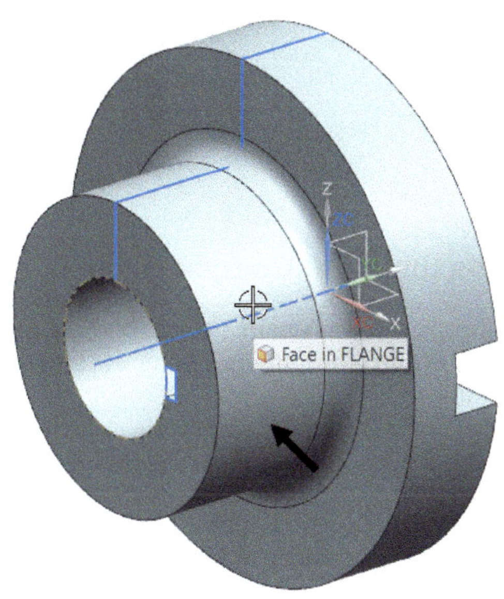

12. Under the **Geometry to Constrain** section, select **Orientation > Align**.
13. Click on the front face of the shaft.

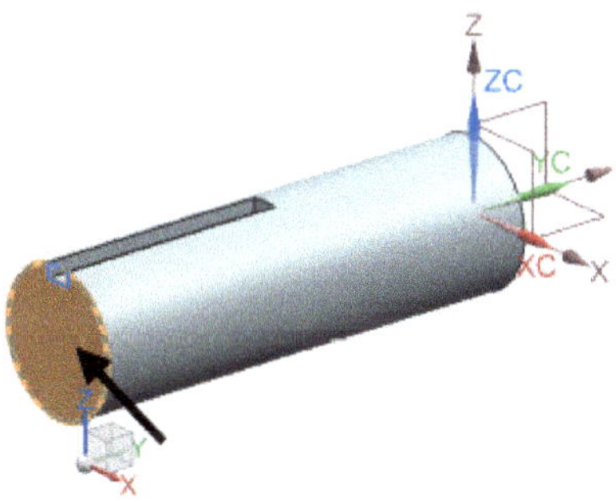

14. Rotate the flange and click on the slot face, as shown in the figure.

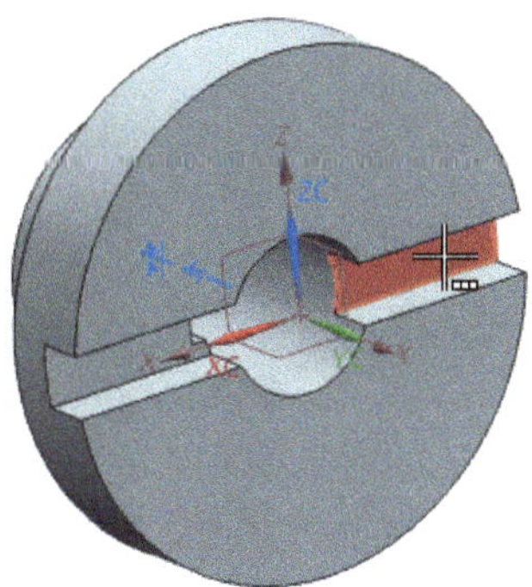

15. Click on the YZ plane of the Shaft.

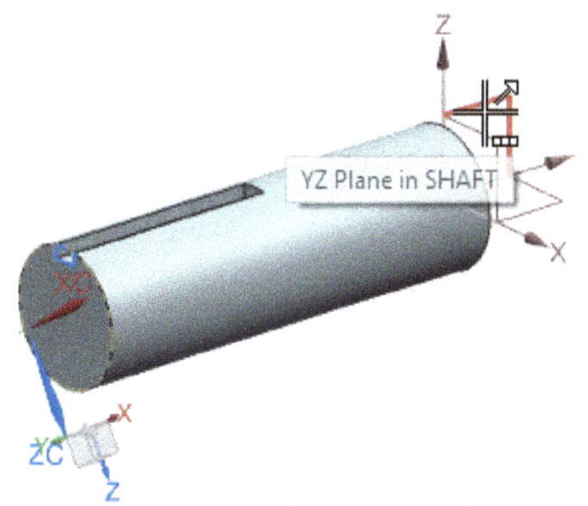

16. Click on the XY plane of the Flange.

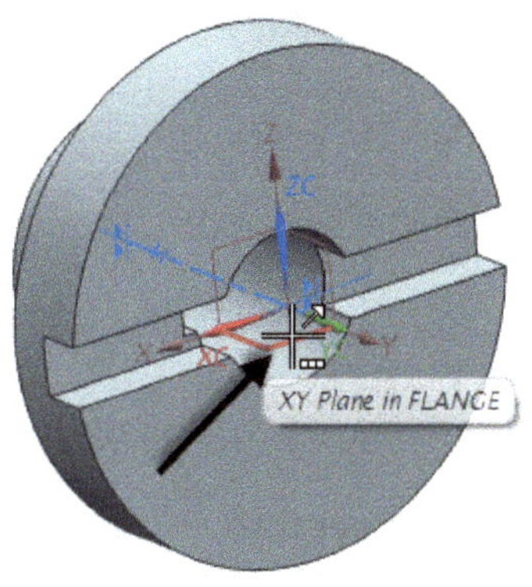

17. Click **OK** to assemble the components.

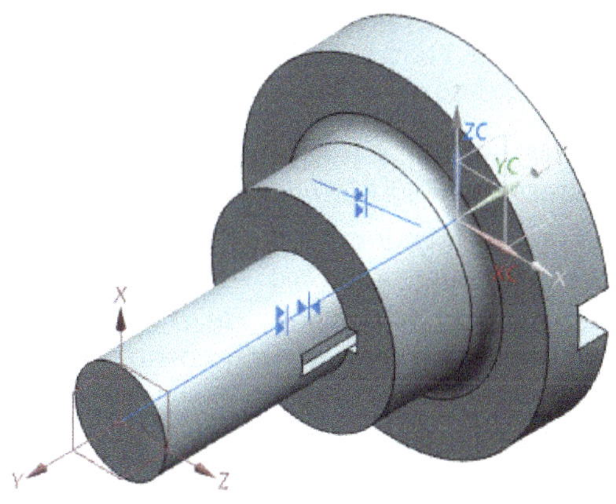

Checking the Degrees of the Freedom

1. To check the degrees of freedom of a component, click **Assemblies > Position > More > Show Degrees of Freedom**.
2. Click on the Flange to display the degrees of freedom.

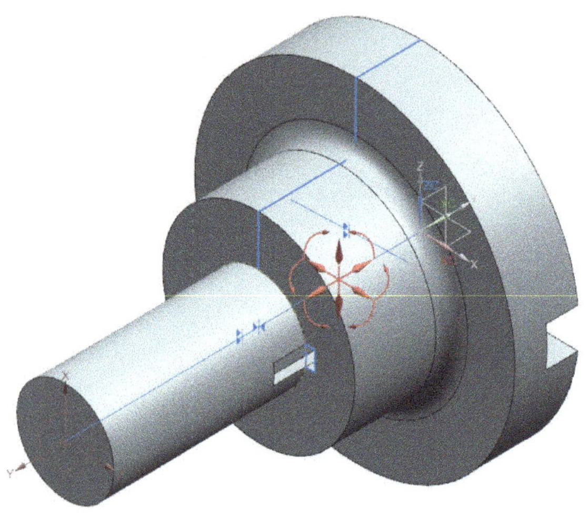

You will notice that the Flange has six degrees of freedom.

Fixing the Flange

1. To fix the flange, click **Assemblies > Position > Assembly Constraints** on the ribbon.
2. On the **Assembly Constraints** dialog, click **Type > Constraint > Fix**.
3. Click on the Flange, and then click **OK**.
4. On the ribbon, click **View > Operation > More > View Operation > Refresh**.
5. To view the degrees of freedom, click **Show Degrees of Freedom** on the **Position** group and select the Flange and Shaft.

You will notice that they are fully constrained.

Hiding the Flange

1. To hide the Flange, click on it and select **Hide** from the contextual toolbar.

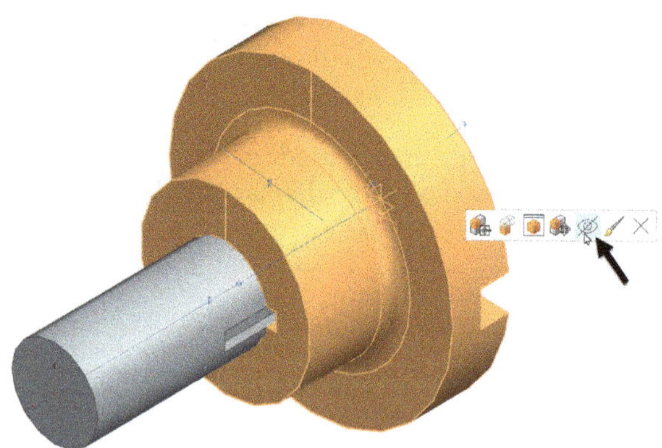

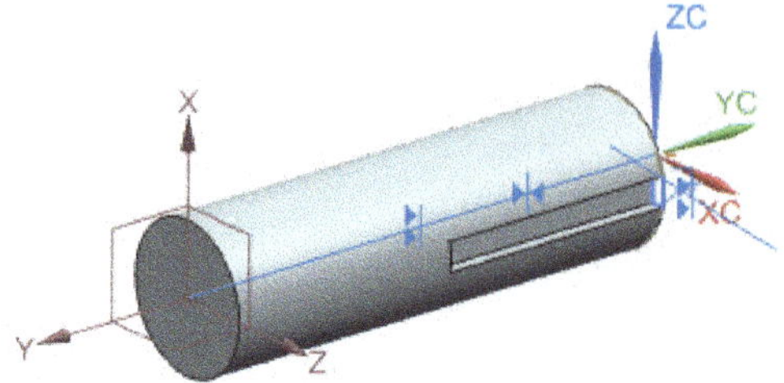

Adding the Third Component

1. Click **Add Component** on the **Base** group.
2. On the **Add Component** dialog, click the **Open** button.
3. Double-click on the **Key.prt**.
4. In the **Placement** section of the dialog, select **Constraint Type > Touch Align**.
5. Under the **Geometry to Constraints** section, select **Orientation > Align**.
6. Click **Select Two Objects** in the **Geometry to Constrain** section.
7. Click on the front face of the Key and front face of the Shaft.

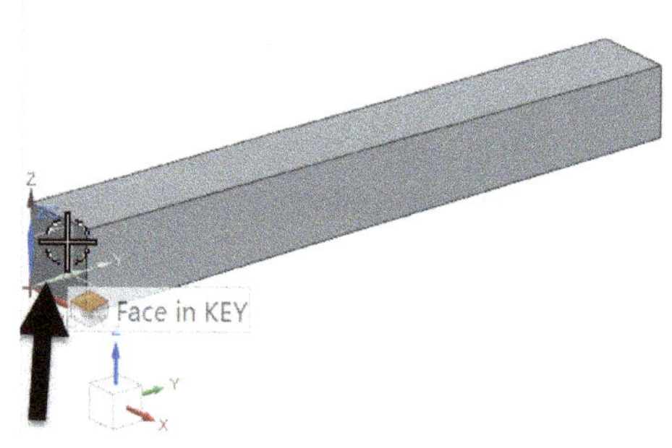

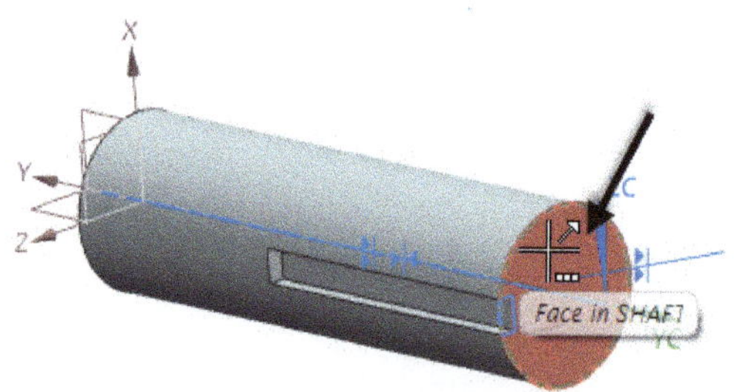

8. Click on the XY plane of the Key.

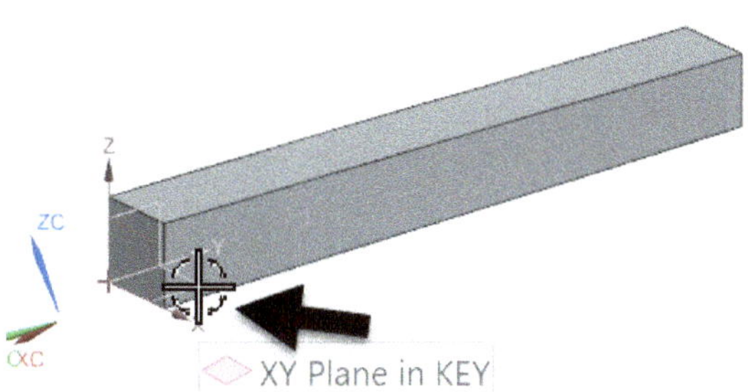

9. Click on the face on the shaft, as shown in the figure.

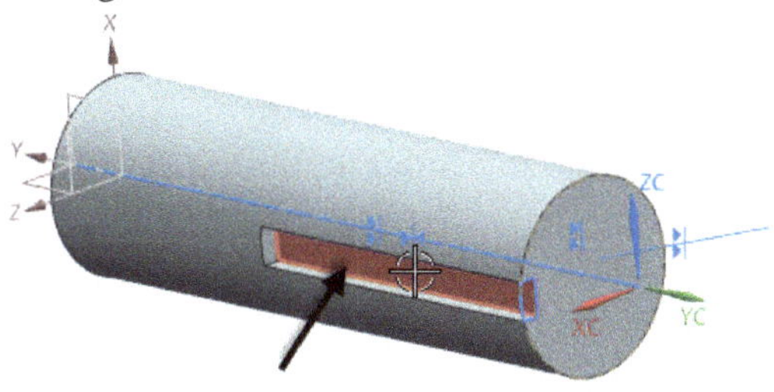

10. Under the **Geometry to Constrain** section, select **Orientation > Touch**.
11. Click on the side face of the Key and select the face on the shaft, as shown in the figure.

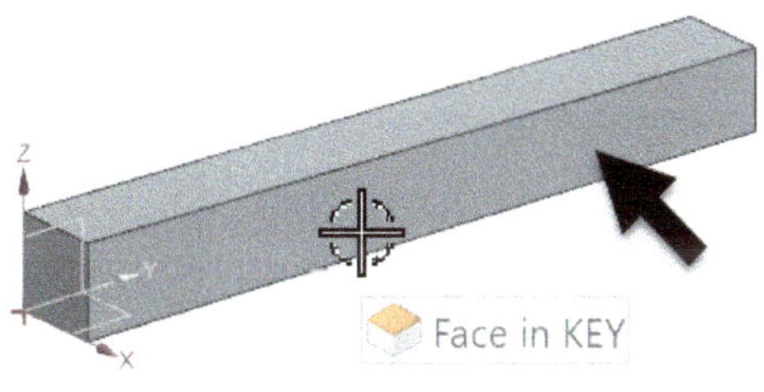

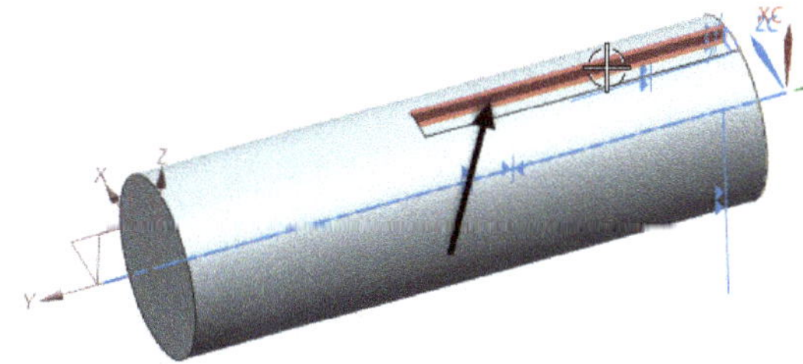

12. Click **OK**.

Showing the Hidden Flange

1. To show the hidden flange, click the **Assembly Navigator** tab, right click on the Flange, and then select **Show**.

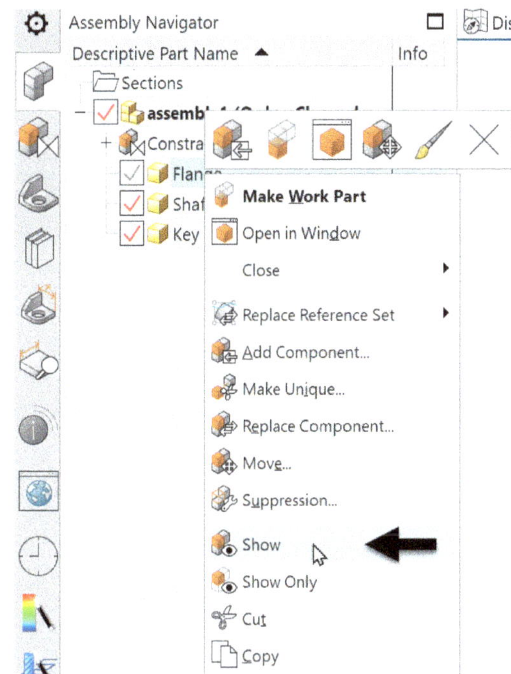

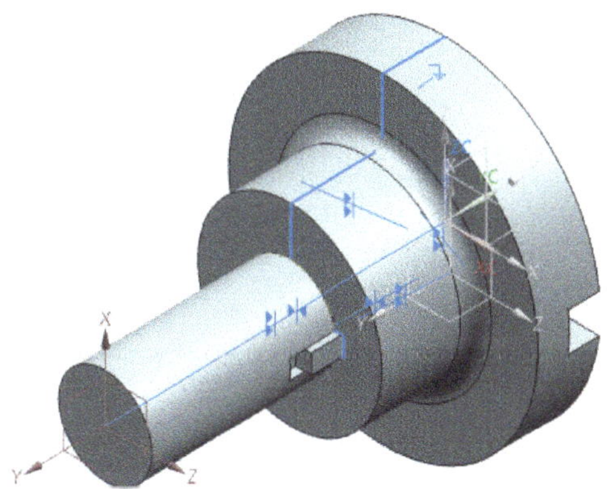

Hiding the Reference Planes, sketches, and Constraint symbols

1. To hide the reference planes, sketches, and constraint symbols, click **View > Content > Show and Hide** on the ribbon.
2. On the **Show and Hide** dialog, click the hide icons in the **Sketches**, **Datums**, and **Assembly Constraints** rows.

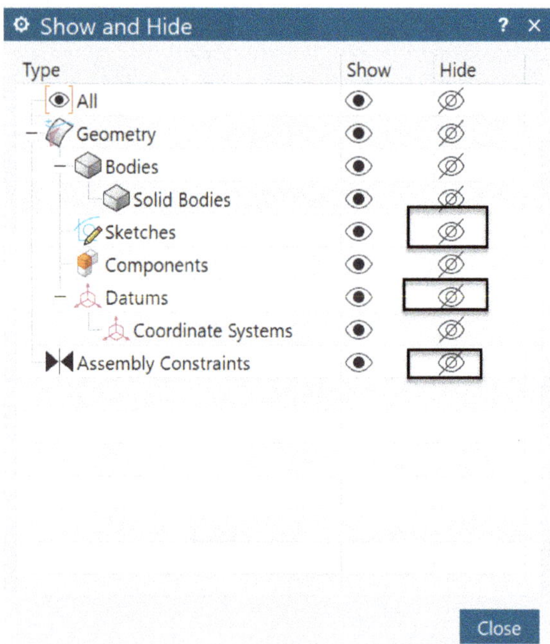

3. Click **Close** on the dialog.

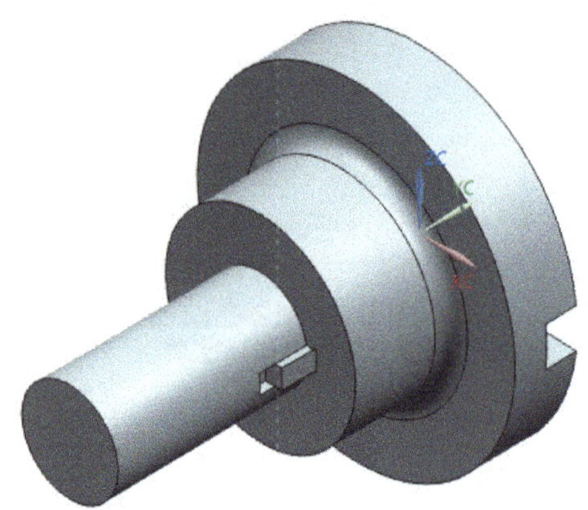

Saving the Assembly

1. Click **File > Save > Save**; the **Name Parts** dialog appears.
2. Type-in **Flange_subassembly** in the **Name** box and click the **Folder** button.
3. Browse to the NX/C3/Oldham_Coupling folder and then click the **OK** button twice.
4. Click **File > Close > All Parts.**

Starting the Main assembly

1. Click **File > New** on the ribbon.
2. On the **New** dialog, click the **Assembly** template.
3. Type-in **Main_assembly** in the **Name** box and click the **Folder** button.
4. Browse to NX/C3/ Oldham_Coupling folder and then click **OK** button twice; the **Assemble** dialog appears.
5. Click **Cancel** on the **Assemble** dialog.

Adding Disc to the Assembly

1. On the ribbon, click **Assemblies > Base > Add Component** .
2. Click the **Open** button.
3. Double-click on **Disc.prt**.
4. Under the **Location** section, select **Component Anchor** > **Absolute**.
5. Select **Assembly Location > WCS**.
6. Set **Reference Set** to **Model** under the **Settings** section.
7. Click **OK** to place the Disc at the origin.
8. Click **Yes** on the **Create Fix Constraint** message box.

Placing the Sub-assembly

1. Click the **Add Component** button on the **Base** group.
2. Click the **Open** button.
3. Double-click on **Flange_subassembly.prt.**
4. On the **Add Component** dialog, select **Placement** > **Constrain.**
5. Set **Constraint Type** to **Touch Align** .
6. Set **Orientation** to **Touch** .
7. Click **Select Two Objects** from the **Geometry to Constrain** section.
8. Click on the face of the flange, as shown in figure.

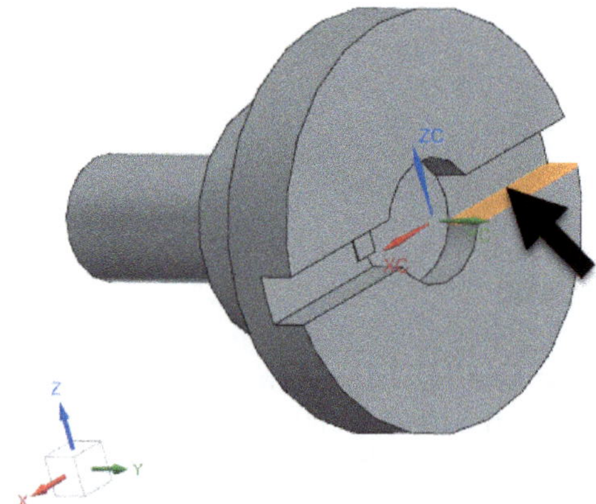

9. Click on the face of the Disc, as shown in the figure.

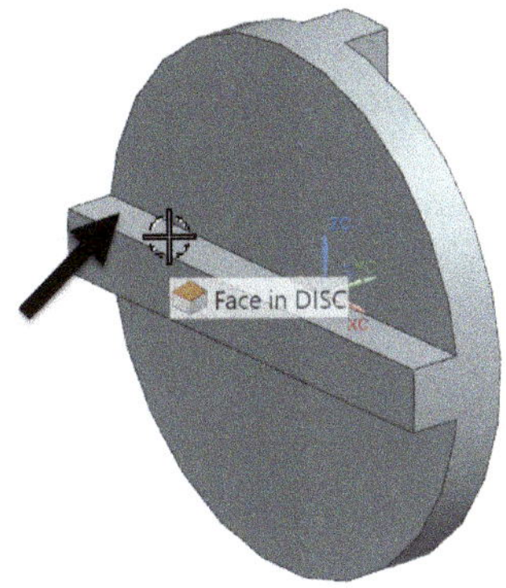

10. Set **Constraint Type** to **Concentric** 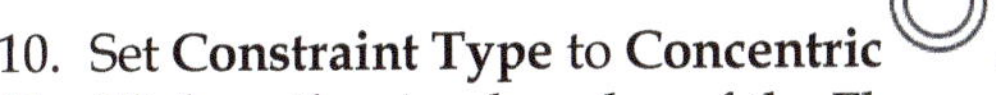 .
11. Click on the circular edge of the Flange.

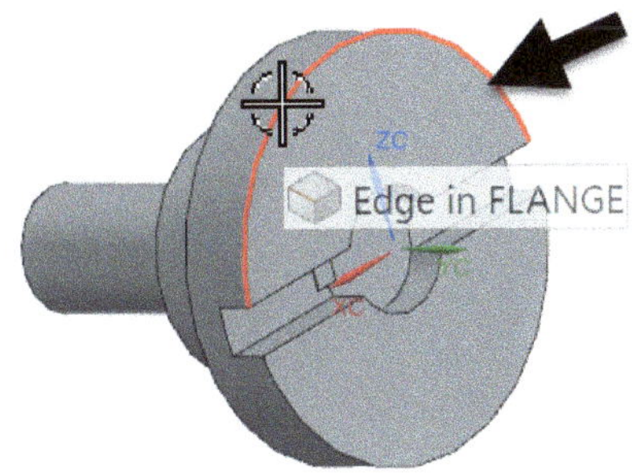

12. Click on the circular edge of the Disc.

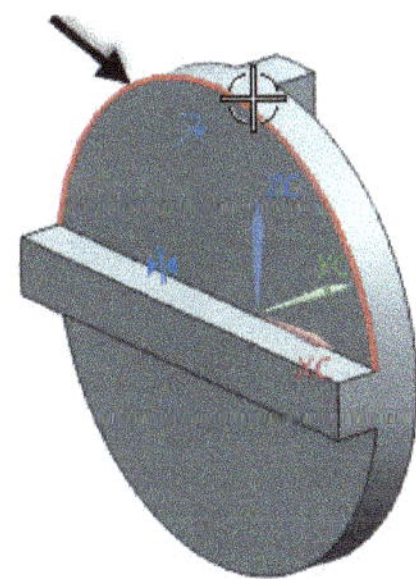

13. Click **OK** to assemble the subassembly.

Placing the second instance of the Sub-assembly

1. Insert another instance of the Flange subassembly.
2. Apply the **Touch Align** and **Concentric** constraints. Note that you have to click the **Reverse Last Constraint** button while applying the **Concentric** constraint.

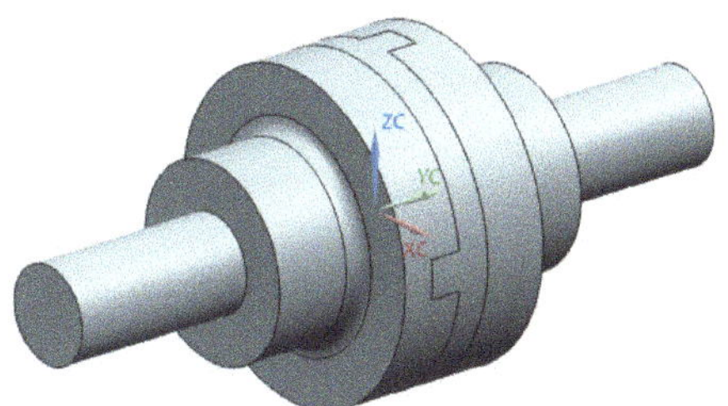

Saving the Assembly

1. Click **Save** on the **Quick Access Toolbar** or click **File > Save**.

TUTORIAL 2

In this tutorial, you produce the exploded view of the assembly created in the previous tutorial.

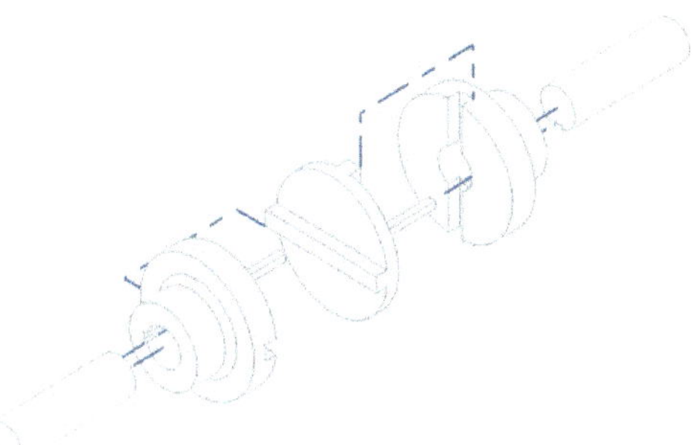

Producing the Exploded view

1. On the **Assembly Navigator**, click the right mouse button on Flange_subassembly x 2.

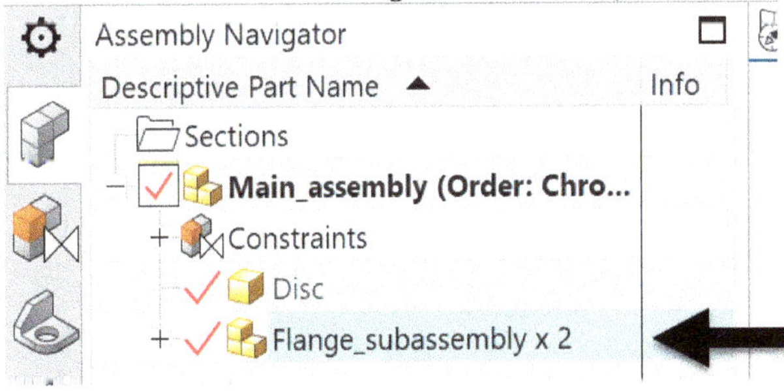

2. Select **Unpack**.
3. On the ribbon, click **Assemblies > Explosions > Explosions**.

Explosions ▾

4. Click **New Explosion** on the **Explosions** dialog; the **Edit Explosion** dialog appears.
5. Select Flange_subassembly from the **Assembly**

Navigator.

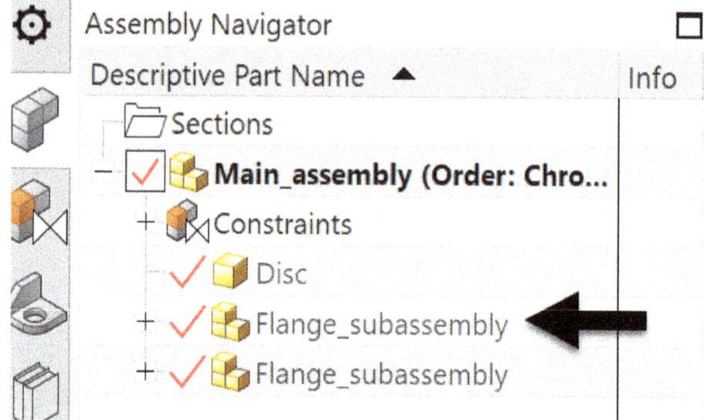

6. Click **Specify Orientation** on the dialog; the dynamic triad appears on the flange subassembly.

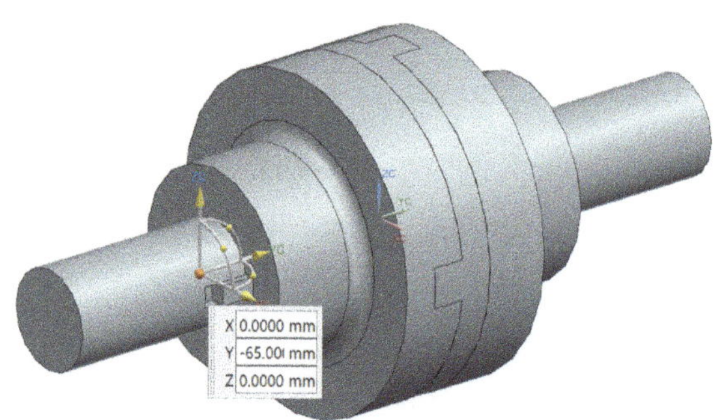

7. Click the **Y-Handle** on the dynamic triad.
8. Enter **-100** in the **Distance** box.

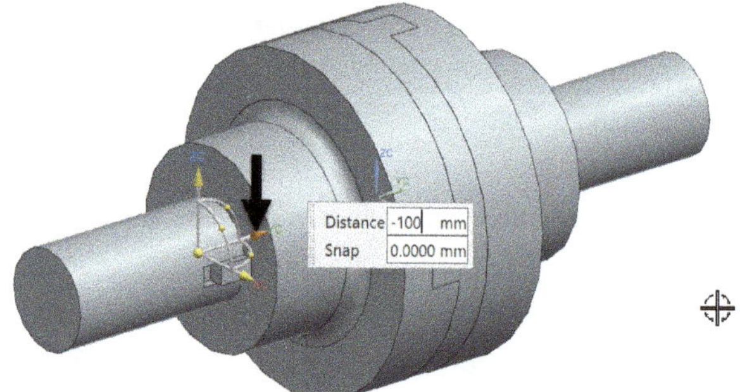

9. Click **OK** to explode the flange subassembly.

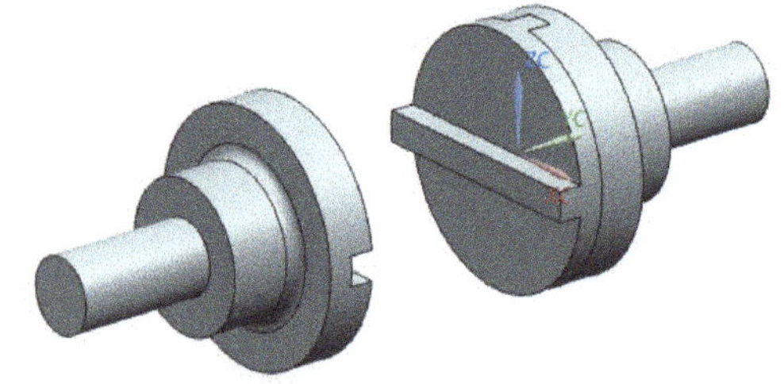

10. Click **Edit Explosion** button on the **Explosions** dialog.
11. Click **Select Components** on the **Edit Explosion** dialog.
12. Select the Key from the assembly.
13. Click **Specify Orientation** on the dialog.
14. Click the **Y-Handle** on the dynamic triad.
15. Enter **-80** in the **Distance** box.

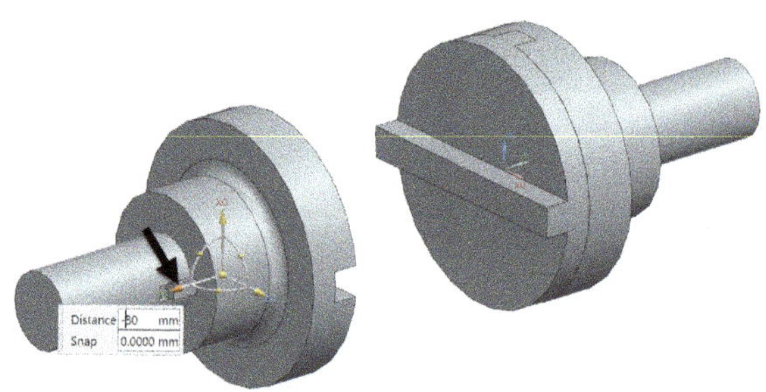

16. Click **Apply** to explode the Key.

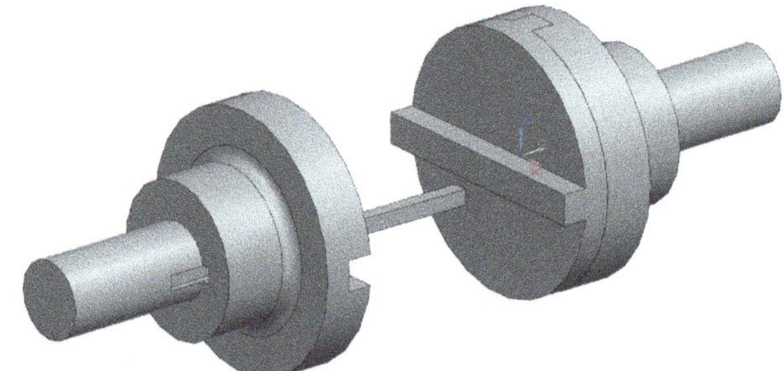

17. Activate the **Edit Explosion** dialog.
18. Explode the shaft in Y-direction up to the distance of **80 mm**.

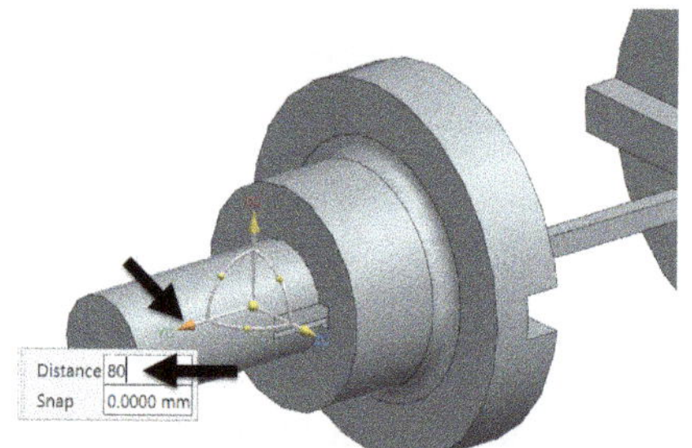

19. Likewise, explode the other flange subassembly and its parts in the opposite direction. The explosion distances are the same.

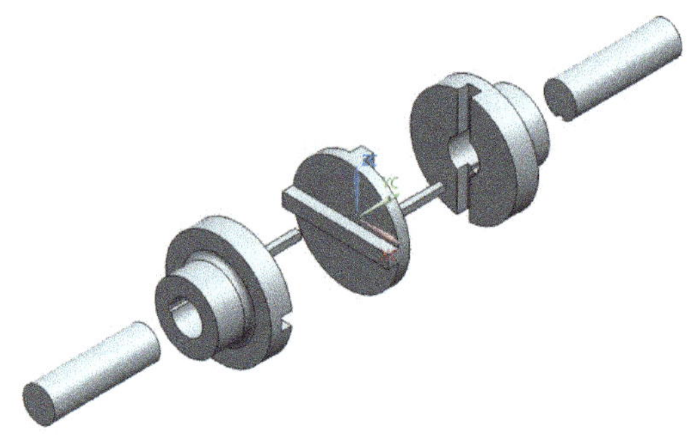

Creating Tracelines

1. Click **Tracelines** on the **Explosions** dialog; the **Tracelines** dialog appears.
2. Click on the center point of the Flange.

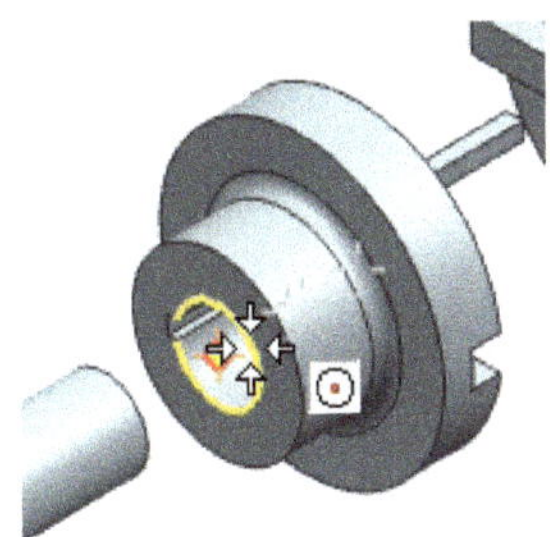

3. On the **Tracelines** dialog, select **End Object > Point**.
4. Click on the center point of the circular edge of the shaft.

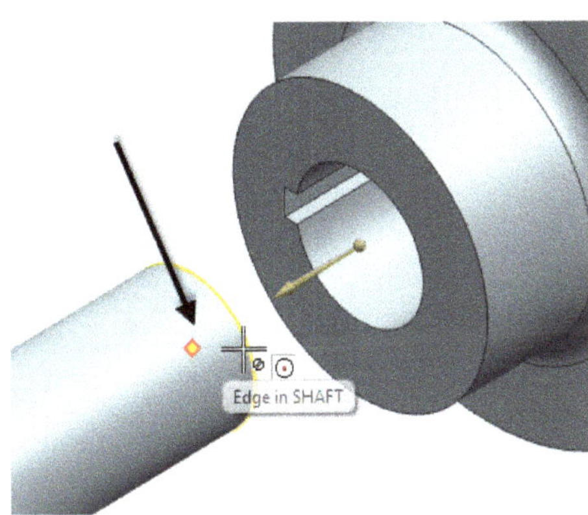

5. Click **OK** to create the trace line.

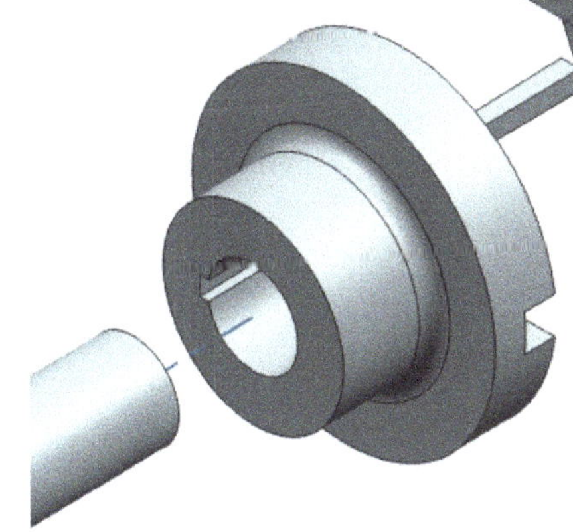

6. Click the **Tracelines** button on the **Explosions** dialog.
7. Under the **Start** section, select **Inferred > End Point** .
8. Select the edge on the keyway of the shaft.

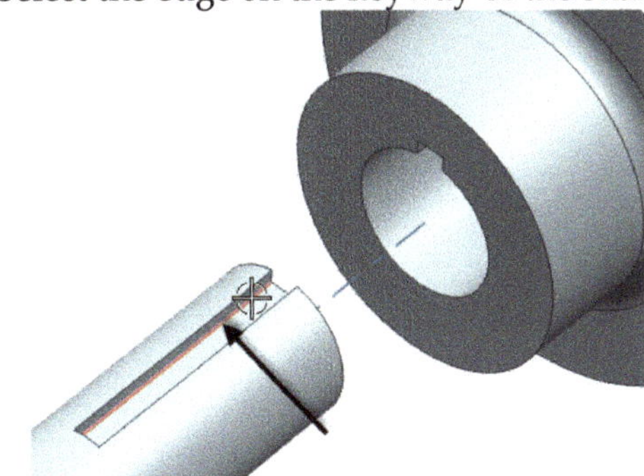

9. Double-click on the arrow displayed on the edge to reverse the direction.
10. Under the **End** section, select **Inferred > End Point**.
11. Click on the edge on the key.

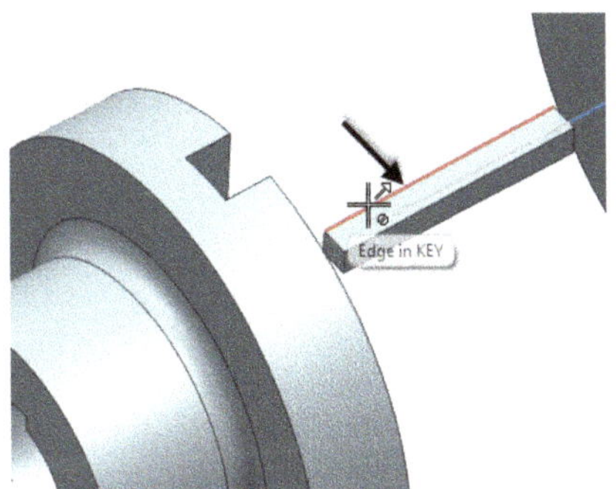

12. Double-click on the arrow to reverse the direction.

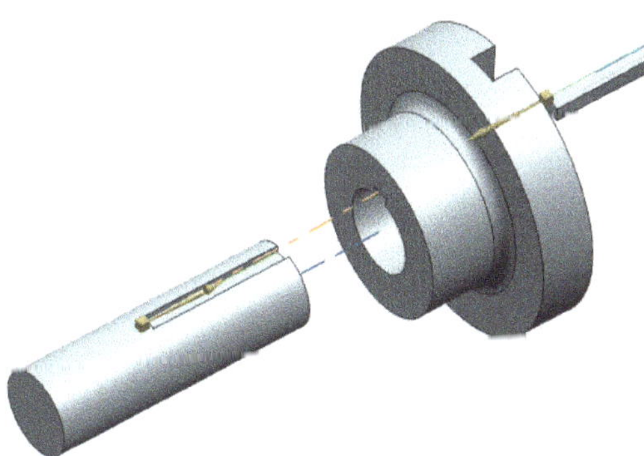

13. Click **OK** to create the trace line.
14. Create tracelines between the other parts.
15. Click Close on the Explosions dialog.
16. Change the view to **Wireframe with Hidden Edges**.

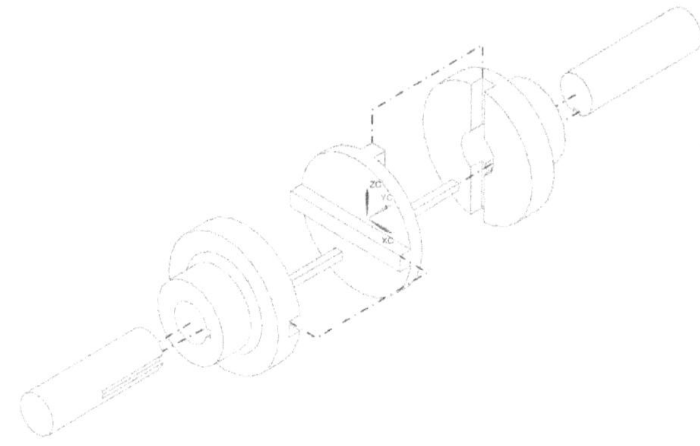

17. Click **Save** on the **Quick Access Toolbar** or click **File > Save**.
18. Close the assembly.

Chapter 4: Generating Drawings

In this chapter, you generate drawings of the parts and assembly from previous chapters.

In this chapter, you will:

- Open and edit a drawing template
- Insert standard views of a part model
- Add model and reference annotations
- Add another drawing sheet
- Insert exploded view of the assembly
- Insert the bill of materials of the assembly
- Apply balloons to the assembly

TUTORIAL 1

In this tutorial, you generate drawings of parts constructed in previous chapters.

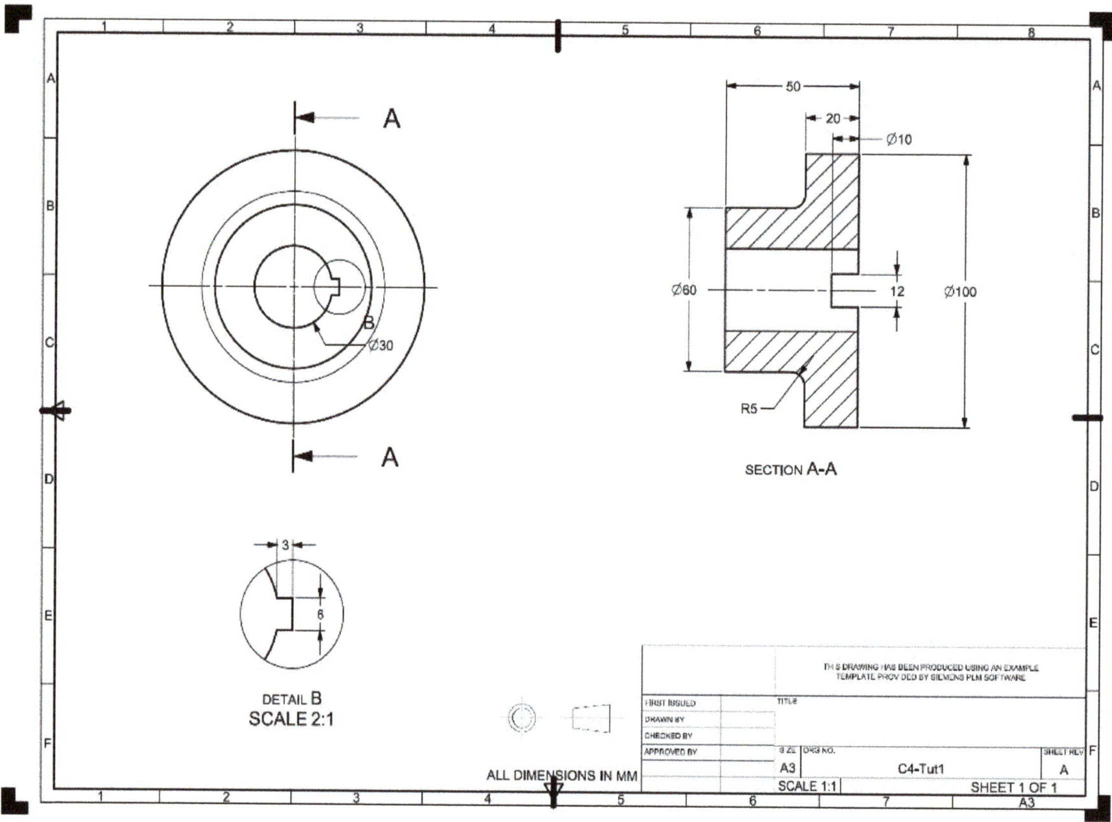

Opening a New Drawing File

1. Start NX.
2. To open a new drawing, click the **New** button on the **Standard** group, or click **File > New**.
3. On the **New** dialog, select the **Drawing** tab.
4. Click **A3-Size** in the **Templates** section.
5. Click **OK**; a new drawing window appears. Also, the **Populate Title Block** dialog appears.
6. Select the individual labels and type-in their values.
7. Click the **Close** button on this dialog.

Editing the Drawing Sheet

1. To edit the drawing sheet, click **Home > Sheet > New Sheet > Edit Sheet** on the ribbon; the **Sheet** dialog appears.
2. Click the gear icon located at the top left corner of the dialog and select **Sheet (More)**.
3. Expand the **Settings** section and set **Units** to **Millimeters**.
4. Set the **Projection** type to **3rd Angle Projection** .
5. Click **OK** on the **Sheet** dialog.

Generating the Base View

1. To generate the base view, click **Base View** on the **View** group; the **Base View** message box appears.
2. Click **Yes** on the message box; the **Part Name** dialog appears.
3. On the **Part Name** dialog, browse to the location NX/C3/Oldham_Coupling and double-click on **Flange.prt**; the **Base View** dialog appears.

   Also, the view appears along with the pointer.

4. On the **Base View** dialog, under the **Model View** section, select **Model View to Use > Front**.
5. Place the view, as shown in the figure; the **Projected View** dialog appears.
6. Click **Close** to close the dialog.

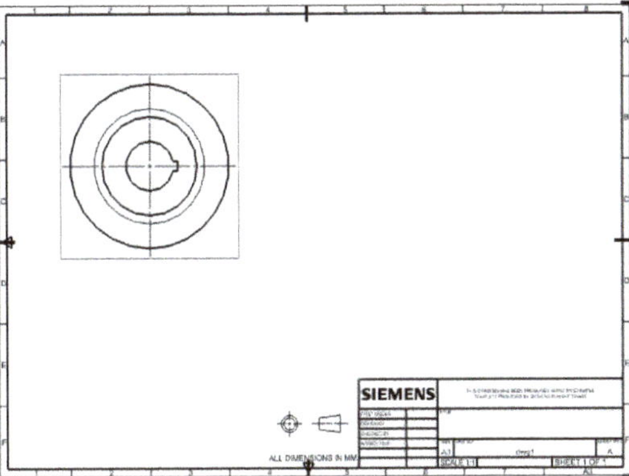

Generating the Section View

1. To generate a section view, click **Home > View > Section View** on the ribbon; the **Section View** dialog appears.
2. Click on the base view; the section line appears.
3. Click on the center point of the base view.

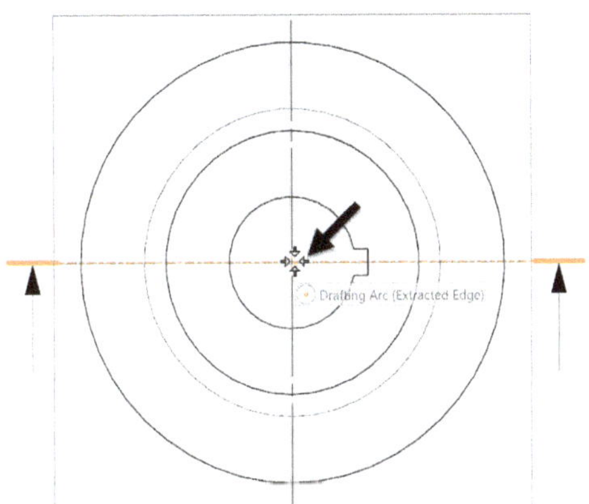

4. Drag the pointer toward the right and click to position the section view.

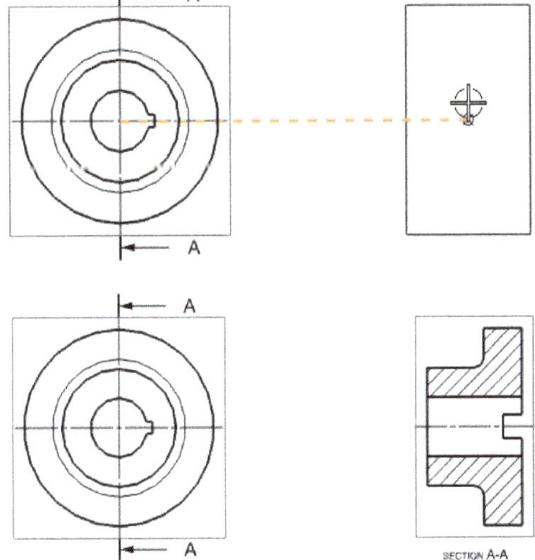

5. Click **Close** on the **Section View** dialog.

Generating the Detailed View

Now, you need to generate a detailed view of the keyway that appears on the front view.

1. To generate a detailed view, click the **Detail View** button on the **View** group.
2. On the **Detail View** dialog, select **Type > Circular**.
3. Specify the center point and boundary point of the detail view, as shown.

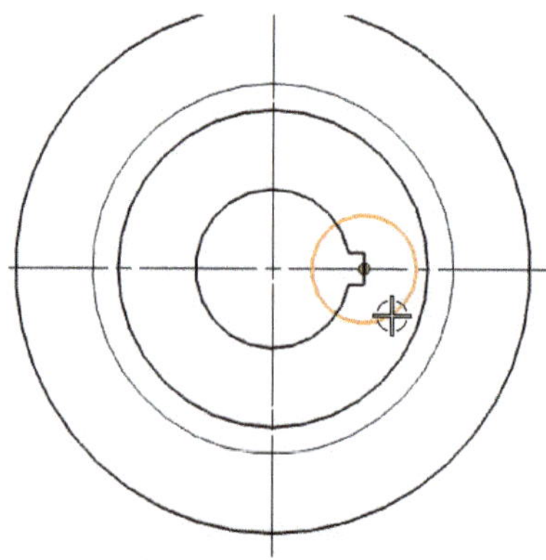

4. Under the **Scale** section, select **Scale > 2:1**.
5. Position the detail view below the base view.
6. Close the **Detail View** dialog.

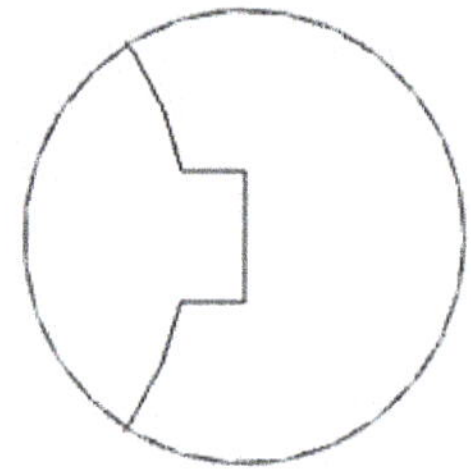

DETAIL B
SCALE 2:1

Setting Annotation Preferences

1. To set the annotation preferences, click **File > Preferences > Drafting**; the **Drafting Preferences** dialog appears.

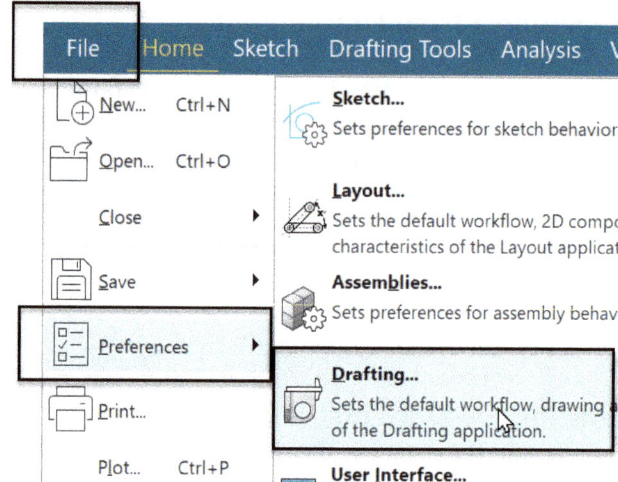

2. On the dialog, type-in **Orientation and Location** in the **Find** box and press Enter.
3. Set the **Orientation** value to **Horizontal text**.

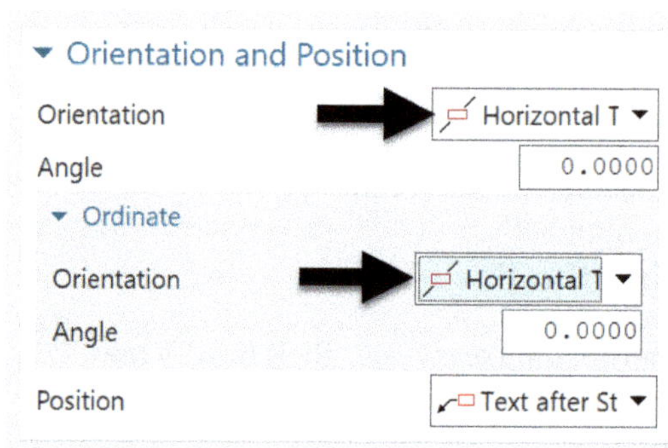

4. On the dialog, select **Dimension > Text > Units** from the tree.
5. Set the **Decimal Delimiter** value to . **Period**.

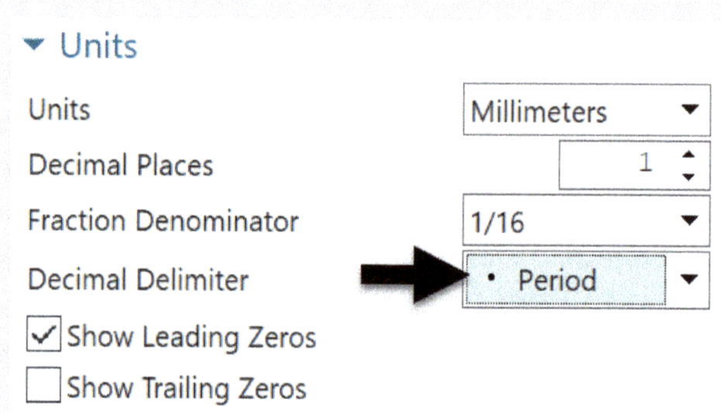

6. On the dialog, select **Dimension > Text > Dimension Text** from the tree.
7. Under the **Format** section, type-in 3.5 in the **Height** box.
8. Select **Common > Line/Arrow > Arrowhead** from the tree.

9. Under the **Workflow** section, check the **Automatic Orientation** option.
10. Under the **Format** section, type-in **3.5** and **30** in the **Length** and **Angle** boxes, respectively.
11. Click **Common > Line/Arrow > Extension Line**.
12. Type-in **1** in the **Gap** boxes.
13. Type in **2** in the **Extension Line Overhang**.
14. Click **Common > Lettering**.
15. Under the **Text Parameters** section, type-in **3.5** in the **Height** box,
16. Click **OK**.

Dimensioning the Drawing Views

1. To add dimensions, click **Home > Dimension > Rapid Dimension** on the ribbon.
2. On the section view, click the horizontal line located at the top.

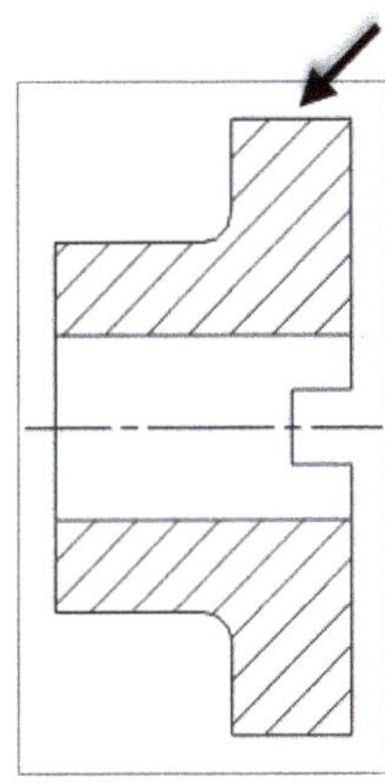

3. Drag the pointer up and click to position the dimension.

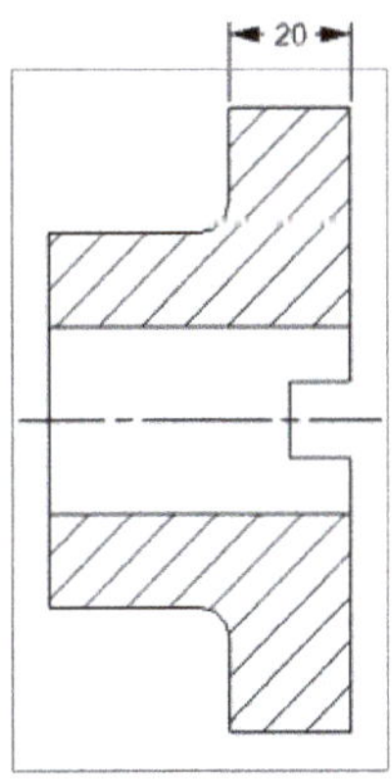

4. Click on the ends of the section view, as shown.

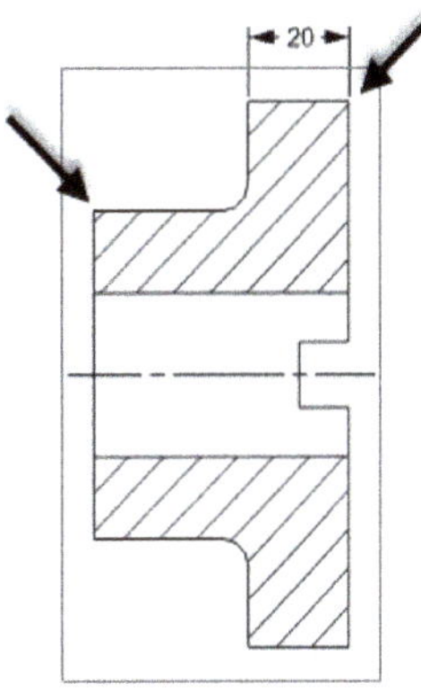

5. Drag the pointer up and click to position the dimension.

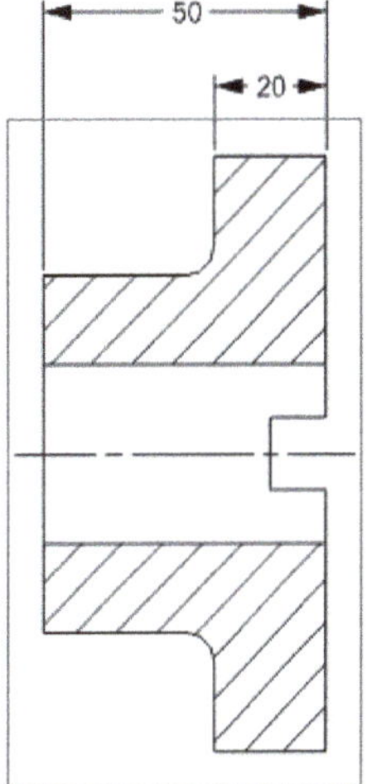

6. Add another linear dimension to the section view.

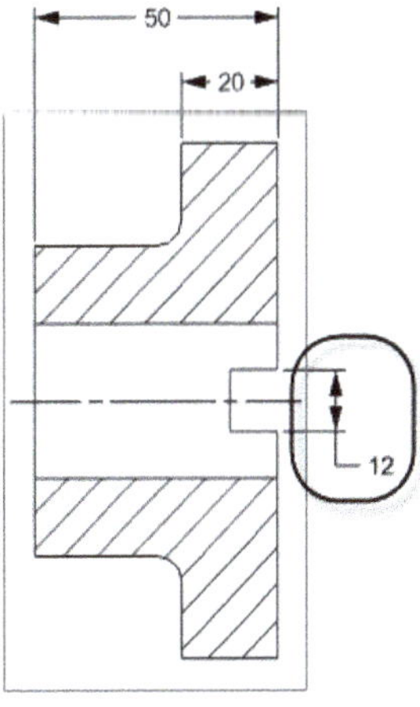

7. On the section view, click on the arc located at

the bottom.

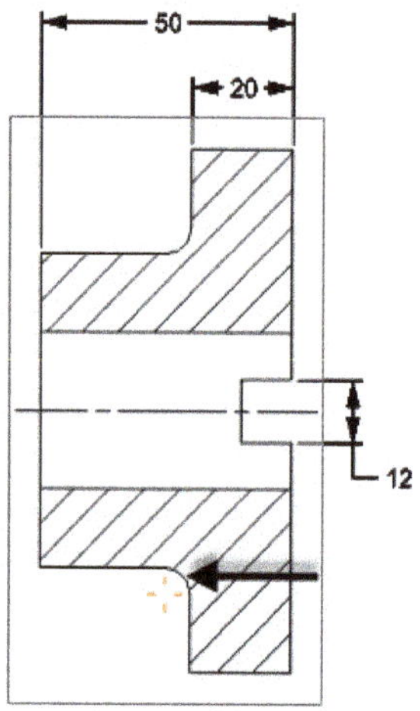

8. Drag the pointer downward and click to position the radial dimension.

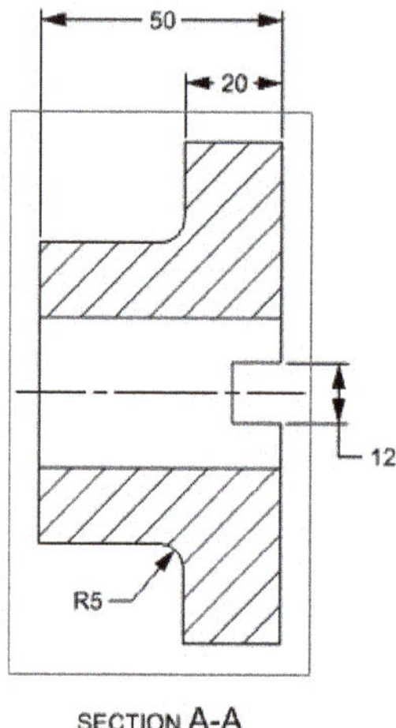

9. On the **Rapid Dimension** dialog, under the **Measurement** section, select **Method > Cylindrical**.

10. Click on the ends of the section view, as shown.

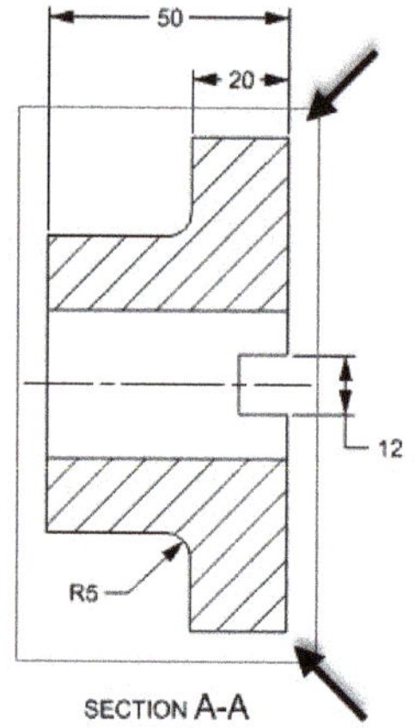

11. Drag the pointer rightwards and click to position the dimension.

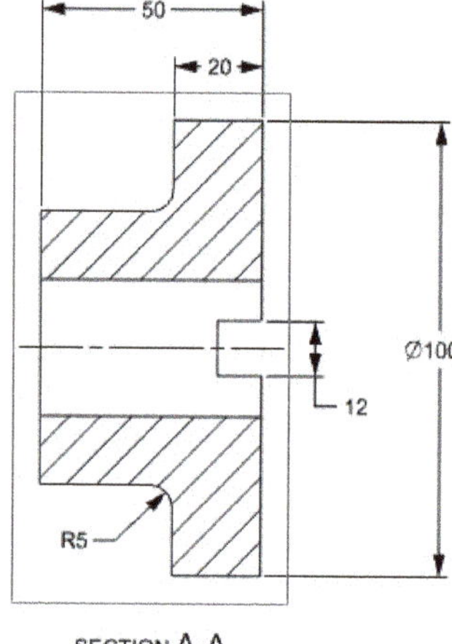

12. Create the other dimensions on the section view, as shown.

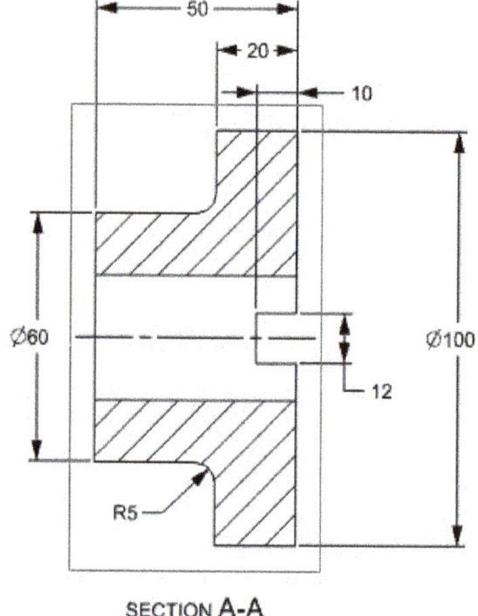

13. Create the radial dimension on the front view, as shown.

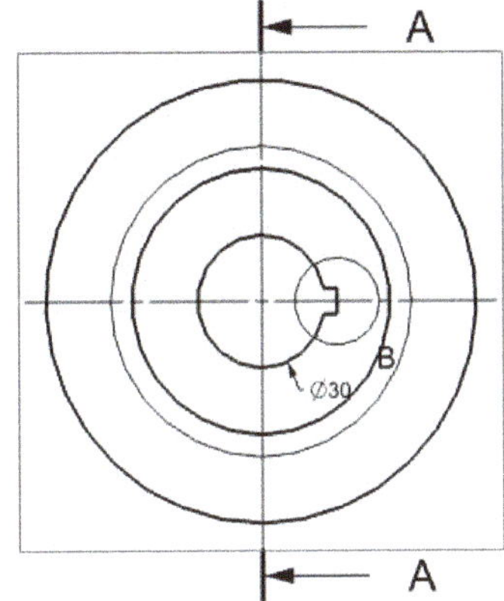

14. Create the dimensions on the detail view, as shown.

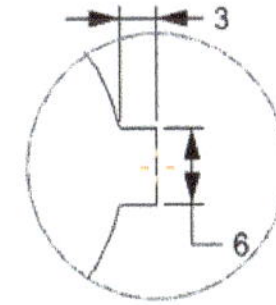

DETAIL B
SCALE 2:1

Saving the Drawing

1. On the **Quick Access Toolbar**, click **Save**; the **Name Parts** dialog appears.
2. Type-in **Flange Drawing** in the **Name** box and click the **Folder** button.
3. Browse to NX/C3 folder and then click **OK** button twice
4. Close the drawing.

TUTORIAL 2

In this tutorial, you generate the drawing of the Disc constructed in Chapter 1.

Creating a custom template

1. Close the NX application window.
2. Type NX in the search bar located on the Taskbar.
3. Right click on the **NX** icon and select **Run as administrator**.
4. Click **Yes** on the message box.
5. On the ribbon, click the **New** button.
6. On the **New** dialog, click the **Model** tab.
7. Double-click on the **Model** template.
8. On the ribbon, click **Application > Document > Drafting** .
9. On the **Sheet** dialog, select **Standard Size**.
10. Set **Size** to **A3 - 297 x 420**.
11. Set **Scale** to **1:1**.
12. Under the **Settings** section, set **Units** to **Millimeters**.
13. Select **3rd Angle Projection** and uncheck **Always Start Drawing View Command**.
14. Click **OK** to open a blank sheet.

Adding Borders and Title Block

1. On the ribbon, click **Drafting Tools > Drawing Format > Borders and Zones** .
2. On the **Borders and Zones** dialog, leave the default settings, and click **OK**.

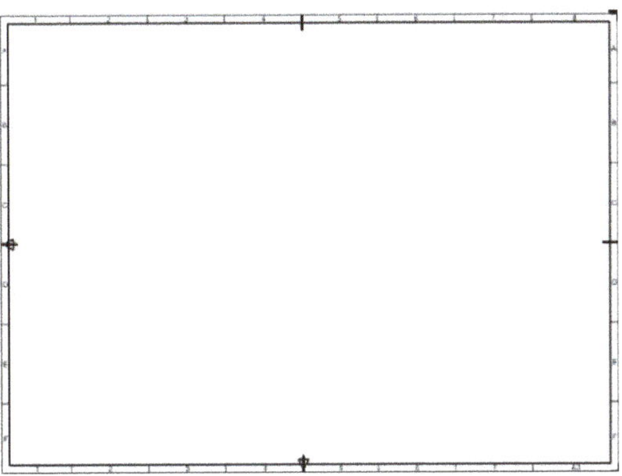

3. On the ribbon, click **Home > Table > Tabular Note** .
4. On the **Tabular Note** dialog, expand the **Settings** section and click the **Settings** icon.
5. On the **Tabular Notes Settings** dialog, click **Common > Section** under the tree view.
6. Under the **Format** section, select **Alignment Position > Bottom Right**.
7. Click **Close**.
8. On the **Tabular Note** dialog, Under the **Table Size** section, set **Number of Columns** to **3** and **Number of Rows** to **2**.
9. Type-in **50** in **Column Width** box.
10. Click on the bottom right corner of the sheet border.

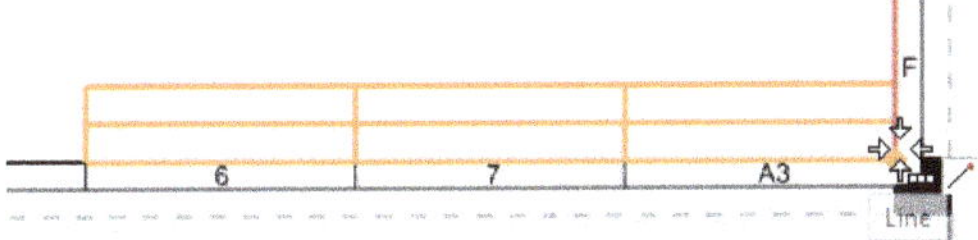

11. Click **Close** on the **Tabular Note** dialog.
12. Click on the left vertical line of the tabular note.

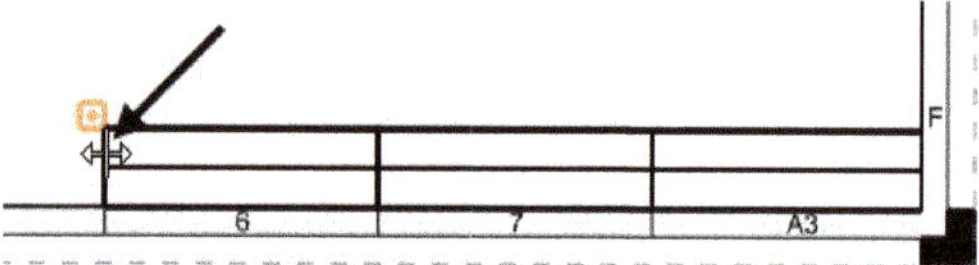

13. Press the left mouse button and drag toward the right.
14. Release the left mouse button when the column width is changed to 35.

15. Likewise, change the width of the second and third columns.

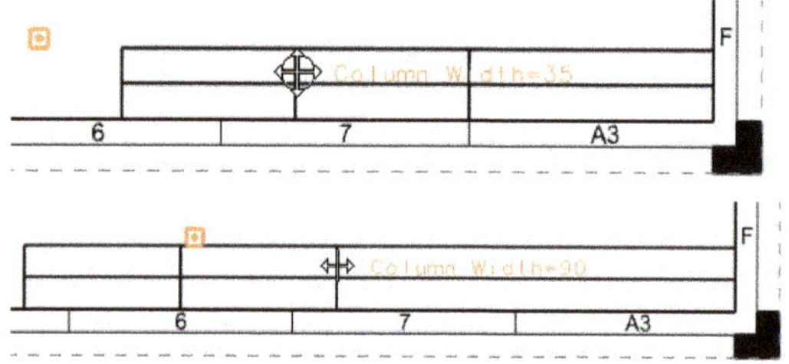

16. Click inside the second cell of the top row.
17. Press the left mouse button and drag it to the third cell.

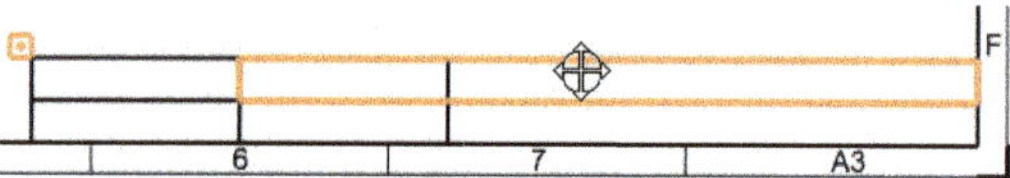

18. Click the right mouse button in the selected cells and select **Merge Cells**.

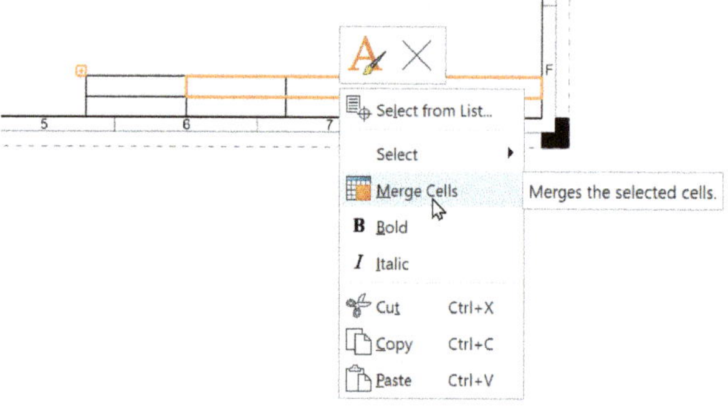

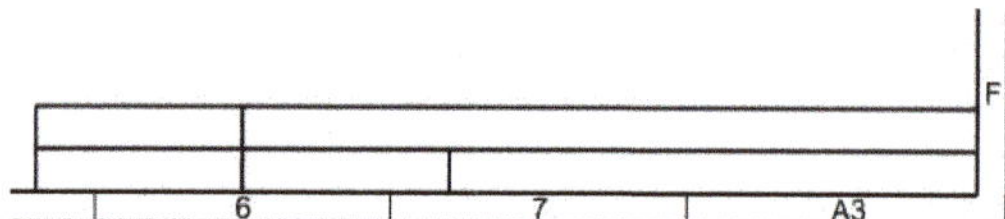

19. Change the height of the top row to 20.

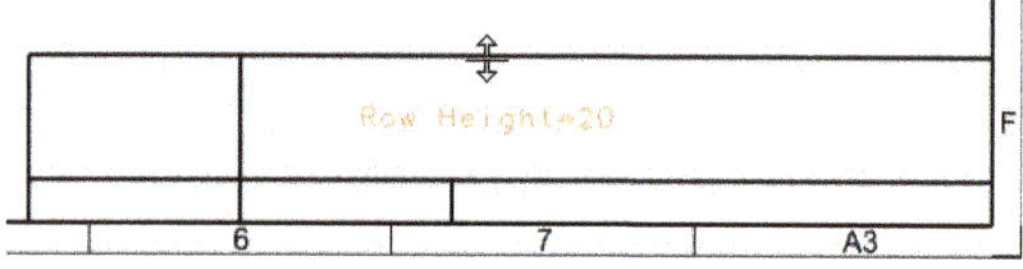

20. Click **Yes** on the message box.
21. Click the right mouse button in the second cell of the top row. Select **Settings** .
22. On the **Settings** dialog, select **Prefix/Suffix** from the tree.
23. Type-in **Title:** in the **Prefix** box.
24. Click **Close**.

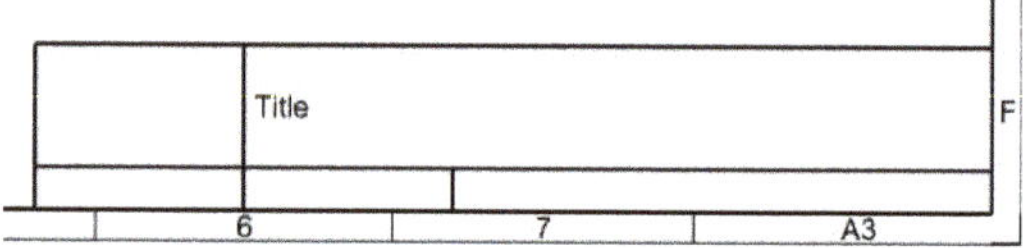

25. Likewise, add prefixes to other cells.

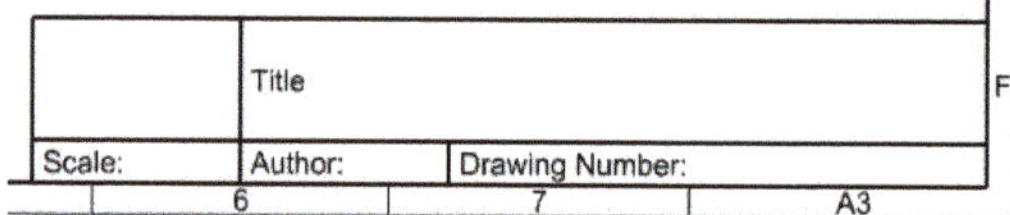

26. Click the right mouse button in the first cell of the top row.
27. Click **Import > Image**.
28. Select your company logo image and click **OK**. Make sure that the size of the image is less than the cell size.
29. On the ribbon, click **Drafting Tools > Drawing Format > Define Title Block** .
30. Click on the table, and then click **OK**.
31. On the ribbon, click **Drafting Tools > Drawing Format > Mark as Template** .
32. On the dialog, select **Mark as Template and Update PAX File**.
33. Under the **PAX File Settings** section, type-in **Custom Template** in the **Presentation Name** box.
34. Select **Template Type > Reference Existing Part**.
35. Click the **Browse** icon.
36. Go to *C:\Program Files\Siemens\NX 2206\LOCALIZATION\prc\english\startup*
37. Right-click on the **ugs_drawing_templates** file and select **Properties**.
38. Uncheck the **Read-Only** option, then click **OK**.
39. Click **OK**.
40. On the **Input Validation** box, click **Yes**.
41. Click **OK** twice.
42. Save and close the file.

Opening a new drawing file using the custom template

1. On the ribbon, click the **New** button on the **Home** tab of the ribbon.

2. On the **New** dialog, under the **Drawing** tab, select **Relationship > Reference Existing Part**.
3. Under the **Templates** section, select **Custom Template**.
4. Under the **Part to create a drawing of** section, click the **Browse** button.
5. On the **Select master part** dialog, click **Open**.
6. Go to the location of Disc.prt and double-click on it.
7. Click **OK** twice.
8. On the **Populate Title Block** dialog, type-in values, as shown.
9. Click **Close**.

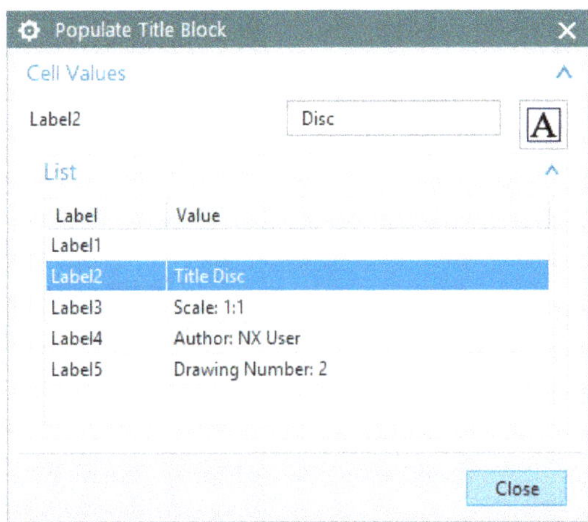

Generating Drawing Views

1. On the **Base View** dialog,
2. Select **Scale > 1:1**.
3. Select **Model View to Use > Front**.
4. Place the view, as shown.

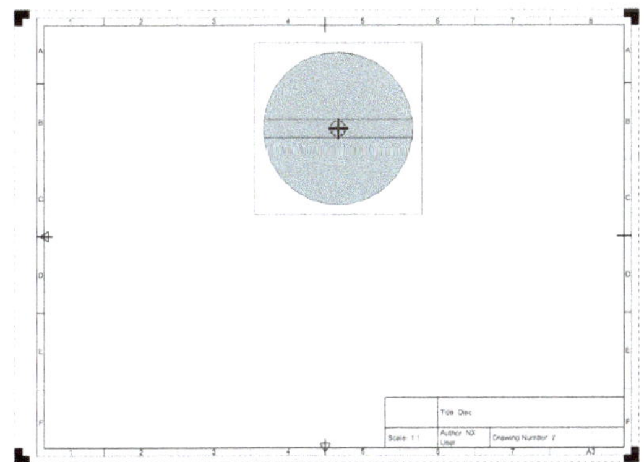

5. Move the pointer downward and click to place the projected view.

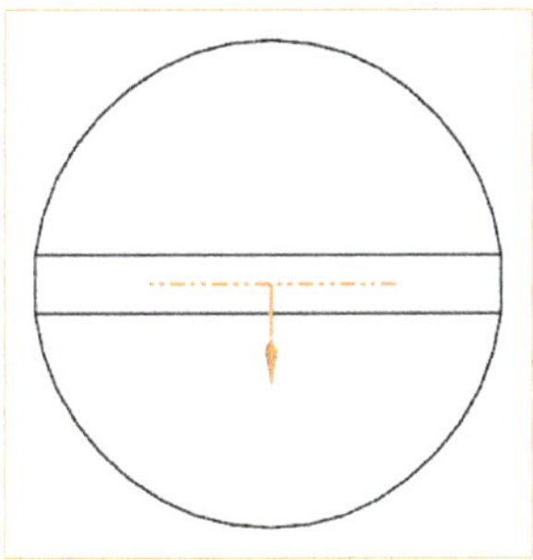

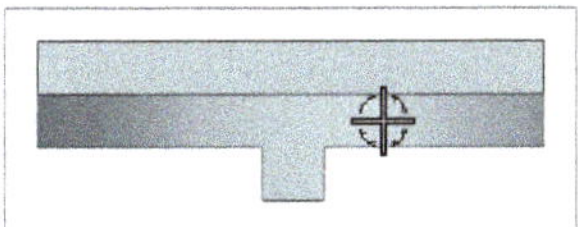

6. Click **Close** on the **Projected View** dialog.

Adding Dimensions

1. Add centerlines and dimensions to the drawing.
2. Save and close the drawing file.

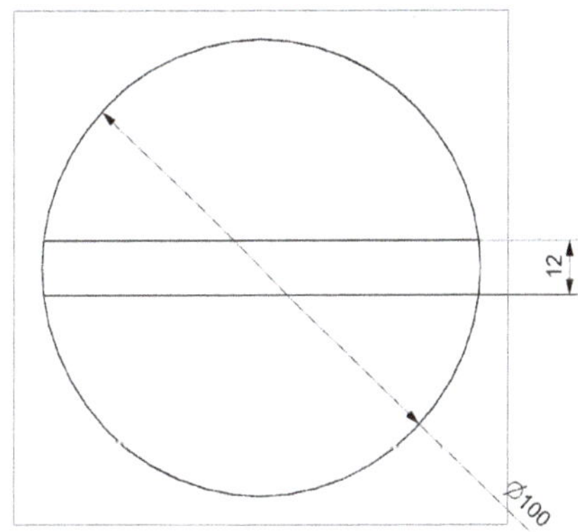

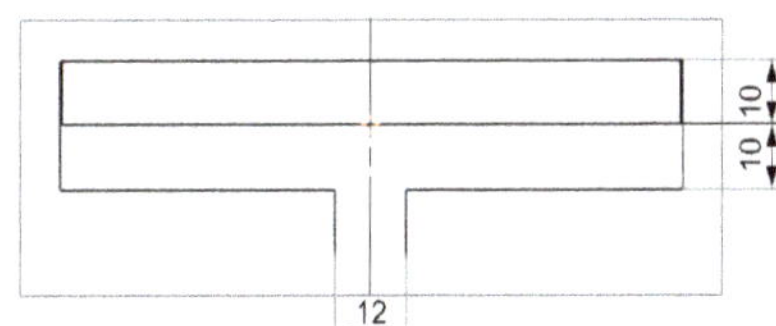

TUTORIAL 3

In this tutorial, you generate the drawing of the Oldham coupling assembly created in the previous chapter.

Creating the assembly drawing

1. Open the Main_assembly.prt file.
2. Click **Applications > Document > Drafting**.
3. On the **Sheet** dialog, select **Standard Size**.

4. Set **Size** to **A3 -297 x 420**.
5. Set **Scale** to **1:2**.
6. Under the **Settings** section, check **Always Start View Creation.**
7. Select **Base View command.**
8. Click **OK**.
9. On the **Base View** dialog, under the **Model View** section, select **Model View to Use** > **Isometric.**
10. Under the **Scale** section, select **Scale > 1:2.**
11. Click on the left side of the drawing sheet.
12. Click **Close** on the **Projected View** dialog.

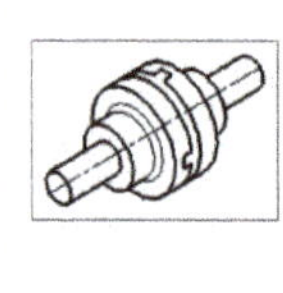

Generating the Exploded View

1. On the ribbon, click **Home > View > Base View.**
2. On the **Base View** dialog, select **Model View to Use >Trimetric.**
3. Click on the right side of the drawing sheet.
4. Click **Close.**

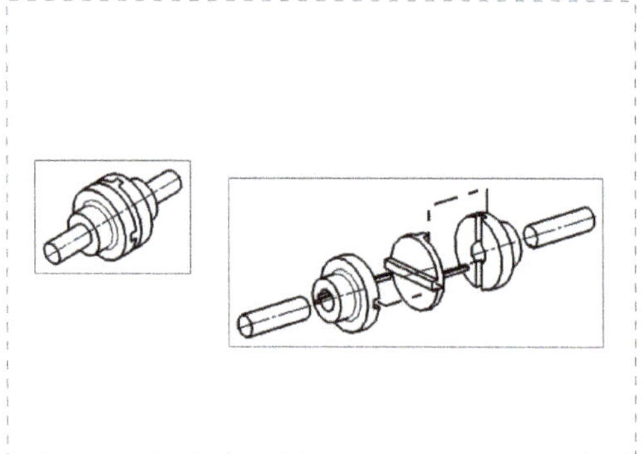

Generating the Part list and Balloons

1. To generate a part list, click **Home > Table > Part List** on the ribbon.
2. In the **Contents** section, select **Scope > Leaves Only.**

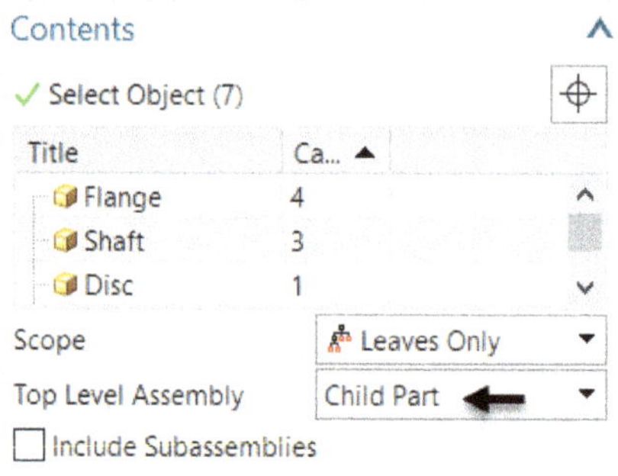

3. Expand the **Balloons** section and check the **Show** option.
4. Select the **Trimetric@2** view from the View list
5. Click **Specify Location** on the **Origin** section of the **Parts List** dialog.
6. Place the part list at the top-right corner.
7. Arrange the balloons by dragging them.
8. Save and close the file

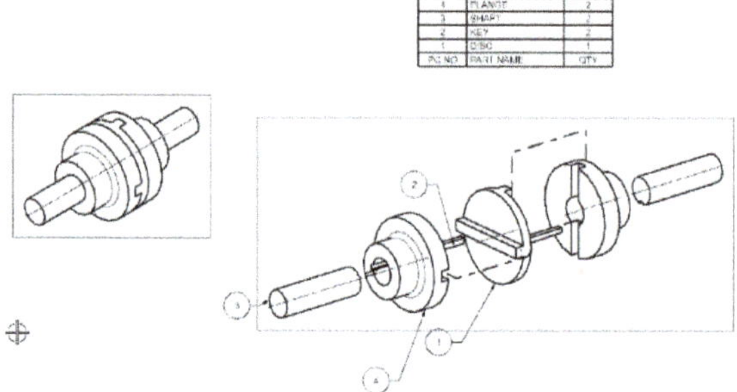

Chapter 5: Sketching

In this chapter, you learn the sketching tools. You learn to create:

- Rectangles
- Polygons
- Resolving Sketch
- Geometric Constraints
- Studio Splines
- Ellipses
- Circles
- Arcs
- Trim
- Fillets and Chamfers

TUTORIAL 1 (Creating Rectangles)

A rectangle is a four-sided 2D object. You can create a rectangle by just specifying its two diagonal corners. However, there are various methods to create a rectangle. These methods are explained next.

1. Start a new file using the **Model** template.
2. On the ribbon, click **Construction > Sketch** and select the Front plane.
3. Click **OK** on the **Create Sketch** dialog.
4. On the ribbon, click **Home > Curve > Rectangle** .
5. Select the origin point to define the first corner.
6. Move the pointer and click to define the second corner.

You can also type the **Width** and **Height** values to create the rectangle.

7. On the **Rectangle** toolbar, click the **By 3 Points** icon under the **Rectangle Method** section. This option creates a slanted rectangle.
8. Select two points to define the width and inclination angle of the rectangle.

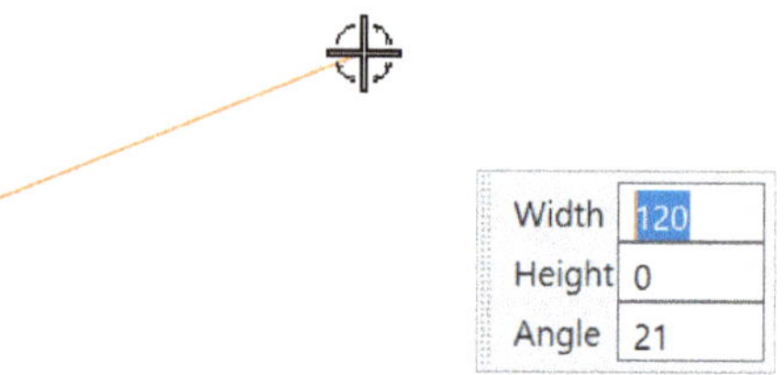

9. Select the third point to define its height.

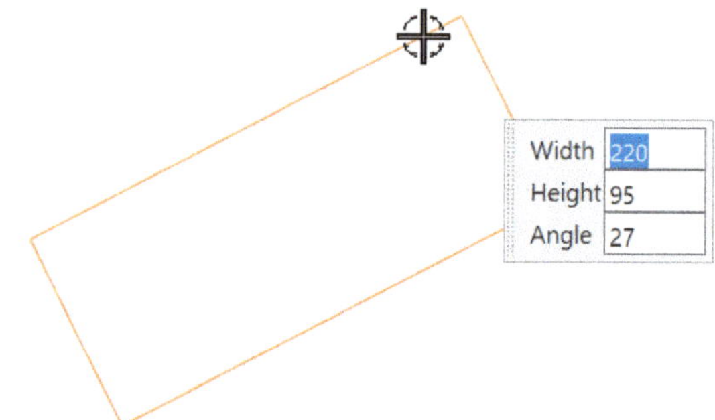

10. On the **Rectangle** toolbar, click the **From Center** icon under the **Rectangle Method** section.
11. Click to define the center point of the rectangle.
12. Move the pointer and click to define the midpoint of one side. Also, the inclination angle is defined.

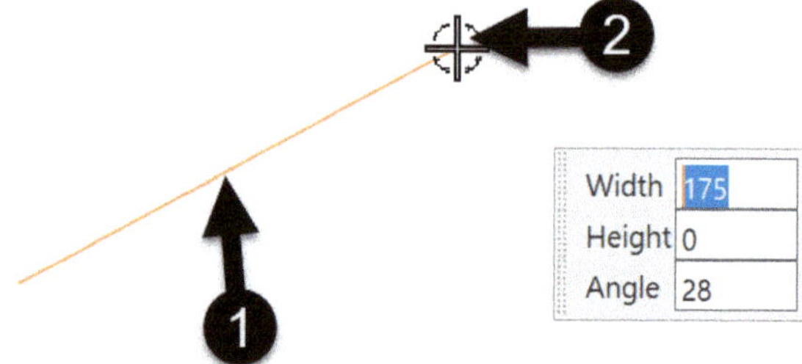

13. Move the pointer and click to define the corner point.

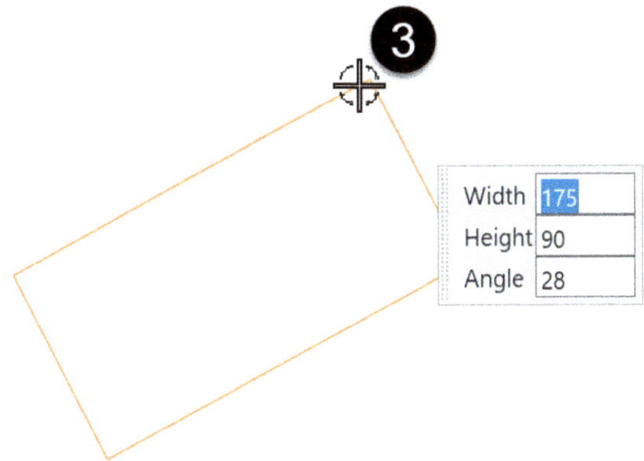

14. Click **Close** on the **Rectangle** toolbar.

Multi-Selection Gesture Drop-down

This drop-down is available on the Top Border Bar and has options to select multiple objects. The **Rectangle** option helps you to select multiple elements by dragging a rectangle covering them.

The **Lasso** option helps you to select multiple elements by dragging the pointer around them.

The **Circle** option helps you to select multiple elements by clicking and dragging a circle covering the elements.

1. On the Top Border Bar, select **Lasso** from the **Multi-Selection Gesture** Drop-down.

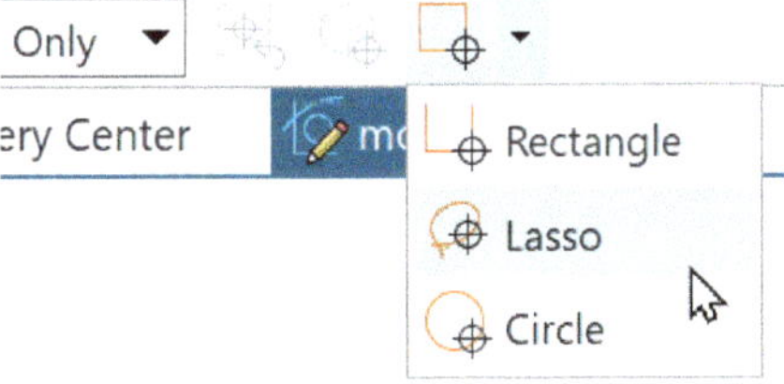

2. On the Top Border Bar, **Selection Scope** to **Within Active Sketch Only**.

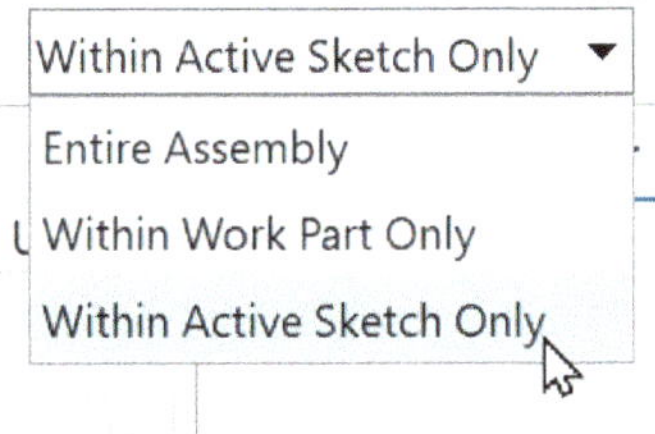

3. Press and hold the left mouse button and drag the pointer covering the slanted rectangles.

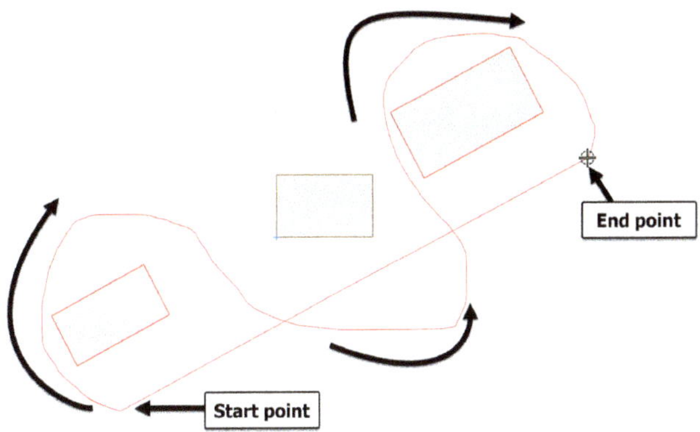

4. Press **Delete** to erase the rectangles.
5. Click **Undo** on the **Quick Access Toolbar**.

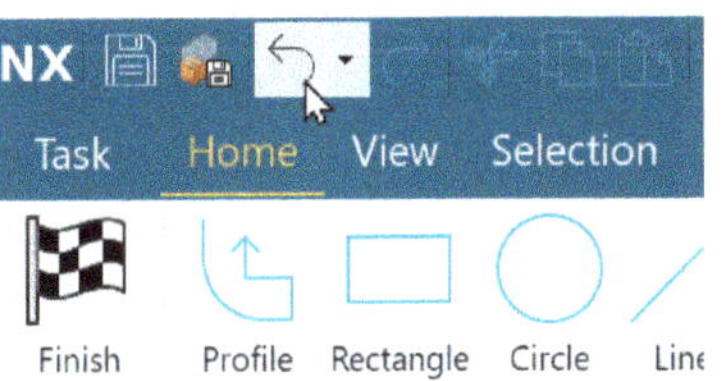

6. On the Top Border Bar, select **Circle** from the **Multi-Selection Gesture** Drop-down.

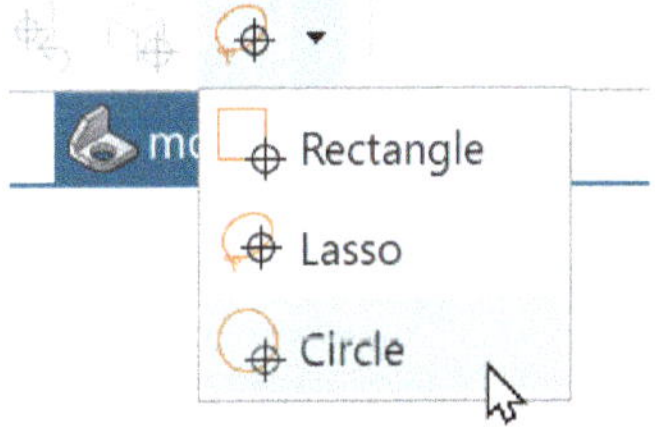

7. On the Top Border Bar, select **Curve** from the **Selection Filter** Drop-down.

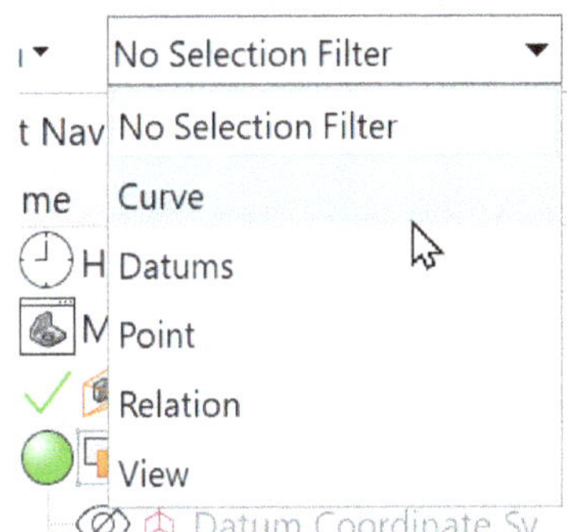

8. Click and drag a selection circle covering all the sketch elements.

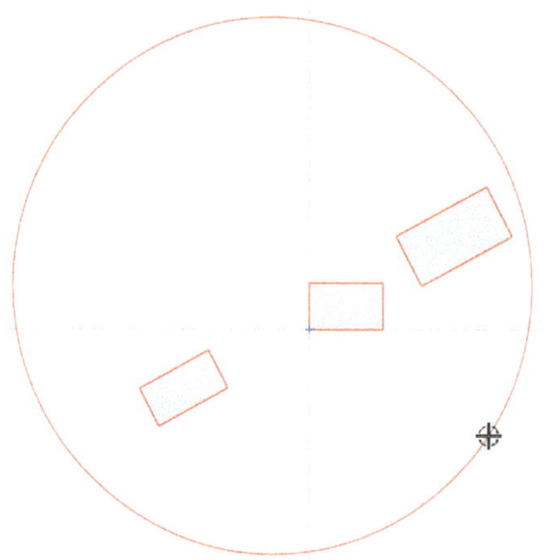

9. Press **Delete** to erase the rectangles.

TUTORIAL 2 (Creating Polygons)

A Polygon is a shape having many sides ranging from 3 to 513. In NX, you can create regular polygons having sided with equal length. Follow the steps given next to create a polygon.

1. Activate the **Sketch Task** environment.
2. On the ribbon, click the down-arrow located at the bottom-right corner of the **Curve** group. Next, select the **Move Gallery** option.

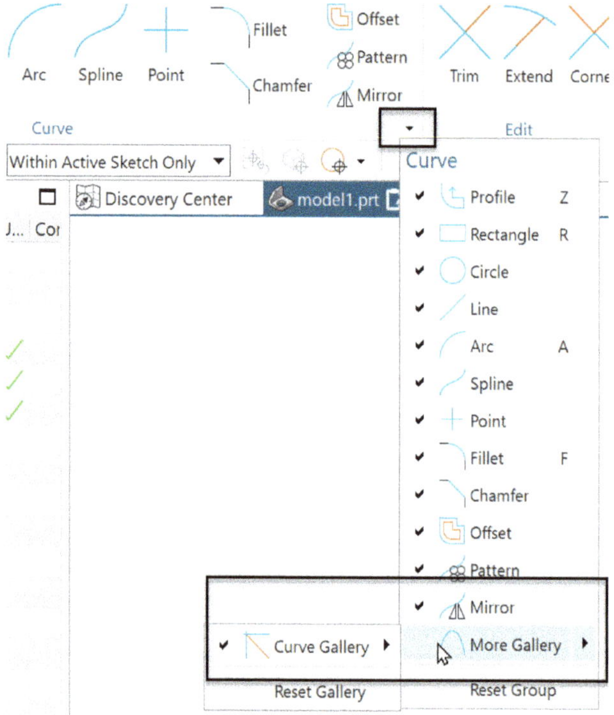

3. On the ribbon, click **Home > Curve > More Gallery > Polygon**.

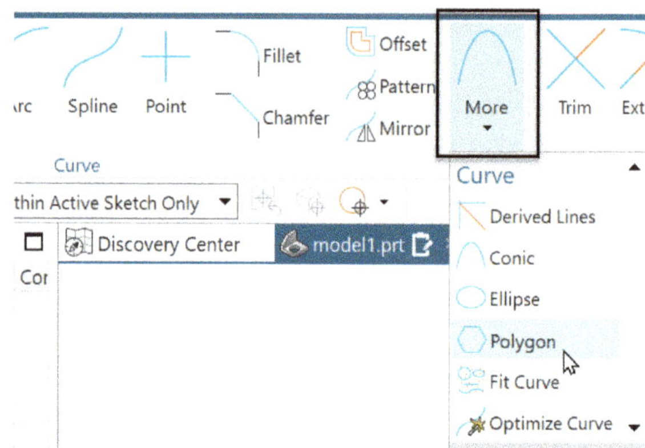

4. On the **Polygon** dialog, type **8** in the **Number of Sides** box under the **Sides** section.
5. Under the **Size** section, select **Size > Inscribed Radius**. This option creates a polygon with its sides touching an imaginary circle. You can also select the **Circumscribed Radius** or **Side Length** options. The **Circumscribed Radius** option helps you to create a polygon with its vertices touching an imaginary circle. The **Side Length** option allows you to create a polygon by specify the length of anyone of its side.
6. Click to define the center of the polygon.
7. Type **0** in the **Rotation** box.
8. Move the pointer and notice that the rotation of the polygon is constrained.
9. Type 50 in the **Radius** box and press Enter.

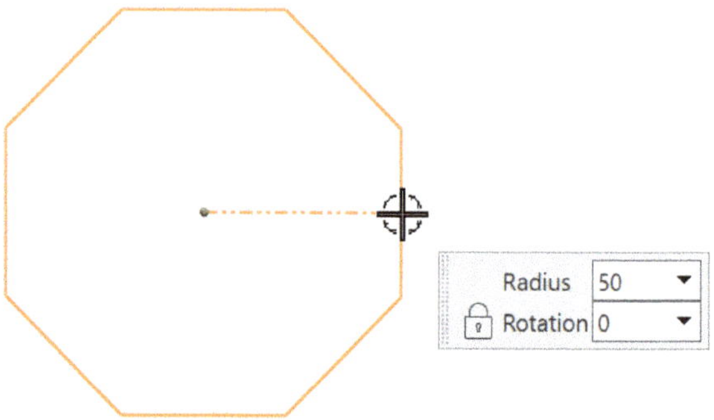

10. Click **Close** on the dialog to deactivate the tool.

Circle by 3 Points

1. On the ribbon, click **Home > Curve > Circle** .
2. On the **Circle** toolbar, click **Circle by 3 Points** icon under the **Circle Method** section.

3. Click on the vertices of the polygon. A circle is created, passing through the vertices.

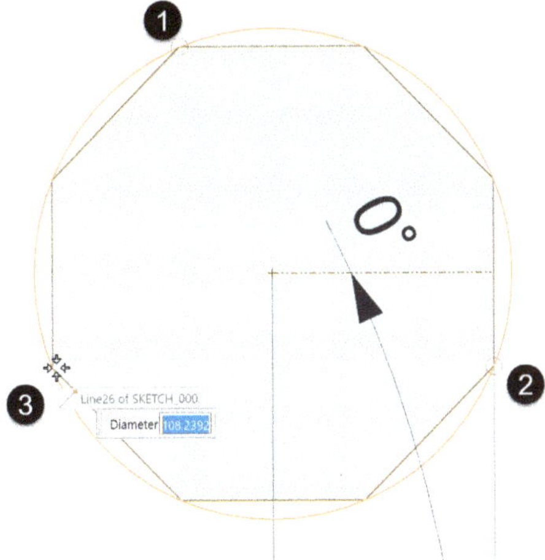

TUTORIAL 3 (Studio Splines)

Studio Splines are non-uniform curves, which are used to create irregular shapes. In NX, you can create studio splines by using two methods: **Through Points**, and **By Pole**.

1. Download the **Studio-spline example.jpg** file from http://www.onlineinstructor.org/shop/nx-tutorial/.
2. On the Top Border Bar, click **Menu > Insert > Datum > Raster Image**.

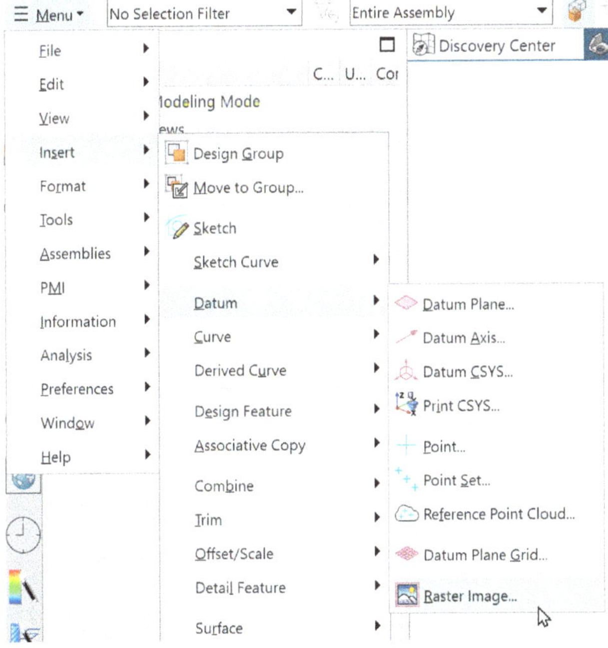

3. On the **Raster Image** dialog, click the **Choose Image File** icon.
4. Go to the location of the downloaded image file and double-click on it.
5. Select the XZ Plane from the Datum Coordinate System.
6. Under the **Orientation** section, select **Basepoint > Bottom Center**.
7. Set the **Reference Direction** to **Vertical**.
8. Enter 180 in the **Rotation** box.

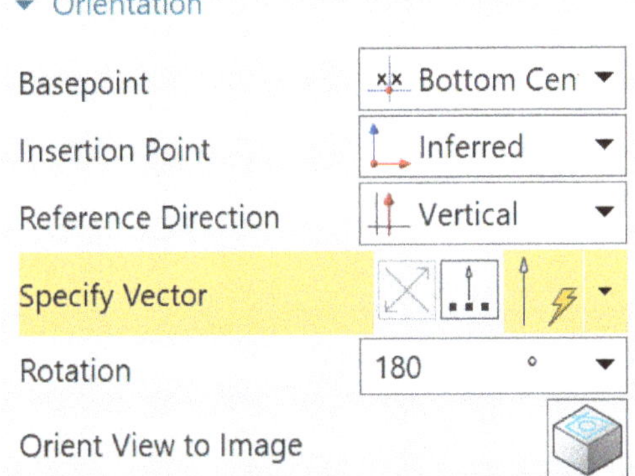

9. Expand the **Image Settings** section and set the **Overall Translucency** to 50.
10. Click **OK**.
11. Activate the **Sketch** command and select the Front Plane.
12. On the Ribbon, click **Home > Curve > Spline**

.

13. On the **Studio Spline** dialog, select **Type > Through Points**.
14. Select the five points, as shown.

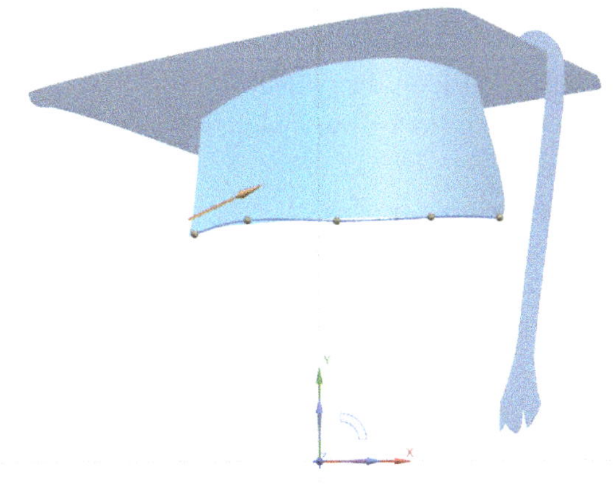

15. Select the three points, as shown.

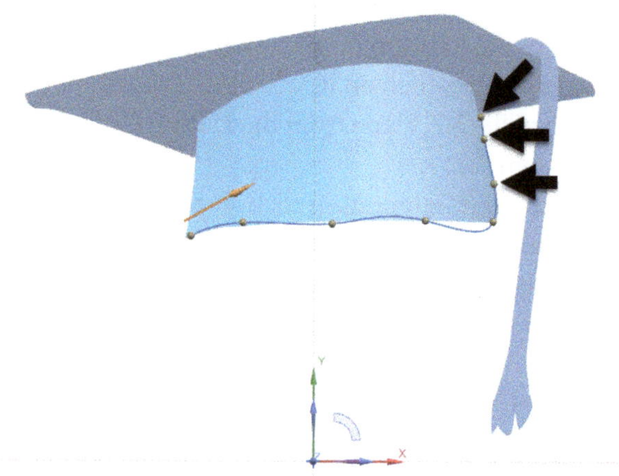

16. Likewise, select other points, as shown.

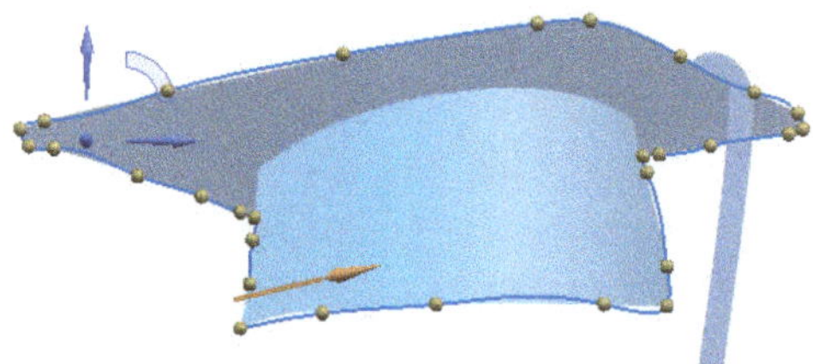

17. Under the **Parameterization** section, set the **Degree** value to 2, and check the **Closed** option.
18. Click **OK**.
19. Click **Yes** on the **Continuous Auto Dimensioning** message box. The auto dimensions are not created.

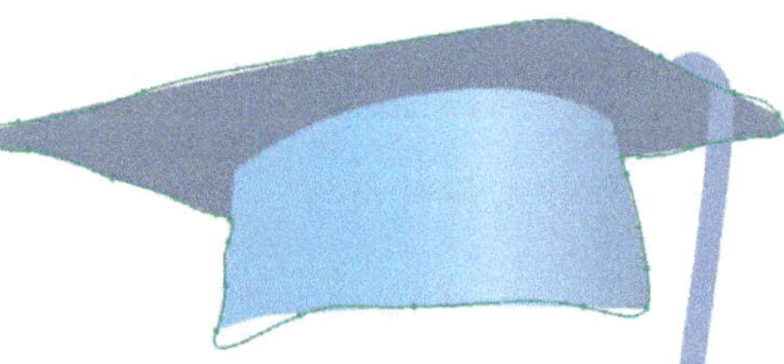

20. Double-click on the spline.
21. On the **Studio Spline** dialog, select **Type > By Poles**.
22. Drag the pole, as shown.

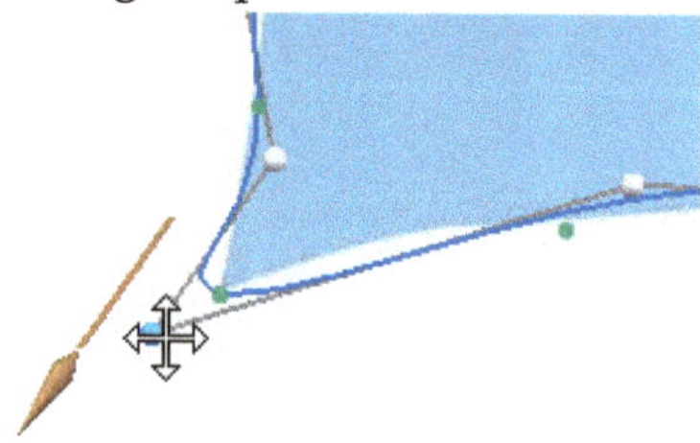

23. Likewise, modify the other pole locations, as shown.

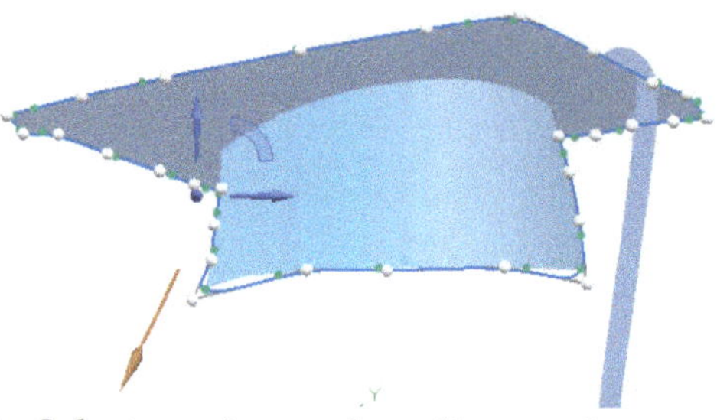

24. Select a point on the spline, as shown. A new pole is added.

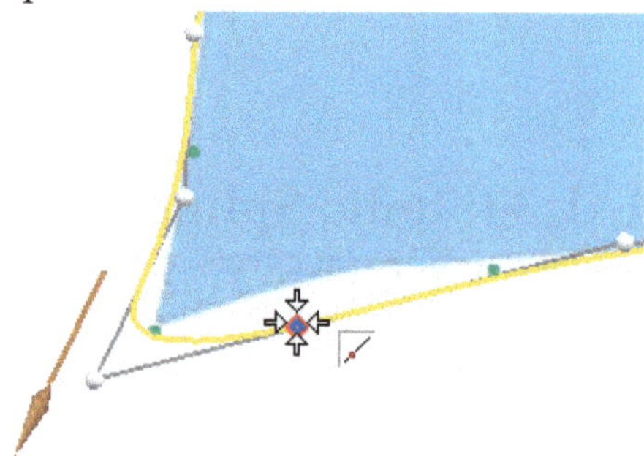

25. Drag the new pole to modify the spline.

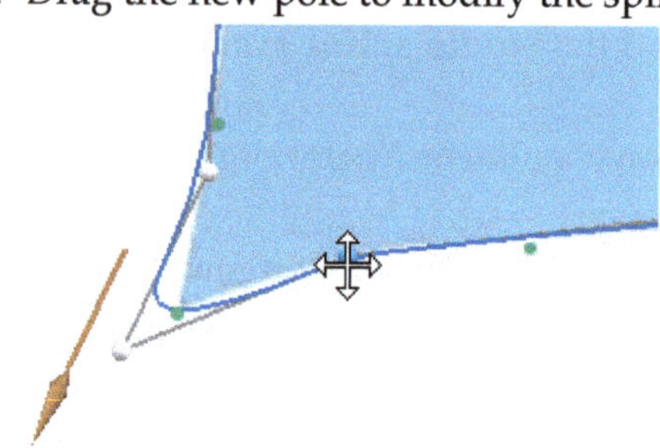

26. Likewise, add poles wherever they are required and modify their position.
27. Click **OK**.
28. Click on the image and select **Hide**.

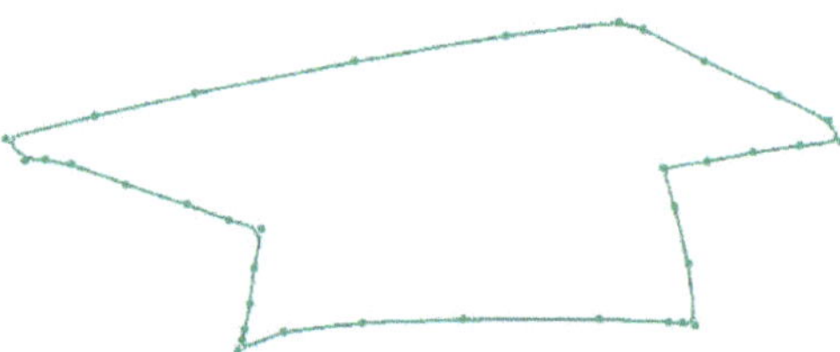

29. Click **Finish** on the **Sketch** group.

TUTORIAL 4 (Geometric Constraints)

1. Activate the **Sketch Task** environment.
2. On the ribbon, click **Home > Curve > Profile**

.

3. Select the sketch origin.
4. Move the pointer towards right horizontally and click.
5. Move the pointer up vertically and click.
6. Move the pointer toward the left and click. The Horizontal and Vertical constraints are created automatically.
7. Move the pointer up vertically and click.

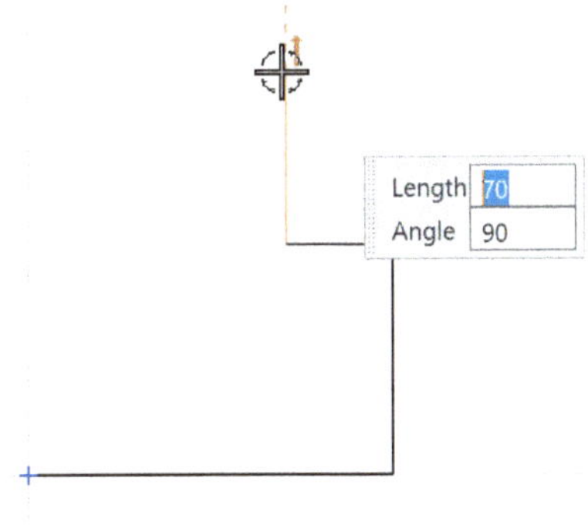

8. On the **Profile** toolbar, click the **Arc** icon.
9. Move the pointer to the endpoint of the previous line, and then move it toward left. An arc normal to the line appears.

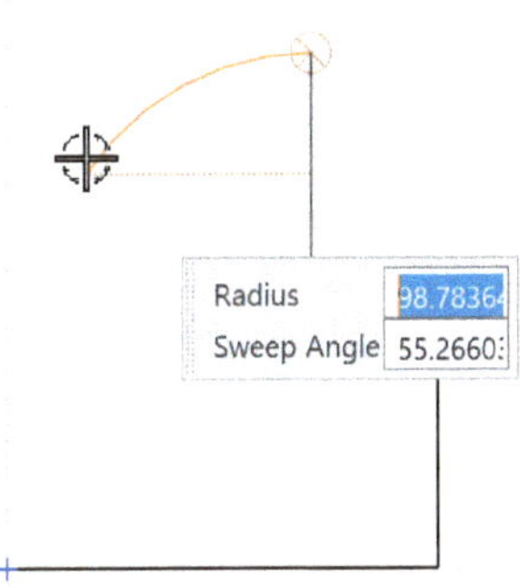

10. Move the pointer to the endpoint of the previous line, move toward up, and left. Notice that an arc tangent to the previous line appears.

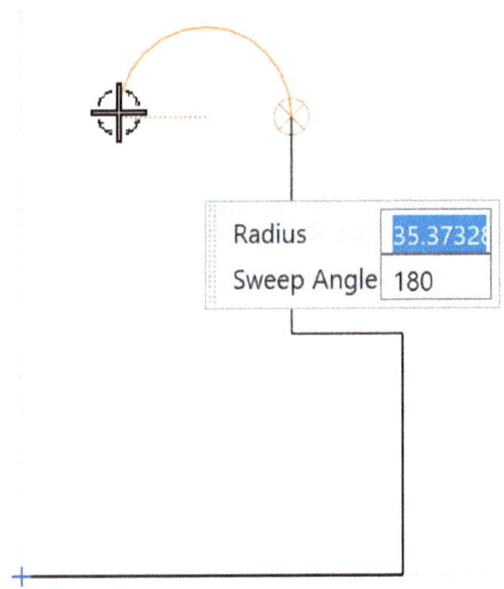

11. Click to create a tangent arc.
12. Move the pointer downward and notice the Tangent constraint.

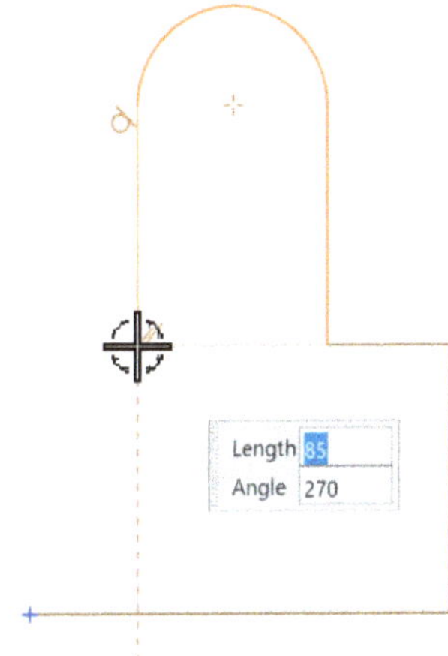

13. Click when a dotted line appears from the horizontal line.
14. Move the pointer toward the left and click when a dotted line appears from the sketch origin.

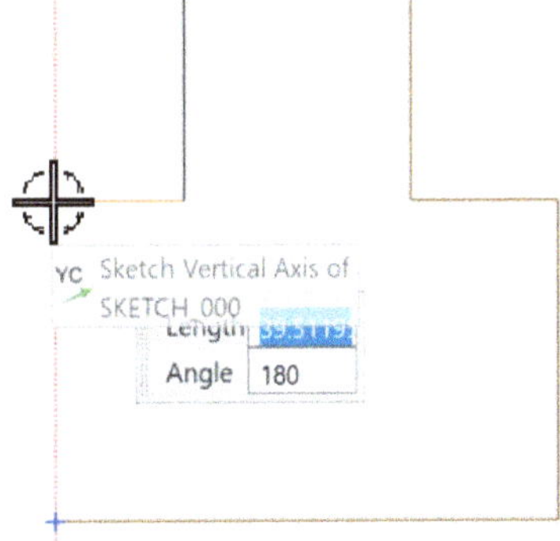

15. Move the pointer downward and click the sketch origin.

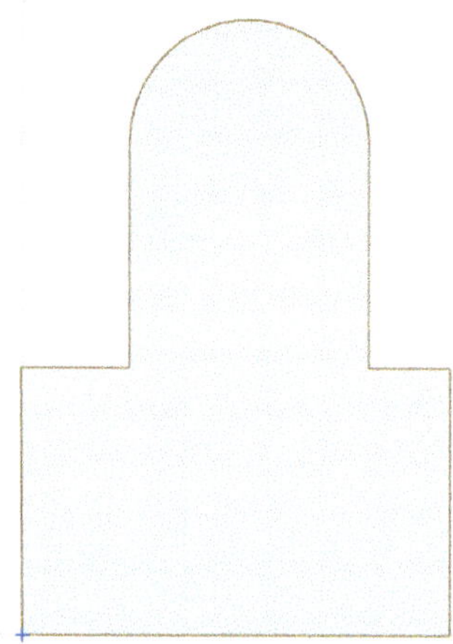

16. On the ribbon, click **Home > Curve > Circle**.
17. On the **Circle** toolbar, click **Circle Method > Circle by Center and Diameter**.
18. Select the center of the tangent arc, move the pointer outward, and click. A concentric constraint is created between the circle and the arc.

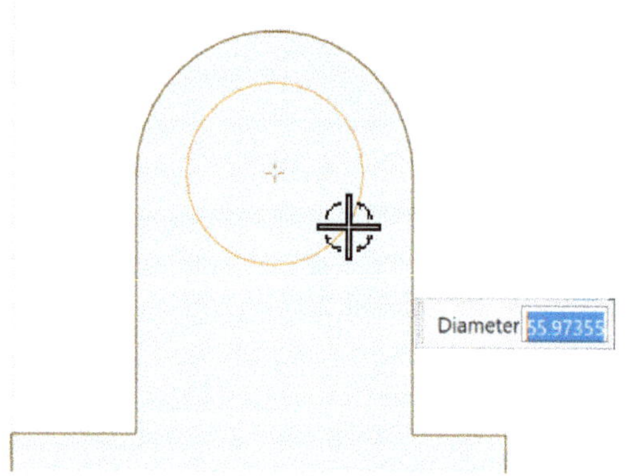

19. Place the pointer on the midpoint of the left vertical line and move the pointer.
20. Click when a horizontal dotted line appears.

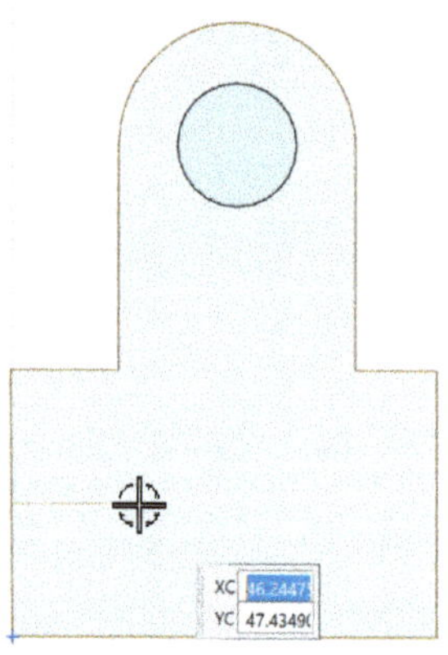

21. Move the pointer and click to create a circle.
22. Likewise, create another circle.
23. Press Esc.

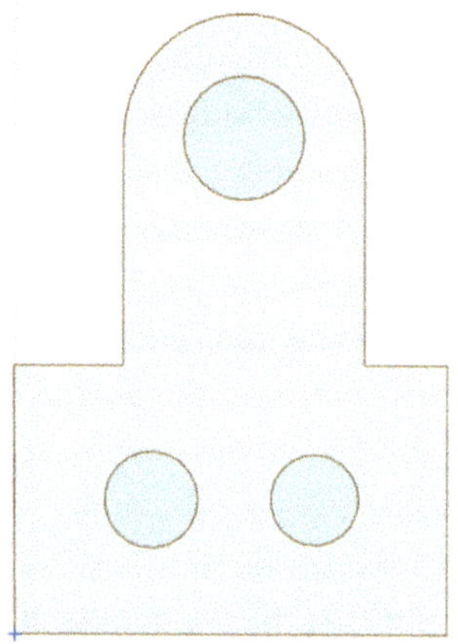

Adding Constraints

Geometric Constraints are used to control the shape of a sketch by establishing relationships between the sketch elements. You can add relations using the **Geometric Constraints** tool.

1. Select the line connected to the tangent arc and click **Vertical** from the **Sketch scene bar**. The vertical constraint is applied to the line.

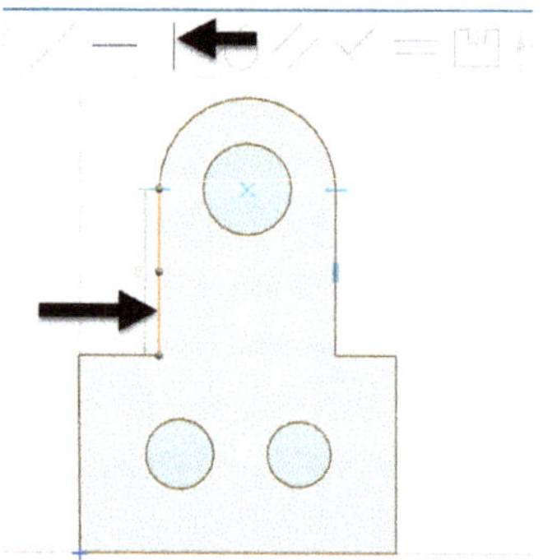

2. Select the lower vertical lines.
3. Click the **Equal Length** = icon on the **Sketch Scene bar** to make the lines equal.
4. Press Esc.
5. Select the two horizontal lines, as shown.
6. Click the **Equal Length** = icon on the **Sketch Scene bar** to make the lines equal.

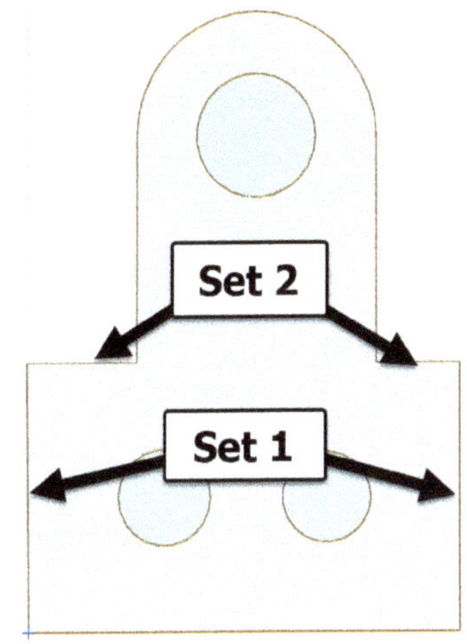

7. Press Esc.
8. Select the other two vertical lines and click the **Equal Length** icon to make them equal.
9. Press Esc.
10. Select the two circles located at the bottom.
11. Click the **Equal Length** icon on the **Sketch Scene bar**.
12. Select the center point of the circle and the left vertical line.
13. Click the **Midpoint** icon on the Sketch Scene bar. The midpoint of the vertical line and the center point of the circle become collinear.

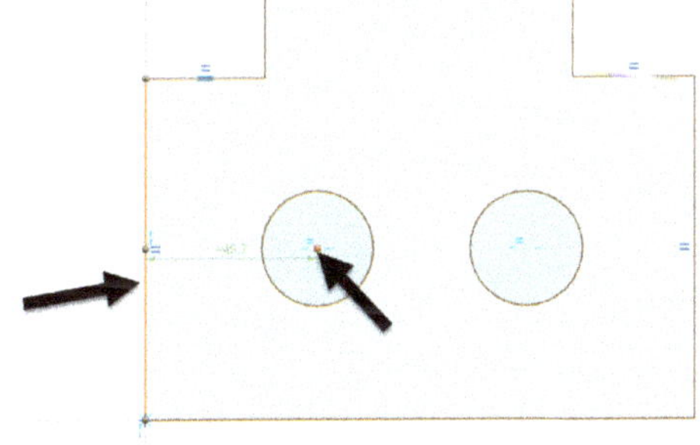

14. Likewise, make the other circle collinear with the midpoint of the right vertical line.

Adding Dimensions

1. Select the lower right vertical line.
2. Double-click on the dimension of the lower right vertical line, type 30, and press Enter.

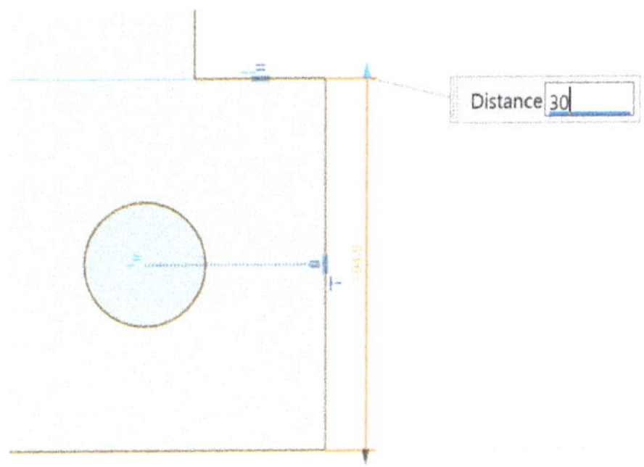

3. Click **Yes**.
4. Likewise, change the dimension of the upper vertical line to 35.
5. Select the lower horizontal line and double-click on the dimension.
6. Type 40 and press Enter.
7. Likewise, add other dimensions to the sketch to constrain it fully.

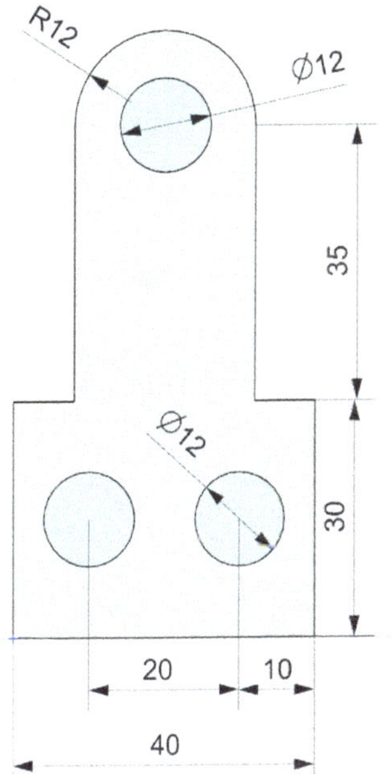

TUTORIAL 5 (Conics)

1. Activate the **Sketch Task** environment.
2. Create a triangle using the **Polygon** tool.

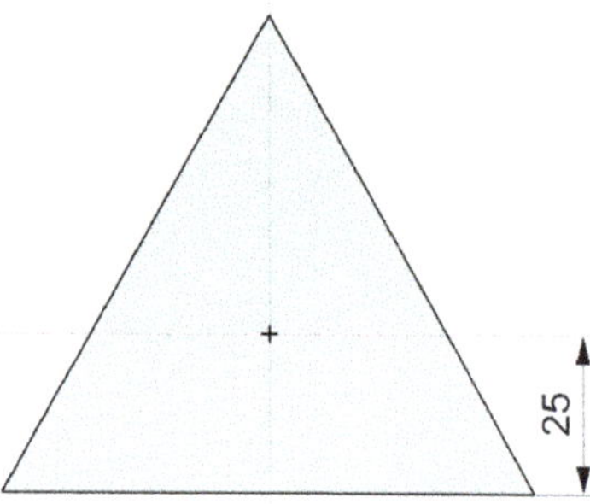

3. On the ribbon, click **Home > Curve > More Gallery Conic** .
4. Select the start and end limits and control point, as shown.

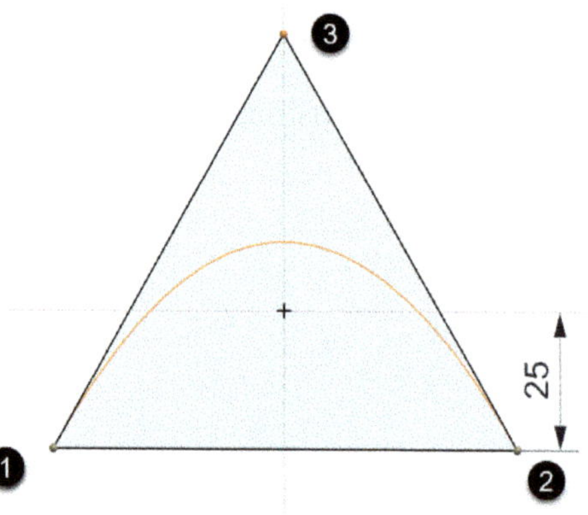

5. Set the Rho **Value** to **0.25**.
6. Check the **Preview** option and click **Show Result**.

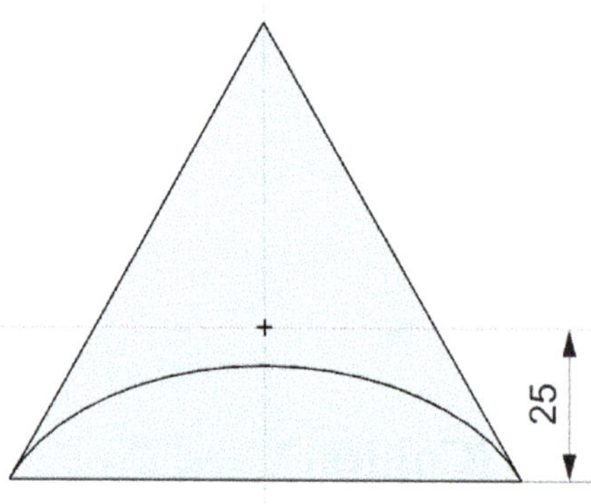

7. Click **Undo Result** on the dialog.
8. Set the Rho **Value** to **0.75** and click **Show Result**.

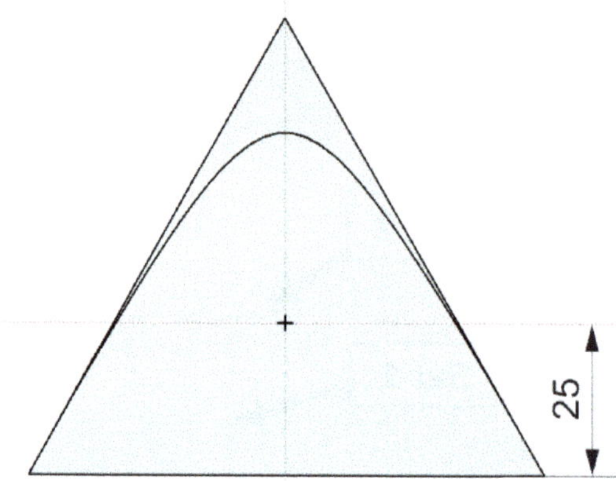

9. Click **OK**.

TUTORIAL 6 (Extend, Trim, Corner, and Offset Curve)

The **Extend** tool is similar to the **Trim** tool, but its use is the opposite of the **Trim** tool. This tool is used to extend lines, arcs, and other open entities to connect to other objects.

1. Create a sketch, as shown below.

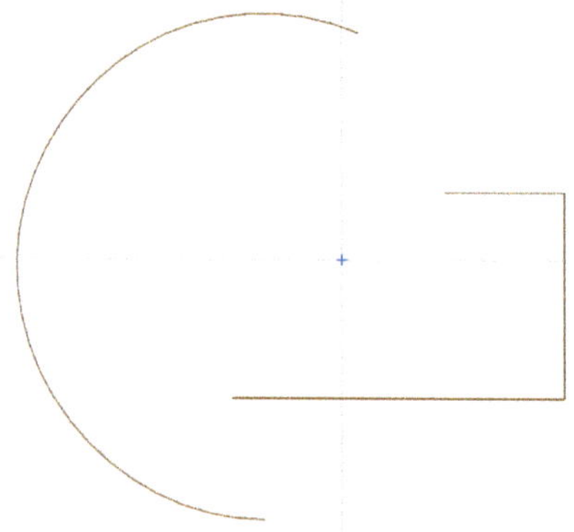

2. Click **Home > Edit > Extend** on the ribbon.
3. Select the horizontal open line; the line extends up to arc.

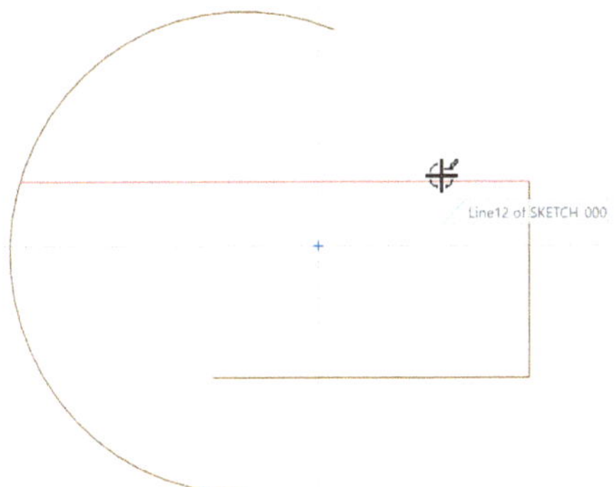

4. Likewise, extend the other elements, as shown.

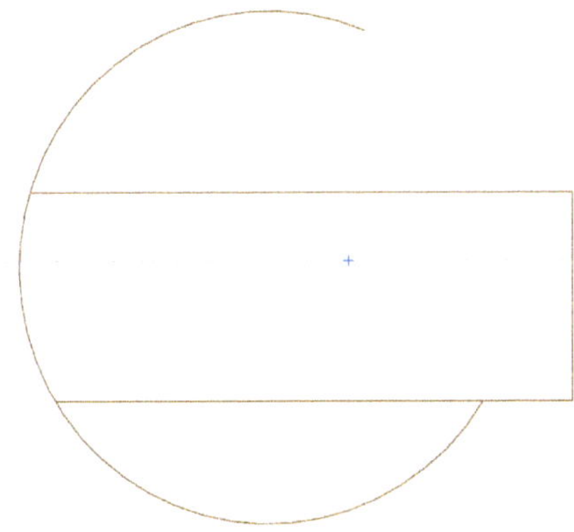

5. Close the **Extend** dialog.

Corner

1. On the ribbon, click **Home > Edit > Corner** .
2. Click on the ending portion of the arc.
3. Click on the starting portion of the horizontal line.

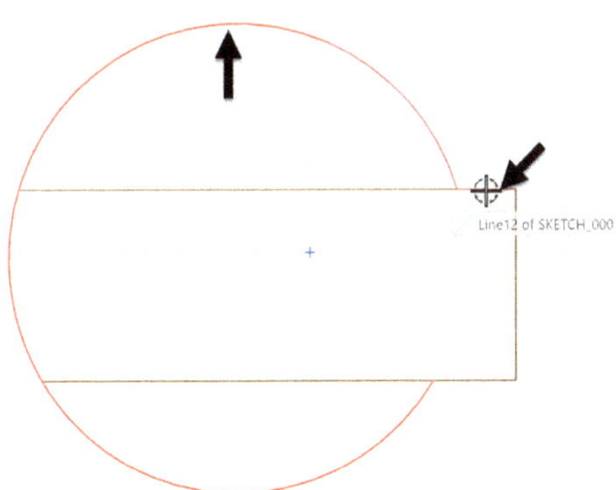

4. Close the **Corner** dialog.

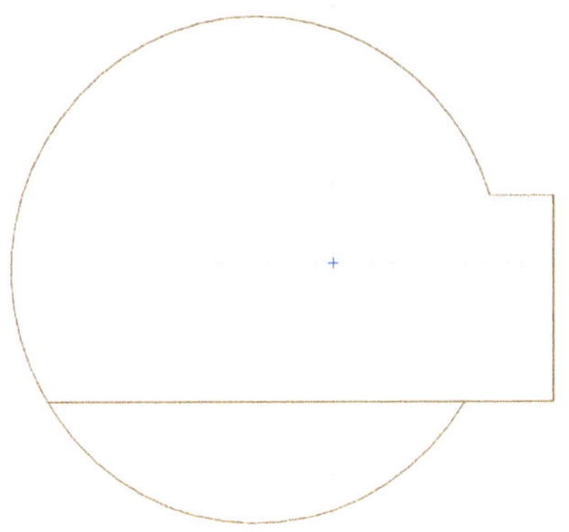

Trim

1. On the ribbon, click **Home > Edit > Trim** .
2. Select the horizontal line.

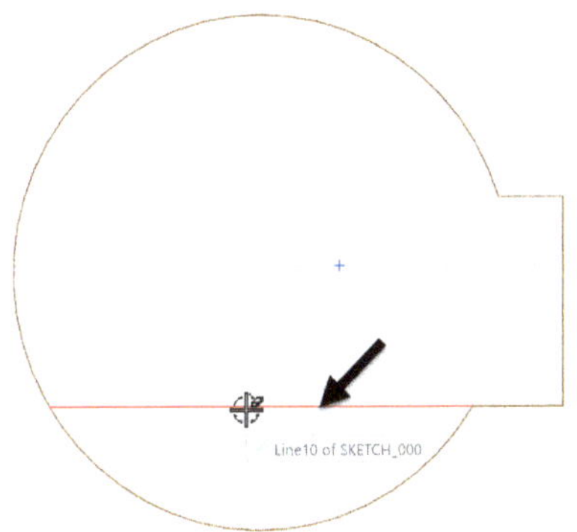

3. Close the **Trim** dialog.

Offset Curve

The **Offset Curve** tool creates parallel copies of lines, circles, arcs, and so on.

1. On the ribbon, click **Home > Curve > Offset Curve** .
2. Select an entity and notice that all the connected entities are selected.
3. Type-in a value in the **Distance** box on the **Offset Curve** dialog (or) drag the arrow that appears on the offset curve.
4. Click the **Reverse Direction** icon to reverse the offset side.
5. Click **OK**.

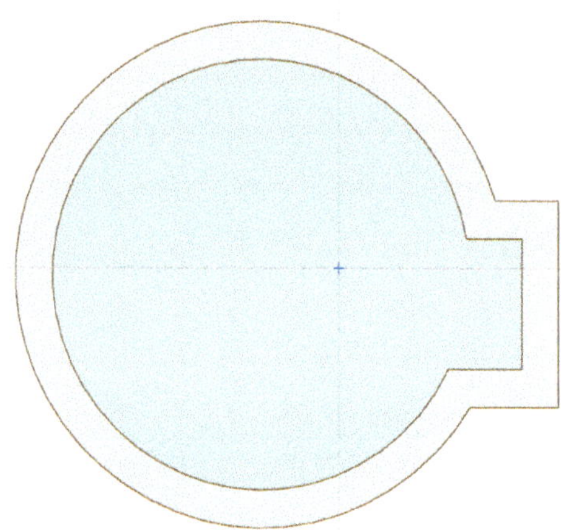

TUTORIAL 7

This tutorial teaches you to use **Fillet, Chamfer, and Mirror Curve** tools.

Fillet

The **Fillet** tool converts the sharp corners into round corners.

1. Draw the lines, as shown below.

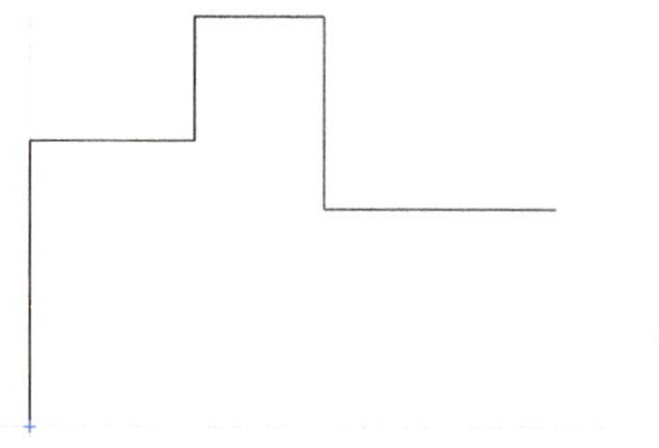

2. Click **Home > Curve > Fillet** on the ribbon.
3. Click on the corner, as shown.
4. Move the pointer and click to define the radius. You can also type the radius value.

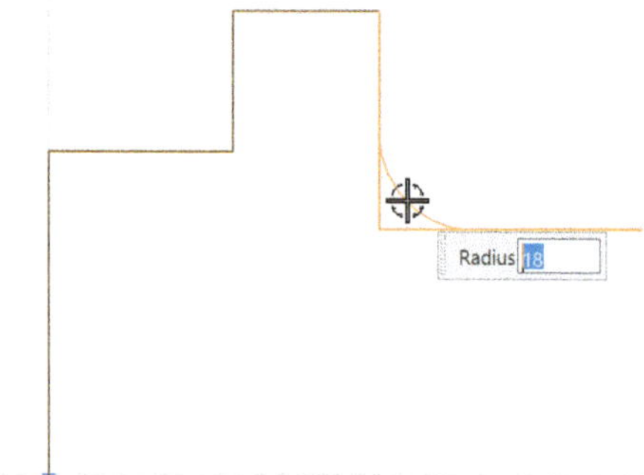

5. On the **Fillet** toolbar, click the **Delete Third Curve** icon.
6. Select the right and left vertical lines.
7. Move the pointer and select the horizontal line connecting the two vertical lines.

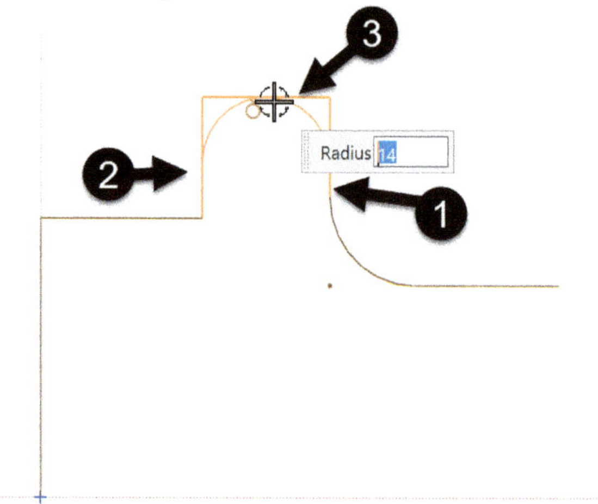

8. Close the **Fillet** dialog.

Chamfer

The **Chamfer** tool replaces the sharp corners with an angled line. This tool is similar to the **Fillet** tool, except that an angled line is placed at the corners instead of a round.

1. Click **Home > Curve > Chamfer** on the Ribbon.
2. On the **Chamfer** dialog, select **Chamfer > Symmetric.**
3. Click on the corner, as shown.

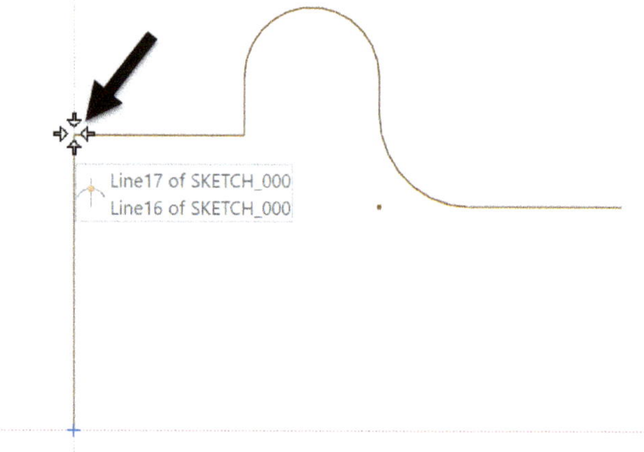

4. Type-in a value in the **Distance** box and press Enter.
5. Close the dialog.

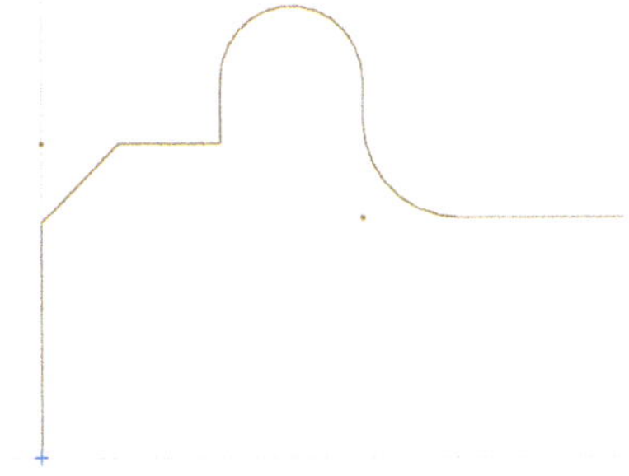

Mirror Curve

The **Mirror Curve** tool creates a mirror image of objects. You can create symmetrical sketches using this tool.

1. On the ribbon, click **Home > Curve > Mirror** .
2. Create a selection window covering all the sketch entities.

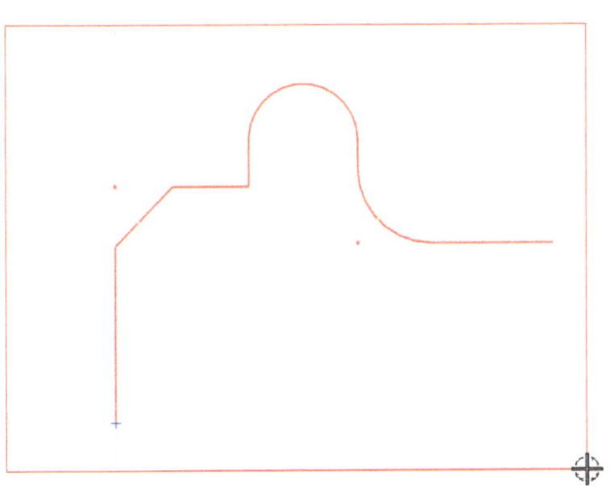

3. On the **Mirror Curve** dialog, click **Select Centerline** and select the horizontal axis.
4. Click **OK** to mirror the selected entities.

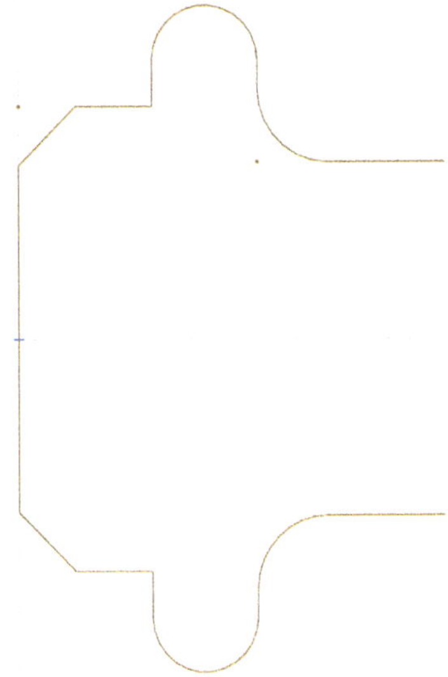

5. On the Ribbon, click **Home > Curve > Arc** .
6. Select the start and endpoints of the arc, as shown.

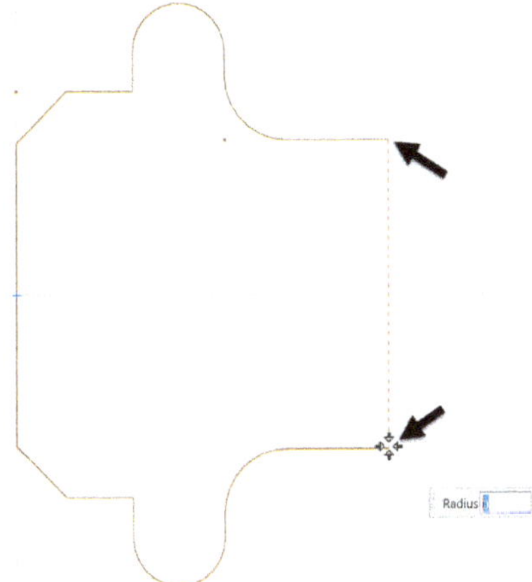

7. Move the pointer rightwards and click when the **Tangent** glyph appears.

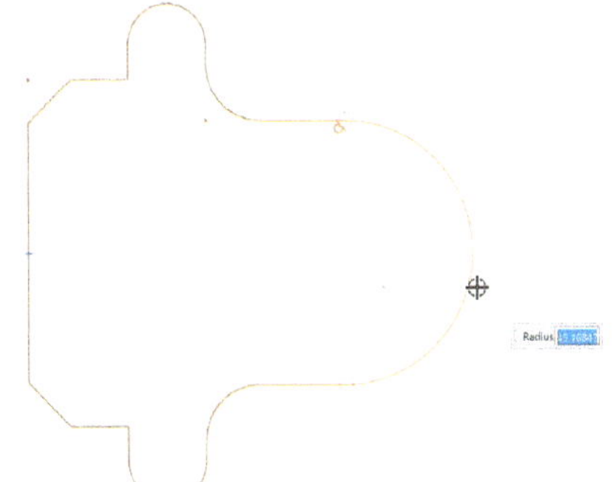

8. Close the **Arc** toolbar.

Adding Dimensions

1. Select the arc located at the top.
2. Double-click on the radial dimension, as shown.
3. Type 15 and press Enter.

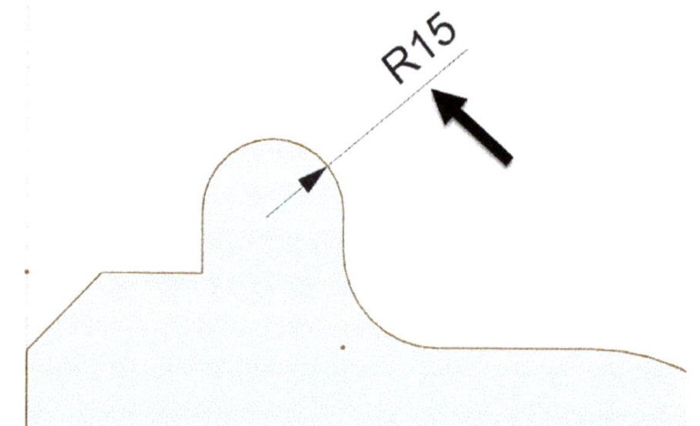

4. Select the leftmost vertical line and the center point of the arc, as shown.
5. Double-click on the dimension displayed.
6. Type 125 and press Enter.

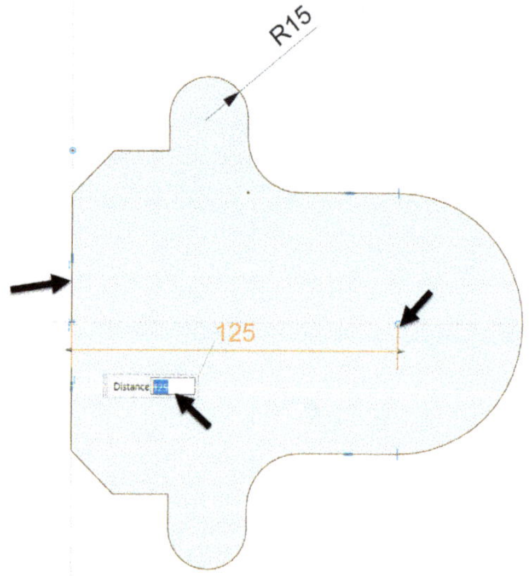

7. Click in the graphics window.
8. Select the fillet and double-click on the dimension displayed.
9. Type 5, and press Enter.
10. Likewise, create other dimensions, as shown.

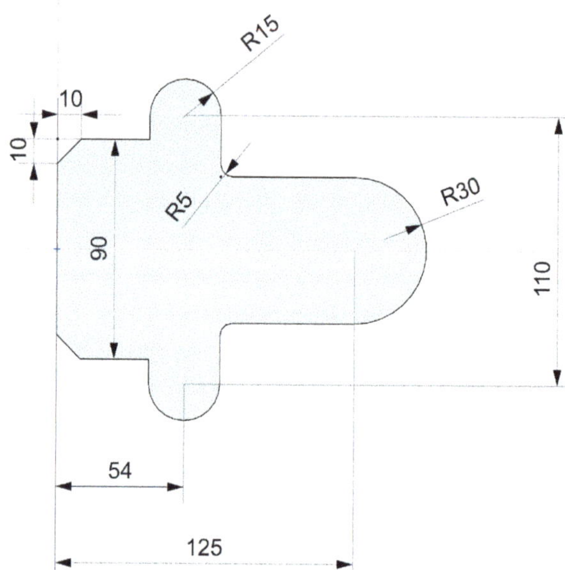

11. Click **Finish** on the **Sketch** group.

Chapter 6: Additional Modeling Tools

In this chapter, you will:

- Construct a Sweep feature
- Construct a Swept feature along guide curves
- Create Holes
- Add Grooves and Slots
- Make Pattern Features
- Construct Tube features
- Apply Boolean operations
- Add chamfers

TUTORIAL 1

In this tutorial, you will construct a helical spring using the **Helix** and **Sweep along Guide** tools.

Constructing the Helix

1. Open an NX file using the **Model** template.
2. To construct a helix, click **Curve > Advanced > Helix** on the ribbon.
3. On the **Helix** dialog, select **Type > Along Vector**.
4. Specify the settings in the **Size** section, as given next.

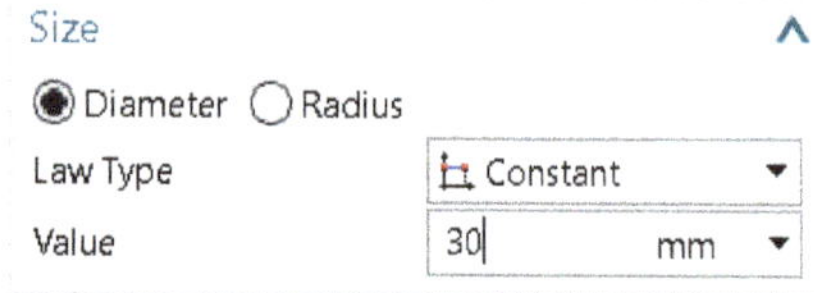

5. Specify the settings in the **Pitch** section, as given next.

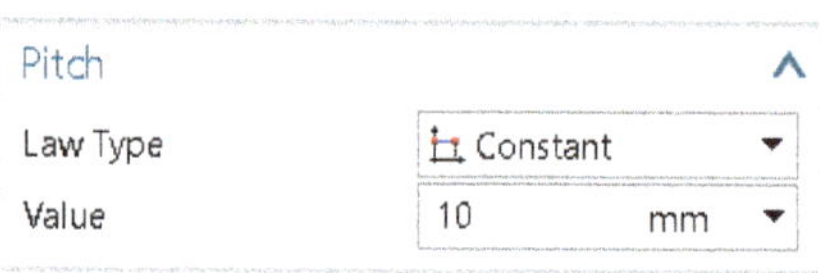

6. Specify the settings in the **Length** section, as given next.

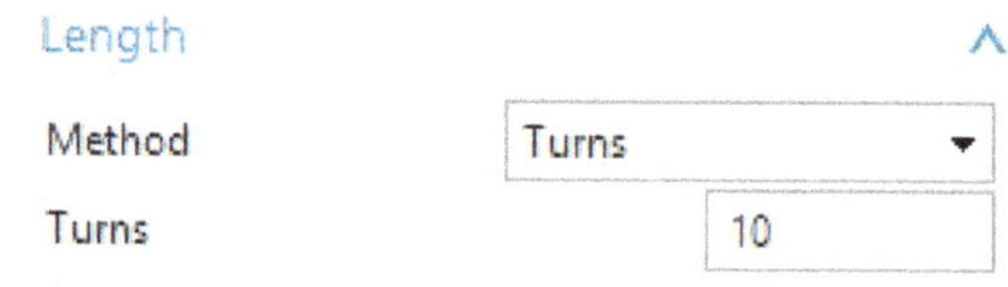

7. Expand the dialog and specify the settings in the **Settings** section, as given next.

8. Click **OK** to construct the helix.

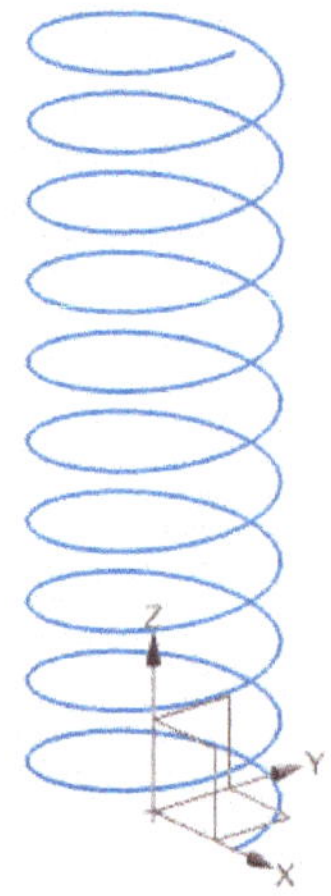

Adding the Datum Plane

1. To add a datum plane, click **Home > Construction > Datum Plane** on the ribbon.
2. On the **Datum Plane** dialog, select **Type > On Curve**.
3. Select the helix from the graphics window.
4. Under the **Location on Curve** section, select **Location > Through Point**.
5. Select the end of the helix.

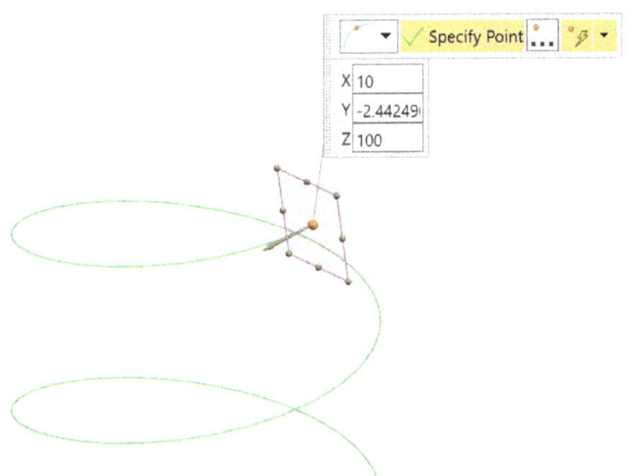

6. Under the **Orientation on Curve** section, select **Direction > Normal to Path**.
7. Leave the default values and click **OK**.

Constructing the Sweep feature

1. On the ribbon, click **Home > Construction > Sketch**.
2. Select the plane created normal to the helix.
3. Expand the Create Sketch dialog.
4. Select **Origin Method** > **Specify Point**.
5. Click the Point dialog button in the **Specify Origin Point**.

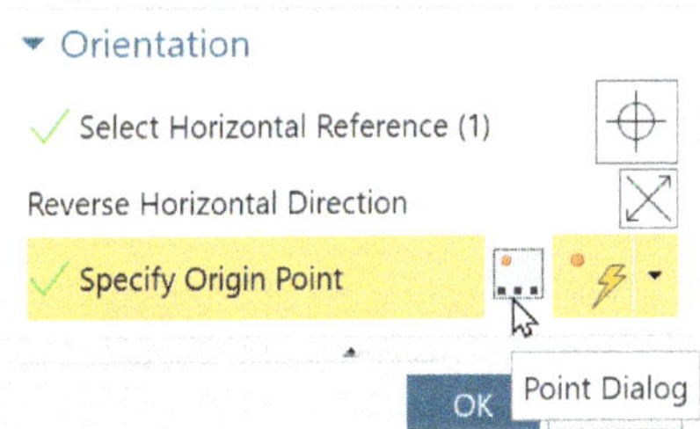

6. Select the endpoint of the helix to define the sketch origin.

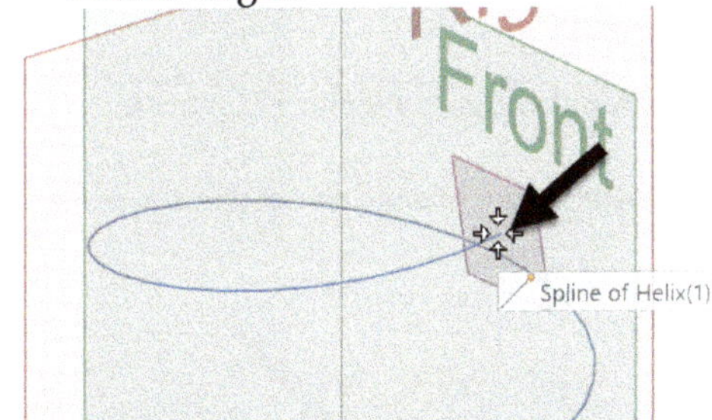

7. Click **OK** twice.
8. Draw a circle of 4 mm in diameter on the sketch origin.

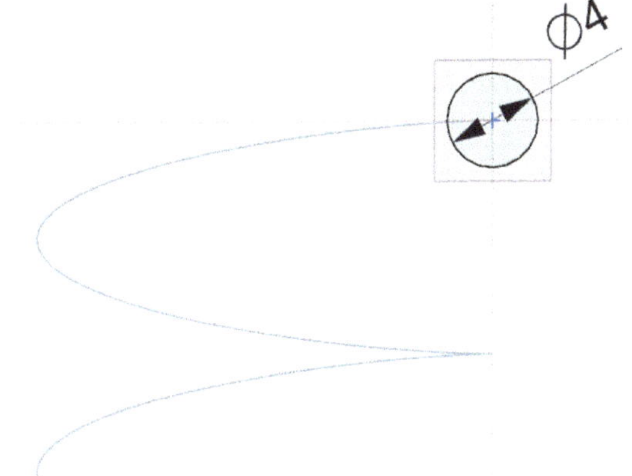

9. Right-click and select **Finish Sketch** .
10. To construct a sweep feature, click **Surface > Base > More > Sweep along Guide** on the ribbon.
11. Select the circle to define the section curve.
12. Under the **Guide** section, click **Select Curve**.
13. Select the helix.
14. Leave the default settings and click **OK** to construct the sweep feature.
15. Click on the plane and select **Hide**.

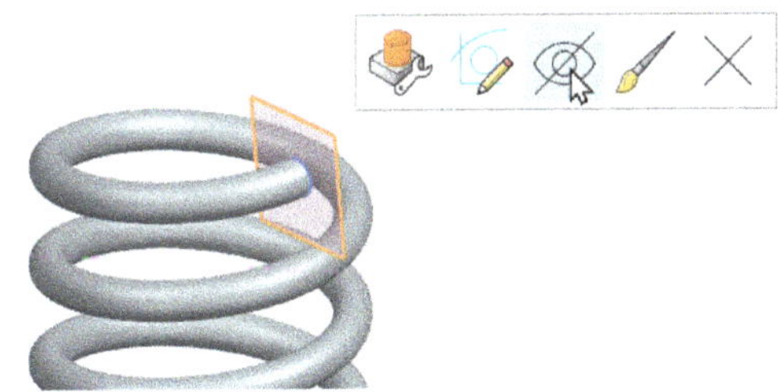

Also, hide the sketch.

16. Save and close the file.

TUTORIAL 2

In this tutorial, you construct a pulley wheel using the **Revolve** and **Groove** tools.

1. Open a file in the **Modeling** Environment.
2. Construct the sketch on the Right plane, as shown in the figure.

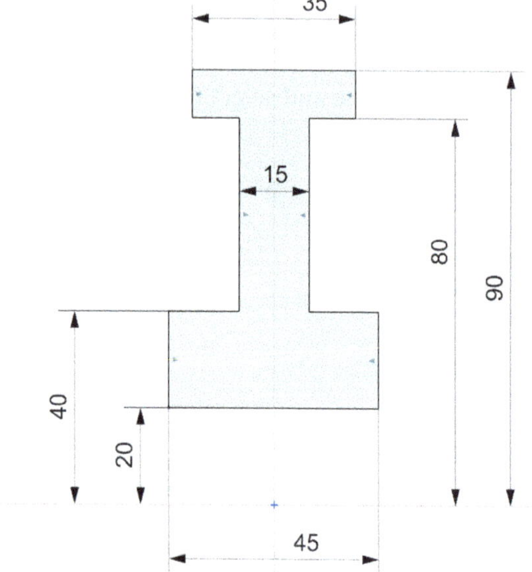

3. Finish the sketch.
4. Construct the revolved feature.

Constructing the Groove feature

1. To construct a groove feature, click **Home > Base > More > Design Feature > Groove** on the ribbon.

Note

Some tools do not appear on the ribbon. You can select them from the menu, as shown in the figure.

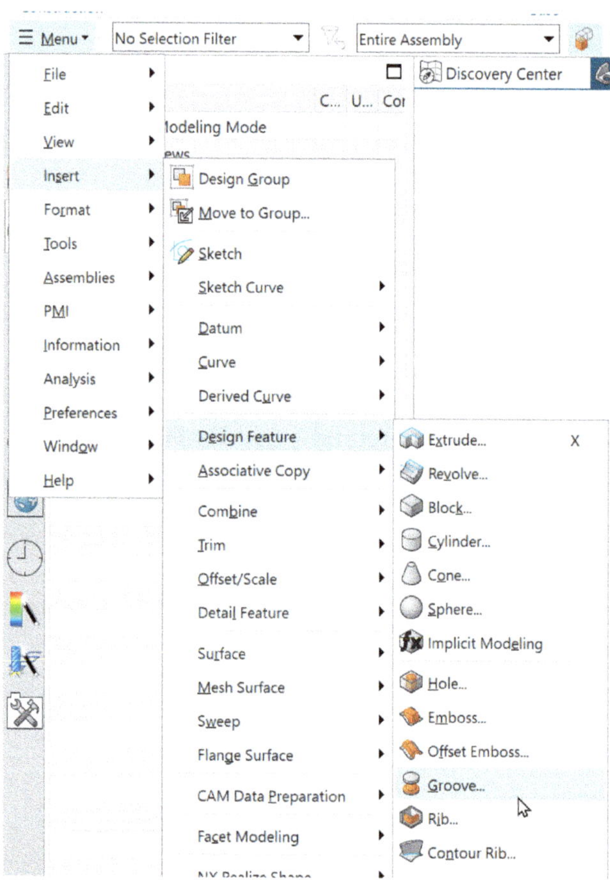

2. On the **Groove** dialog, click the **U Groove** button.
3. Select the outer cylindrical face of the revolved feature.

4. Specify the values on the **U Groove** dialog, as shown in the figure.

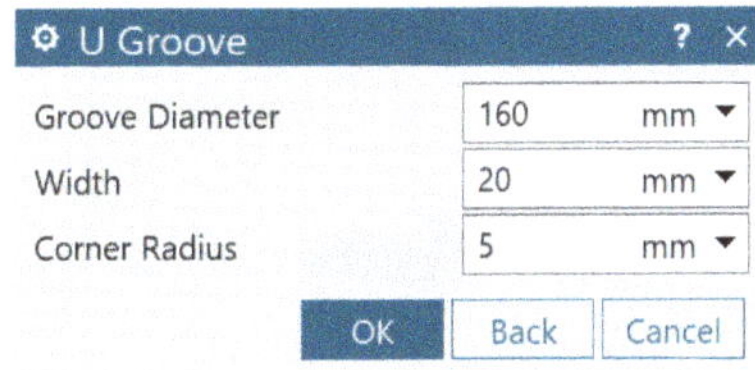

5. Click **OK**; the **Position Groove** dialog appears.
6. Click on the round edges of the model and groove preview, as shown.

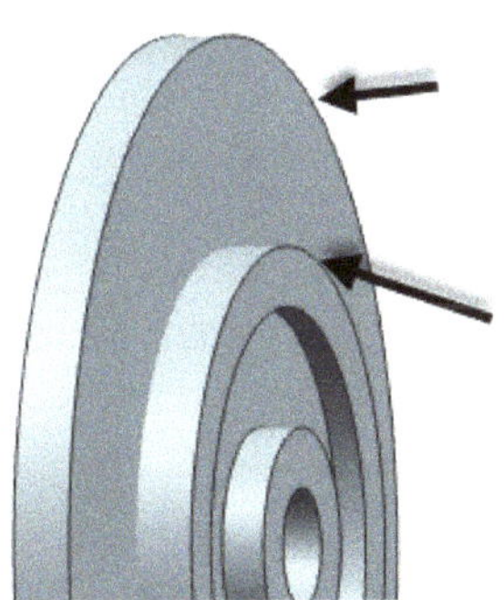

7. Enter **7.5** on the **Create Expression** dialog.

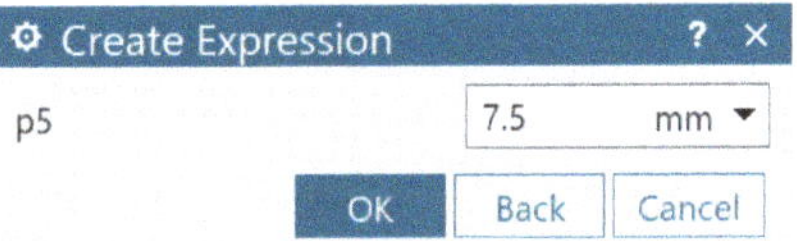

8. Click **OK** to add the groove.

9. Click **Cancel**.
10. Save and close the model.

TUTORIAL 3

In this tutorial, you construct a shampoo bottle using the **Swept**, **Extrude**, and **Thread** tools.

Creating Sections and Guide curves

To construct a swept feature, you need to create sections and guide curves.

1. Open a file in the **Modeling** Environment.
2. On the ribbon, click **Home > Construction > Sketch**.
3. Select the Top plane.
4. On the **Create Sketch** dialog, click **OK** to start the sketch.
5. On the ribbon, click **Home > Curve > More > Ellipse** .
6. Select the origin point of the coordinate system.
7. Specify **Major Radius** as 50 mm.
8. Specify **Minor Radius** as 20 mm.
9. Specify **Angle** as 0.
10. Leave the default settings and click **OK**.

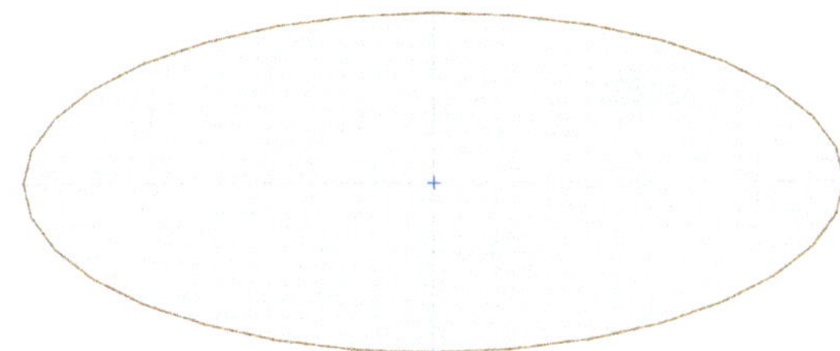

11. Select the Ellipse and the horizontal axis.
12. Double-click on the dimension displayed between the ellipse and the horizontal axis.
13. Type 20 and press ENTER.
14. Click in the graphics window.
15. Select the Ellipse and the vertical axis.
16. Double-click on the dimension.
17. Type 50 and press ENTER.

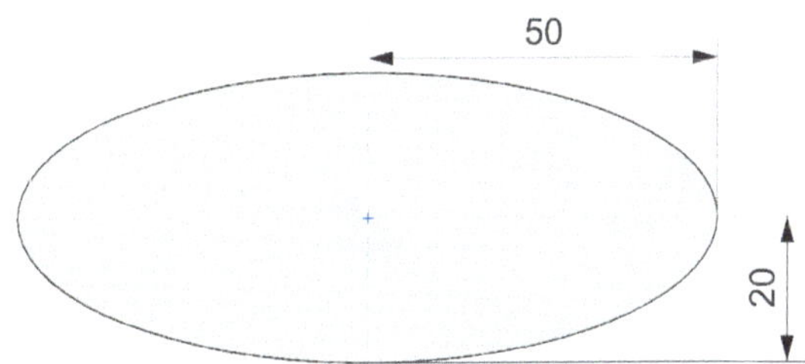

18. Click **Finish** on the **Sketch** group.
19. On the ribbon, click **Home > Construction > Sketch**.
20. Select the Front plane.
21. Click **OK**.
22. On the ribbon, click **Home > Curve > Studio Spline** .
23. On the **Studio Spline** dialog, select **Type > Through Points**.
24. Draw a spline similarly to the one shown in figure (refer to TUTORIAL 3 of Chapter 5: Sketching).

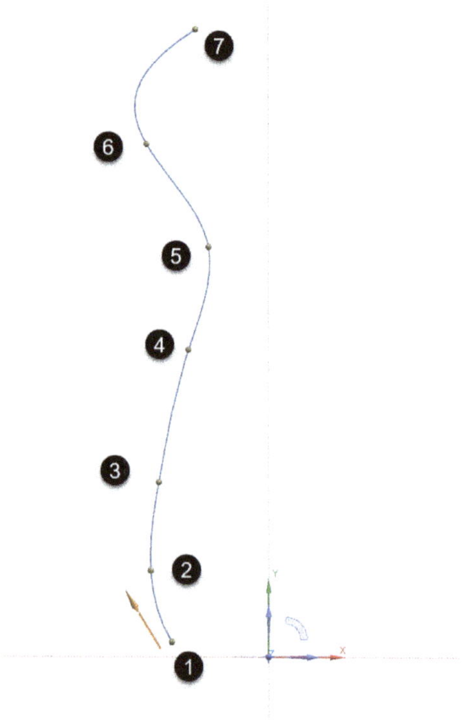

25. Click **OK**.
26. Select the first point of the spline and the origin point.
27. Select **Make Horizontal** from the Sketch Scene bar.

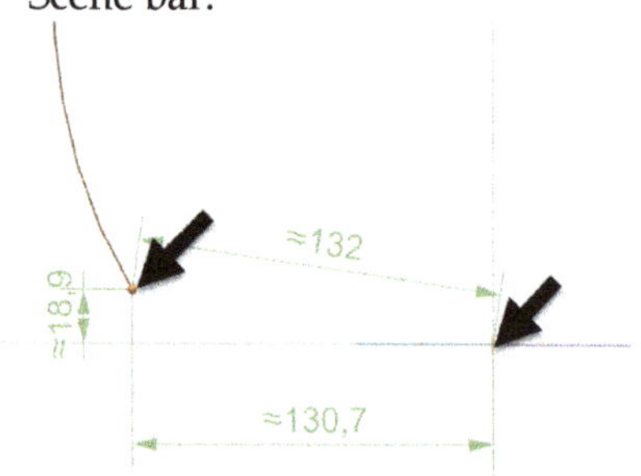

28. Select the spline, and then click on the second point from the bottom.
29. Select the vertical axis; a dimension is displayed between the vertical axis and the spline.

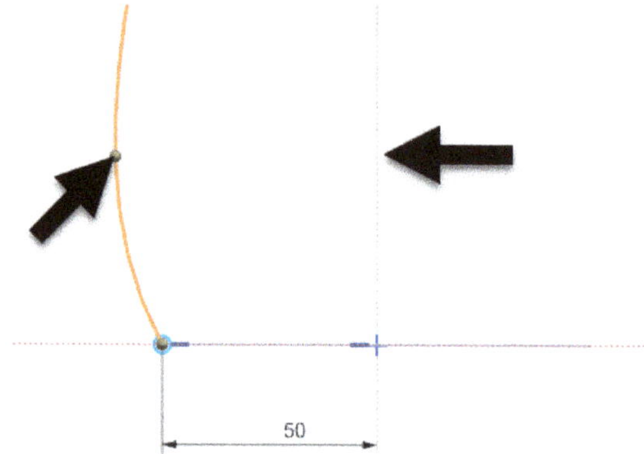

30. Double-click on the dimension, type 65 and press ENTER.
31. Apply dimensions to the spline, as shown in the figure.

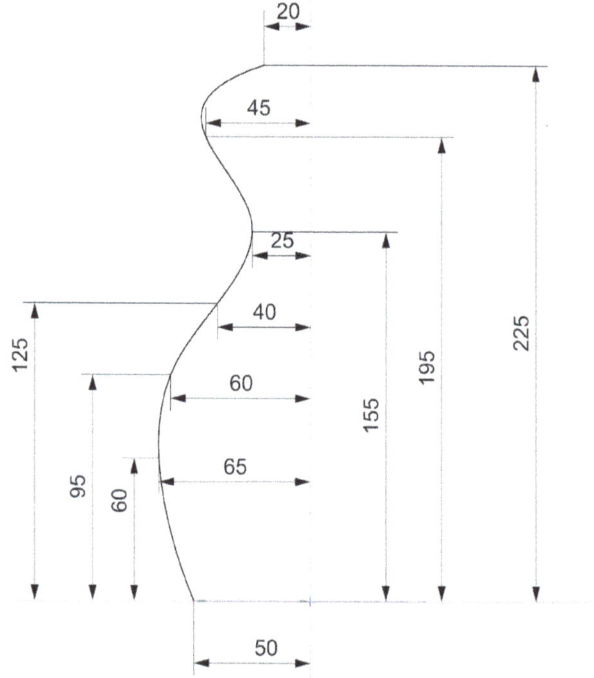

32. On the ribbon, click **Home > Curve > Mirror Curve** .
33. Select the spline.
34. On the **Mirror Curve** dialog, click **Select Centerline** and then select the vertical axis of the sketch.
35. Click **OK**.

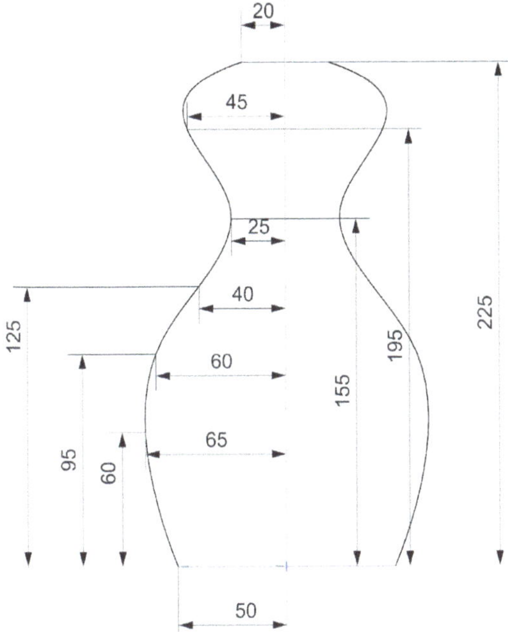

36. Click **Finish** on the **Sketch** group.

Creating another section

1. On the ribbon, click **Home > Feature > Datum Plane**.
2. On the **Datum Plane** dialog, select **Type > At Distance**.
3. Select the XY plane from the coordinate system.
4. Type-in **225** in the **Distance** box.

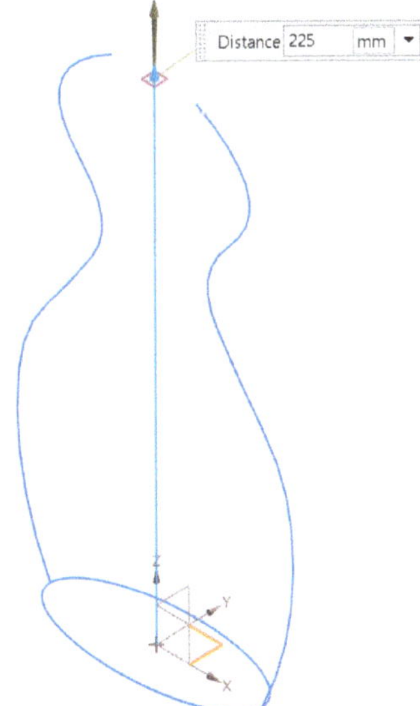

5. Click **OK**.
6. Start a sketch on the new datum plane.
7. Draw a circle of 40 mm in diameter.

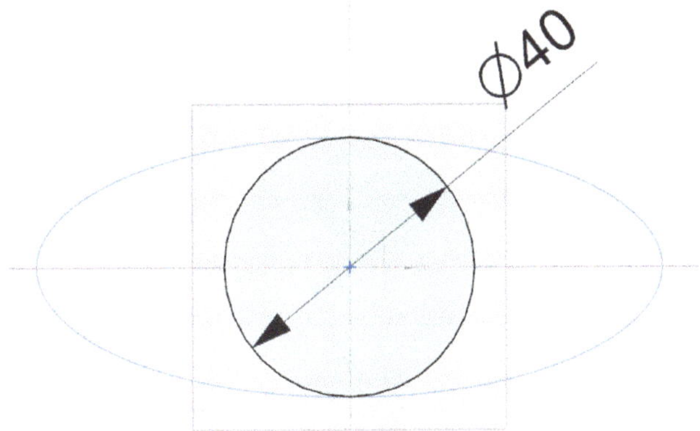

8. Click **Finish** on the **Sketch** group.

Constructing the swept feature

1. On the ribbon, click **Home > Surface > Swept** .
2. Select the circle and click the middle mouse button.

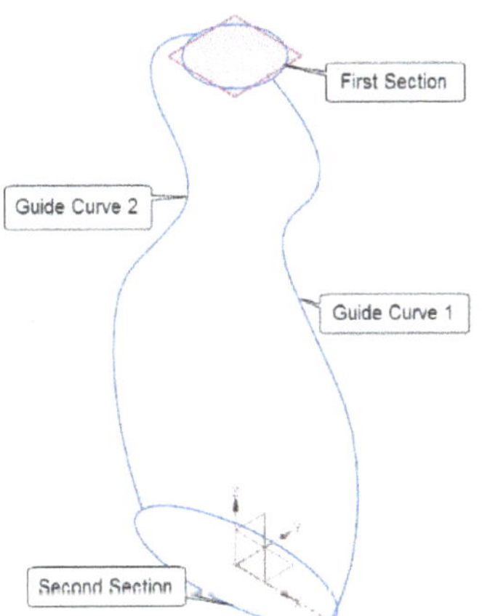

3. Select the ellipse.

Ensure that the arrows on the circle and the ellipse point in the same direction. Use the **Reverse Direction** button in the **Sections** section to reverse the direction of arrows.

4. Click **Select Curve** in the **Guides (3 maximum)** section.
5. On the Sketch Scene Bar, select **Curve Rule > Single Curve**.

6. Select the first guide curve and click the middle mouse button.

7. Select the second guide curve.
8. Click **OK** to construct the swept feature.

Constructing the Extruded feature

1. Click on the circle on the top of the sweep feature.
2. Click **Extrude** on the contextual toolbar.

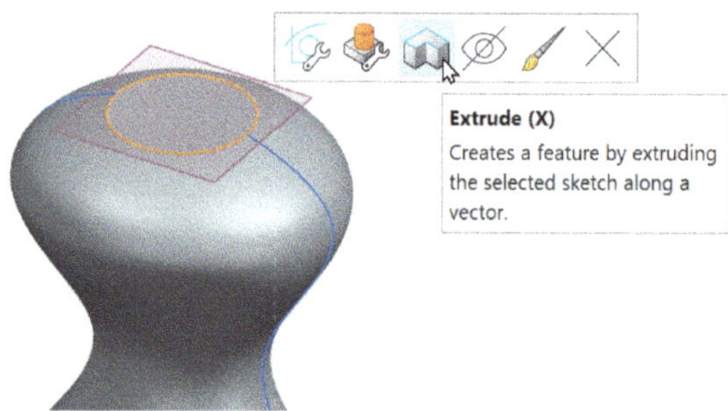

3. On the **Extrude** dialog, under the **Boolean** section, select **Boolean > Unite**.
4. Extrude the circle up to 25 mm.

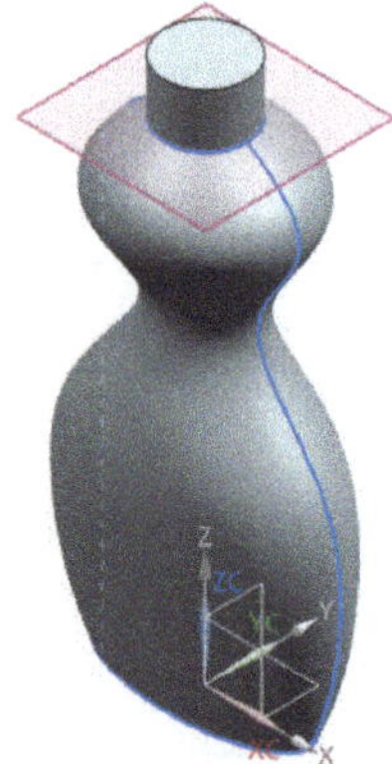

Adding the Emboss feature

1. On the **Construction** group, click the **Datum Plane** button.
2. On the **Datum Plane** dialog, select **Type > At Distance**.
3. Select the XZ plane from the coordinate system.
4. Enter **50** in the **Distance** box.
5. Click **Reverse Direction** to create the plane, as shown. Click **OK**.

6. Create a sketch on the plane, as shown in the figure. The major and minor radii of the ellipse are 50 and 20, respectively.

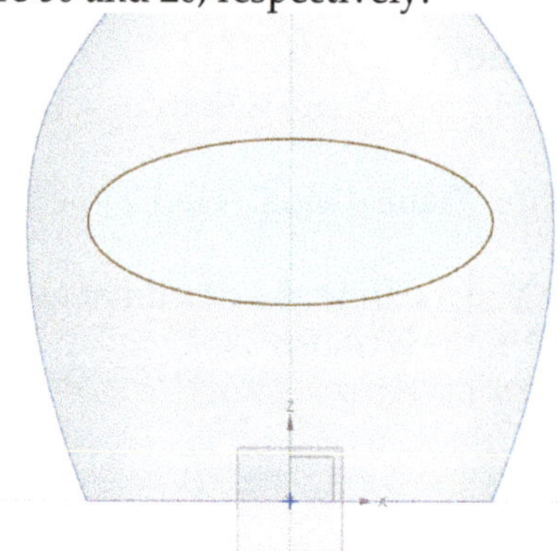

7. Make sure that the center point of the ellipse is coincident with the vertical axis.
8. Select the horizontal axis and the center point of the ellipse.
9. Double-click on the dimension displayed between the two selections.
10. Type 60 and press ENTER.
11. Select the vertical axis of the sketch and the ellipse.
12. Double-click on the dimension, type 50 and press ENTER.
13. On the Top Border Bar, select **Menu > Insert > Dimension > Rapid Dimension**.
14. Select the center point of the ellipse and its top quadrant point.
15. Move the pointer toward right and click.

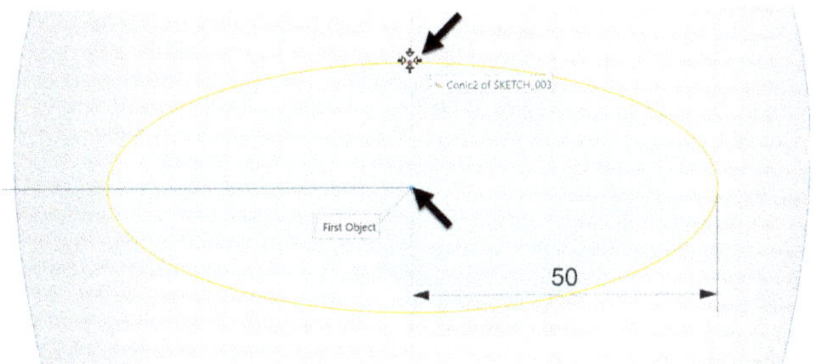

16. Type 20 and press ENTER.
17. Apply constraints and dimensions to fully constrain the sketch (refer to TUTORIAL 6 of Chapter 5: Sketching).

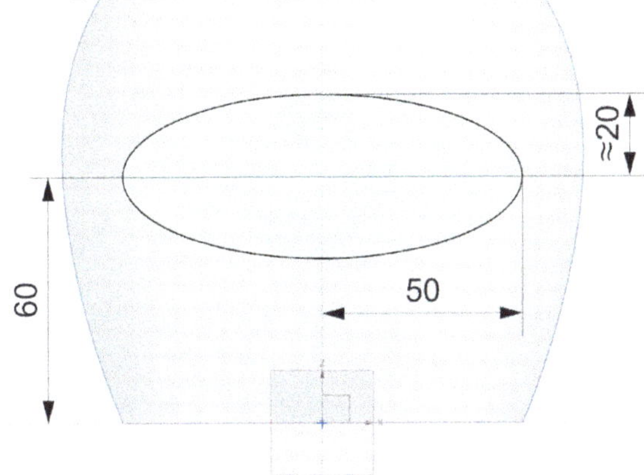

18. Click **Finish** on the **Sketch** group.
19. On the ribbon, click **Home > Base > More > Detail Feature > Emboss** .
20. Select the sketch.
21. On the **Emboss** dialog, under **Face to Emboss**, click **Select Face**.
22. Select the swept feature.

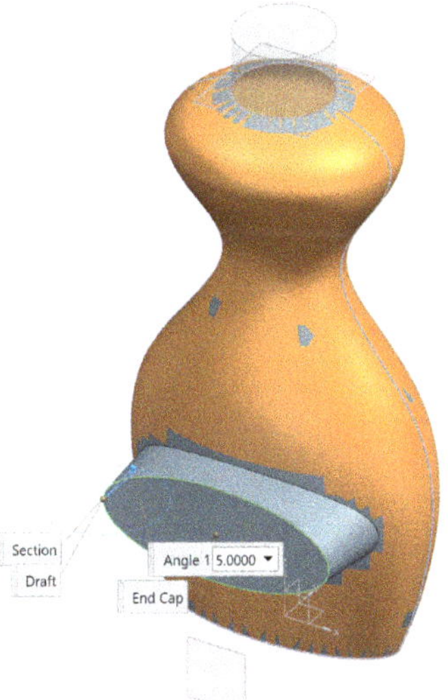

23. Expand the **End Cap** section, specify the settings, as given in the figure.

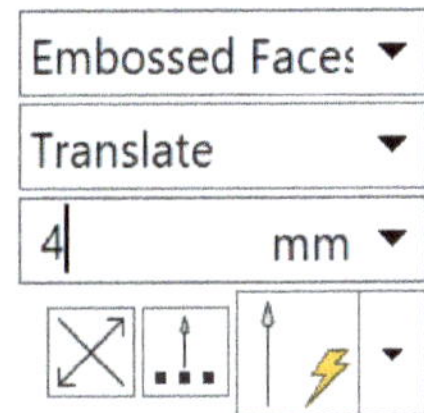

24. Leave the default settings and click **OK** to add the embossed feature.

Adding Edge Blend

1. On the ribbon, click **Home > Base > Edge Blend**.
2. Click on the bottom and top edges of the swept feature.
3. Set **Radius 1** to 5 mm.

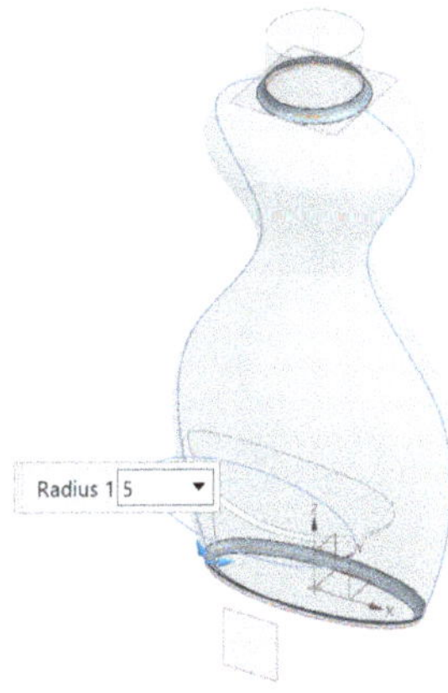

4. Click **Apply** to add the blend.
5. Set **Radius 1** to 1 mm.
6. Select the edges of the emboss feature and click **OK**.

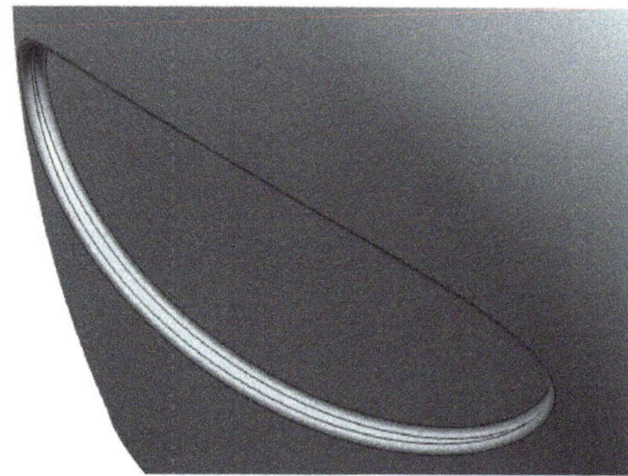

Shelling the Model

1. On the ribbon, click **Home > Base > Shell**.
2. On the **Shell** dialog, select **Type > Open.**
3. Set **Thickness** to 2 mm.
4. Select the top face of the cylindrical feature.

5. Click **OK** to shell the geometry.

Adding Threads

1. On the ribbon, click **Home > Base > More > Thread**.
2. On the **Thread** dialog, set **Thread Type** to **Detailed.**
3. Select the round face.

4. On the **Form** section, select **Input > Manual.**
5. Set **Pitch** to 8 mm.
6. On the **Limit** section, select **Thread Limit > Full.**
7. Leave the other default settings and click **OK** to add the thread.

8. Save the model and close it.

TUTORIAL 4

In this tutorial, you construct a patterned cylindrical shell.

Constructing a cylindrical shell

1. Start a new file using the **Model** template.
2. On the ribbon, click **Home > Base > More > Design Feature > Cylinder**.
3. On the **Cylinder** dialog, select **Type** > **Axis, Diameter, and Height.**
4. Select the Z-axis from the triad.

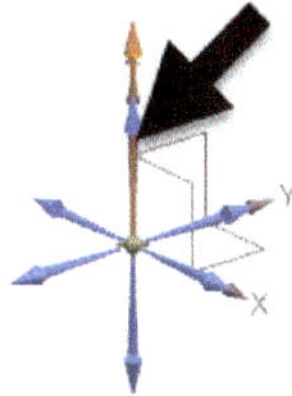

5. Specify **Diameter** and **Height** as **50** and **100**, respectively.
6. Leave the default settings and click **OK**.

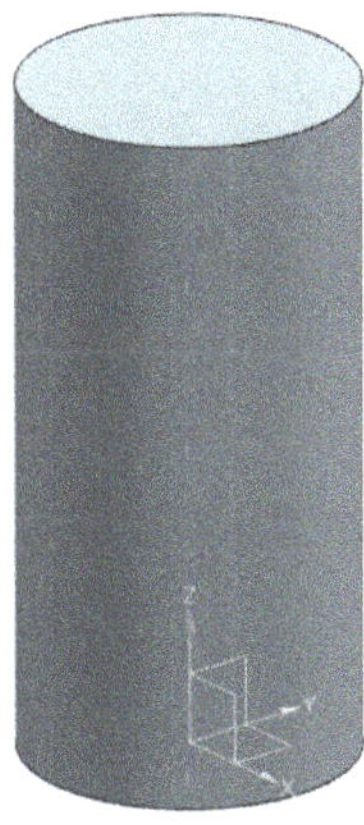

7. On the ribbon, click **Home > Base > Shell**.
8. Set **Thickness** to 3 mm.
9. Select the top and bottom faces of the cylindrical feature.
10. Click **OK** to shell the geometry.

Adding slots

1. On the ribbon, click **Home > Base > Extrude**.
2. Click on the YZ plane; the Sketch Task Environment is displayed.

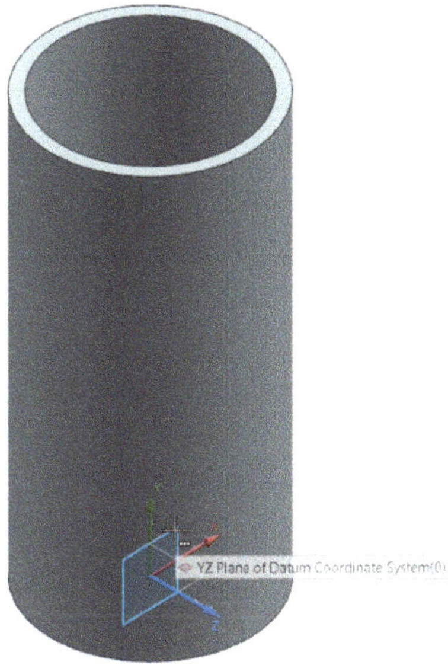

3. On the ribbon, click **Home > Curve > Profile**.
4. Click to specify the first point of the line.
5. Move the pointer upward, and then click to create a vertical line.

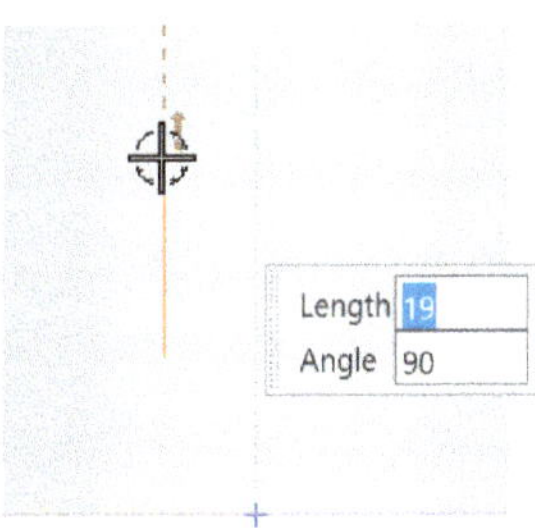

6. On the **Profile** dialog, click the **Arc** icon.
7. Move the pointer toward the right, and then click.

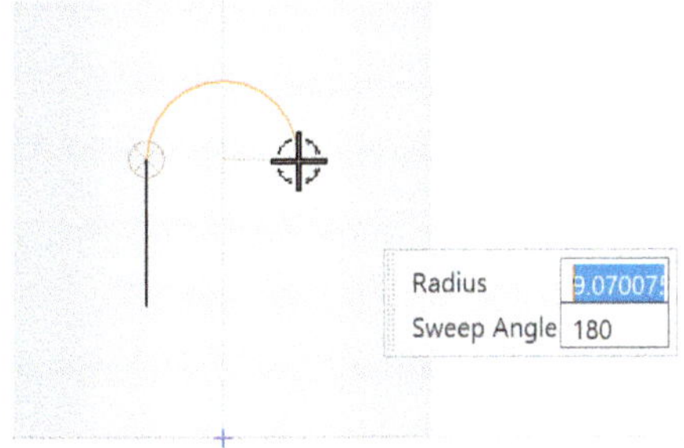

8. Move the pointer vertically downward, and then click.

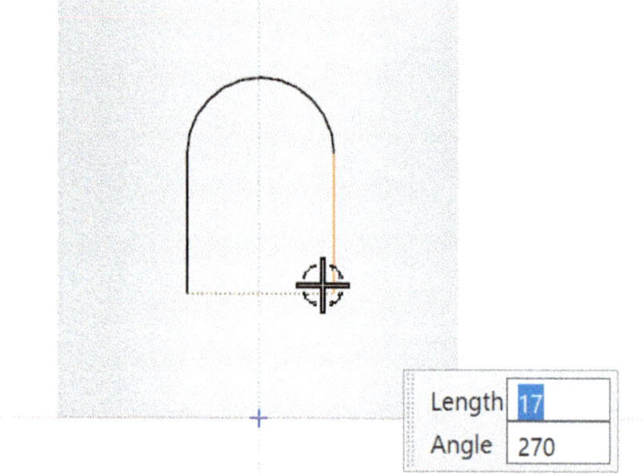

9. On the **Profile** dialog, click the **Arc** icon.
10. Select the start point of the sketch.

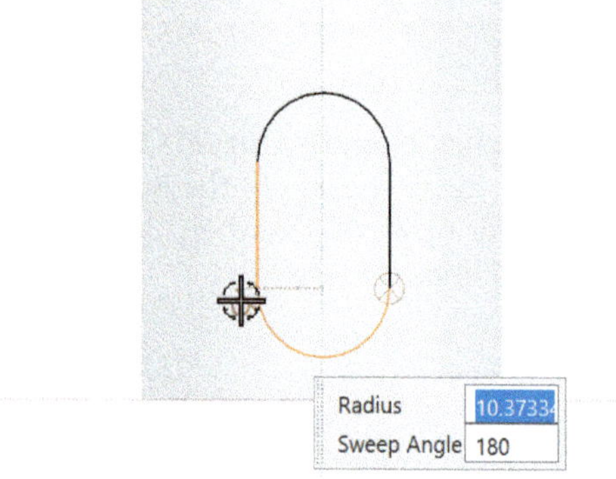

11. Press Esc to deactivate the **Profile** command.
12. Select the two arcs of the sketch, and then select the **Make Equal** icon on the **Sketch Scene Bar**.
13. Select the centerpoint of the arc and the Vertical axis of the sketch.
14. Click the **Make Coincident** option on the **Sketch Scene Bar**.
15. Add dimensions to the sketch, as shown.

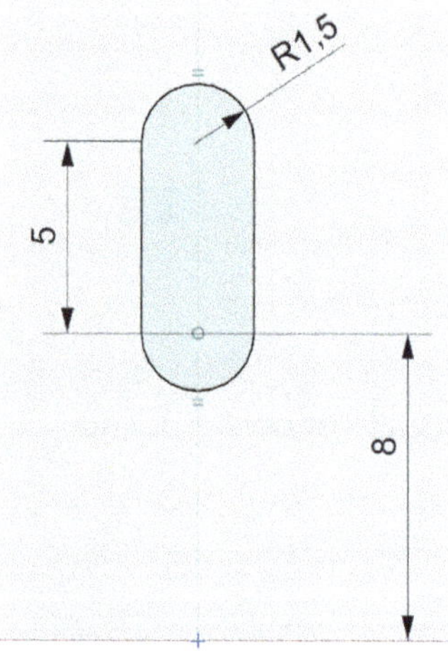

16. Click **Finish** on the **Sketch** group of the **Home** tab.
17. On the **Extrude** dialog, select **End > Until Selected** from the **Limits** section.
18. Click on the outer cylindrical surface of the model.
19. Select the **Boolean > Subtract** from the **Boolean** section.

20. Click **OK** on the **Extrude** dialog.

Constructing the Linear pattern

1. On the ribbon, click **Home > Base > Pattern Feature**.
2. On the **Pattern Feature** dialog, select **Layout > Linear**.
3. Select the Extrude feature.
4. Under the **Pattern Definition** section, select **Direction 1 > Specify Vector**.
5. Select the Z-axis vector.

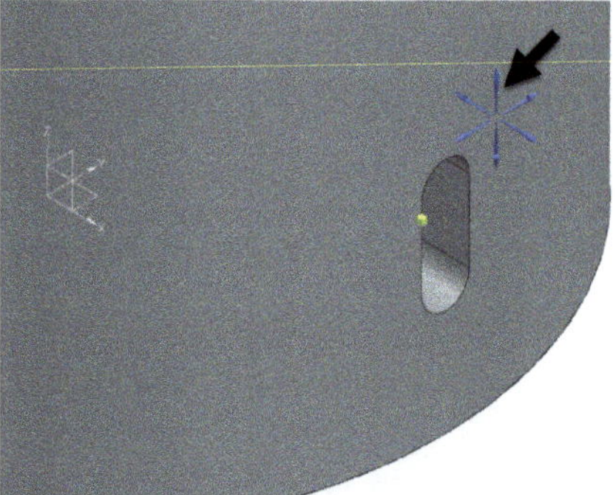

6. Select **Spacing > Count and Pitch**.
7. Type-in **6** in the **Count** box.
8. Enter **16** in the **Pitch Distance** box.
9. Click **OK** to make the linear pattern.

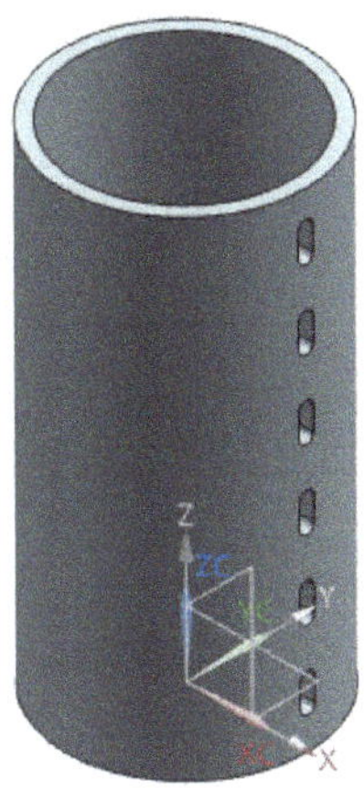

Constructing the Circular pattern

1. On the ribbon, click **Base > Pattern Feature** .
2. On the **Pattern Feature** dialog, select **Layout > Circular** .
3. Press and hold the Ctrl key, and then select the linear pattern and the extrude feature from the **Part Navigator**.
4. Under the **Pattern Definition** section, select **Rotation Axis > Specify Vector**.
5. Select the Z-axis vector.

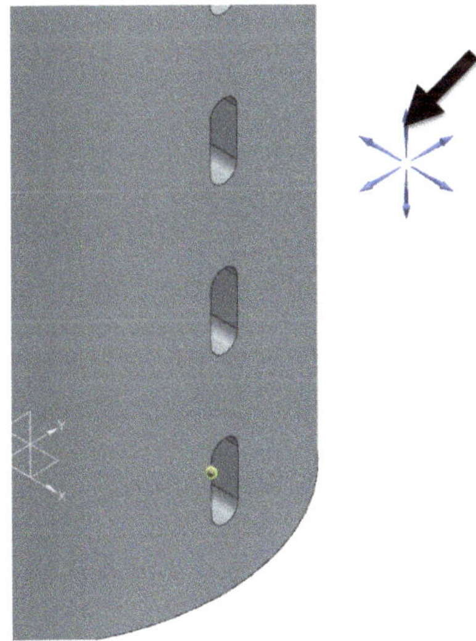

Now, you have to specify the point through which the rotation axis passes.

6. Click on the circular edge of the cylindrical feature (to select the center point of the cylinder).

7. Select **Spacing > Count and Span**.
8. Type-in **12** in the **Count** box.
9. Type-in **360** in the **Span Angle** box.
10. Click **OK** to make the circular pattern.

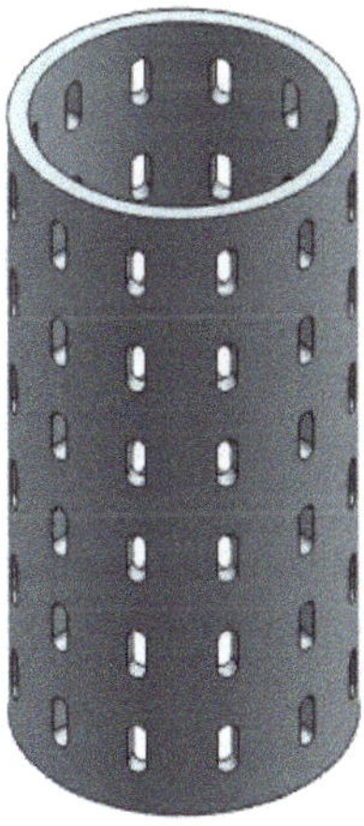

11. Save and close the model.

TUTORIAL 5

In this tutorial, you will construct a chain.

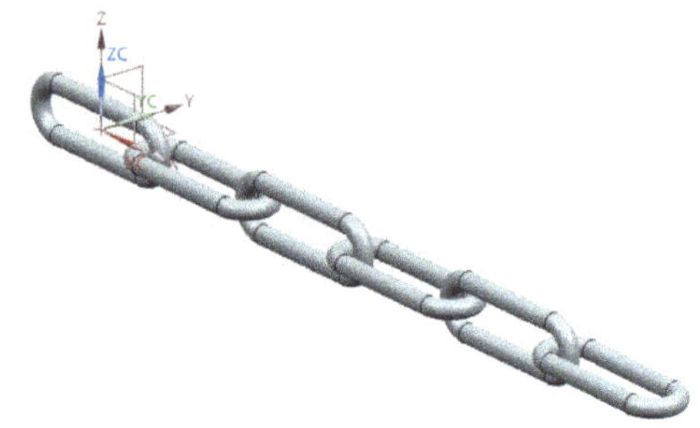

Constructing the Tube feature

1. Open a new file using the **Model** template.
2. On the ribbon, click **Home > Construction** > **Sketch**.
3. Select the Front plane.
4. Click **OK** on the **Create Sketch** dialog.
5. On the ribbon, click **Home > Curve > Rectangle**.
6. Click the **From Center** icon on the Rectangle toolbar.
7. Select the sketch origin to define the center point of the retangle.
8. Move the pointer toward right and click on the horizontal axis of the sketch.
9. Move the pointer upward up to a small distance and click.

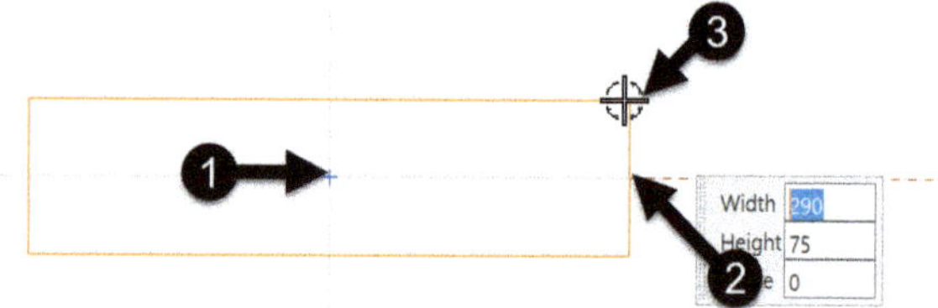

10. On the ribbon, click **Home > Curve > Arc**.
11. Click the **Arc by 3 Points** icon on the **Arc** toolbar.
12. Select the lower left corner of the rectangle.
13. Select the upper left corner of the rectangle.
14. Move the pointer toward left and click when the Tangent constraint glyph is displayed.

15. Likewise, create another tangent arc at the right of the rectangle, as shown.

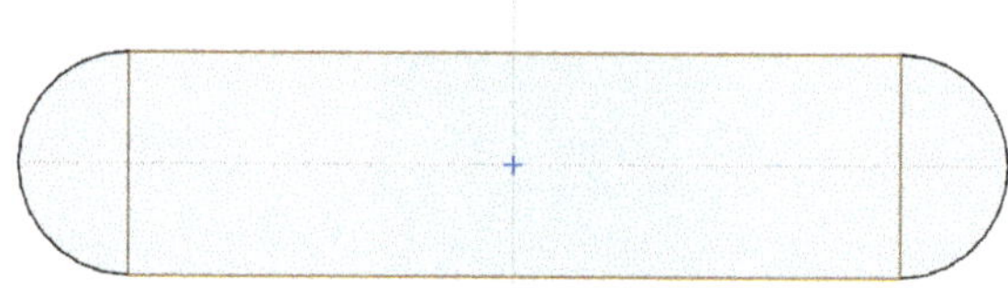

16. On the ribbon, click Home > Edit > Trim.
17. Select the two vertical lines of the rectangle.

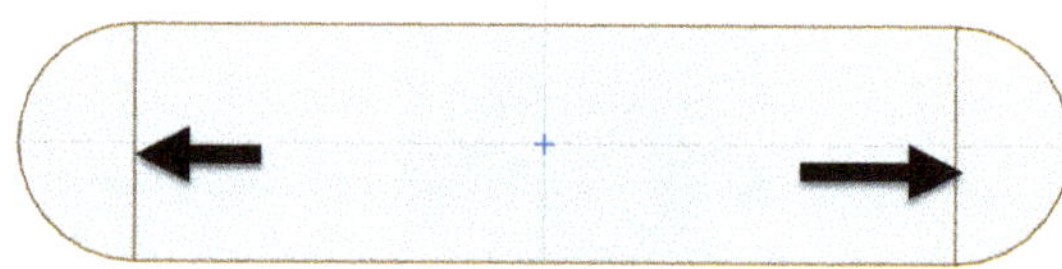

18. Close the **Trim** dialog.

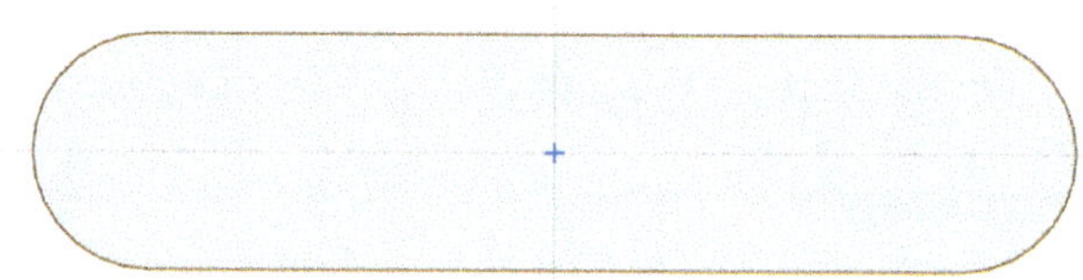

19. Add dimensions to the sketch.

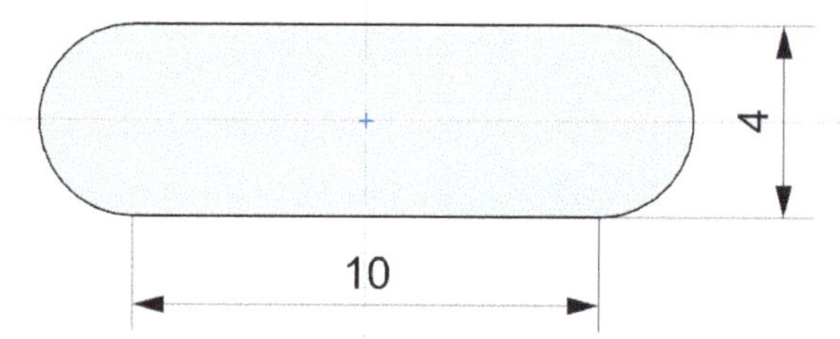

20. Click **Finish** on the **Sketch** group.
21. To construct a tube feature, click **Surface > Base > More > Sweep > Tube** on the ribbon.
22. Select the sketch.
23. On the **Tube** dialog, type-in 1.5 and 0 in the **Outer Diameter** and **Inner Diameter** boxes, respectively.
24. Click **OK** to construct the tube feature.

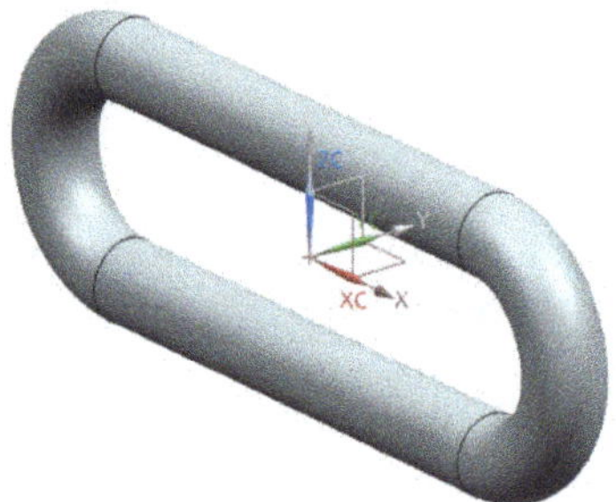

Patterning the Tube geometry

1. On the ribbon, click **Home > Base > Pattern Feature**.
2. On the **Pattern Feature** dialog, select **Layout >**

Linear and click on the tube feature.

3. Under the **Pattern Definition** section, select **Direction 1 > Specify Vector**.
4. Select the X-axis vector.

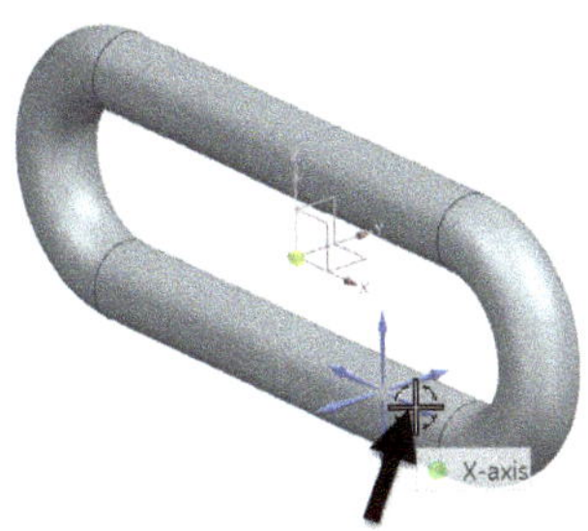

5. Under **Direction 1**, select **Spacing > Count and Pitch**.
6. Type-in **6** and **12** in the **Count** and **Pitch** boxes, respectively.
7. Expand the **Orientation** section and select **Orientation > CSYS to CSYS**.
8. Under **Orientation**, select **Specify From CSYS > CSYS Dialog** .
9. On the **CSYS** dialog, select **Type > Dynamic**.
10. Accept the default position of the Dynamic CSYS and click **OK**.

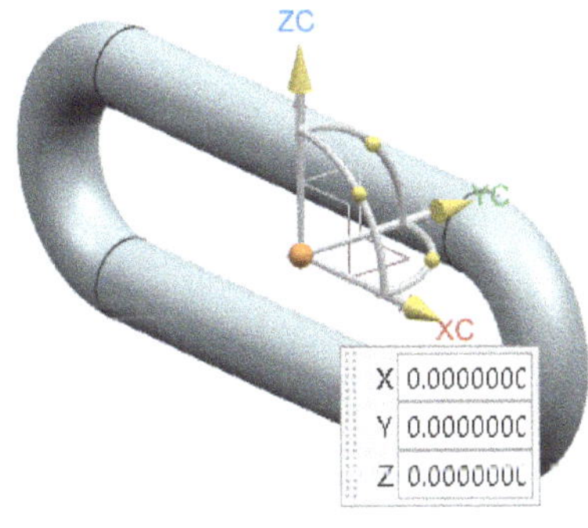

11. On the **Pattern Feature** dialog, under **Orientation**, select **Specify To CSYS > CSYS Dialog**.
12. Rotate the Dynamic CSYS about the X-axis. The rotation angle is -90 degrees.

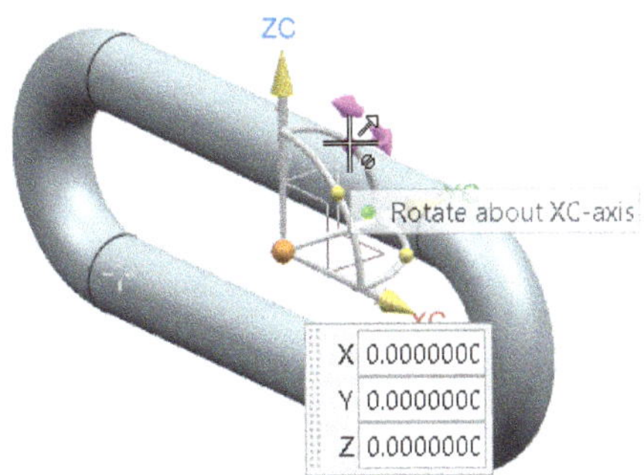

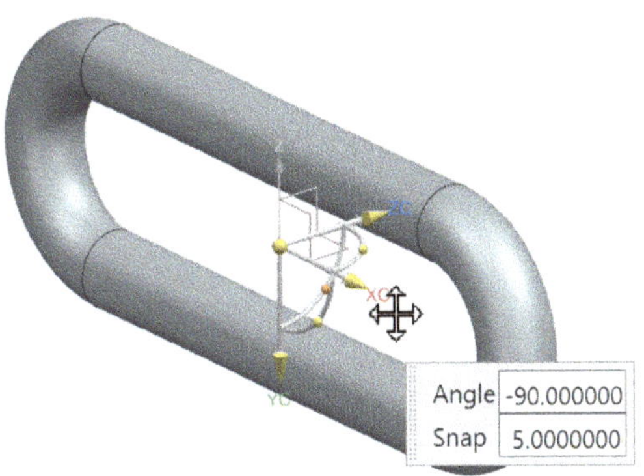

13. Click **OK**.
14. On the **Pattern Feature** dialog, under the **Orientation** section, check the **Repeat Transformation** option.
15. Click **OK** to make a pattern of the tube.

16. Save and close the file.

Boolean Operations

Types of Boolean operations.

Unite
Subtract
Intersect

These tools combine, subtract, or intersect two bodies. Activate these tools from the **Base** group.

Unite: This tool combines the **Tool Body** and the **Target Body** into a single body.

Subtract: This tool subtracts the **Tool body** from the **Target body**.

Intersect: This tool keeps the intersecting portion of the tool and target bodies. Activate this tool from the **Trim Body** drop-down available on the **Base** group.

TUTORIAL 6

In this tutorial, you will construct the model shown in the figure.

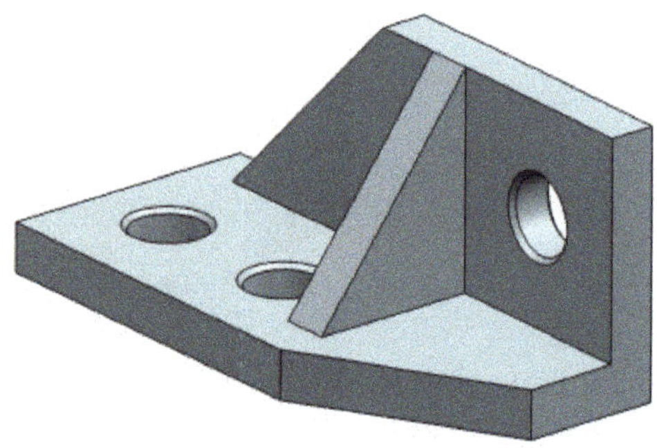

Constructing the first feature

1. Open a new part file.
2. Construct the first feature on the Top plane (create a rectangular sketch and extrude it up to a distance of 10 mm).

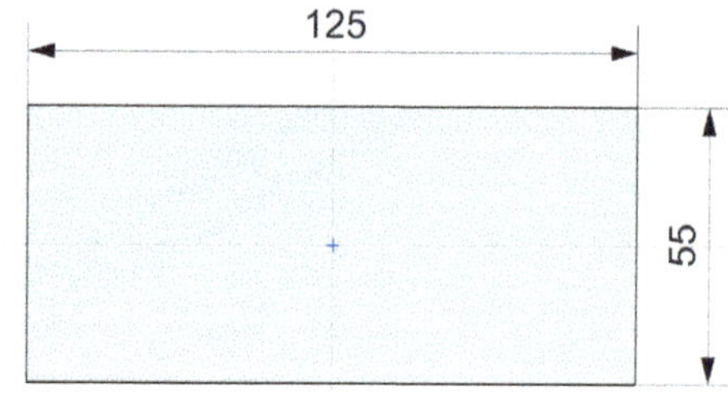

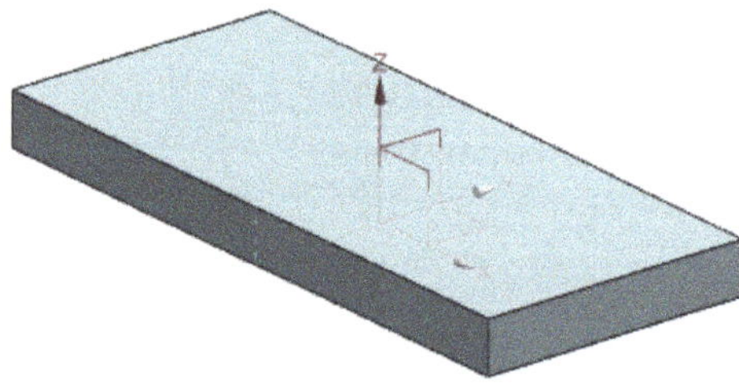

Constructing the Second Feature

1. Draw the sketch on the top face of the first feature.

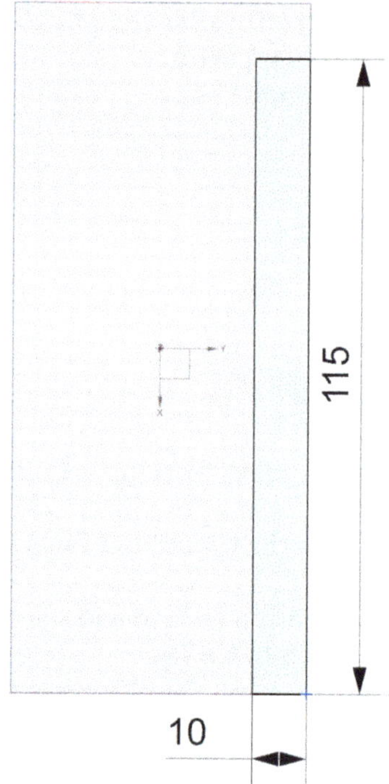

2. On the ribbon, click **Home > Base > Extrude.**
3. Select the sketch.
4. Type-in **45** in the **End** box.

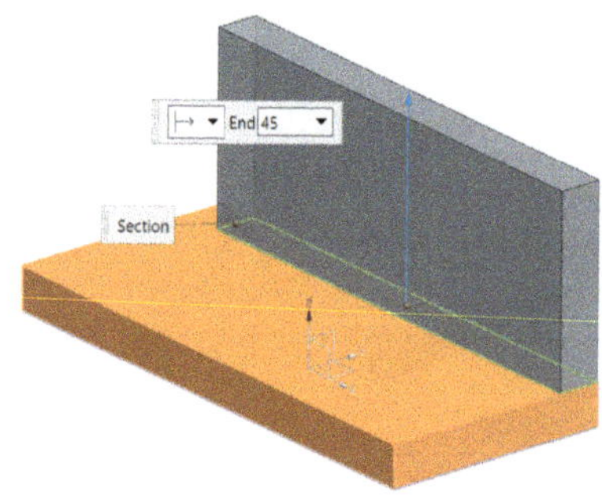

5. Under the **Boolean** section, select **Boolean > Unite.**
6. Click **OK.**

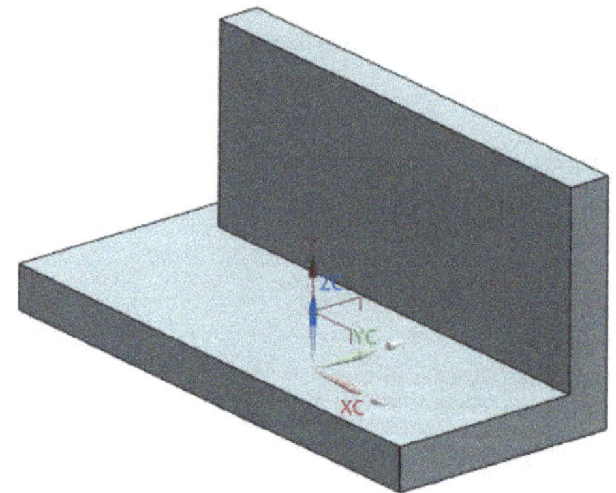

Constructing the third feature

1. On the ribbon, click **Home > Construction > Datum Plane**.
2. On the **Datum Plane** dialog, select **Type > At Distance** .
3. Click on the right-side face of the model geometry.
4. Type-in **50** in the **Distance** box and click the **Reverse Direction** icon on the **Datum Plane** dialog.

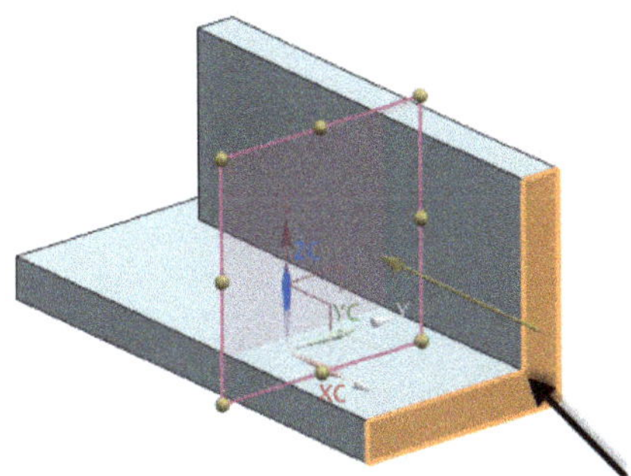

5. Click **OK**.
6. On the ribbon, click Home > Construction > Sketch.
7. Select the newly created datum plane.
8. On the ribbon, click **Home > Include > More > Project Curve**.
9. Select the right vertical edge, as shown.

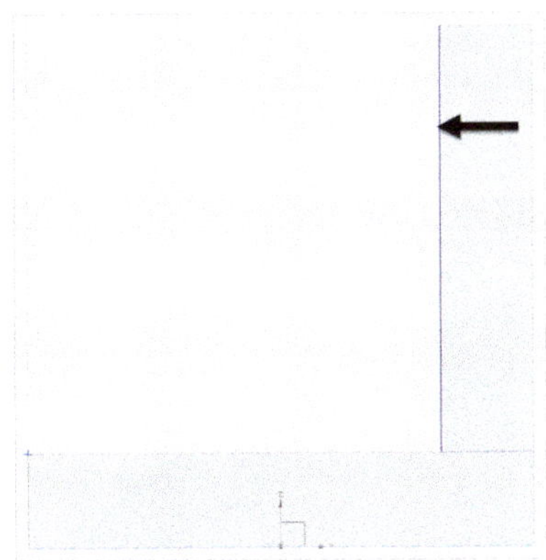

10. Click the **Line** icon on the **Curve** group.
11. Select the top endpoint of the projected curve.
12. Click on the horizontal axis.

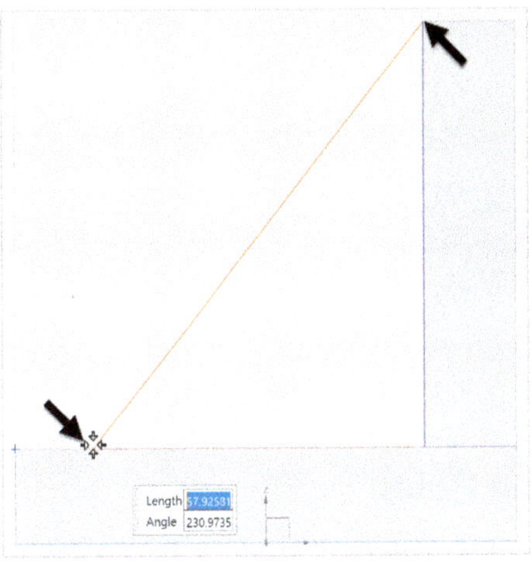

13. Add dimension between the sketch origin and the lower endpoint of the inclined line.
14. Select the projected curve and click the **Convert to Reference** icon on the Shortcuts toolbar.

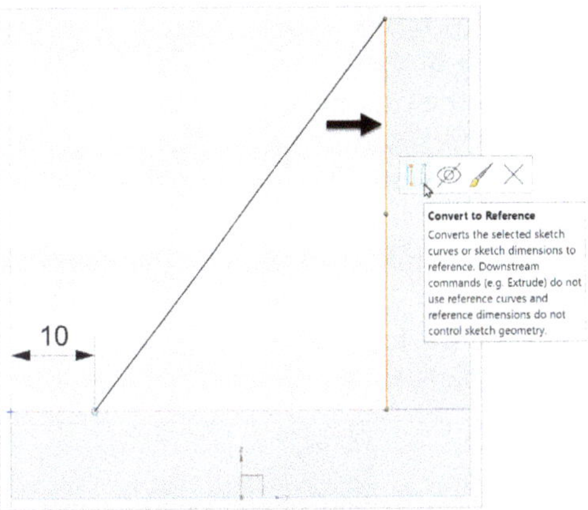

15. Click **Finish** on the **Sketch** group of the **Home** tab.
16. On the ribbon, click **Home > Base > More > Detail Feature > Rib** .
17. Select the sketch.
18. On the **Rib** dialog, select **Walls > Parallel to Section Plane**.
19. Under the **Walls** section, select **Dimension > Symmetric** and type-in **10** in the **Thickness** box.
20. Check **Combine Rib with Target**.
21. Click **OK**.

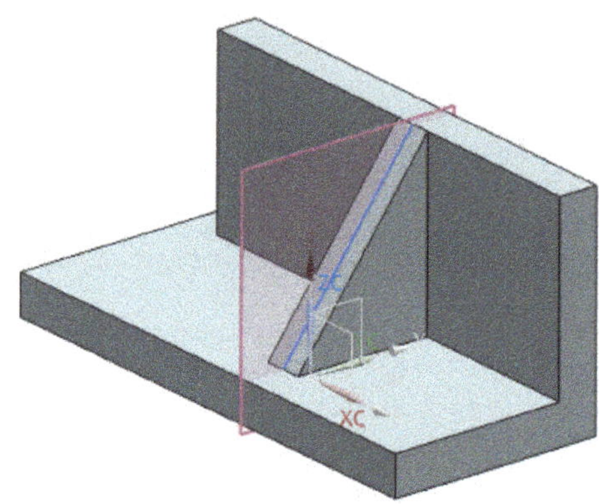

Drilling Holes

1. To drill holes, click **Home > Base > Hole** on the ribbon.
2. On the **Hole** dialog, select **Type > Simple**.
3. On the **Form** section, select **Hole Size > Drill Size**.
4. Under the **Form** section, select **Size > 16**.
5. Under the **Limit** section, select **Depth Limit > Through Body**.
6. Expand the **Chamfer** sub-section in the Form section.
7. Check the **Start Chamfer** and **End Chamfer** options.
8. Click **Sketch Section** icon on the **Position** section.
9. Click on the top face of the model.

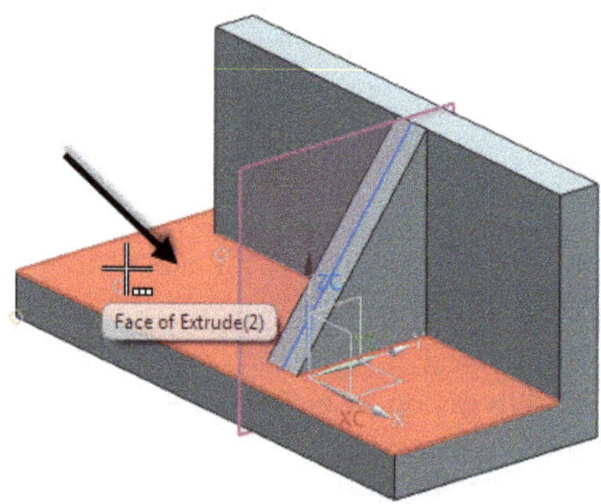

10. Click **OK** on the **Create Sketch** dialog.
11. Place two points and click the **Close** button on the **Sketch Point** dialog.
12. Add dimensions and constraints to the points to define the hole location.

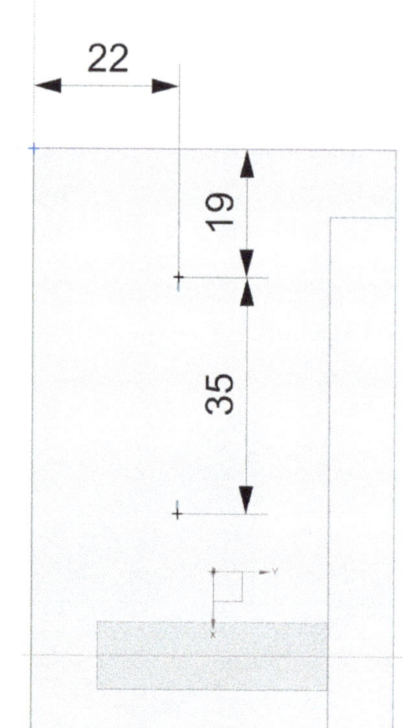

13. Click **Finish** on the ribbon.

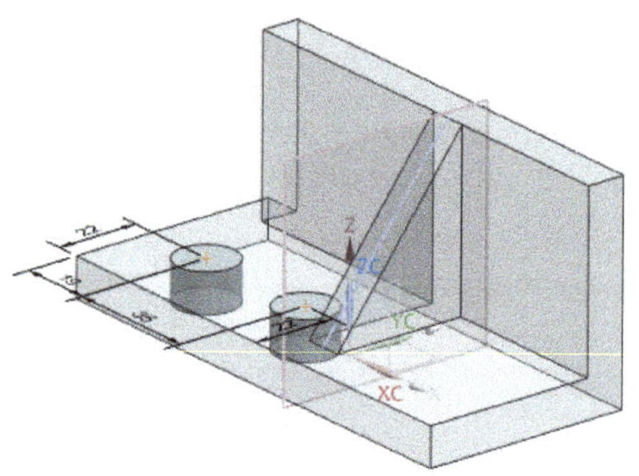

14. Click **Apply** to create the hole.

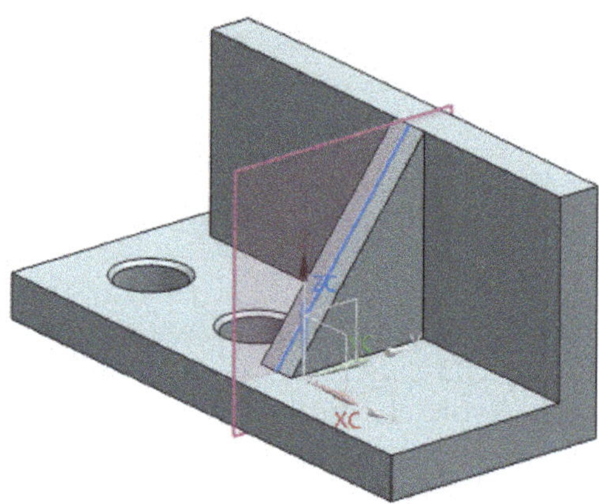

15. Drill another hole on the front face of the second feature.

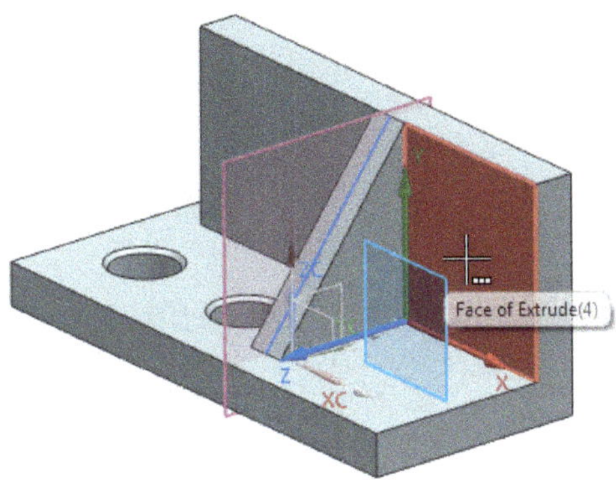

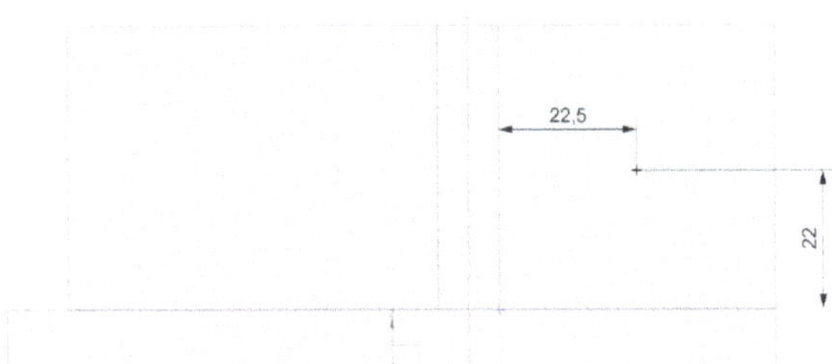

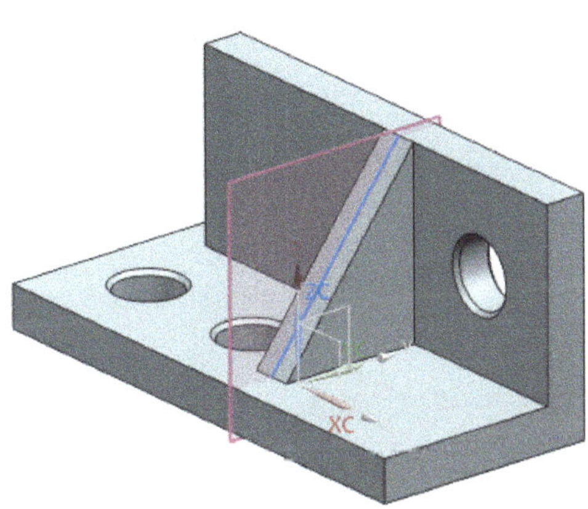

Adding Chamfers

1. To add a chamfer, click **Home > Base > Chamfer** on the ribbon.
2. On the **Chamfer** dialog, select **Cross-section > Asymmetric**.
3. Type-in **25** and **45** in the **Distance 1** and **Distance 2** boxes.
4. Click on the corner edge of the first feature.

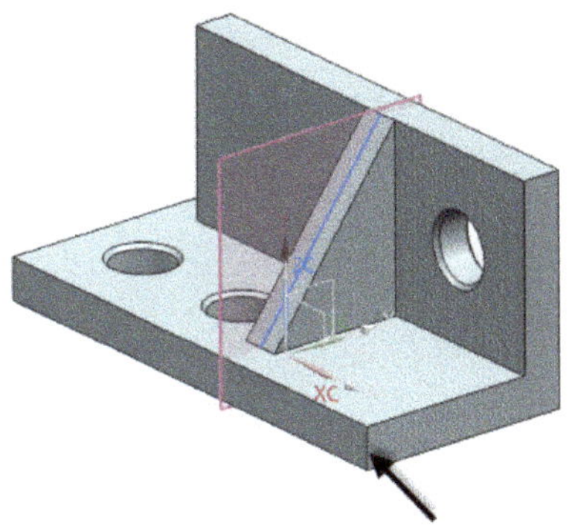

5. Click **Apply** add the chamfer.

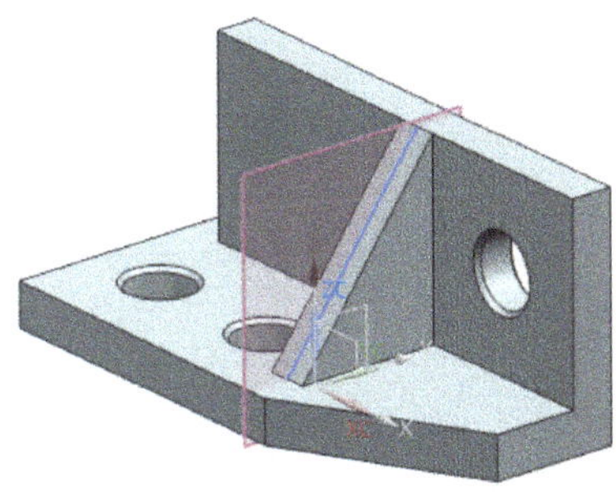

6. On the **Chamfer** dialog, select **Cross Section > Symmetric**.
7. Type-in **45** in the **Distance** box.
8. Click on the corner edge of the second feature.

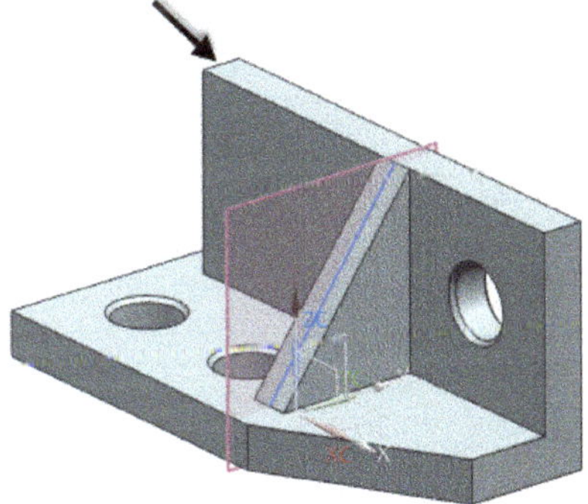

9. Click **OK**.

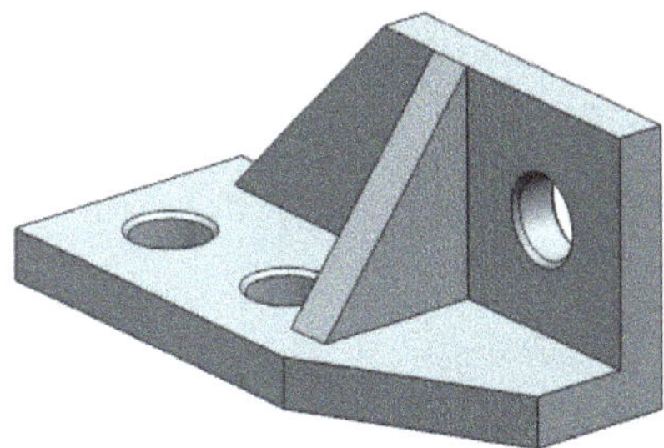

10. Save the model.

Edit Parameters

1. Click on the Drilled hole and select **Edit with**

Rollback from the Shortcuts toolbar.

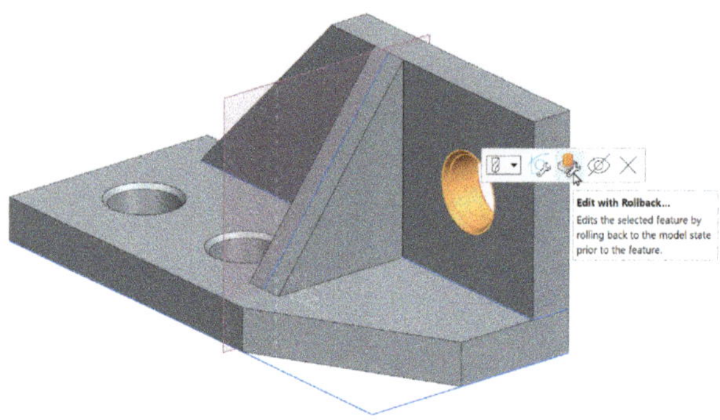

2. On the **Hole** dialog, select **Type > Counterbored.**
3. Set the dimensions and options of the counterbored hole in the **Form** section, as shown.

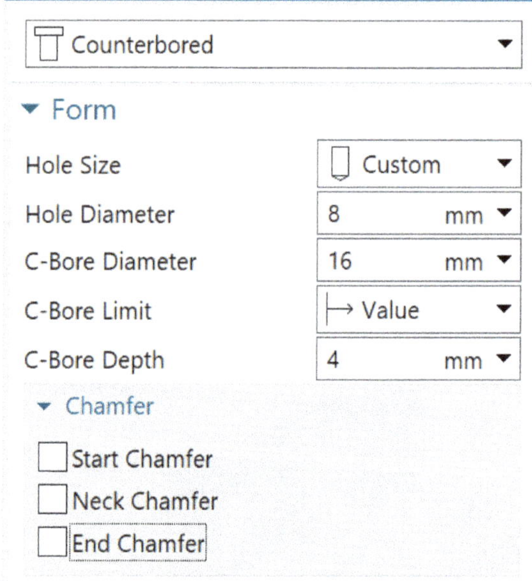

4. Click **OK.**

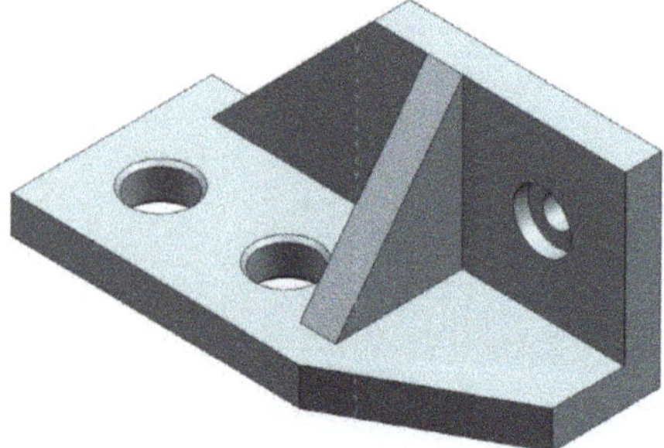

Show Dimensions

1. In the Part Navigator, right-click on the first Extruded feature and select **Show Dimensions**.
2. Double click on the linear dimension of the extrude feature.

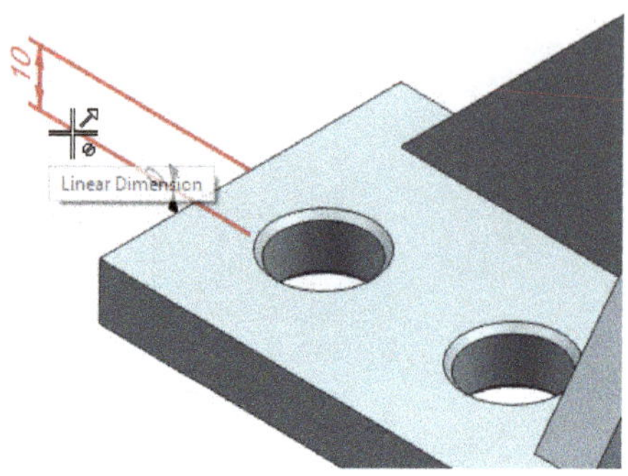

3. On the **Feature Dimension** dialog, type-in 20 in the value box and click **OK.**

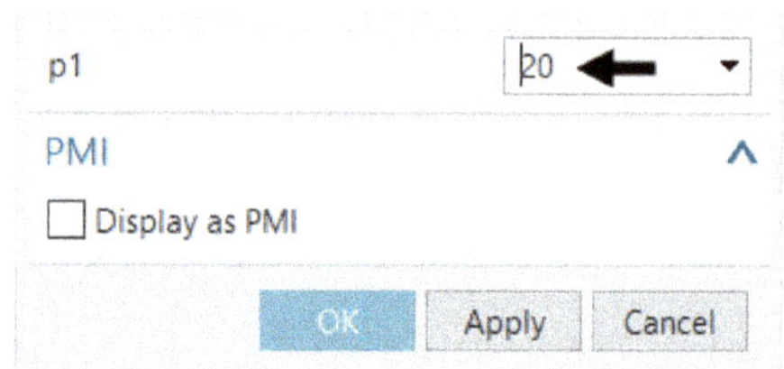

4. Right click and select **Refresh** or press F5.

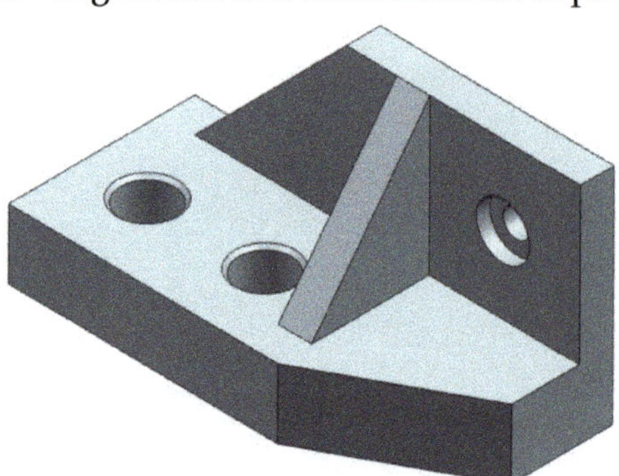

Editing Features by Double-clicking

1. Double-click on the chamfer.

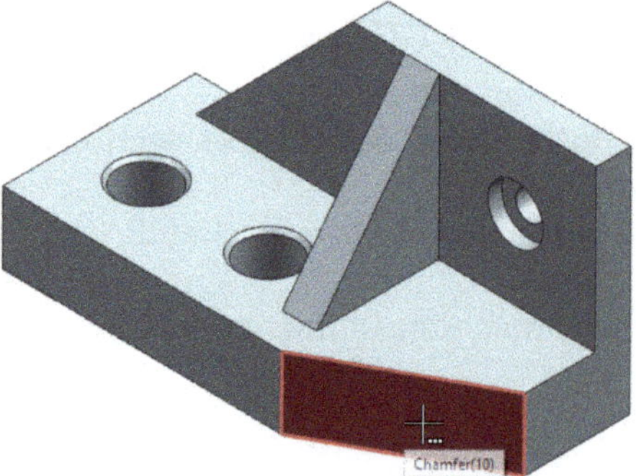

2. On the **Chamfer** dialog, type-in 30 in the **Distance 1** box and click **OK.**

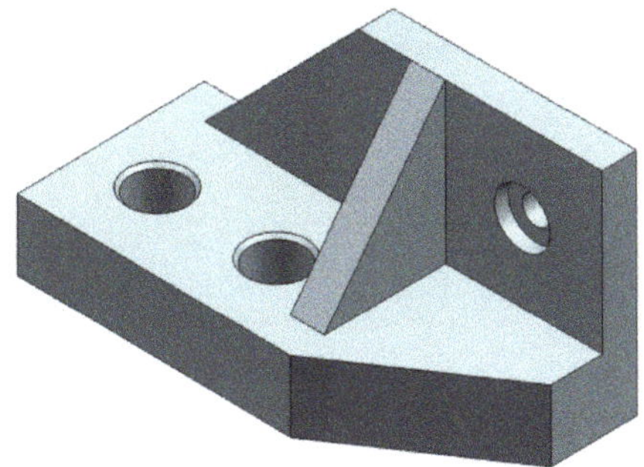

Suppress Features

1. In the Part Navigator, right-click on the last Chamfer feature and select **Suppress**.

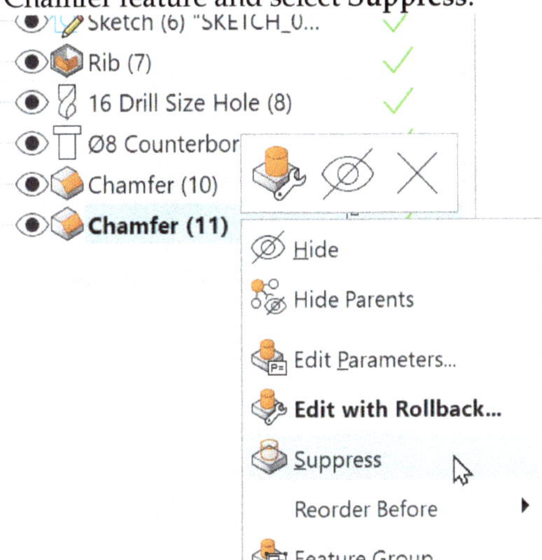

2. On the Part Navigator, right-click on the **Chamfer** feature and select the **Unsupress** option.

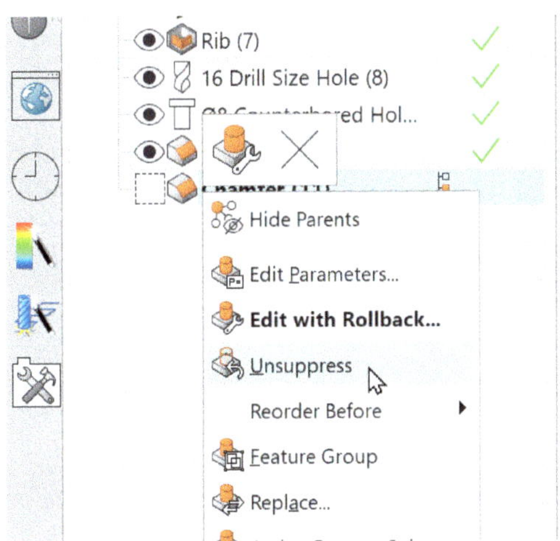

3. On the Part Navigator, right click on the Sketch of the base feature and select **Edit**.
4. Select the **125** dimension, and click the **Edit Annotation** option.

5. On the **Linear Dimension** dialog, check the **Expression** option in the **Driving** section.
6. Type **Length** in the **Expression** box.

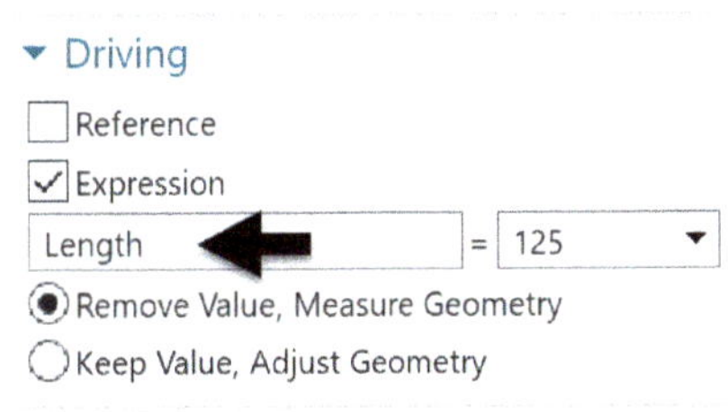

7. Click **OK**.
8. Click **Finish** on the ribbon.
9. On the Top Border Bar, click **Menu > Edit > Feature > Suppress by Expression**.

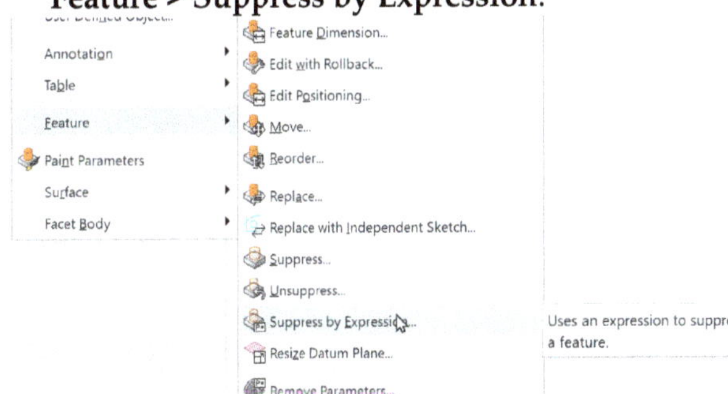

10. Select the previously unsuppressed chamfer and click **Apply**.
11. Click **Show Expressions** on the dialog. The **Information** window appears showing the chamfer expression. The value 1 indicates that it is currently unsuppressed.

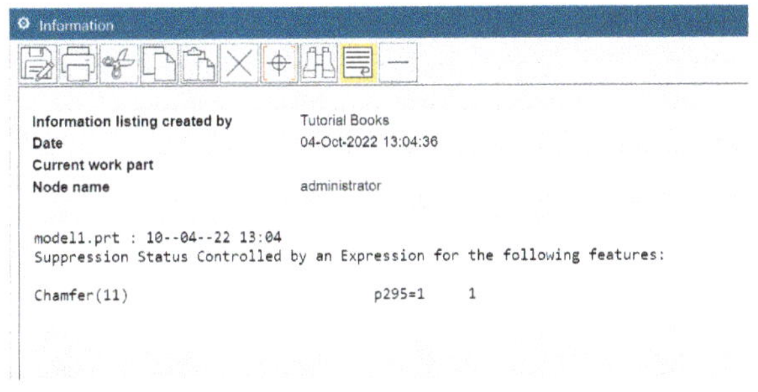

12. Close the **Information** window and the **Suppression By Expression** dialog.
13. On the ribbon, click **Tools > Utilities > Expression**.

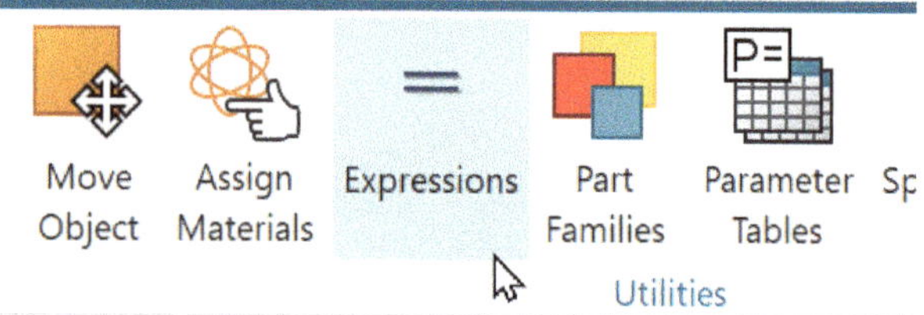

14. On the **Expressions** dialog, select **Show > All Expressions**.
15. Scroll down and select **p295** from the listed expressions.

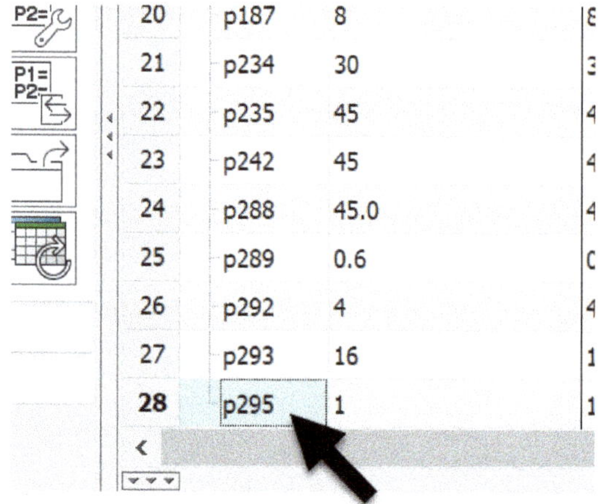

Note: The expression number may differ in your case.

16. Double click in the **Name** box and enter **Chamfer_Suppression**.
17. Enter **if (Length=>125) (1) else (0)** in the **Formula** box.

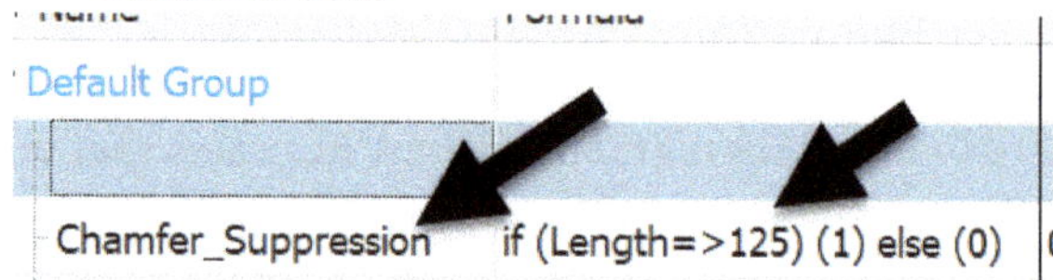

18. Click **OK**.
19. On the Part Navigator, right click on the Sketch of the base feature and select **Edit Parameters**.
20. On the **Edit Parameters** dialog, select the 125 dimension, and change its value to **124**.

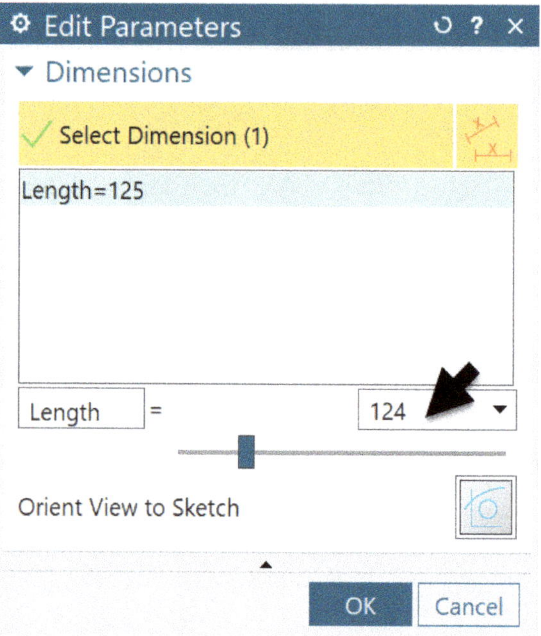

21. Click **OK**. The chamfer is suppressed as the length value is less than 125.

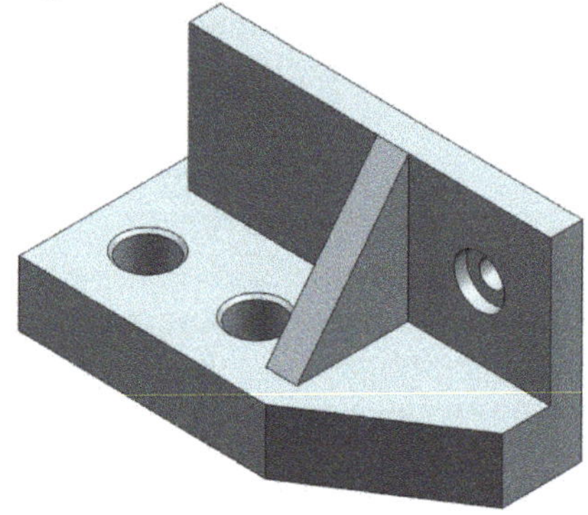

22. Close the file.

TUTORIAL 7

In this tutorial, you create the model shown in the figure.

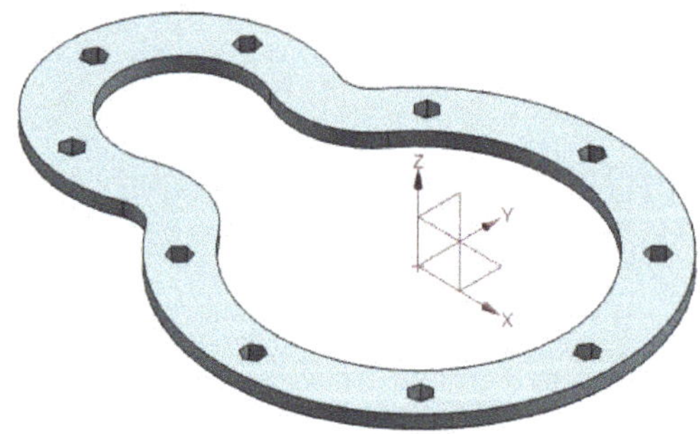

Constructing the first feature

1. Open a new part file.
2. On the ribbon, click **Home > Base > Extrude**.
3. Click on the XY plane.
4. Construct two circles and add dimensions to them.

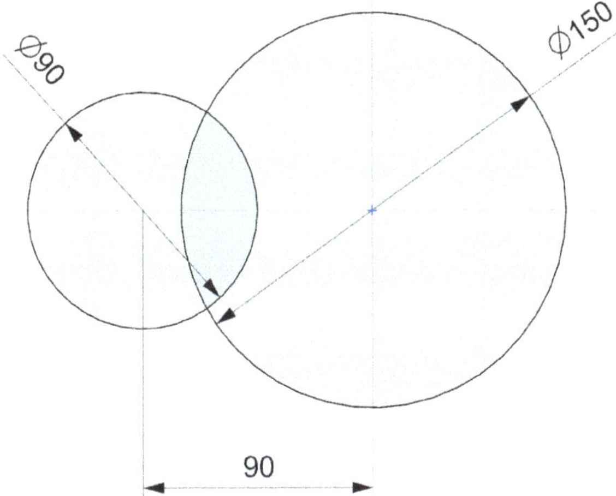

5. On the ribbon, click **Home > Curve > Trim** and trim the intersecting entities.

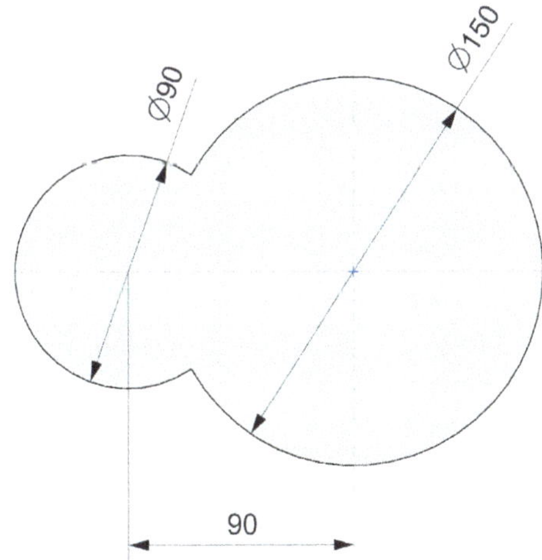

6. On the ribbon, click **Home > Curve > Fillet** and set the **Radius** value to 10.
7. Select the intersecting corners of the circles.

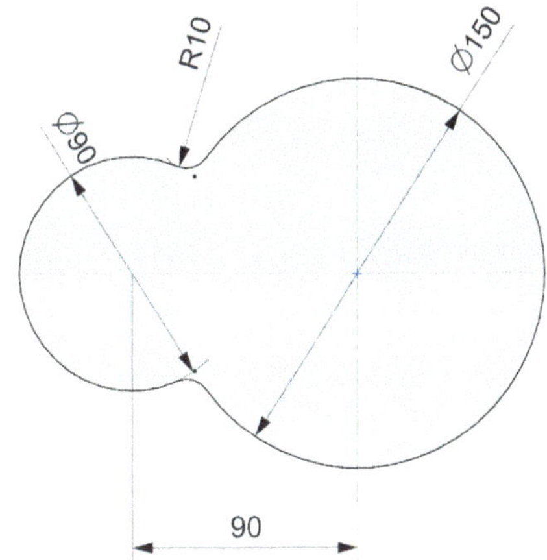

8. Click **Finish**.
9. Extrude the sketch up to 5 mm distance.

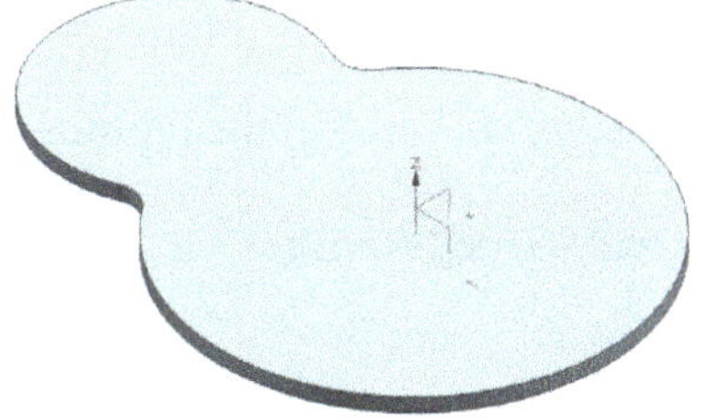

Constructing the Extruded cut

1. On the ribbon, click **Home > Base > Extrude**.
2. Click on the top face of the model.
3. On the ribbon, click **Home > Curve > Offset Curve**.
4. On the Top Border Bar, select **Selection Scope > Within Work Part Only**.
5. Click on any edge of the top face.
6. On the **Offset Curve** dialog, set the **Distance** value to **20**.
7. Click the **Reverse Direction** button.
8. Expand the **Settings** section and check the **Create Persistent Relations** option.
9. Click **OK**.

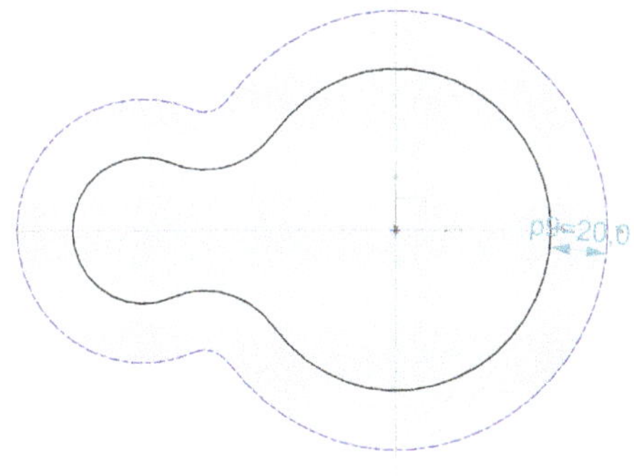

10. Click **Finish**.
11. On the **Extrude** dialog, click the **Reverse Direction** button under the **Direction** section.
12. Click **OK**.

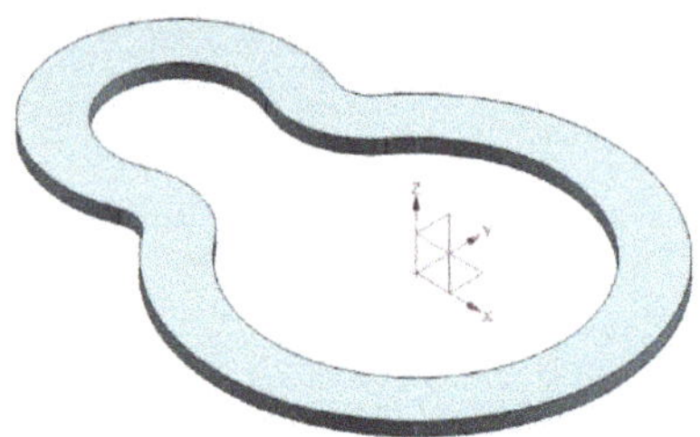

Constructing the Extruded cut

1. On the ribbon, click **Home > Base > Extrude**.
2. Click on the top face of the model geometry.
3. On the ribbon, click **Home > Curve > More > Polygon**.
4. On the **Polygon** dialog, type-in **6** in the **Number of Sides** box.
5. Select **Size > Circumscribed Radius**.
6. Set the **Radius** to **4**.
7. Set the **Rotation** to **0**.
8. Click on the horizontal axis to define the center point of the polygon.

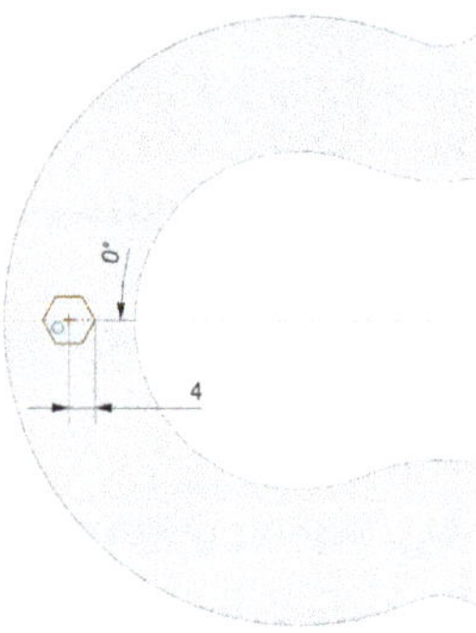

9. Close the **Polygon** dialog.
10. Add a dimension between the center point of the polygon and the origin.

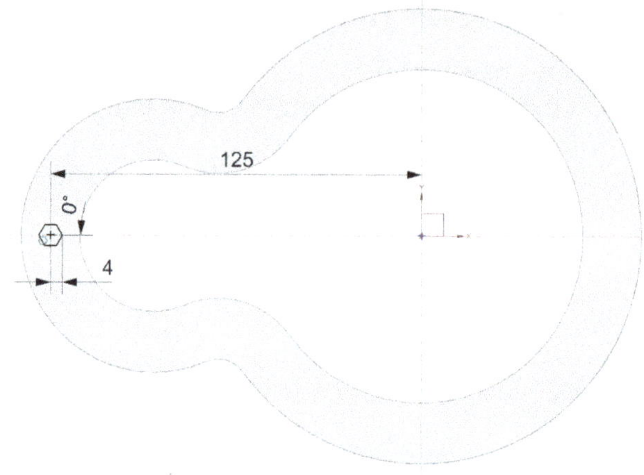

11. Click **Finish**.
12. Create the cut throughout the body.

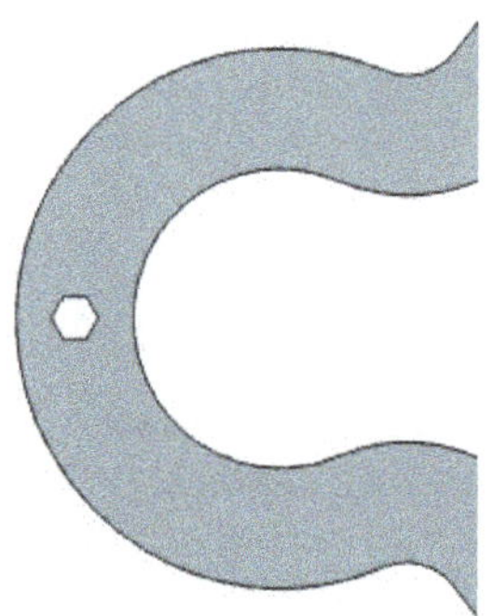

Making the Along Pattern

1. On the ribbon, click **Home** > **Base > Pattern Feature**.
2. Select the polygonal cut to define the feature to pattern.
3. Select **Layout > Along**.
4. Select **Path Method > Offset**.
5. Click **Select Path**.
6. On the Sketch Scene bar, select **Curve rule > Tangent Curves**.
7. Select the outer edge of the top face.

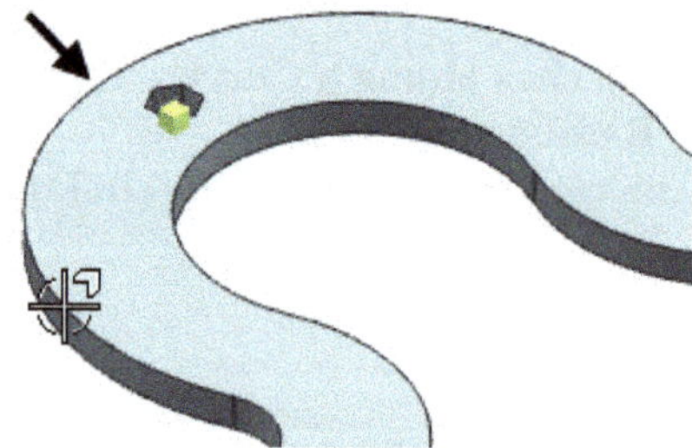

8. Select **Spacing > Count and Span**.
9. Type-in **10** in the **Count** box.
10. Type-in **100** in the % **Span By** box.
11. Under the **Orientation** section, set **Orientation**

to **Normal to Path**.

12. Click **OK**.

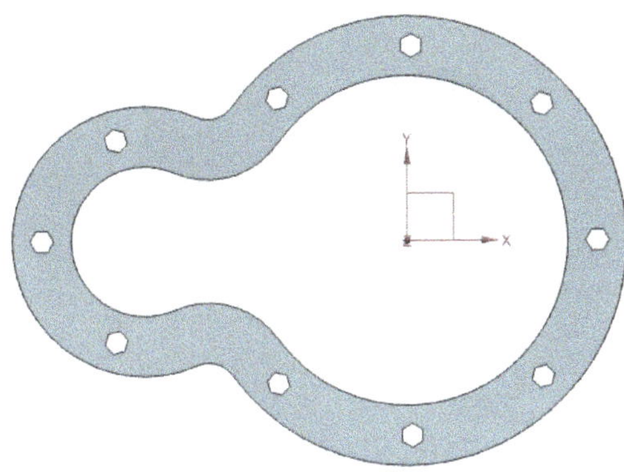

Measuring the Mass Properties

1. On the ribbon, click **Analysis > Measure > Measure.**

2. Place the pointer on the top face of the model. Next, click when three dots are displayed; the **QuickPick** dialog appears.
3. Select **Solid Body of Extrude** from the **QuickPick** dialog; all the properties of the geometry appear.

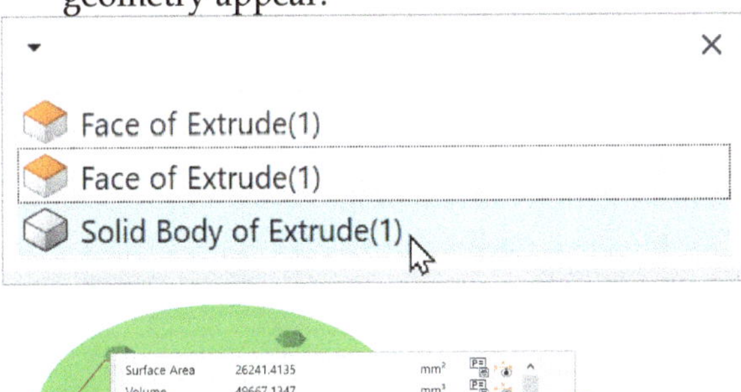

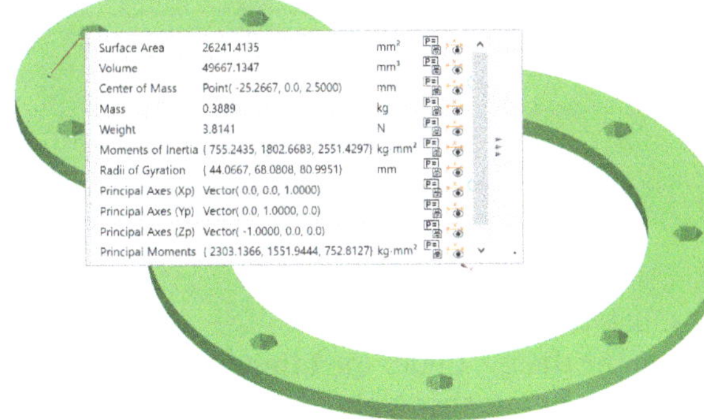

4. Press Esc.
5. On the Top Border Bar, click **Menu > Edit > Feature > Solid Density**.
6. On the **Assign Solid Density** dialog, select **Units > lbm/in3**.
7. Type **0.45** in the **Solid Density** box.
8. Select the geometry and click **OK**.
9. On the ribbon, click **Analysis > Measure > Measure**.
10. Select the geometry and notice the updated mass properties.

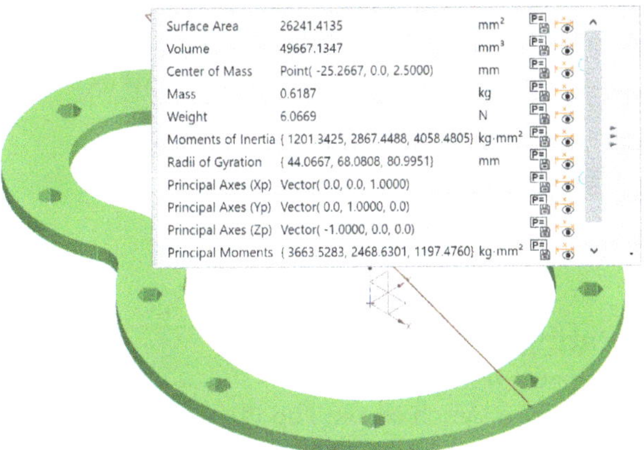

11. Click **Cancel**.
12. On the ribbon, click **Tools > Utilities > Assign Materials**.
13. Select the geometry.
14. Select **Iron_Malleable** from the **Materials** section.
15. Click **Apply**.
16. Right click on the **Iron_Malleable** material and select **Inspect** from the shortcut menu. The **Isotropic Material** dialog appears showing various properties of the material. You can view the Mechanical, Strength, Durability, Formability, and other properties by clicking on each of them.

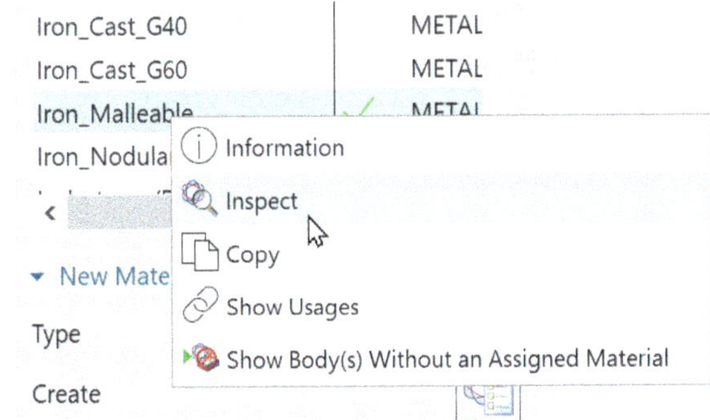

17. Close the **Isotropic Material** dialog and click **OK**.
18. Use the **Measure** tool to see the Mass Properties of the geometry.
19. Save and close the file.

TUTORIAL 8

In this tutorial, you create a plastic casing.

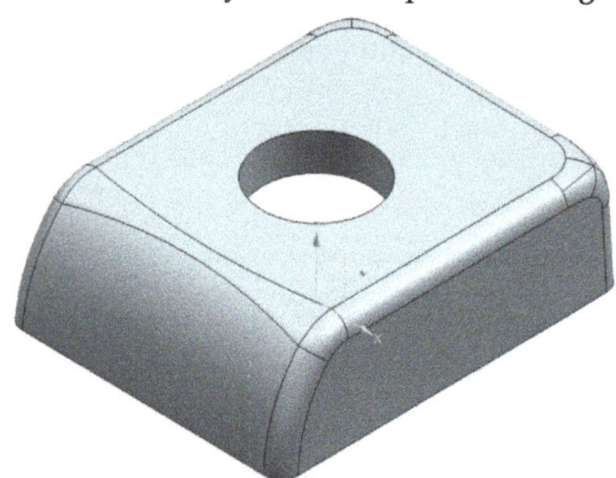

Creating the First Feature

1. Open a new part file.
2. Create a sketch on the Top Plane, as shown in the figure.

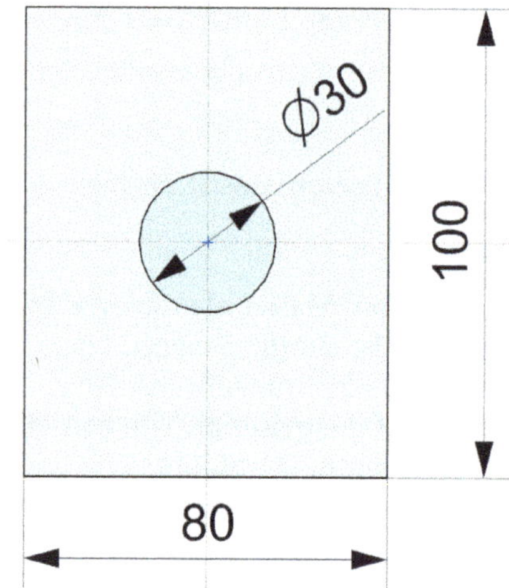

3. Click **Finish** on the **Sketch** group.
4. Click the **Base > Extrude** on the ribbon.
5. Select the sketch.
6. Set the **Distance** to 30.
7. Click the **Dialog Options** (gear) icon located at the top-left corner of the Extrude dialog.
8. Select **Extrude (More)** from the drop-down.
9. Expand the **Draft** section and select **Draft > From Start Limit.**
10. Set the **Angle** to **2**.
11. Click **OK.**

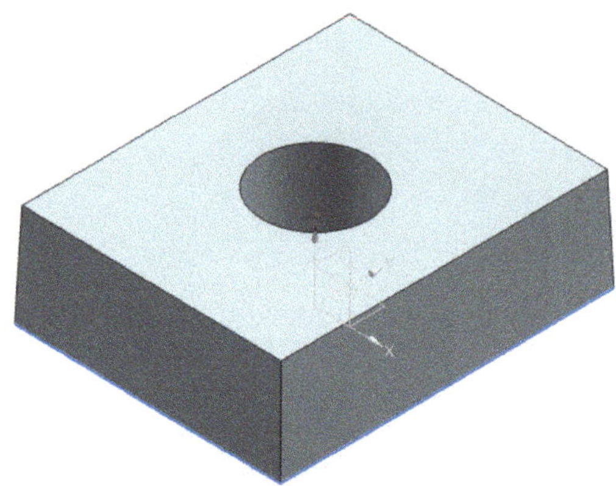

Creating the Extruded surface

1. Click **Base > Extrude** on the ribbon and select the YZ Plane. Next, click **OK.**
2. On the Top Border Bar, select **Selection Scope > Within Work Part Only**.
3. On the ribbon, click Home > Curve > Arc.
4. Select lower left corner of the model, as shown.
5. Click on the top edge of the model.
6. Move the pointer toward left and click when the Tangent constraint glyph is displayed.
7. Press ESC.

8. Select the newly created arc.
9. Double-click on the dimension, type 40 and press ENTER.

10. Click **Finish.**
11. On the dialog, under the **Limits** section, select **Start > Symmetric Value.**
12. Type-in **100** in the **Distance** box and click **OK.**

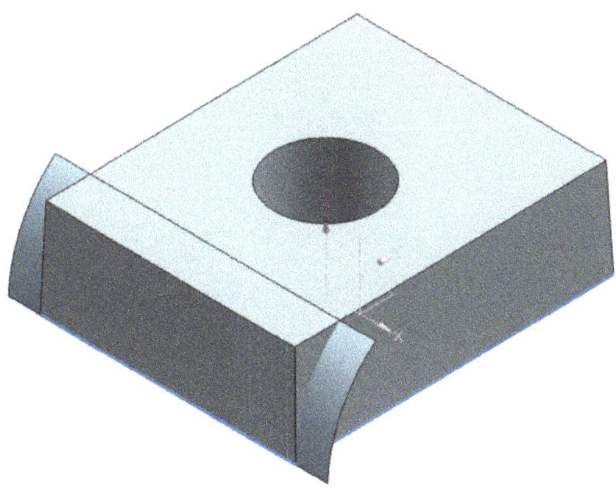

Trim Body

1. On the ribbon, click **Base > Trim Body** .

Now, you need to select the target body.

2. Select the solid body.

Next, you need to select the tool body.

3. Select **Tool Option > Face or Plane**.
4. Click **Select Face or Plane** and select the extruded surface.
5. Make sure that the arrow points towards the front. You can double-click on it to reverse its direction.
6. Click **OK** to trim the solid.

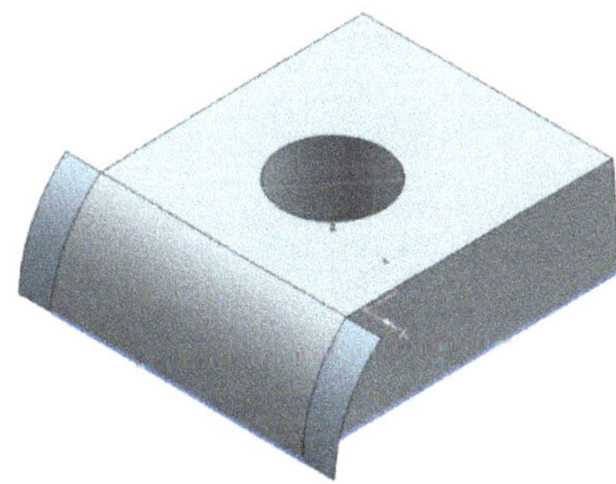

7. Hide the extruded surface by clicking on it and selecting **Hide**.

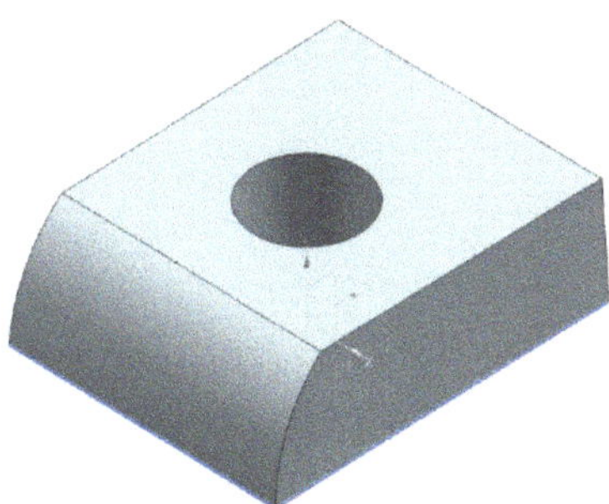

Variable Radius Blend

1. On the ribbon, click **Home > Base > Edge Blend** .
2. Select the edge between the top and curved faces.

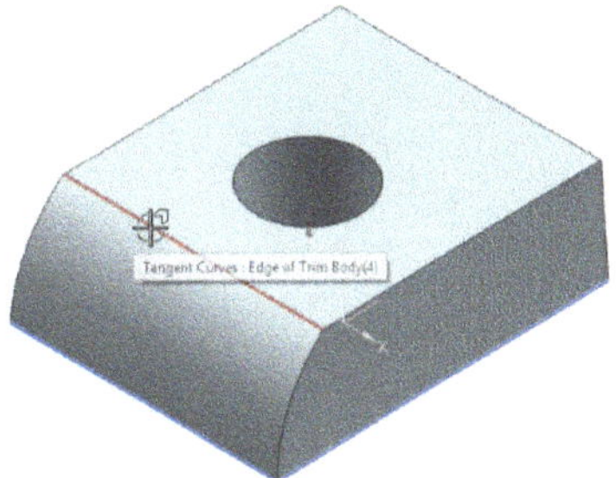

3. Expand the **Variable Radius** section and click **Specify Radius Point**.
4. Select the three points on the edge, as shown.

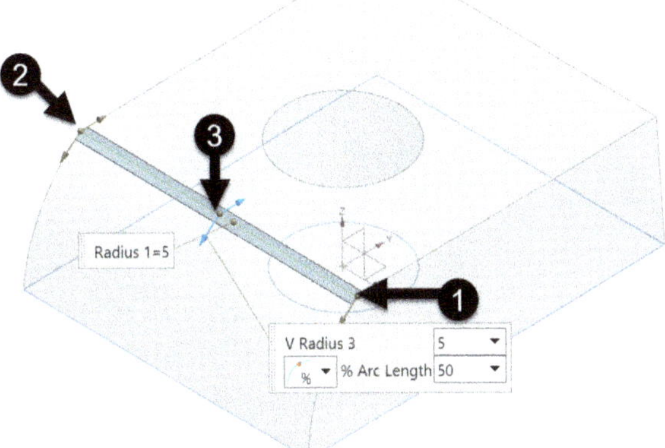

5. Under the **Variable Radius** section, expand the **List** section.
6. Select the radius points one-by-one and change the radius values, as shown.

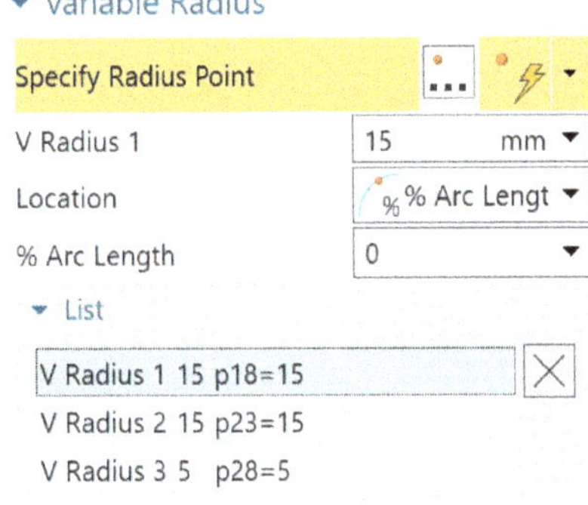

7. Click **OK** to create the variable radius blend.

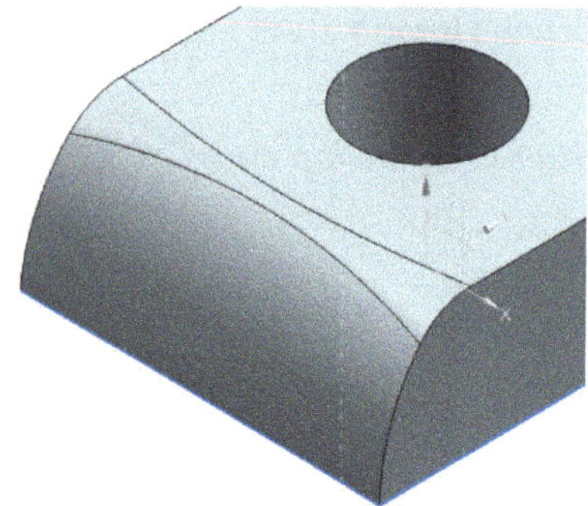

Corner Setbacks

1. On the ribbon, click **Home > Base > Edge Blend** .
2. Set the **Radius 1** to 5
3. Select the edges of the geometry, as shown.

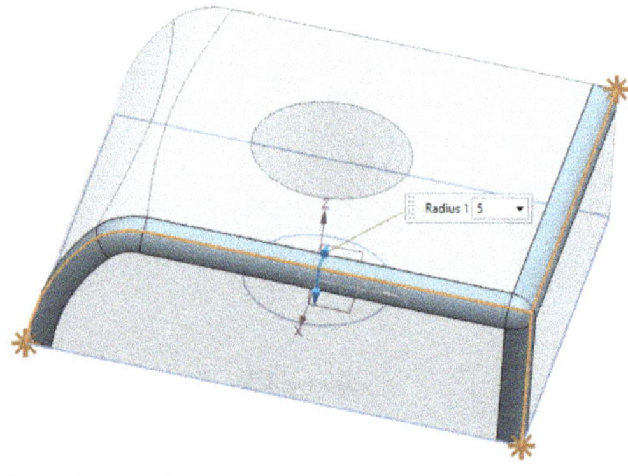

4. Expand the **Corner Setback** section and click **Select End Point.**
5. Select the vertex point, as shown.

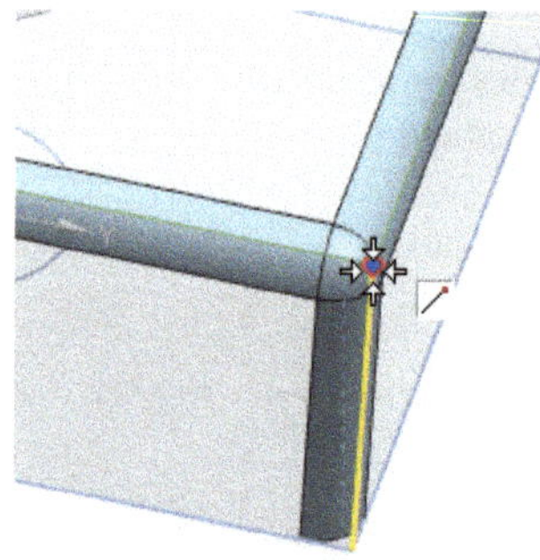

6. Under the **Corner Setback** section, expand the **List** section.
7. Select the setback points one-by-one and change the setback values, as shown. You can also change the setback values on the handle attached to the corner.

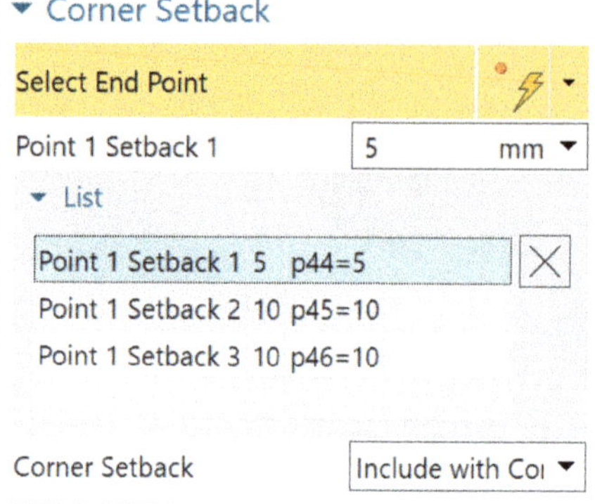

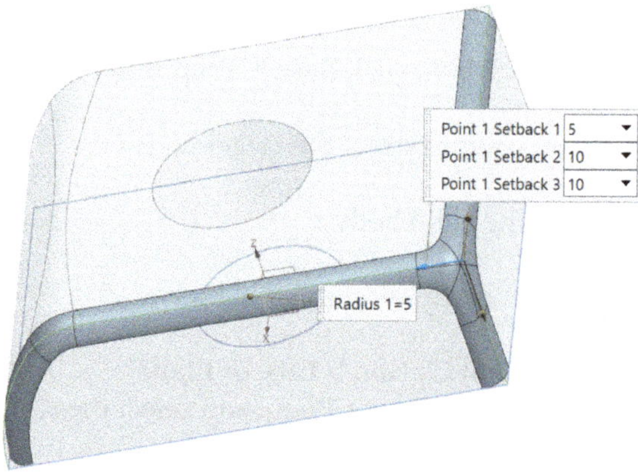

8. Under the **Edge** section, click **Select Edge.**
9. Select the edges, as shown.

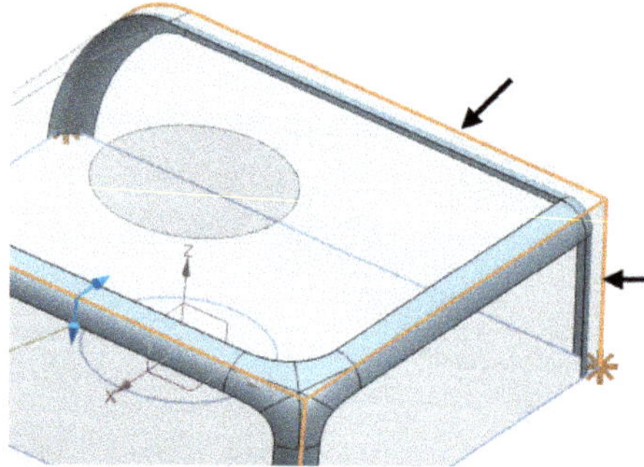

10. Under the **Corner Setback** section, click **Select End Point.**
11. Select the vertex point, as shown.

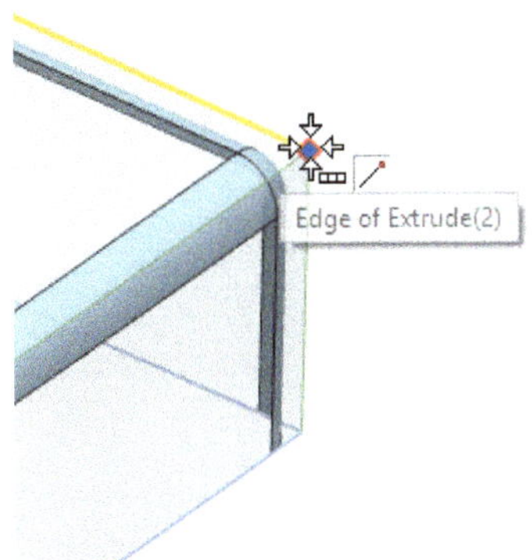

12. Change the setback values on the handle attached to the corner.

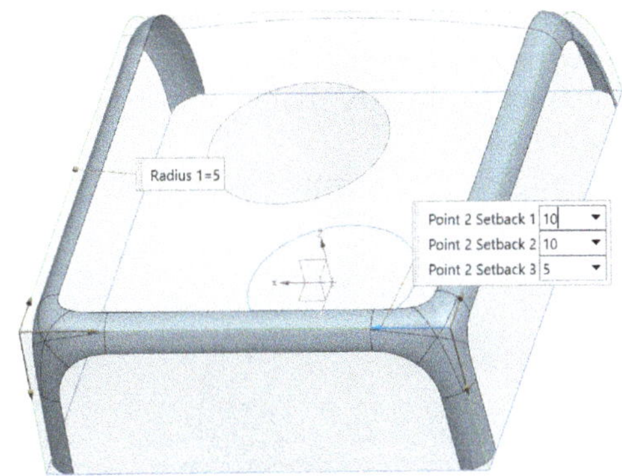

13. Click **OK**.

Shell with an Alternate Thickness

1. On the ribbon, click **Home > Base > Shell**.
2. Select the bottom face of the geometry.
3. Under the **Thickness** section, type-in 2 in the **Thickness** box.
4. Expand the **Alternate Thickness** section and click **Select Face**.
5. Select the round face, as shown.
6. Under the **Alternate Thickness** section, type-in 4 in the **Thickness** box.

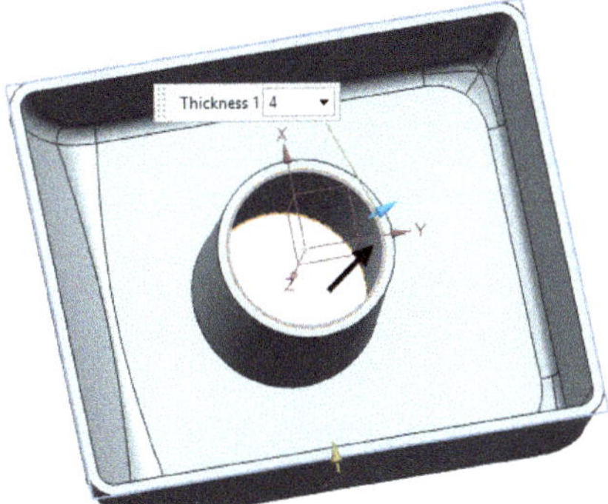

7. Click **OK**.

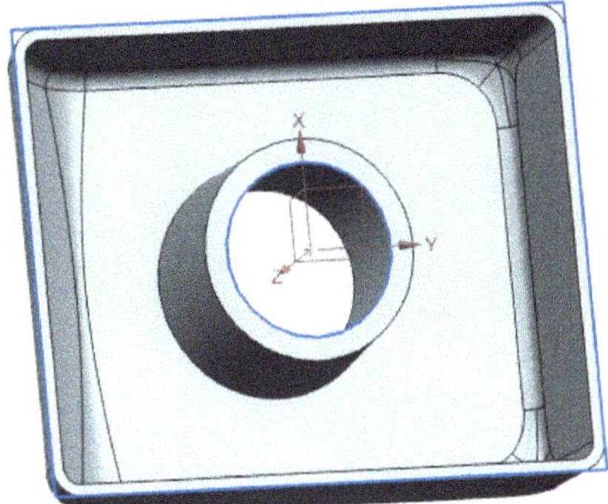

Offset Face

1. On the ribbon, click **Home > Base > More > Offset > Offset Face**.
2. Select the face of the geometry, as shown.

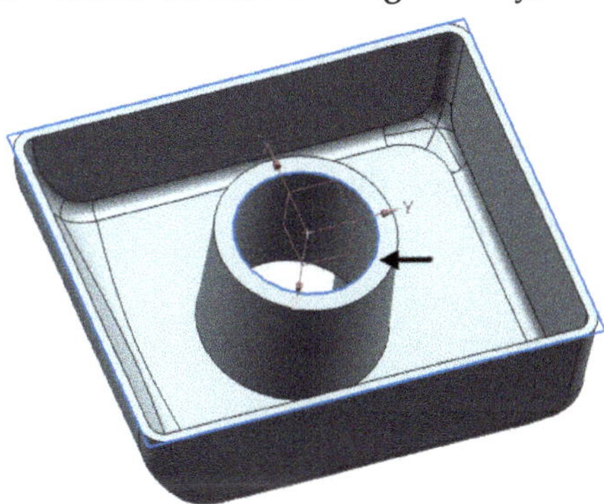

3. Drag the arrow handle downward and release when the offset value is set to 20.

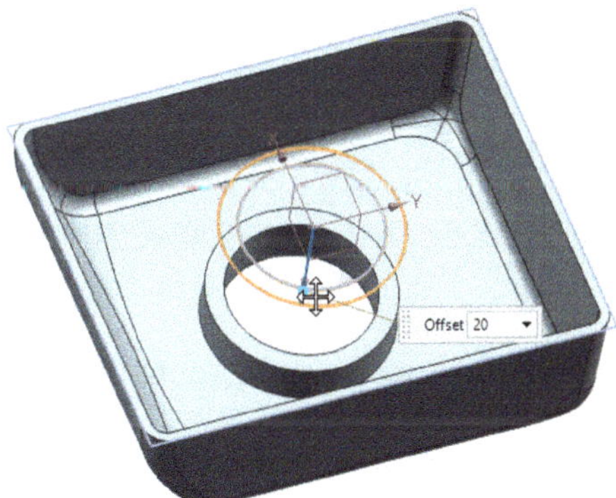

4. Click **OK**.

Scale Body

1. On the ribbon, click **Home > Base > More > Offset > Scale Body**.
2. On the **Scale Body** dialog, select **Type > Uniform**.
3. Select the geometry.
4. Under the **Scale Point** section, click **Specify Point**.
5. Select the center point of the circular edge, as

shown.

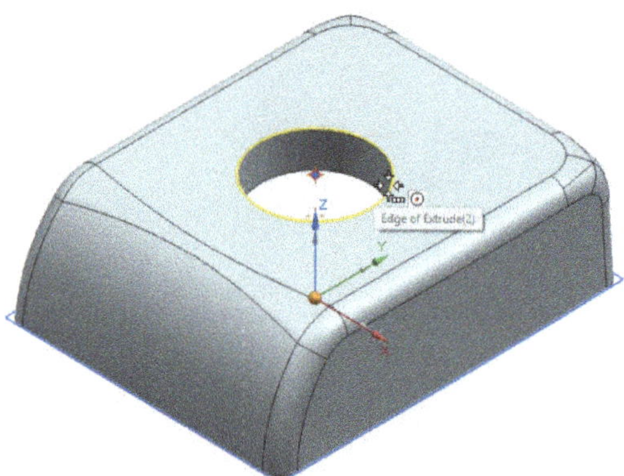

6. Type-in **1.05** in the **Uniform** box.
8. Check the **Preview** option and click **Show Result**.
7. Click the **Undo Result** button.
8. Select **Type > Non-uniform**.
9. Under the **Scale Factor** section, type-in 1.2, 1.5, and 0.8 in the **X Direction, Y Direction**, and **Z Direction** boxes, respectively.
10. Click **Show Result**.

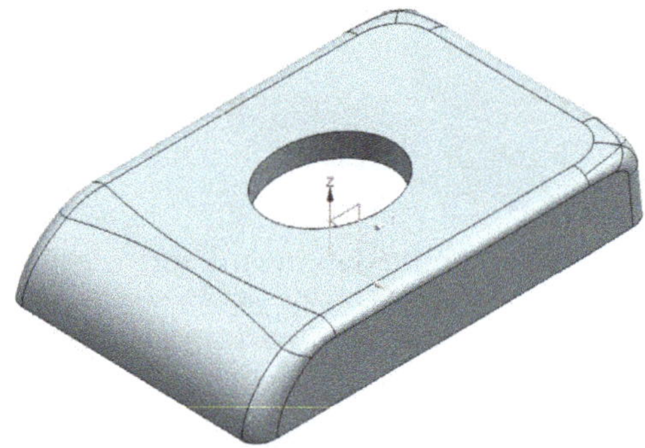

11. Click **Undo Result**.
12. Select **Type > Axisymmetric**.
13. Under the **Scale Axis** section, click **Specify Vector**.
14. Select the Z axis from the triad.
15. Click **Specify Point** and select the center point of the circular edge, as shown.
16. Under the **Scale Factor** section, type-in 2 in the **Along Axis** box.
17. Click **Show Result**.

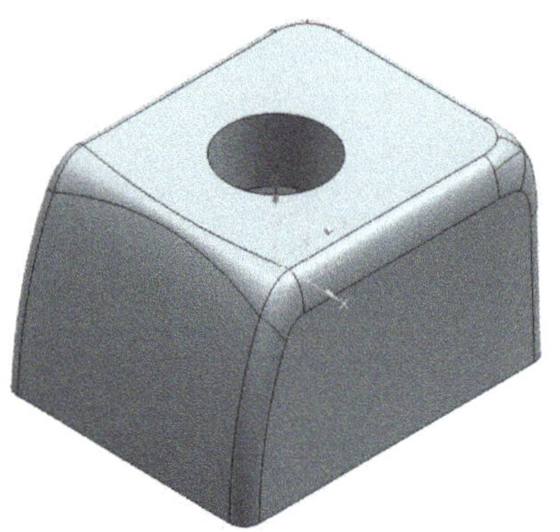

18. Click **Cancel**.

Extract Geometry

1. On the ribbon, click **Home > Base > More > Copy > Extract Geometry**.
2. On the **Extract Geometry** dialog, select **Type > Composite Curve**.
3. Select the edges of the geometry, as shown.

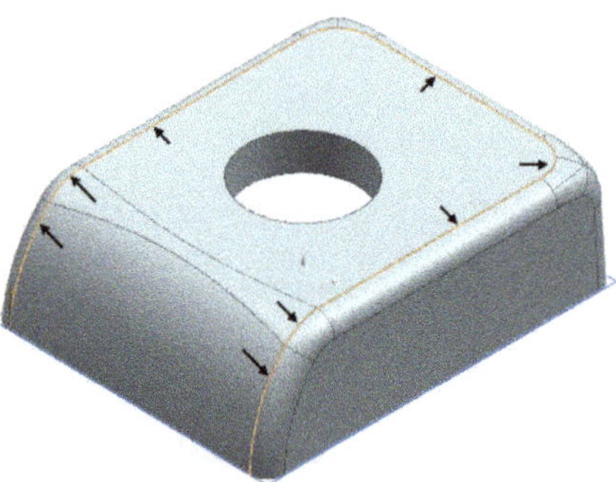

4. Click **OK**.
5. On the Part Navigator, right click on the **Composite Curve** and select **Hide Parents**. The geometry is hidden.

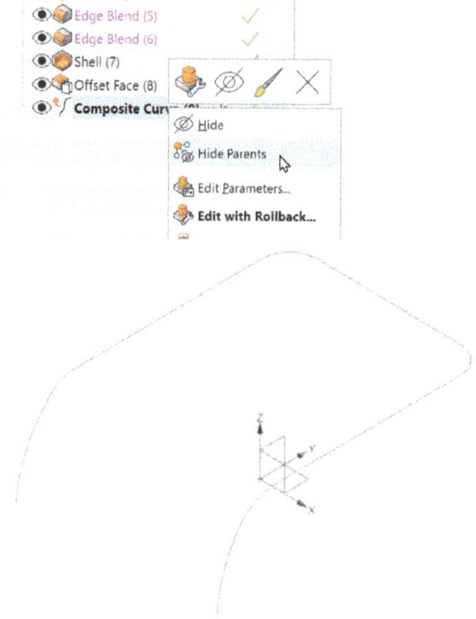

6. Right click on the **Composite Curve** and select **Show Parents**.
7. On the ribbon, click **Home > Base > More > Copy > Extract Geometry**.
8. On the **Extract Geometry** dialog, select **Type > Face**.
9. Select the top face of the geometry and click **OK**.
10. In the Part Navigator, right click on the extracted face and select **Hide Parents**.

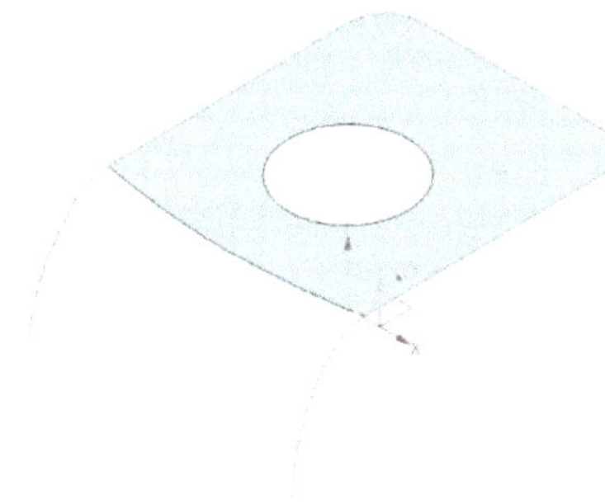

11. Right click on the extracted face and select **Show Parents**.
12. On the ribbon, click **Home > Base > More > Copy > Extract Geometry**.
13. Select **Type > Region of Faces**.
14. Select the inner horizontal face of the shell feature.

15. Select the thin planar face to define the boundary.

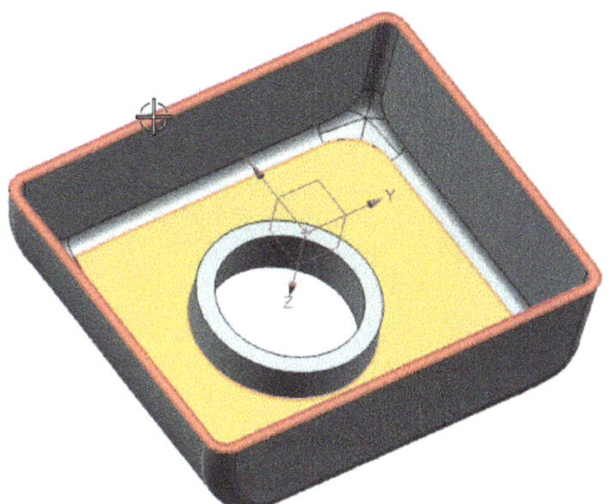

16. Under the **Region Options** section, check the **Traverse Interior Edges** option.
17. Expand the **Preview** section and click **Preview Region**.

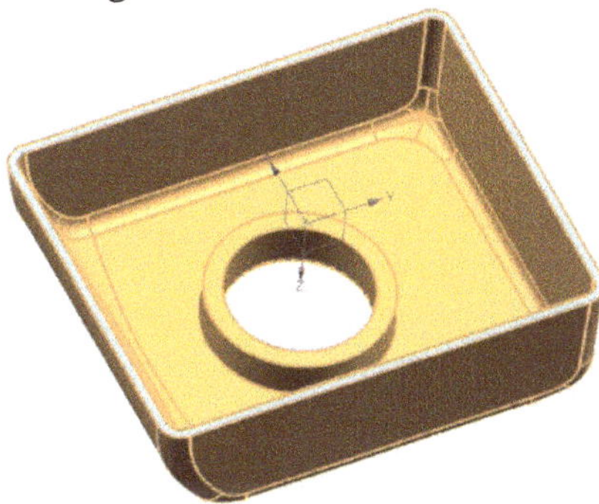

18. Click **Finished Preview**.
19. Uncheck the **Traverse Interior Edges** option.
20. Click **Preview Region**.

21. Click **OK**.
22. Close the file.

TUTORIAL 9

In this tutorial, you will learn the **Reorder Feature**, and **Replace Feature** tools.

1. Download and open the Tutorial 9 file.

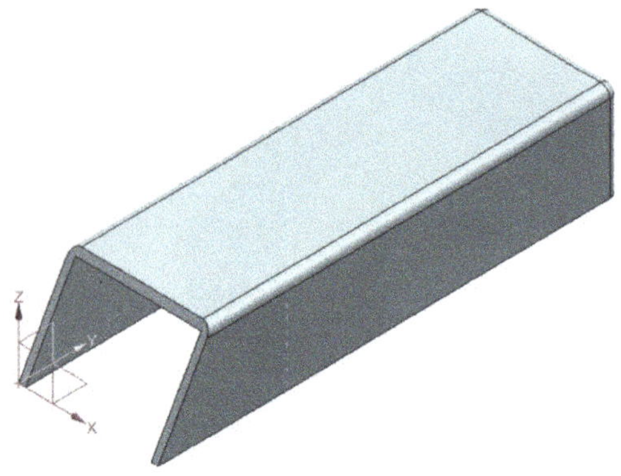

Notice that the edge blend is applied only on the outside edges of the geometry.

2. In the Part Navigator, click the Edge Blend, drag it, and place above the Shell.

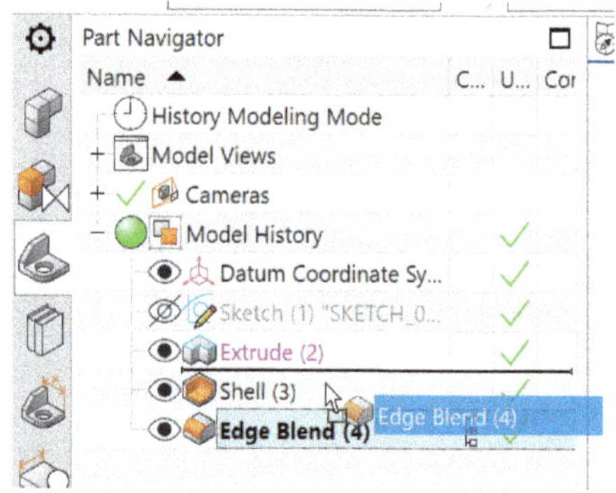

The edge blend is applied to both the inner and outer edges of the shell feature, automatically.

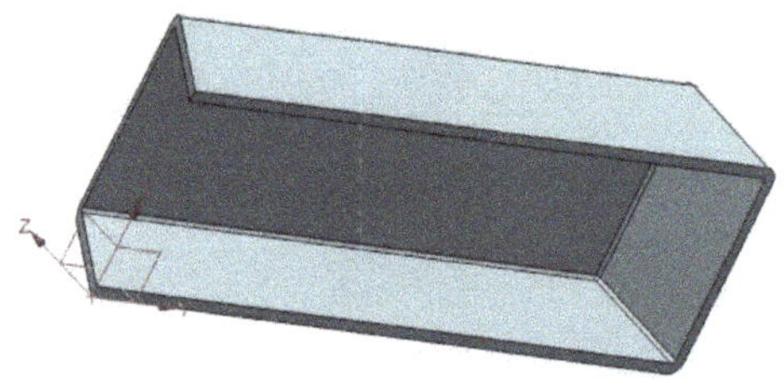

Replace Features

1. In the Part Navigator, right click on the **Extrude** feature and select **Make Current Feature**.
2. Download the Tutorial 9-Replacement.
3. Click **File > Import > Part**.
4. On the **Import Part** dialog, uncheck the **Create Named Group** option, leave the default settings and click **OK**.
5. Browse to the location of the Tutorial 9-Replacement part and double-click on it.
6. On the **Point** dialog, leave the X, Y, and Z values to 0 and click **OK**.

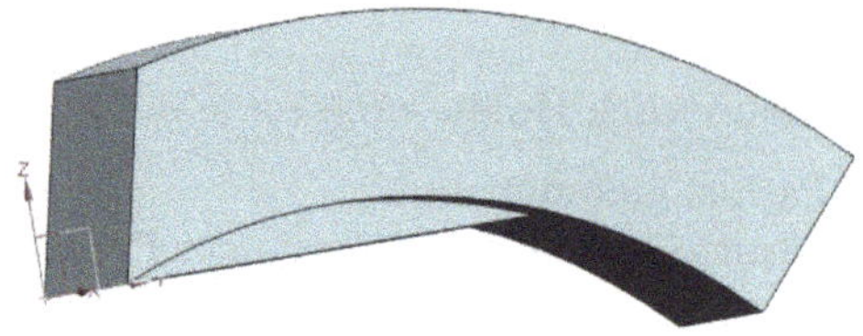

7. Click **Cancel**.
8. In the Part Navigator, right click on the **Shell** feature and select **Make Current Feature**.
9. In the Part Navigator, right click on the first **Extrude** feature and select **Replace**.
10. On the **Replace Feature** dialog, click **Select Feature** under the **Replacement Feature** section.
11. Select the imported geometry.
12. Click the **Next** button in the **Mapping** section until the back edge of the extrude feature is highlighted.

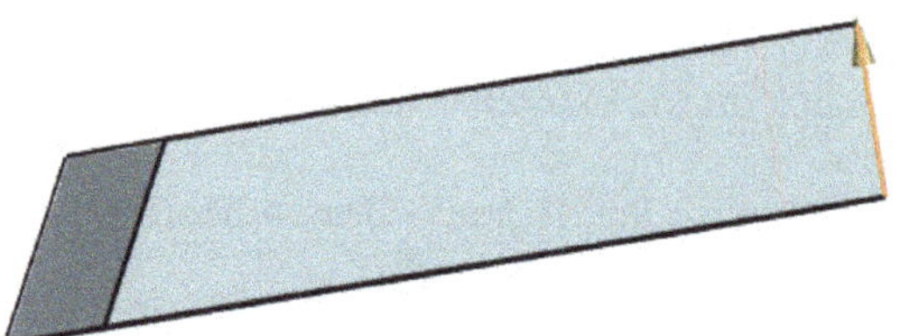

13. Select the corresponding edge on the replacement feature.

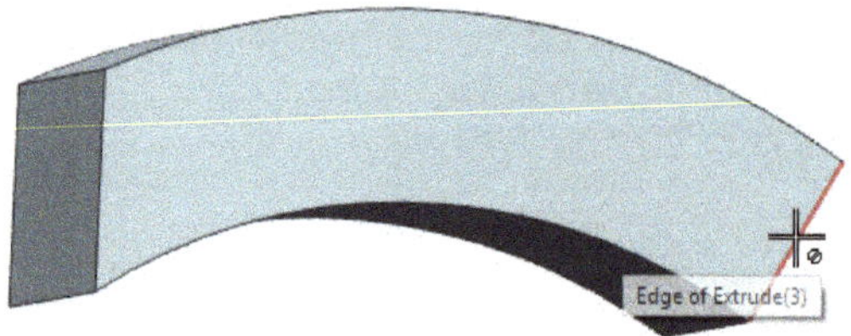

14. Likewise, select the corresponding references on the replacement feature.
15. Expand the **Settings** section and check the **Delete Original Feature** option.
16. Click **OK**.

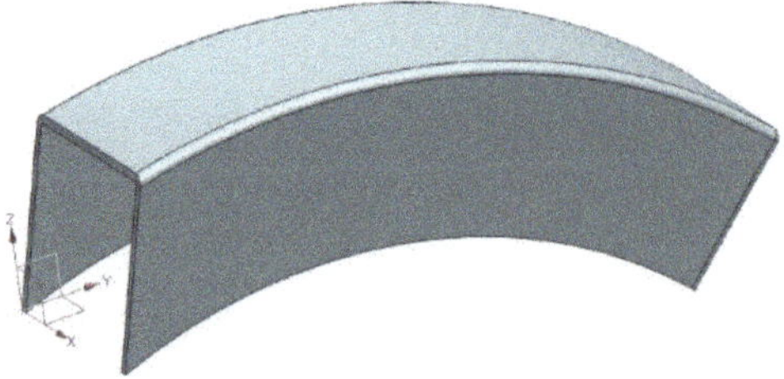

17. Save and close the file.

TUTORIAL 10

In this tutorial, you will learn to divide faces and

apply a draft using the **To Parting Edges** option.

1. Download and open the Tutorial 10 file.

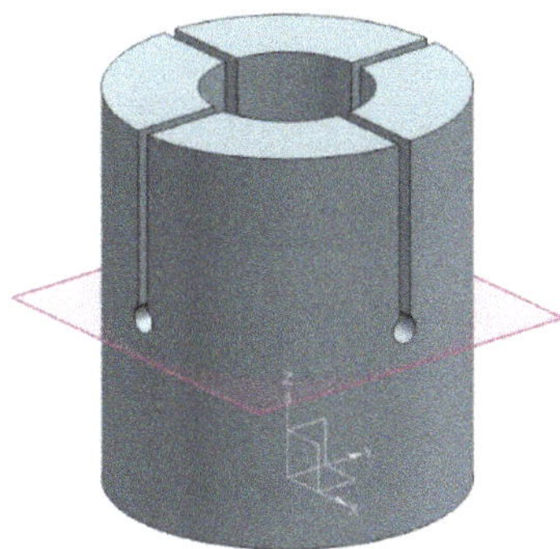

2. On the ribbon, click **Home > Base > More > Trim > Divide Face**.
3. Select the outer cylindrical face of the geometry.
4. Click **Select Object** under the **Dividing Objects** section.
5. Select the datum plane.
6. Leave the **Projection Direction** to **Normal to Face**.
7. Click **OK**. The round face is divided into two parts.

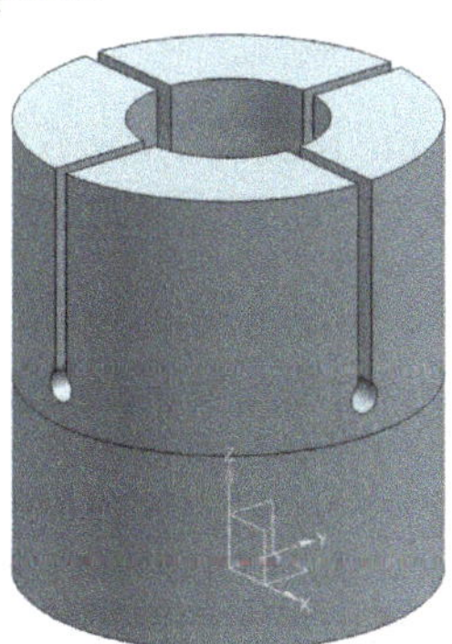

Applying Draft using the Parting Edge option

1. On the ribbon, click **Home > Base > Draft**.
2. On the **Draft** dialog, select **Type > Parting Edge**.
3. Click **Select Plane** under the **Stationary Plane** section.
4. Select any point on the parting edge, as shown.

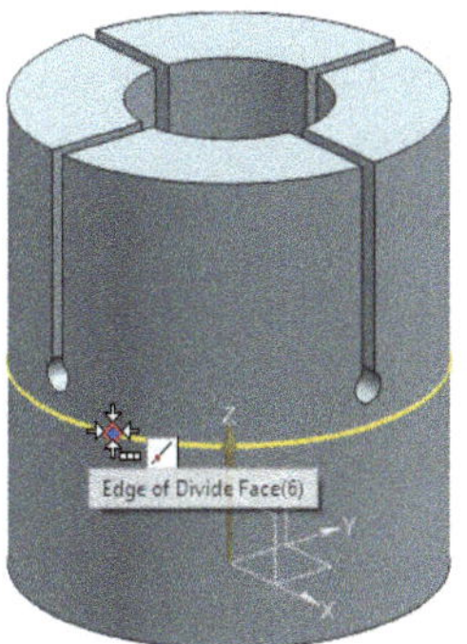

5. Click **Select Edge** under the **Parting Edges** section.
6. Select the parting edge and enter 10 in the **Angle 1** box.

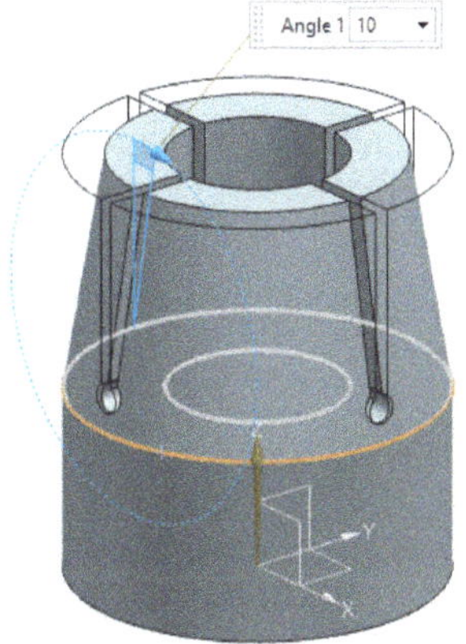

7. Click **OK**.
8. Save and close the file.

TUTORIAL 11

In this tutorial, you will learn to apply a draft using the **Face** option.

1. Download and open the Tutorial 11 file.

2. On the ribbon, click **Home > Base > Draft**.
3. On the **Draft** dialog, select **Type > Face**.
4. Select the Z-axis from the triad to define the drafting direction.
5. Under the **Draft References** section, select **Draft**

Method > Parting Face.

6. Click **Select Stationary Parting Face** under the **Draft References** section.
7. Select the parting surface, as shown.

8. Click **Select Face** under the **Faces to Draft** section.
9. On the Sketch Scene Bar, set the **Face Rule** to **Tangent Faces**.
10. Select any one of the tangentially connected faces, as shown.

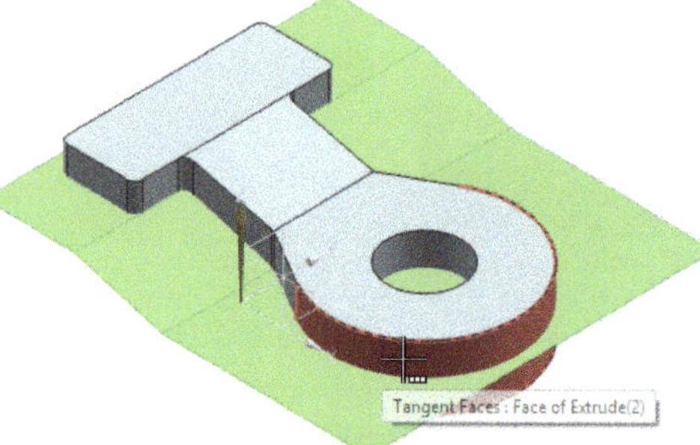

11. Type **10** in the **Angle 1** box.
12. Check the **Draft Both Sides** option under the **Draft References** section.
13. Uncheck the **Symmetric Angle** option under the **Faces to Draft** section.
14. Type **15** in the **Below Angle 1** box.

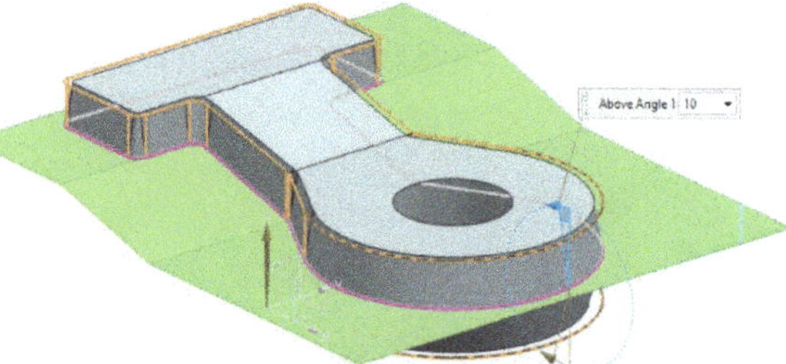

15. Click **OK**.
16. Click on the parting surface and select **Hide**.

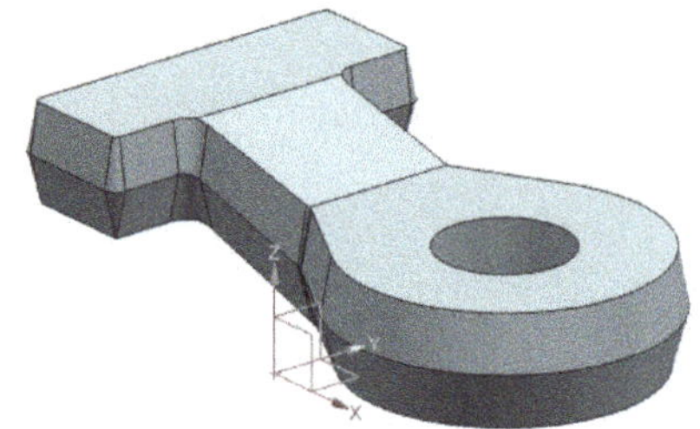

17. Save and close the file.

TUTORIAL 12

In this tutorial, you will learn to apply a draft using the **Tangent to Face** option.

1. Download and open the Tutorial 12 file.

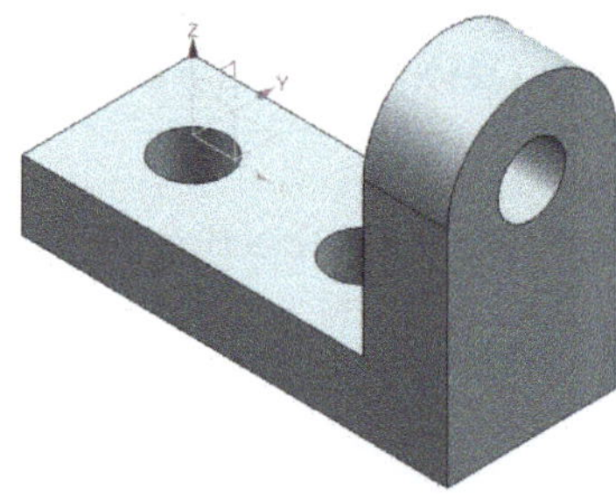

2. On the ribbon, click **Home > Base > Draft**.
3. On the **Draft** dialog, select **Type > Tangent to Face**.
4. Select the Z-axis from the triad to define the drafting direction.
5. Select the round face. The faces connected tangentially to the cylindrical face are drafted

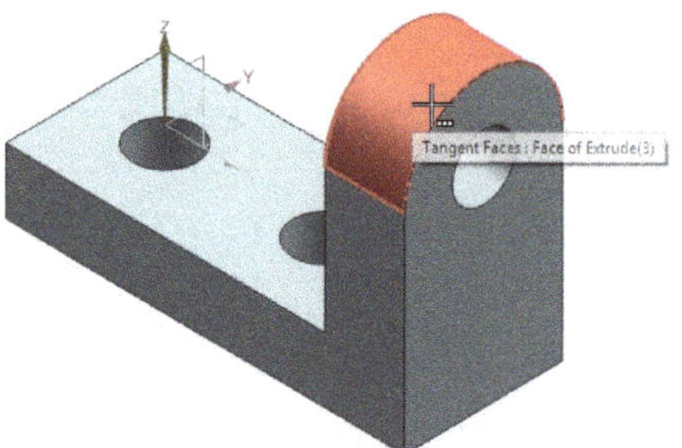

6. Type **10** in the **Angle 1** box and click **OK**.

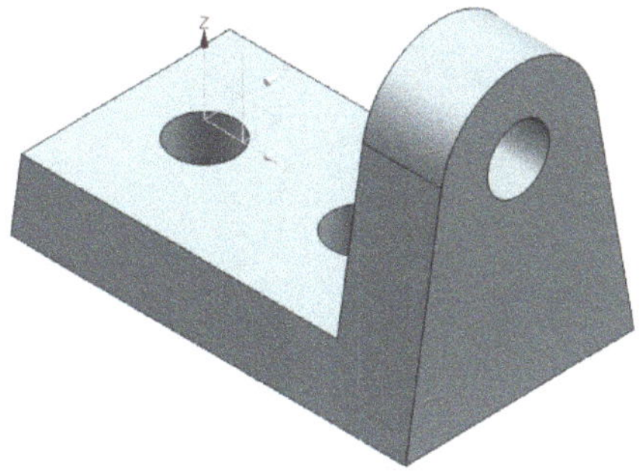

7. Save and close the file.

TUTORIAL 13

In this tutorial, you will learn to create Feature groups.

1. Download and open the Tutorial 13.

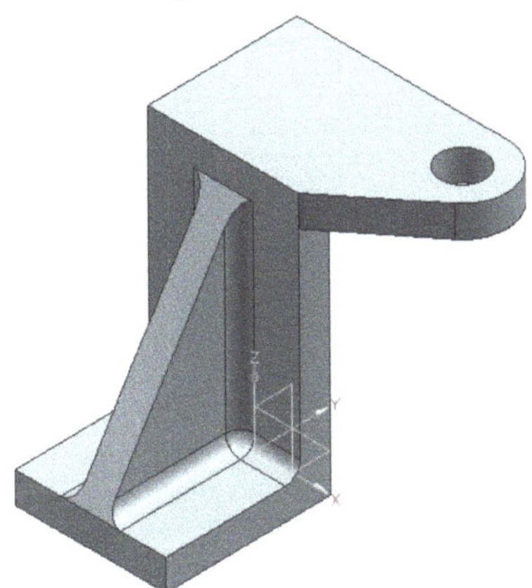

2. On the Top Border Bar, click **Menu > Format > Group > Feature Group**.
3. Type **Rib_with_blends** in the **Feature Group Name**.
4. Press the Ctrl key and select **Rib (3)** and **Edge Blend (4)** from the **Features in Part** list.
5. Click the **Add** icon to add them to the **Features in Group** list.
6. Click **OK**. The feature group appears in the **Part Navigator**.
7. Right-click on the **Feature Group** option in the Part Navigator.
8. Select **Suppress** from the **Shortcuts** toolbar. The **Feature** group is suppressed.
9. Right-click on the **Feature Group** option, and then select **Unsuppress**; the feature group is retained.
10. Save and close the file.

TUTORIAL 14

In this tutorial, you will learn to create a Swept Volume feature.

1. Open a new NX file using the **Model** template.
2. Create a cylindrical feature of 40 mm diameter and 50 mm height.
3. On the ribbon, click **Curve > Advanced > Helix** .
4. Click the Angle handle on the CSYS manipulator, and then type 90 in the Angle box.

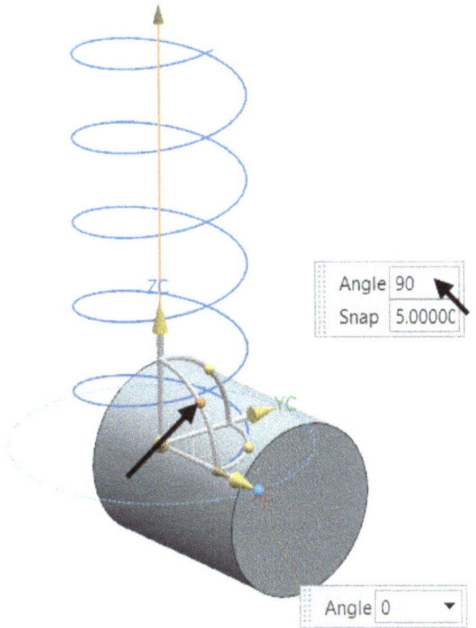

5. On the **Helix** dialog, under the **Size** section, click the down arrow next to the **Value** box, and then select **Measure**.

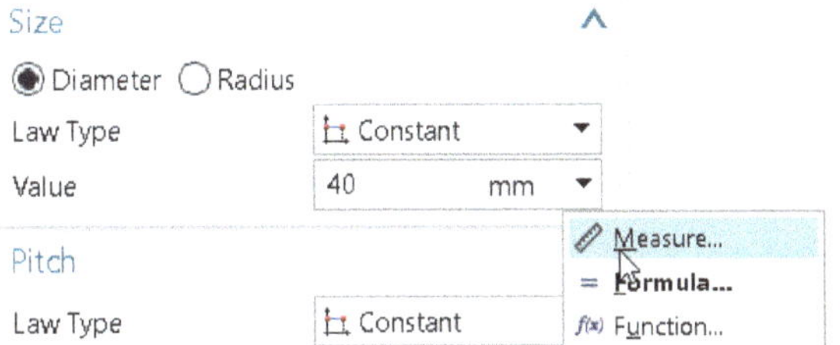

6. Select the cylindrical surface, and then select the **Diameter** option from the callout, as shown.

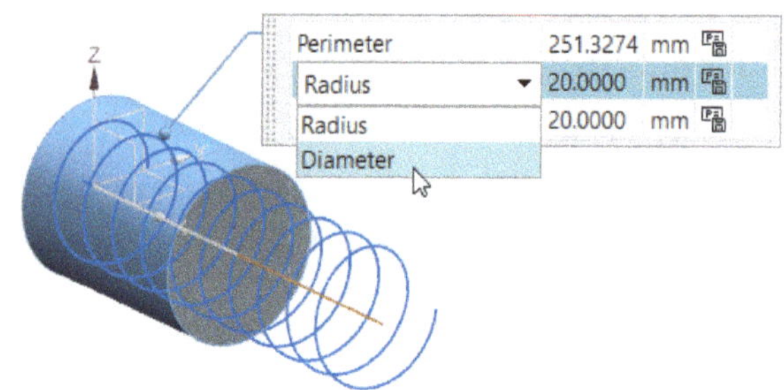

7. Click the **Creates a measurement expression on OK** option on the callout.

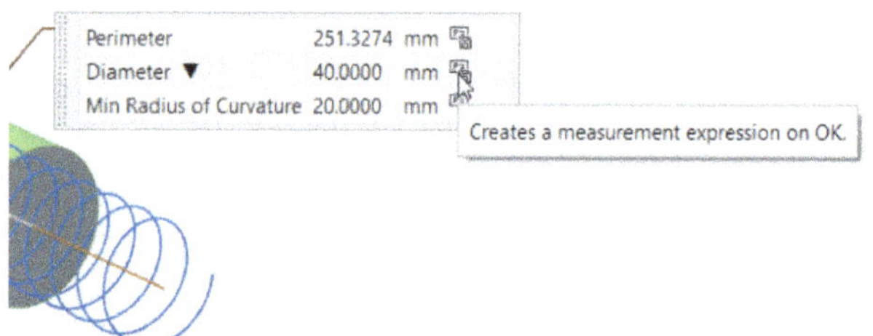

8. Click **OK** on the **Measure** dialog.
9. Enter **10** in the **Value** box of the **Pitch** section.
10. Select **Limits** from the **Method** drop-down.
11. Enter **50** in the **End Limit** box of the **Length** section.
12. Enter **-90** in the **Angle** box of the **Orientation** section.
13. Under the **Settings** section, select **Turn Direction > Right Hand**.

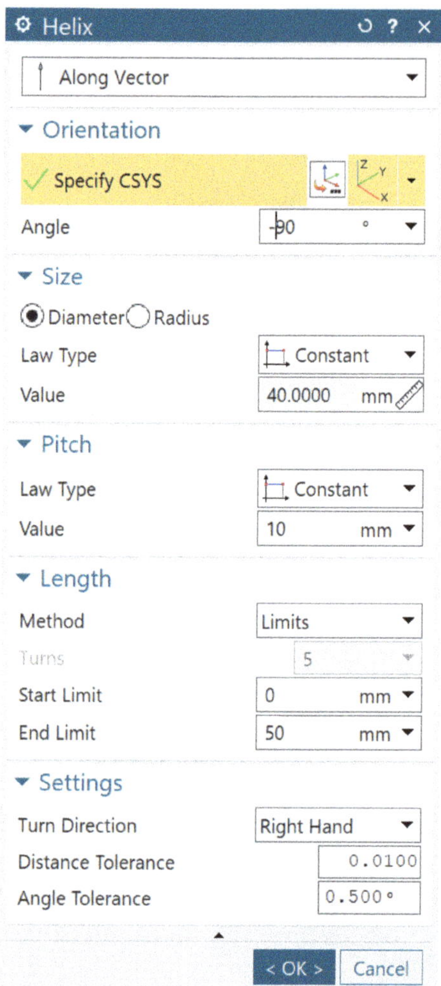

14. Click **OK**.

Creating the Tool Body

1. On the ribbon, click **Home > Construction > Sketch**.
2. Select the XY Plane from the Datum coordinate system, and then click **OK**.
3. Create a sketch, as shown in the figure below.

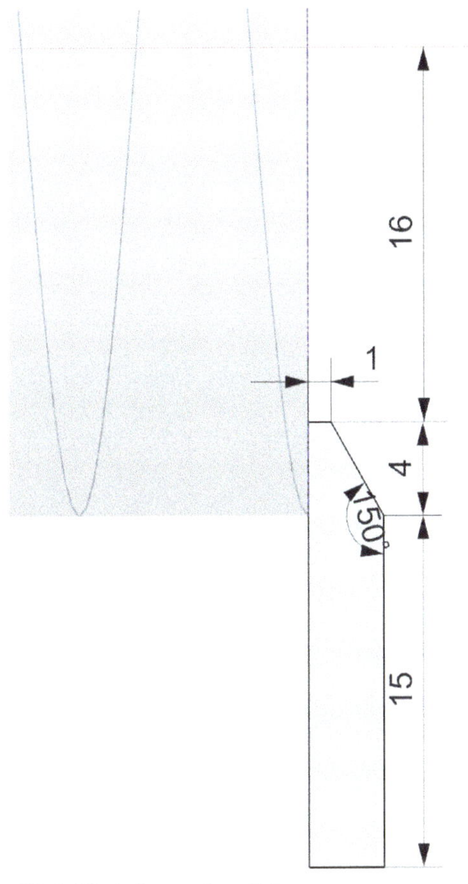

4. Click **Finish** on the ribbon.
5. On the ribbon, click **Home > Base > Revolve.**
6. Select the sketch from the graphics window.
7. On the **Revolve** dialog, click **Specify Vector** in the **Axis** section.
8. Select the vertical line of the sketch, as shown.

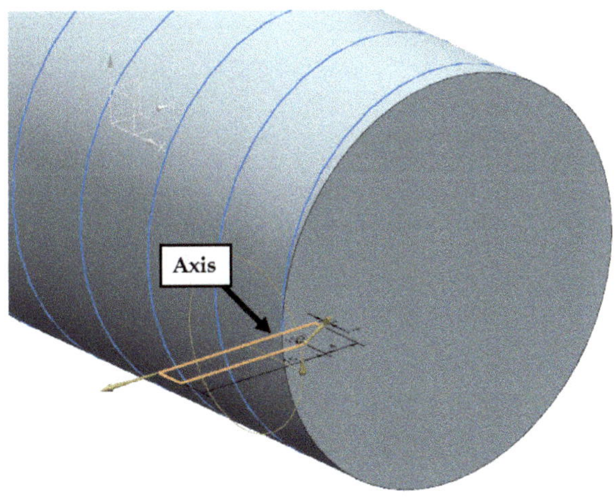

9. Enter 360 in the **End** box attached to the sketch.
10. Under the **Boolean** section, select **Boolean > None**; a separate solid is created.
11. Click **OK**.

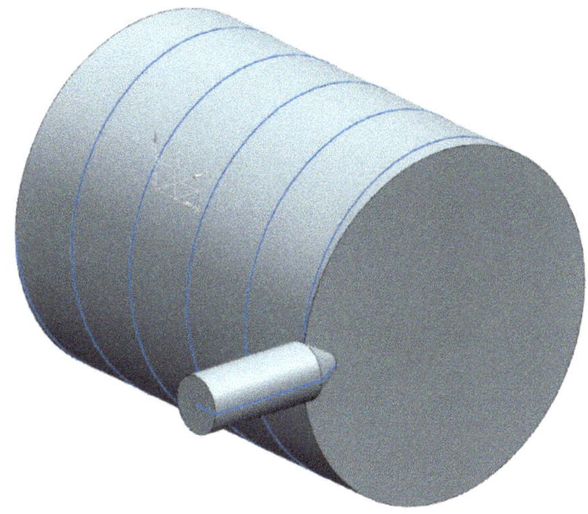

Creating the Swept Volume Feature

1. On the ribbon, click **Surface > Base > More > Sweep > Swept Volume** .
2. Select the Tool body from the graphics window; the target body is selected automatically.
3. Select the helix.
4. Under the **Orientation** section, select **Sweep Orientation > Normal to Path.**
5. Select the X-axis from the triad.

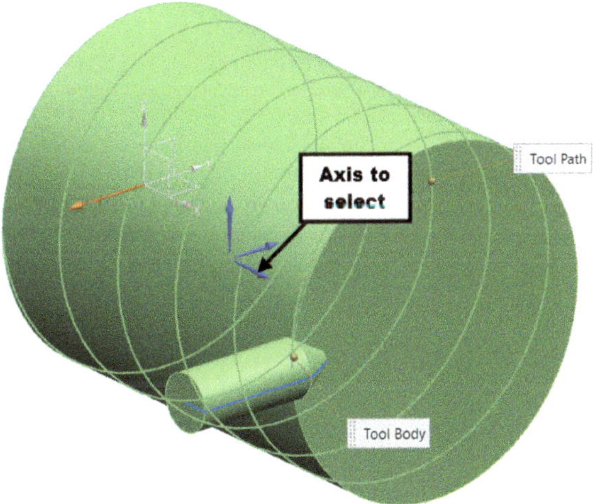

6. Make sure that the **Boolean** type is set to **Subtract**.
7. Click **OK** to create the swept volume feature.

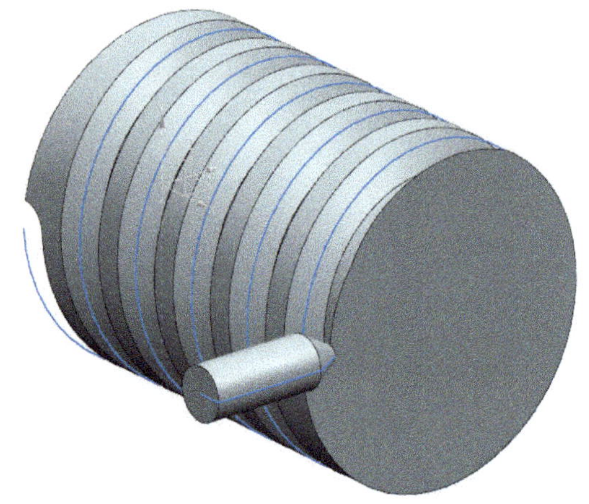

Chapter 7: Expressions

In this chapter, you will:

- Use Program Generated Expressions
- Create Expressions
- Create a Family of Parts
- Create expressions by measuring elements
- Export and Import Expressions

TUTORIAL 1

In this tutorial, you will modify the basic expressions which are automatically created by NX.

1. Start a new file in the Modeling environment.
2. Activate the **Sketch** command and select the XY plane. Next, click **OK**.
3. Create the sketch, as shown.

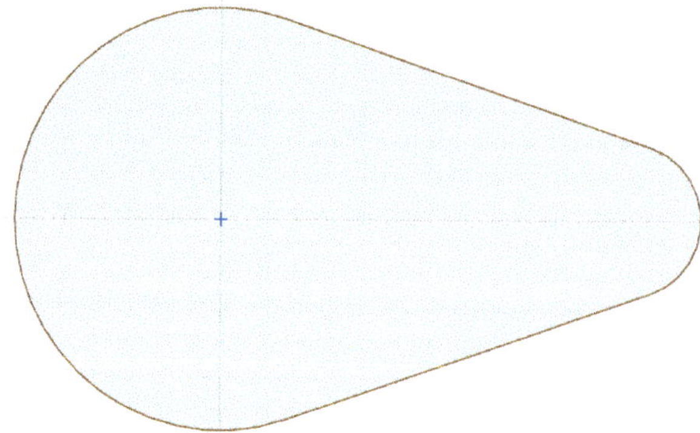

4. Click **Menu > Insert > Dimensions> Rapid** on the Top Border Bar.
5. On the **Rapid Dimension** dialog, select **Measurement > Method > Radial**.
6. Select the large arc.
7. On the **Rapid Dimension** dialog, check the **Expression** on the **Driving** section.
8. Move the pointer and click.
9. Type **30** and press ENTER.
10. Click **Yes** on the message box.
11. Select the small arc.
12. Move the pointer and click.
13. Type **15** and press ENTER.
14. On the **Rapid Dimension** dialog, select **Measurement > Method > Inferred**.
15. Select the Vertical axis and the center point of the small arc.
16. Move the pointer downward and click.
17. Type **60** and press ENTER.

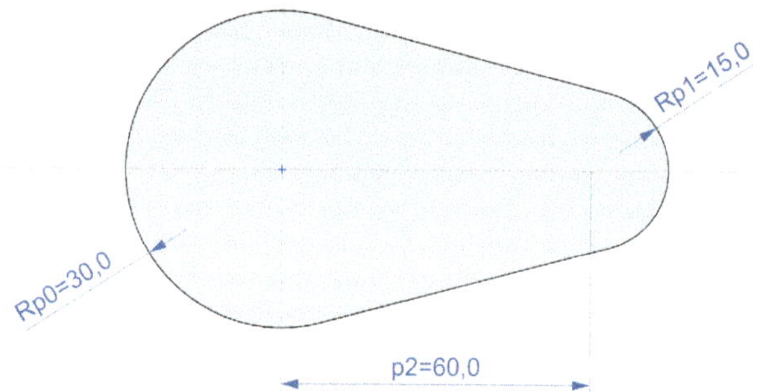

18. Click **Finish** on the ribbon.
19. On the ribbon, click **Home > Base > Extrude**.
20. Select the sketch.
21. On the **Extrude** dialog, set the values in the **Limits** section, as given below:

    Start: Value
    Distance: 0
    End: Value
    Distance: 15

22. Expand the **Offset** section and set the values, as given below:

    Offset: Symmetric
    End: 5

23. Click **OK**.

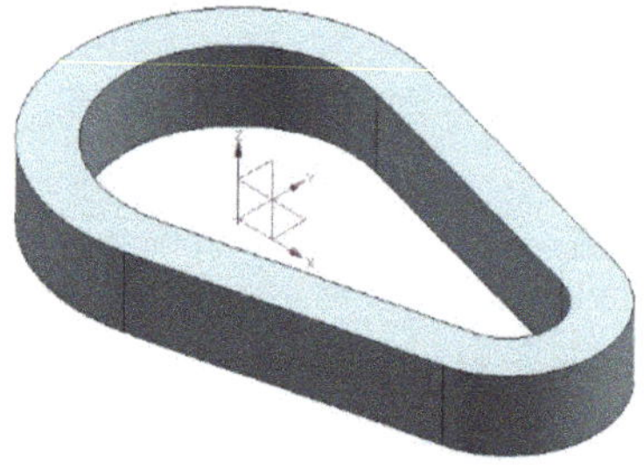

24. On the ribbon, click **Tools > Utilities > Expression** = .
25. On the **Expressions** dialog, select **Show > All Expressions**. All the expressions in the file are displayed.
26. Scroll to **(Extrude (2) Start Offset)** in the **Source** column of the expressions sheet.

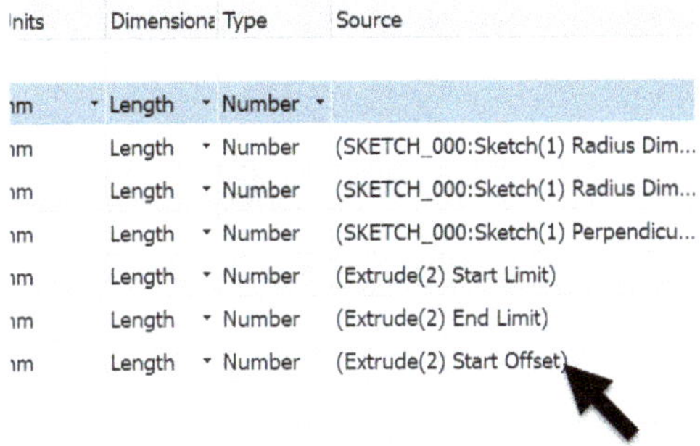

nits	Dimensioni	Type	Source
m	Length	Number	
m	Length	Number	(SKETCH_000:Sketch(1) Radius Dim...
m	Length	Number	(SKETCH_000:Sketch(1) Radius Dim...
m	Length	Number	(SKETCH_000:Sketch(1) Perpendicu...
m	Length	Number	(Extrude(2) Start Limit)
m	Length	Number	(Extrude(2) End Limit)
m	Length	Number	(Extrude(2) Start Offset)

27. Type 3 in the **Formula** box and click **Apply**.

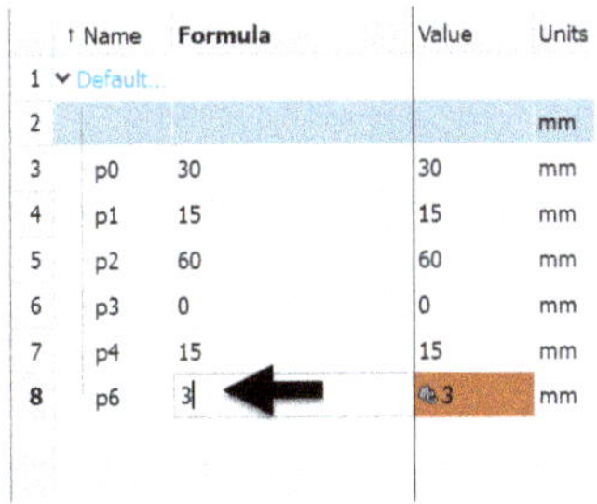

↑	Name	Formula	Value	Units
1	Default			
2				mm
3	p0	30	30	mm
4	p1	15	15	mm
5	p2	60	60	mm
6	p3	0	0	mm
7	p4	15	15	mm
8	p6	3	3	mm

28. Click **OK** to update the model.

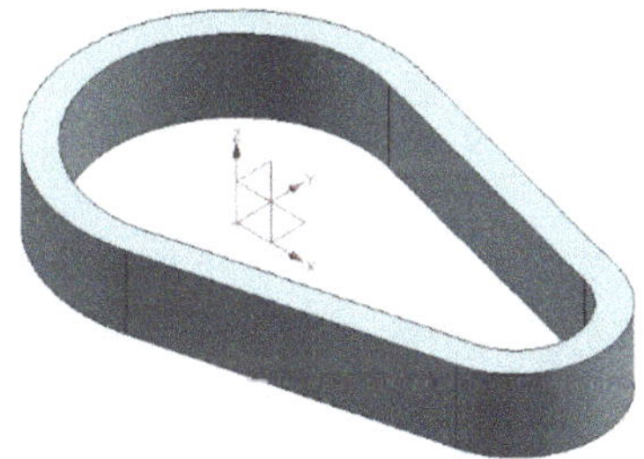

29. Select the **Extrude** feature from the **Part Navigator**.
30. Expand the **Details** section on the **Part Navigator**.
31. Double-click on the **Start Limit** value and type-in 10. The model is updated, as shown.

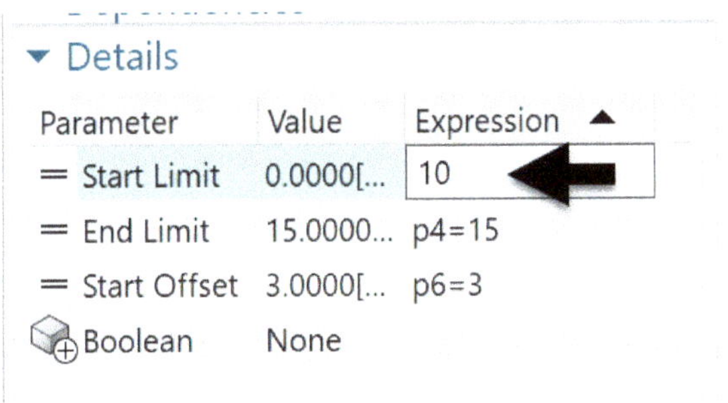

Details

Parameter	Value	Expression
Start Limit	0.0000[...	10
End Limit	15.0000...	p4=15
Start Offset	3.0000[...	p6=3
Boolean	None	

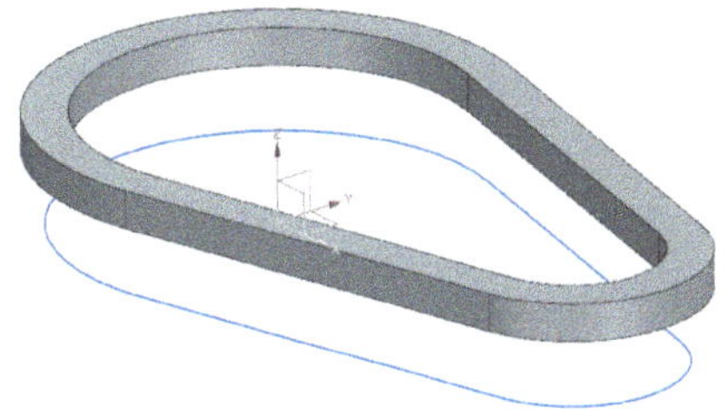

32. Save and close the part file.

TUTORIAL 2

In this tutorial, you will create expressions to drive the parameters of a bolt.

1. Start a new part file.
2. Activate the **Extrude** command and select the YZ plane.
3. Create a circle of 20 mm in diameter. Add the dimension using the **Rapid Dimension** tool.

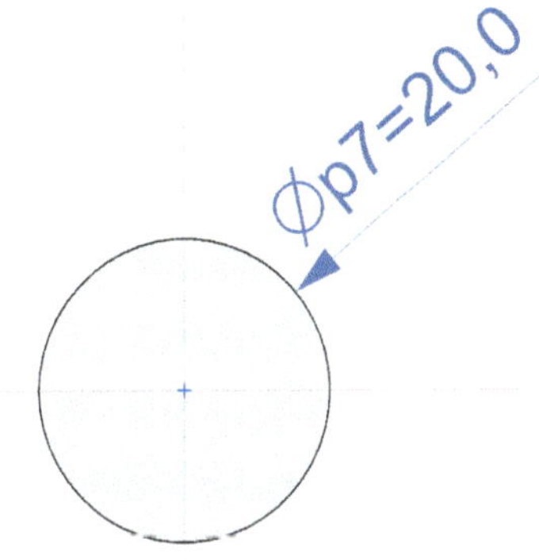

4. Click **Finish**.
5. Extrude the sketch up to 80 mm distance.

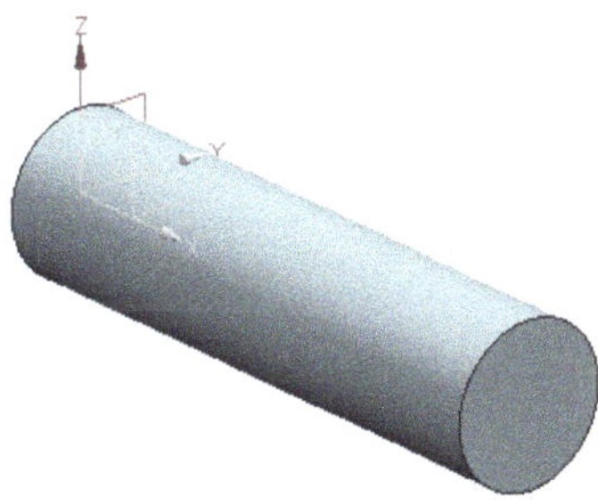

6. Activate the **Extrude** command and select the right end face of the cylinder.
7. Create a hexagon, as shown.
8. Create a dimension between the vertical axis and the right vertex of the hexagon by selecting them.

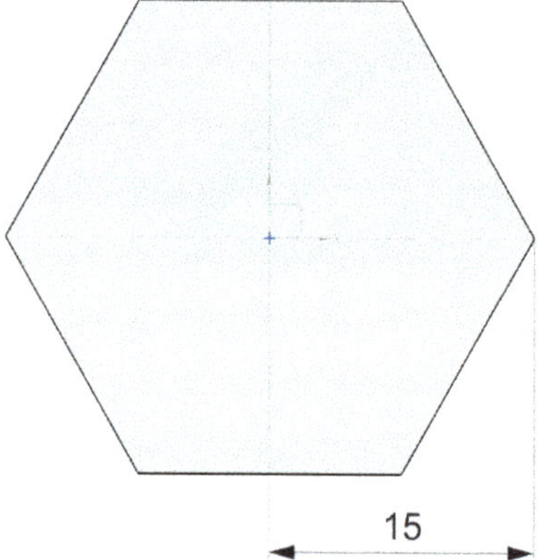

9. Select the dimension and click the **Edit Annotation** icon.
10. On the **Rapid Dimension** dialog, check the **Expression** on the **Driving** section.
11. Click **Close** on the dialog.

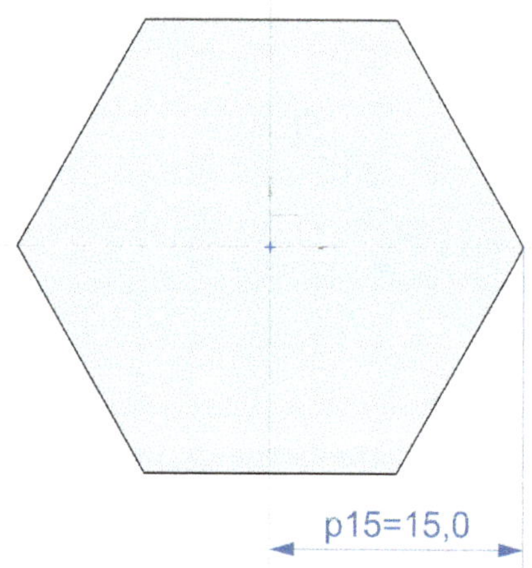

12. Click **Finish**.
13. Extrude the sketch up to 10 mm distance.

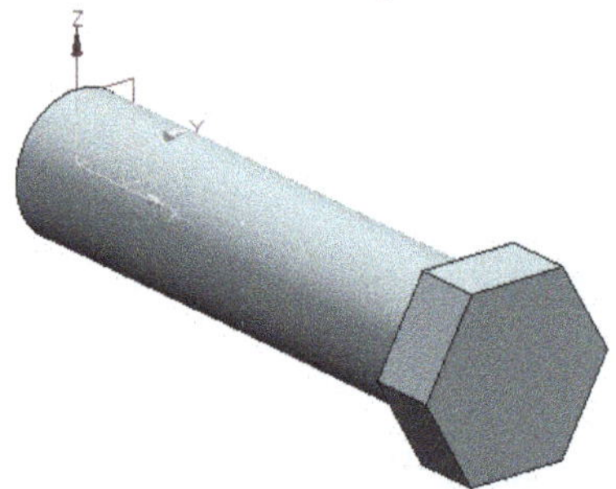

14. On the ribbon, click **Tools > Utilities > Expressions** ═.
15. On the **Expressions** dialog, select **Visibility > Show > All Expressions**.
16. Double click in the **Name** box of **(Extrude (1) Diameter Dimension on Arc1)**.

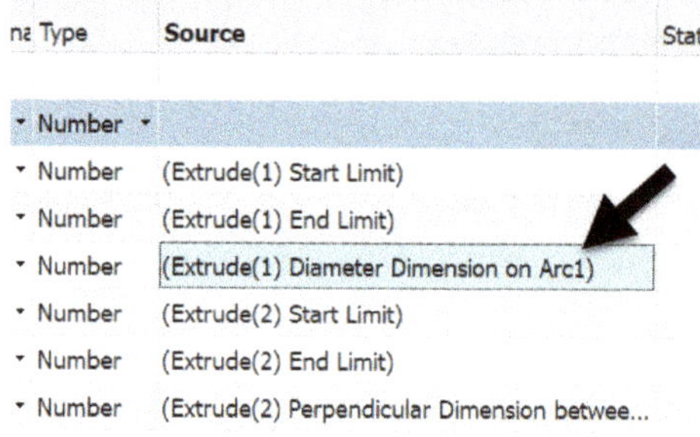

17. Type **Diameter** in the **Name** box and click **Apply**.

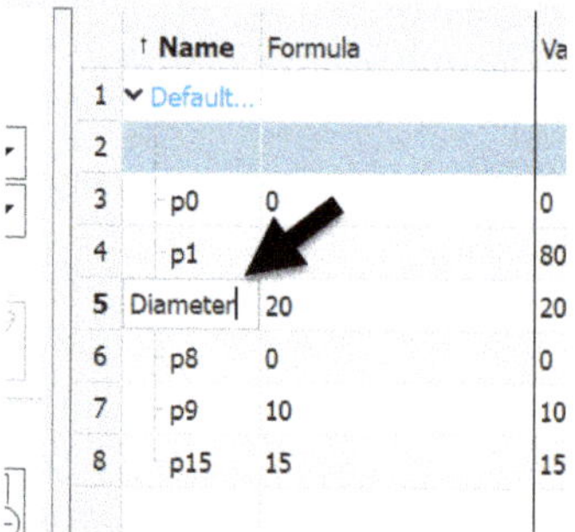

18. Double click in the **Formula** box of **(Extrude (2) Perpendicular Dimension between Line 3 and Line7)**.

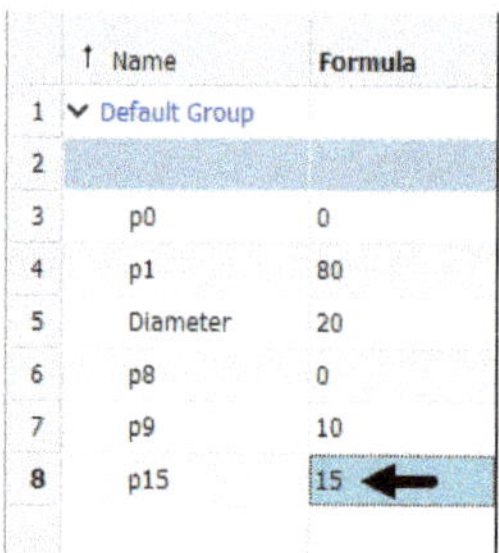

19. Type **Diameter** in the **Formula** box and click **Apply**.

	Name	Formula
1	Default Group	
2		
3	p0	0
4	p1	80
5	Diameter	20
6	p8	0
7	p9	10
8	p15	Diameter

20. Double click in the **Formula** box of **(Extrude (2) End Limit)**.
21. Type **0.75*Diameter** in the **Formula** box and click **Apply**.

	↑ Name	Formula
1		
2	Diameter	20
3	p0	0
4	p1	80
5	p8	0
6	p9	.75*Diameter
7	p15	Diameter

22. Click **OK** to update the model.

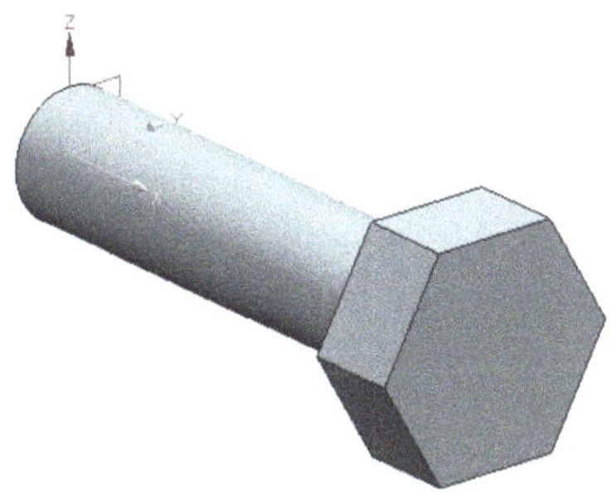

23. Select the **Extrude (1)** feature from the **Part Navigator**.
24. Expand the **Details** section on the **Part Navigator**.
25. Double-click on the **Diameter** value and type 10. The model is updated, as shown.

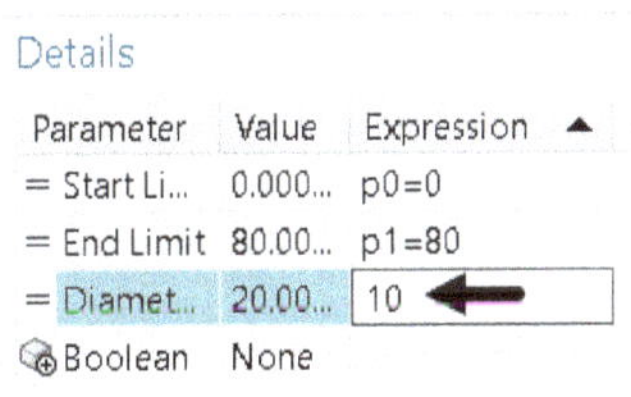

Details

Parameter	Value	Expression
= Start Li...	0.000...	p0=0
= End Limit	80.00...	p1=80
= Diamet...	20.00...	10
Boolean	None	

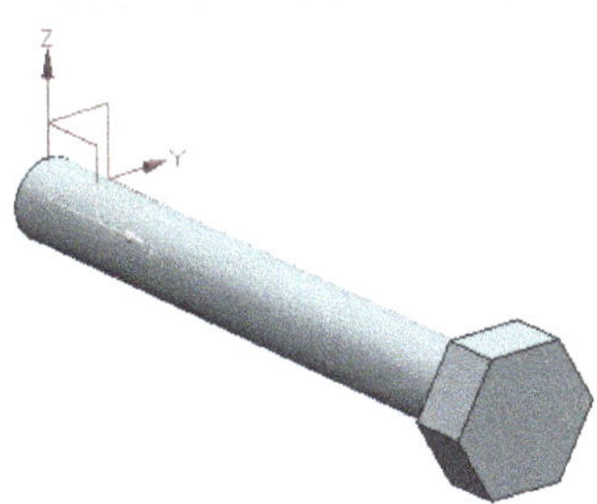

26. On the ribbon, click **Home > Base > More > Design Feature > Thread** .
27. On the **Thread** dialog, set the **Type** to **Detailed**.
28. Select the circular face of the geometry.
29. On the **Thread** dialog, under the **Form** section, select **Input > Manual**.
30. Click **OK** to create the thread.

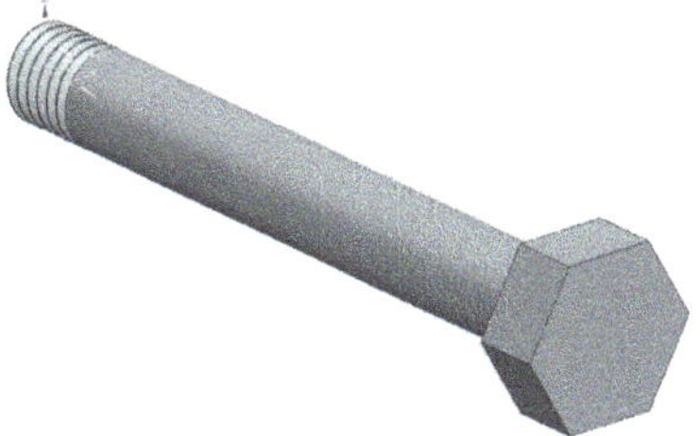

31. Press Ctrl+E to open the **Expressions** dialog.
32. On the **Expressions** dialog, select **Show > Feature Expressions**.
33. Select the **Threads** feature from the **Part Navigator** and notice all the expressions related to it.
34. Double click in the **Name** box of **(Threads (3) Major Diameter).**
35. Type **D** in the **Name** box.
36. Type **Diameter** in the **Formula** box to make the major diameter value equal to the diameter of the cylinder.
37. Double click in the **Name** box of **(Threads (3) Pitch)**.
38. Type **Pitch** in the **Name** box.
39. Double click in the **Name** box of **(Threads (3) Minor Diameter)**.
40. Type **D2** and **D-1.08*Pitch** in the **Name** and **Formula** boxes, respectively.
41. Double click in the **Name** box of **(Threads (3) Length)**.
42. Type **Length** and **2*D** in the **Name** and **Formula** boxes, respectively.
43. Double click in the **Name** box of **(Threads (3) Shaft Size)**.
44. Type **Shaft_Diameter** and **D-0.6495*Pitch** in the **Name** and **Formula** boxes, respectively.
45. Click **Apply** and **OK**. The model is updated, as shown.

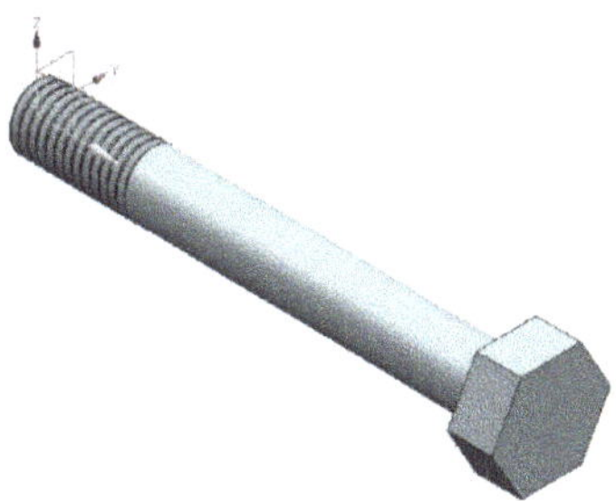

46. Select the **Extrude (1)** feature from the **Part Navigator**.
47. Expand the **Details** section on the **Part Navigator**.
48. Double-click on the **Diameter** value and type 20. The model is updated, as shown.

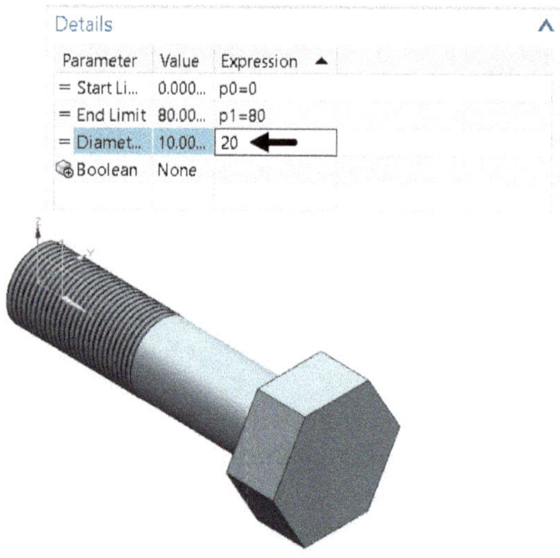

49. Select the **Threads** feature from the **Part Navigator** and change the Pitch value in the **Details** section to 2.5. The pitch and minor diameter of the threads are updated.

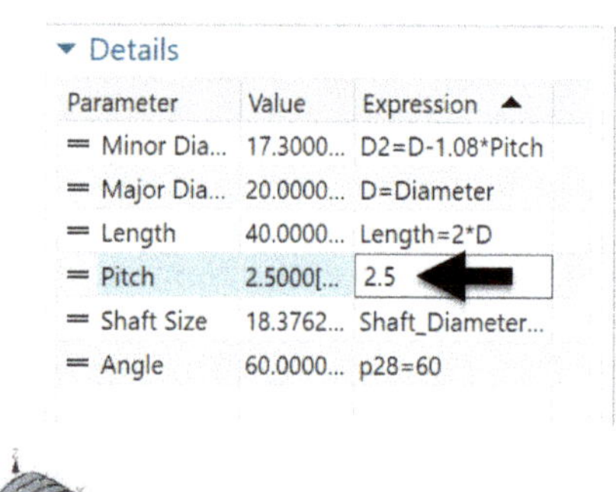

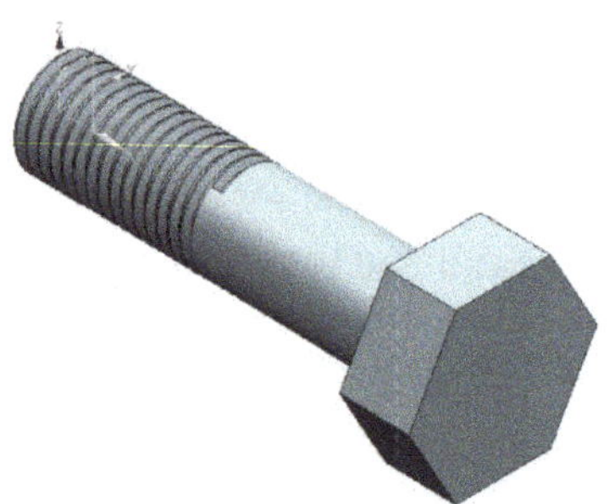

Instead of updating the pitch and diameter values manually, you can use a spreadsheet to change all the values. The following section deals with using a spreadsheet to change the parameters.

Creating Family of Parts

1. On the ribbon, click **Tools > Utilities > Spreadsheet**. The Worksheet in Modeling is opened.
2. In the Worksheet environment, click **ADD-INS > Extract Expr** on the ribbon. The expressions are added to the spreadsheet.
3. Copy the contents of column **B** into columns **C** and **D**.

	A	B	C	D
1	***Parameters***			
2	D	20	20	20
3	_D2	17.3	17.3	17.3
4	Diameter	20	20	20
5	Length	40	40	40
6	Pitch	2.5	2.5	2.5
7	_p0	0	0	0
8	_p1	80	80	80
9	_p8	0	0	0
10	_p9	15	15	15
11	_p15	20	20	20
12	_p18	60	60	60

4. Type M20x2.5, M10x1.25, and M6x0.75 in the first rows of columns B, C, and D, respectively.
5. Click in the second row of column B and change its expression to **=EXPRVAL("Diameter")**

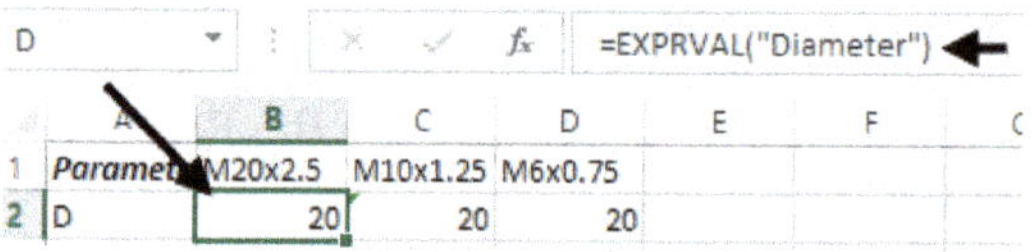

6. Likewise, change the expressions of D values in columns **C** and **D** to **=Diameter**.
7. Edit the values of the highlighted rows, as shown.

	A	B	C	D
1	***Parameter***	M20x2.5	M10x1.25	M6x0.75
2	D	=EXPRVAL("Diameter")	=Diameter	=Diameter
3	_D2	17.3	17.3	17.3
4	Diameter	20	10	6
5	Length	40	40	40
6	Pitch	2.5	1.25	0.75
7	Shaft_Dian	18.37625	18.37625	18.37625
8	_p0	0	0	0
9	_p1	80	60	20
10	_p8	0	0	0
11	_p9	15	15	15
12	_p15	20	20	20
13	_p28	60	60	60

8. Drag the pointer across the A2 and D13 cells.

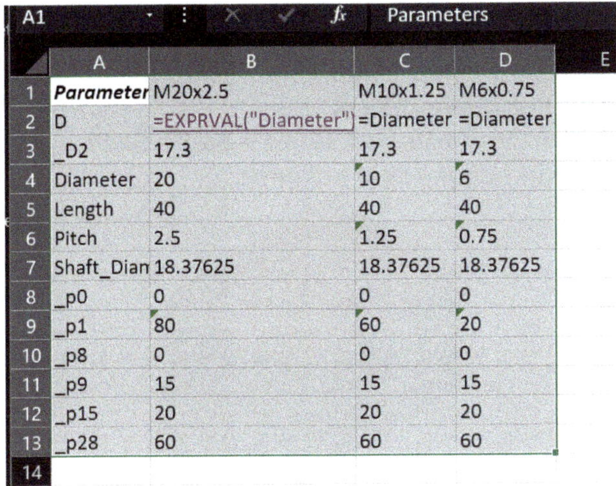

A1 | Parameters

	A	B	C	D	E
1	Parameter	M20x2.5	M10x1.25	M6x0.75	
2	D	=EXPRVAL("Diameter")	=Diameter	=Diameter	
3	_D2	17.3	17.3	17.3	
4	Diameter	20	10	6	
5	Length	40	40	40	
6	Pitch	2.5	1.25	0.75	
7	Shaft_Dian	18.37625	18.37625	18.37625	
8	_p0	0	0	0	
9	_p1	80	60	20	
10	_p8	0	0	0	
11	_p9	15	15	15	
12	_p15	20	20	20	
13	_p28	60	60	60	
14					

9. Click **ADD-INS > Define Expr Rng** on the ribbon.
10. Click **ADD-INS > Options > NX Preferences**.
11. Uncheck the **Use Fixed Update Range** option and click **OK**.
12. Select the contents of column D.

	A	B	C	D
1	Parameter	M20x2.5	M10x1.25	M6x0.75
2	D	=EXPRVAL("Diameter")	=Diameter	=Diameter
3	_D2	17.3	17.3	17.3
4	Diameter	20	10	6
5	Length	40	40	40
6	Pitch	2.5	1.25	0.75
7	Shaft_Dian	18.37625	18.37625	18.37625
8	_p0	0	0	0
9	_p1	80	60	20
10	_p8	0	0	0
11	_p9	15	15	15
12	_p15	20	20	20
13	_p28	60	60	60

13. Click **ADD-INS > Update NX Part**.
14. Save and close the spreadsheet. The part is updated.

15. On the ribbon, click **Tools > Utilities > Spreadsheet**.
16. Select the contents of column C.
17. Click **ADD-INS > Update NX Part**.
18. Save and close the spreadsheet. The part is updated.

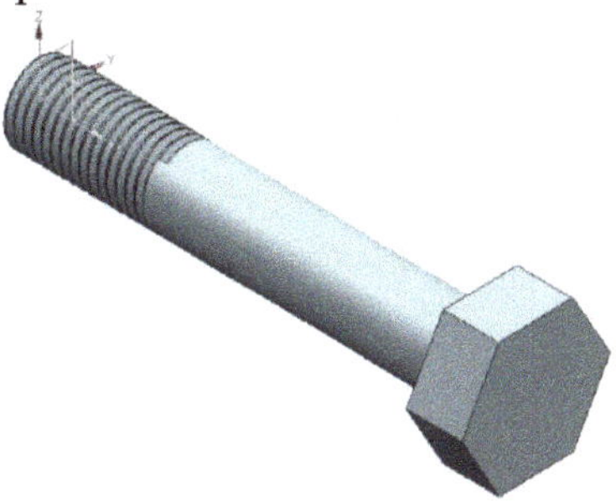

19. On the ribbon, click **Tools > Utilities > Spreadsheet**.
20. Likewise, select the contents of column **B** and click **Update NX Part**.
21. In the spreadsheet, enter the location and part name (for example, C:\Users\Public\Documents\M20x2.5 at the bottom of the B, C, and D columns. The part names should be M20x2.5, M10x1.25, and M6x0.75.

	A	B	C	D
1	Parameter	M20x2.5	M10x1.25	M6x0.75
2	D	=EXPRVAL("Diameter")	=Diameter	=Diameter
3	_D2	17.3	17.3	17.3
4	Diameter	20	10	6
5	Length	40	40	40
6	Pitch	2.5	1.25	0.75
7	Shaft_Dian	18.37625	18.37625	18.37625
8	_p0	0	0	0
9	_p1	80	60	20
10	_p8	0	0	0
11	_p9	15	15	15
12	_p15	20	20	20
13	_p28	60	60	60
14		C:\Users\Public\Documents\M20x2.5	C:\Users\Public\Documents\M10x1.25	C:\Users\Public\Documents\M6x0.75
15				

22. Drag the pointer across the A2 and D14 cells.
23. Click **ADD-INS > Define Fmly Rng** on the ribbon. The selected data will be used to create a part family.
24. Click **ADD-INS > Build Family** on the ribbon.
25. Close the spreadsheet and click **Discard**. The part family is created in the specified folder.

26. Close the part file.

TUTORIAL 3

1. Download the Tutorial 3 file of the Expressions chapter and open it.

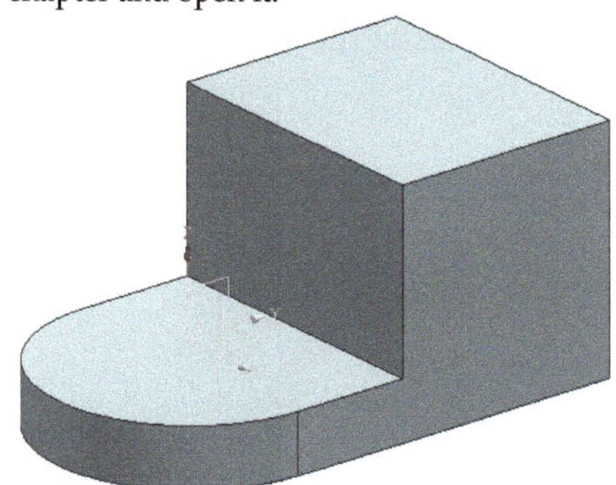

2. On the ribbon, click **Analysis > Measure > Measure**.
3. Select the edge of the geometry, as shown.
4. Click the option on the callout attached to the selected edge, as shown.

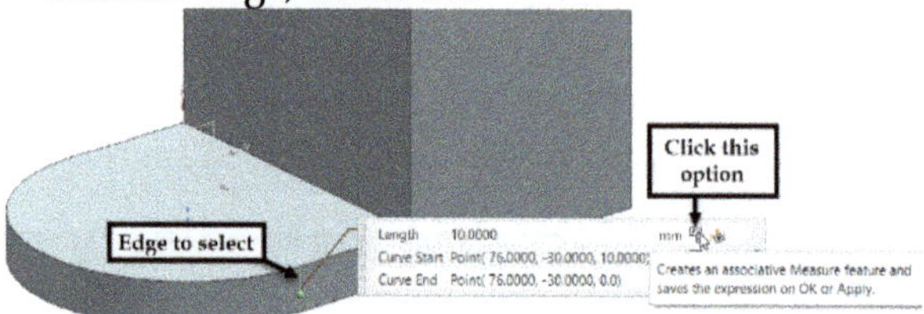

5. Click **OK**; the Measure parameter is displayed in the Part Navigator.

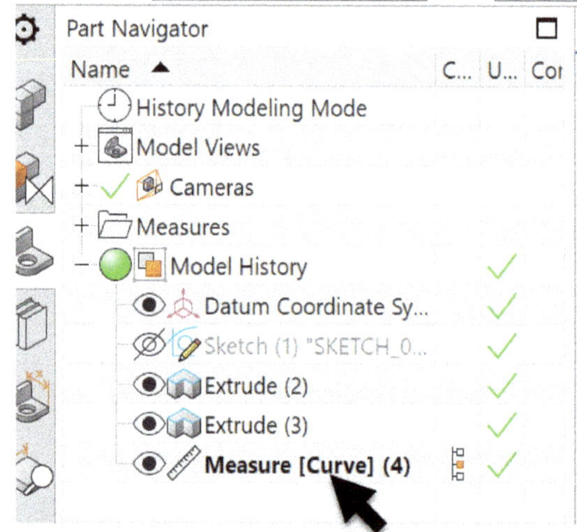

6. On the ribbon, click **Tools > Utilities > Expressions**.
7. On the **Expressions** dialog, select **Show > All Expressions**.
8. Double click in the **Name** box of **(Measure (4))**.
9. Type **Thickness** in the **Name** box.

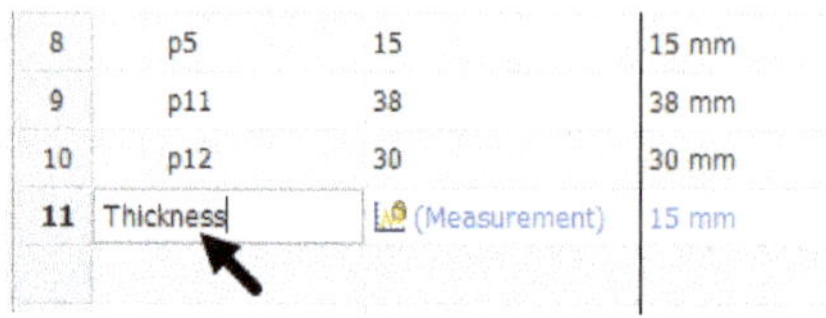

8	p5	15	15 mm
9	p11	38	38 mm
10	p12	30	30 mm
11	Thickness	(Measurement)	15 mm

10. Click **Apply** and **OK**.
11. On the ribbon, click **Home > Base > Shell**.
12. Select the flat face, as shown.

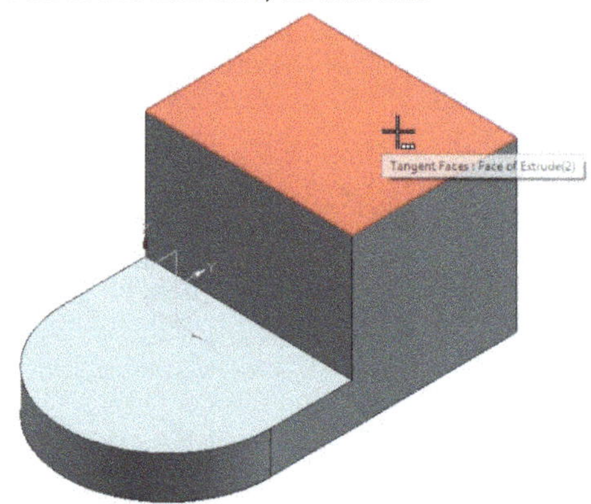

13. Click the down-arrow on Thickness handle and select **Formula**.

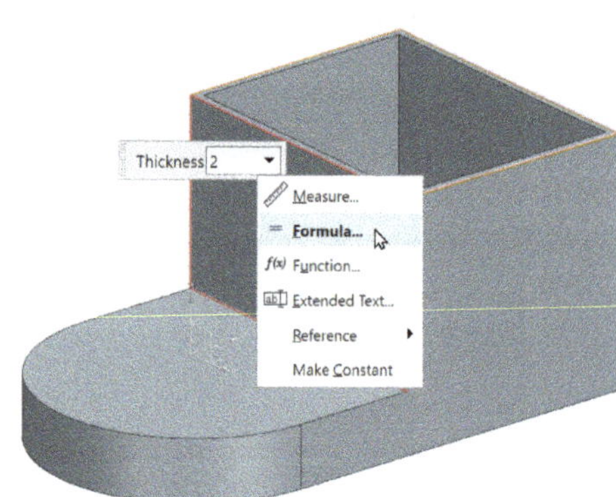

14. On the **Expressions** dialog, type Thickness in the **Formula** box and press Enter.

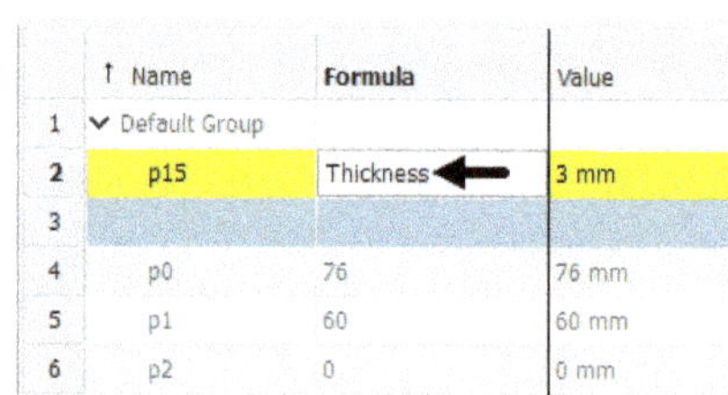

	Name	Formula	Value
1	Default Group		
2	p15	Thickness	3 mm
3			
4	p0	76	76 mm
5	p1	60	60 mm
6	p2	0	0 mm

15. Click **OK** on the **Expressions** and **Shell** dialogs.
16. Click on the second extruded feature and select **Show Dimensions**.
17. Double-click on the linear dimension and change its value to 10.

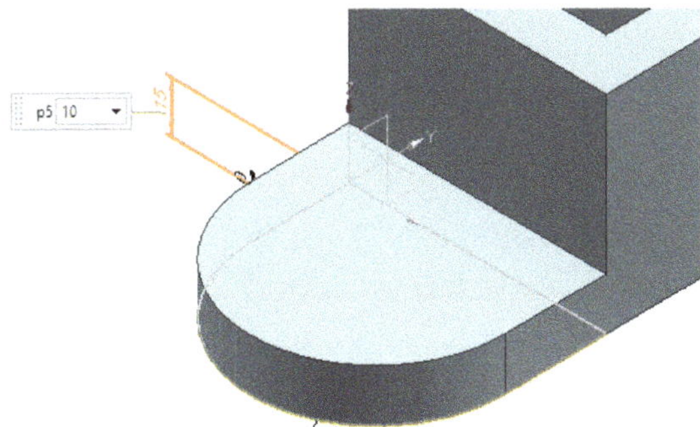

18. Click **OK** on the **Feature Dimension** dialog.
19. Press **F5** on your keyboard.

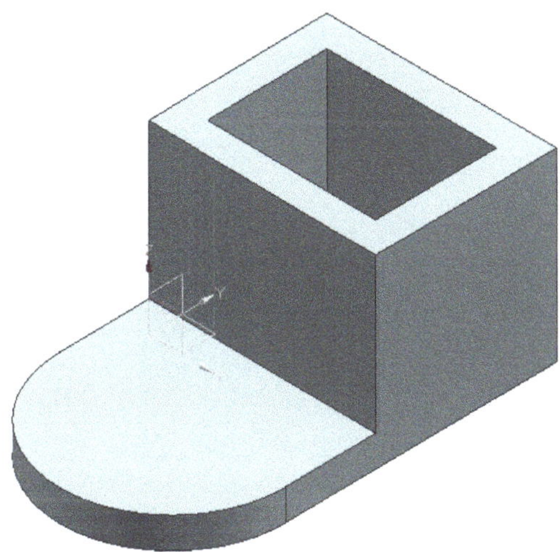

TUTORIAL 4

1. Download the Tutorial 4 file of the Expressions chapter and open it.

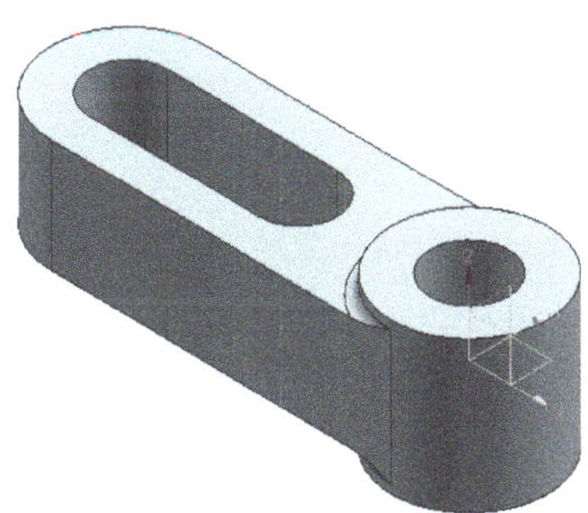

2. On the ribbon, click **Tools > Utilities > Expressions**.
3. On the **Expressions** dialog, select **Show > All Expressions**.
4. On the **Expression** dialog, expand the **Import/Export** section, and then click the **Export Expressions** button.
5. Browse to a location to save the file.
6. Set the **Export Options** to **Work Part**.
7. Type **Tutorial_4** in the **File name** box and click **OK**. The expressions of the model are exported to a text file.
8. Open the **Tutorial_4.exp** file in Notepad or any text editor.
9. Modify the expressions in the text file and save it.

```
[MilliMeter]Diameter=25
[MilliMeter]Extrude1=18
[MilliMeter]Extrude2=0.75*Extrude1
[MilliMeter]Hole_diameter=Diameter/2
[MilliMeter]Parallel_Dimension=90
[MilliMeter]Slot_length=Parallel_Dimension/2
[MilliMeter]Slot_radius=Hole_diameter/2
[MilliMeter]p65=0
[MilliMeter]p73=4
```

10. Switch to the NX application window.
11. On the **Expressions** dialog, click the **Import Expressions**  icon.
12. Go to the location of **Tutorial_4.exp** file and double-click on it.
13. Click **OK** on the **Expressions** dialog.

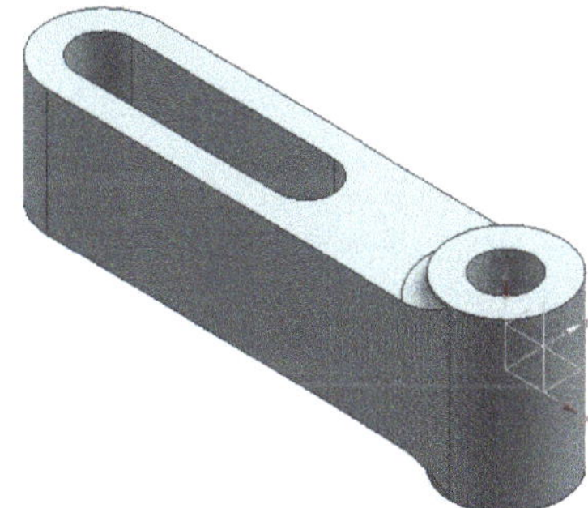

14. Save and close the file.

Chapter 8: Sheet Metal Modeling

This chapter will show you to:

- Construct Tab feature
- Construct Flange
- Contour Flange
- Closed corners
- Louvers
- Beads
- Drawn Cut-outs
- Gussets
- Flat Pattern

TUTORIAL 1

In this tutorial, you construct the sheet metal model shown in the figure.

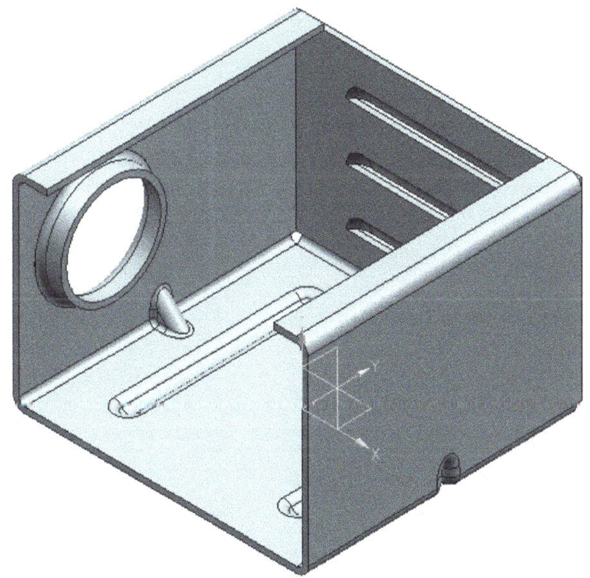

Opening a New Sheet Metal file

1. To open a new sheet metal file, click **Home > New** on the ribbon.
2. On the **New** dialog, click **Sheet Metal**.
3. Click **OK**.

The NX Sheet Metal ribbon appears, as shown below.

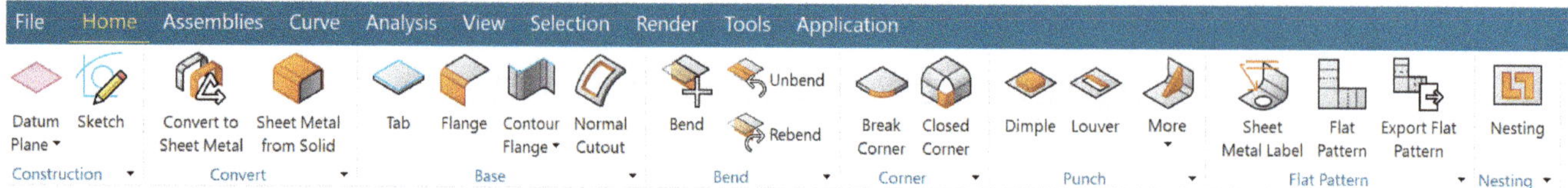

Setting the Parameters of the Sheet Metal part

1. To set the parameters, click **File > Preferences > Sheet Metal**

On the **NX Sheet Metal Preferences** dialog, you can set the preferences of the sheet metal part such as thickness, bend radius, relief depth, and width. In this tutorial, you will construct the sheet metal part with the default preferences. Click **OK** on the dialog.

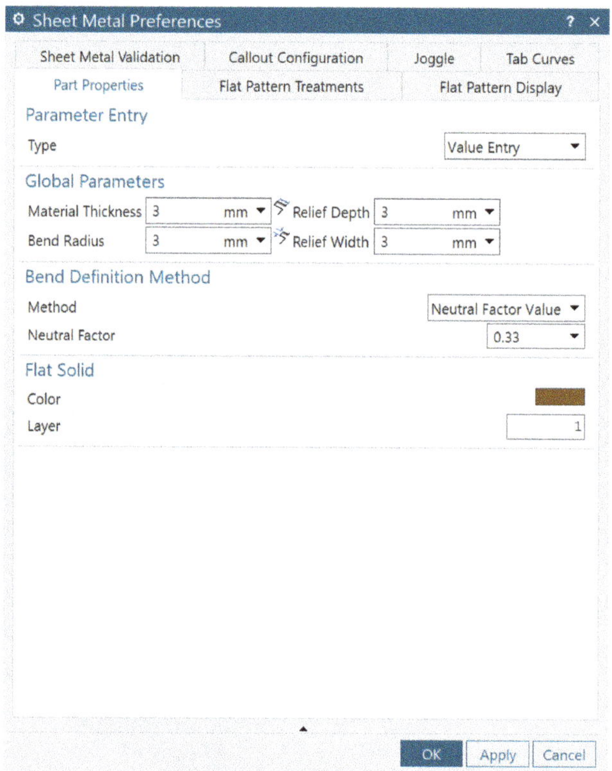

Constructing the Tab Feature

1. To construct the base feature, click **Home > Base > Tab** on the ribbon.
2. Select the XY plane.
3. Construct the sketch, as shown.

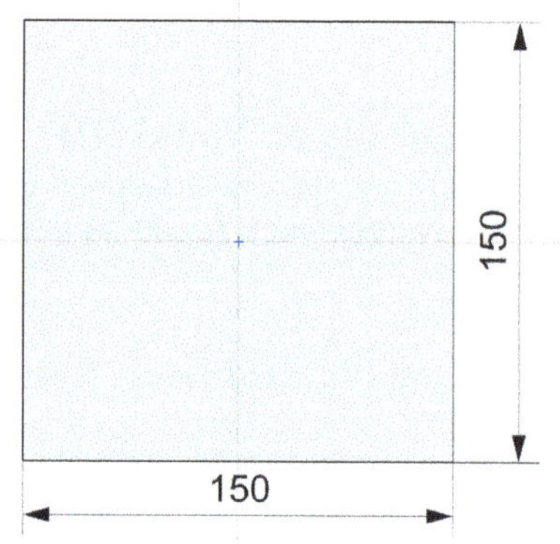

4. Click **Finish.**

5. Click **OK** to construct the tab feature.

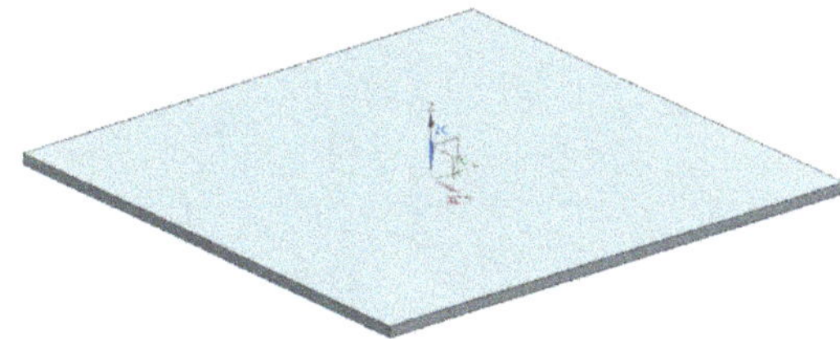

Adding a flange

1. To add the flange, click **Home > Base > Flange** 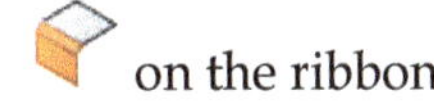 on the ribbon.
2. Select the edge on the top face.

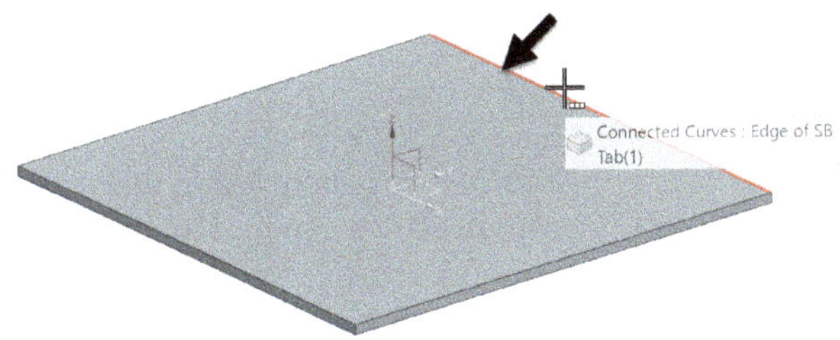

3. On the **Flange** dialog, set **Length** to 100.
4. Click **OK** on the **Flange** dialog to add the flange.

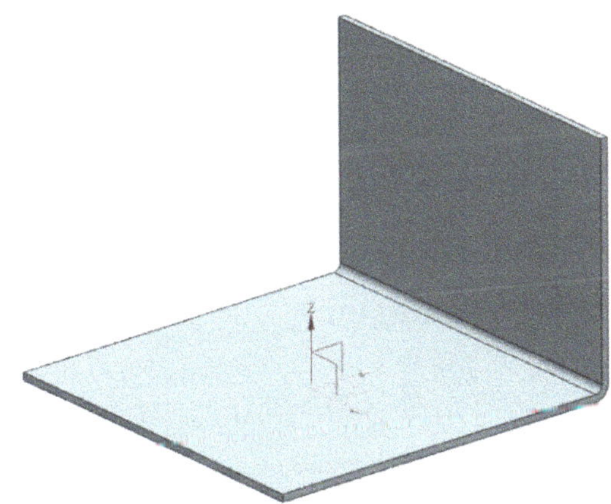

Constructing the Contour Flange

1. To construct the contour flange, click **Home > Base > Contour Flange** on the ribbon.
2. Click the **Reset** icon on the **Contour Flange** dialog.
3. On the **Contour Flange** dialog, click the **Sketch Section** icon.
4. On the Sketch Scene Bar, select **Curve Rule > Single Curve**.

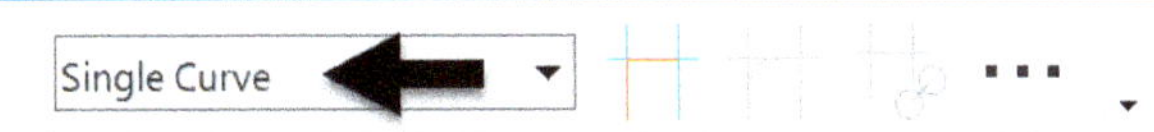

5. Click on the left edge of the top face at the location, as shown.

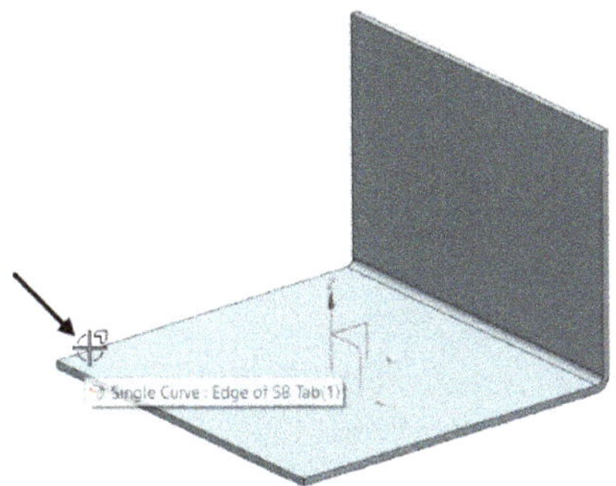

6. On the **Create Sketch** dialog, under the **Plane Location** section, type-in **100** in the **% Arc Length** box.
7. Under the **Plane Orientation** section, click **Reverse Plane Normal**.

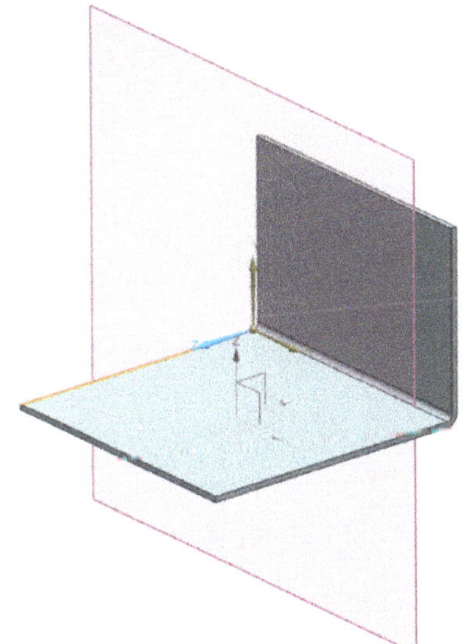

8. Click **OK**.
9. Draw the sketch, as shown.

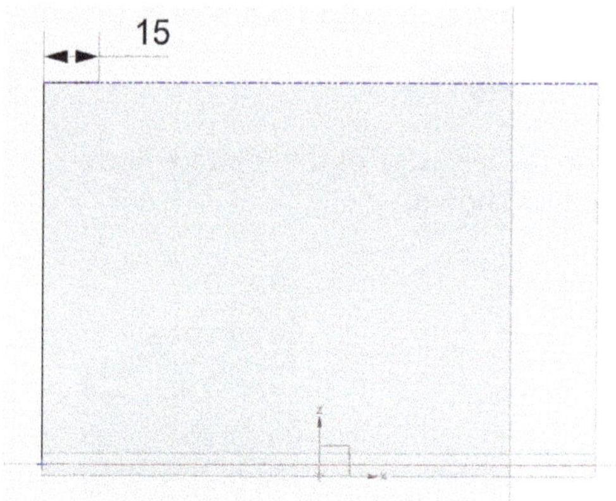

10. Click **Finish**.
11. On the **Contour Flange** dialog, under the **Width** section, select **Width Option** > **To End**.
12. Click on the arrow attached to the sketch, if it points in the direction shown below.

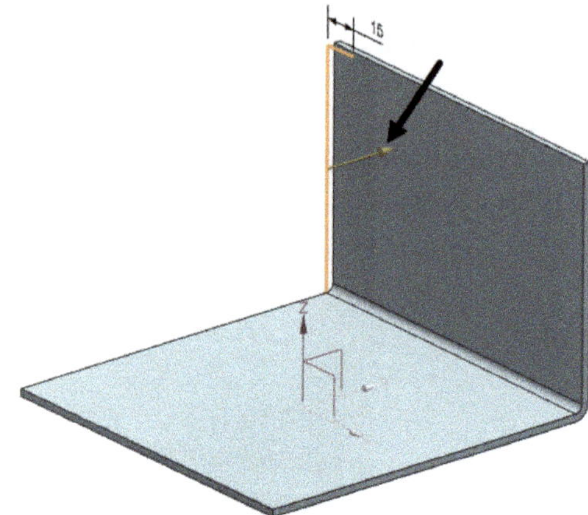

13. Click **OK** to construct the contour flange.

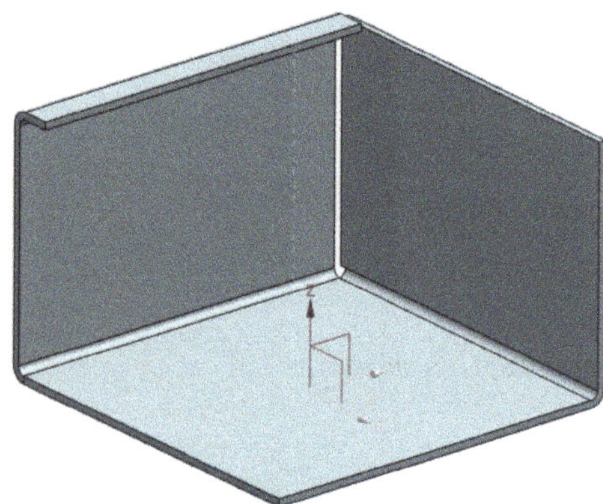

Adding the Closed Corner

1. To add the closed corner, click **Home > Corner > Closed Corner**.
2. Select the two bends forming the corner.

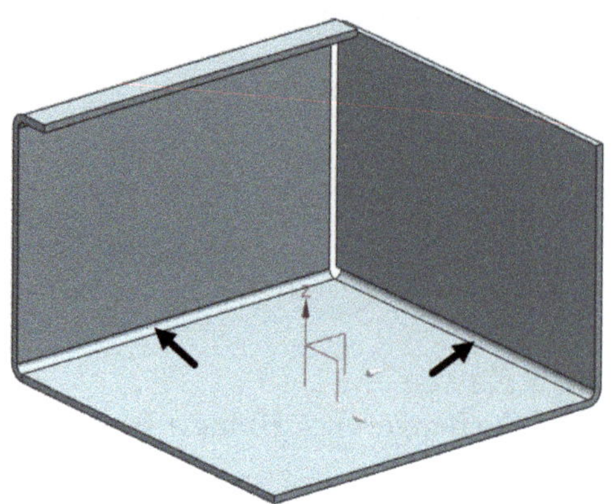

3. On the **Closed Corner** dialog, under the **Corner Properties** section, select **Treatment > Open.**
4. Select **Overlap > None.**
5. Click **OK** to add the open corner.

You can also apply corner treatment using the options in the **Treatments** drop-down. The different types of corner treatments are given next.

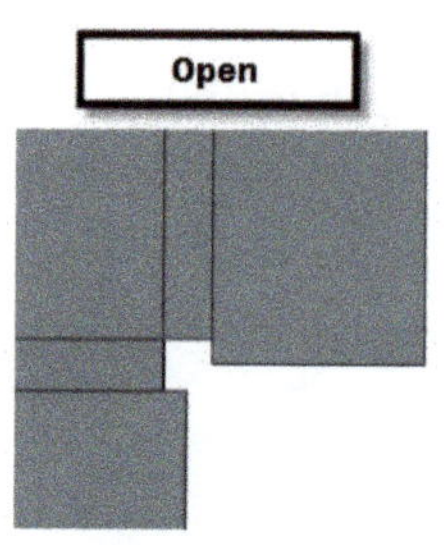

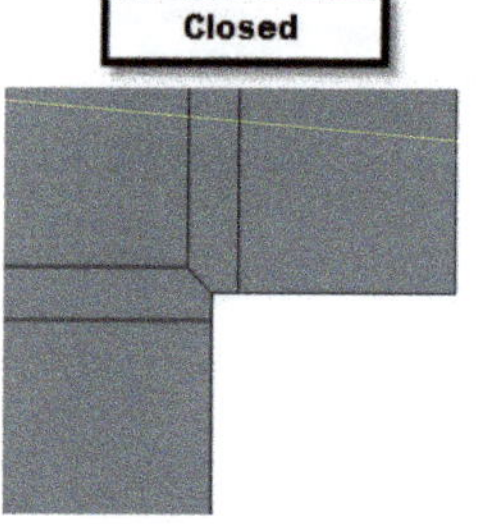

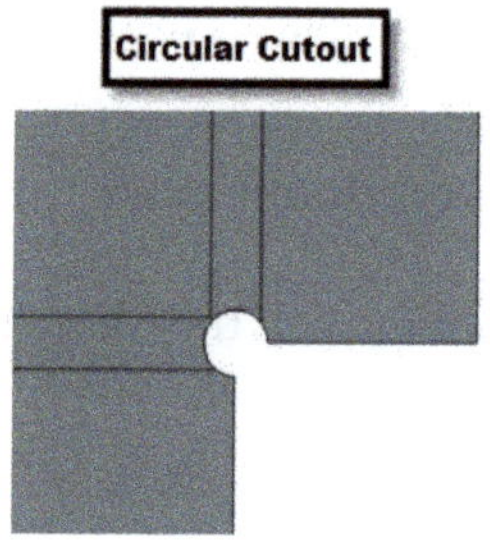

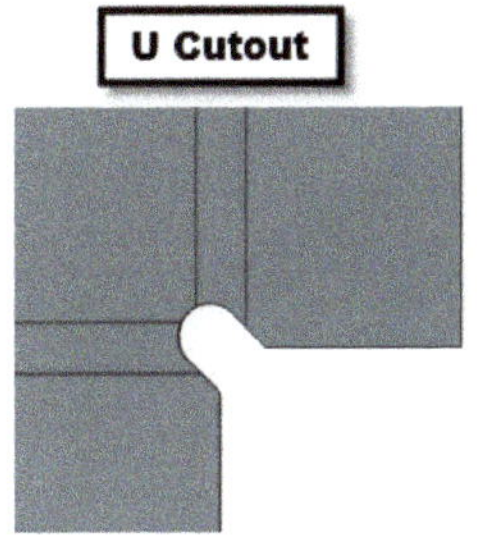

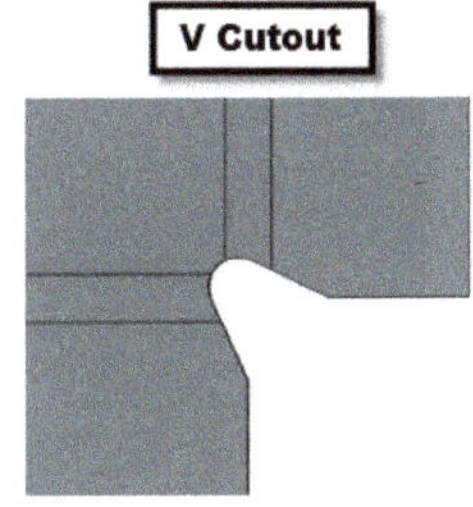

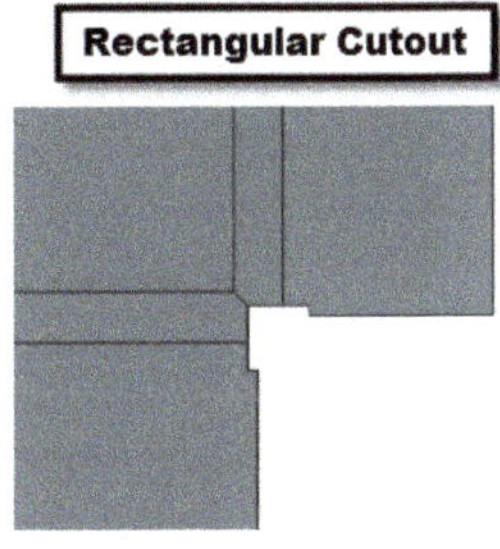

Check the **Miter Corner** option, if you want the result, as shown below.

Adding the Louver

1. To add the louver, click **Home > Punch > Louver** on the ribbon.
2. Click on the front face of the flange at the location shown below.

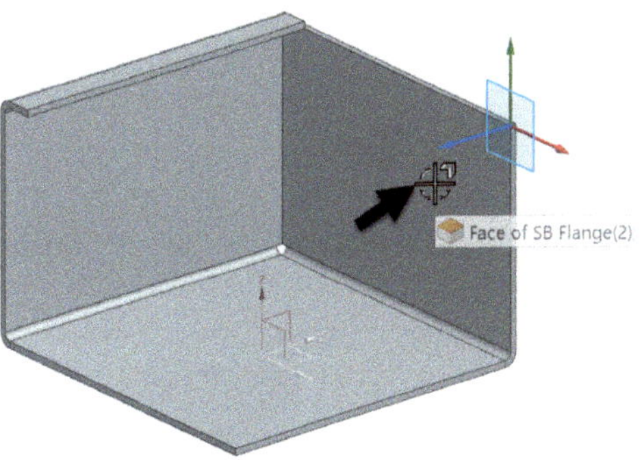

3. Construct the sketch, as shown in the figure.

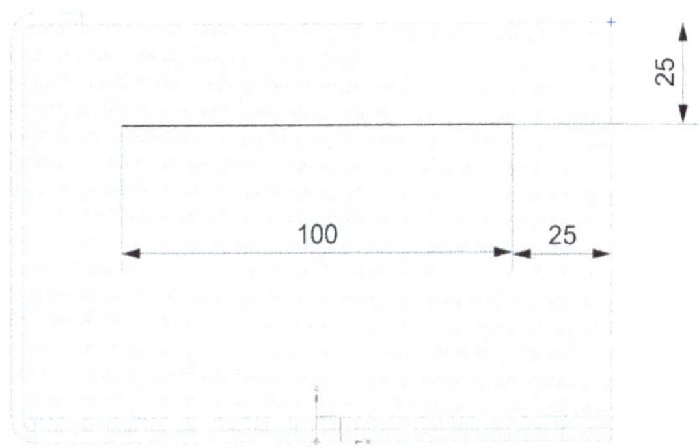

4. Click **Finish**.
5. On the **Louver** dialog, select **Louver Shape > Formed**.
6. Type-in **5** in the **Depth** box and click the **Reverse Direction** icon next to it.
7. Type-in **10** in the **Width** box and click the **Reverse Direction** icon next to it.
8. Click **OK** to add the louver.

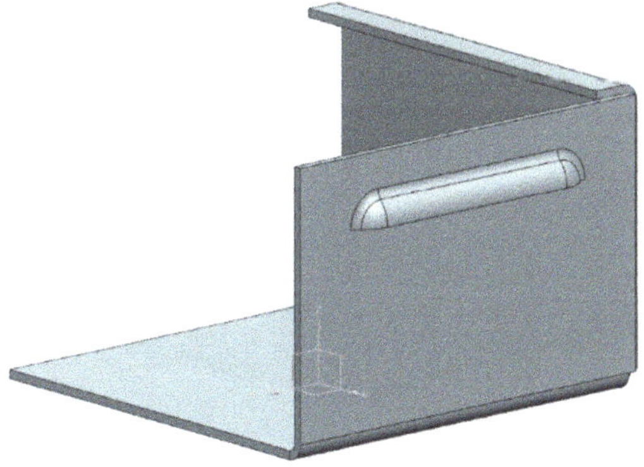

Making the Pattern Along the curve

1. On the Top Border Bar, click **Menu > Insert > Associative Copy > Pattern Feature** .
2. Select the louver feature.
3. On the **Louver** dialog, under the **Pattern Definition** section, select **Layout > Along**.
4. Under the **Direction 1** section, click **Select Path**.
5. On the Sketch Scene Bar, select **Curve Rule >**

Single Curve.

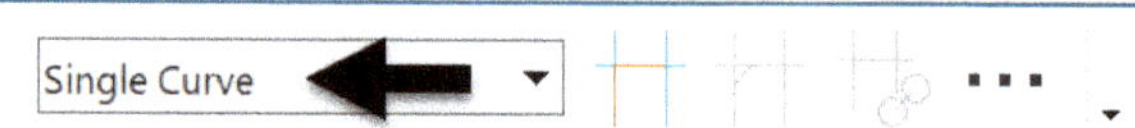

6. Select the vertical edge of the flange feature.

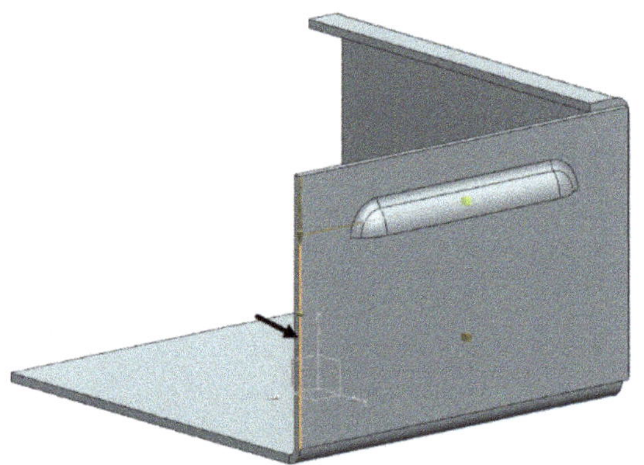

7. Under the **Direction 1** section, select **Spacing > Count and Span.**
8. Set **Count** to 3.
9. Set % **Span By** as 60.
10. Make sure that the arrow points downwards. You can double-click on it to reverse its direction.
11. Under the **Pattern Method** section, select **Method > Variational.**
12. Click **OK** to construct the pattern along the curve.

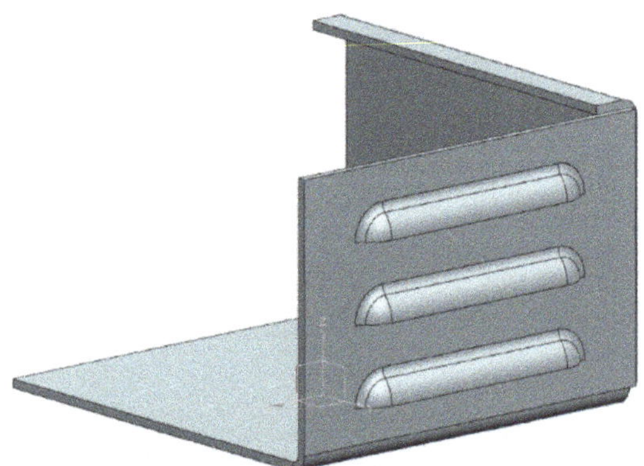

Adding the Bead

1. To add the bead, click **Home > Punch > More > Bead** on the ribbon.
2. Click on the top face of the tab feature at the location, as shown.

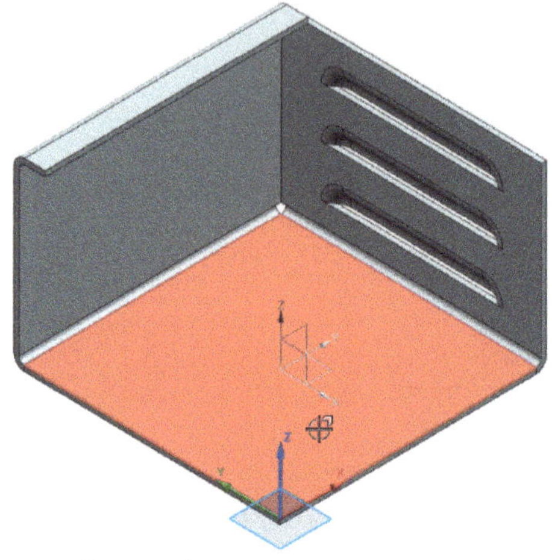

3. Draw a line and dimension it.

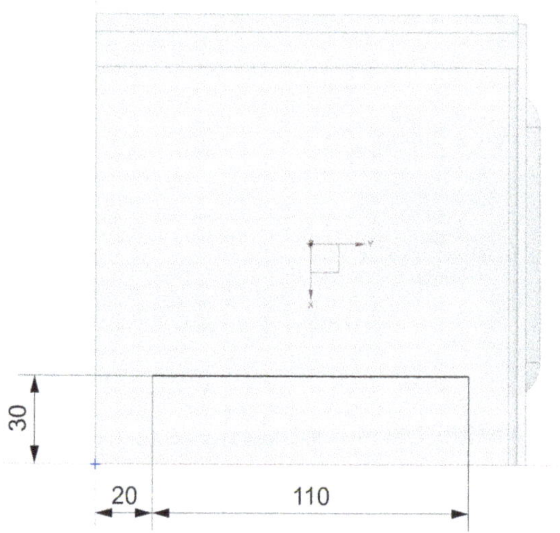

4. Click **Finish** on the ribbon.
5. Under the **Bead Properties** section, select **Cross Section > Circular.**
6. Set **Depth** to 4 and click the **Reverse Direction** icon next to the **Depth** box.
7. Set **Radius** to 4.
8. Select **End Condition > Formed.**
9. Click **OK** to add the bead.

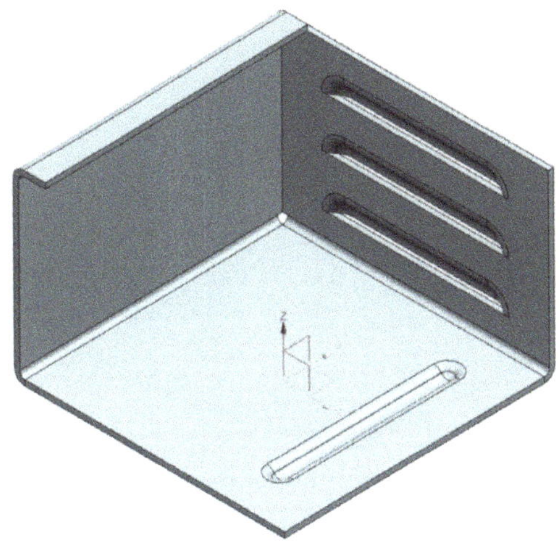

Adding the Drawn Cutout

1. To add the drawn cutout, click **Home > Punch > More > Drawn Cutout** on the ribbon.
2. Click on the face of the contour flange at the location shown below.

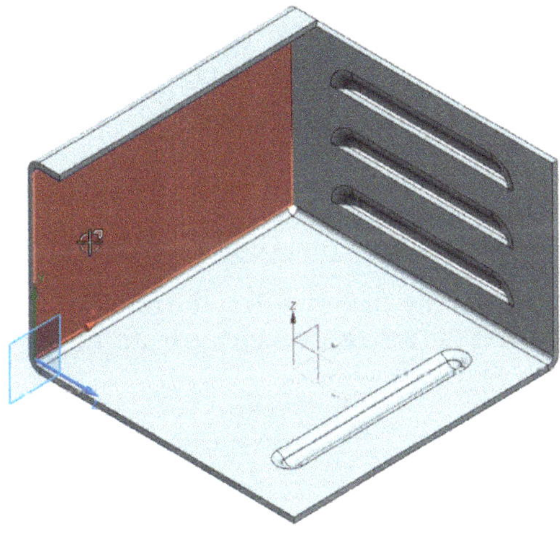

3. Draw a circle and dimension it.

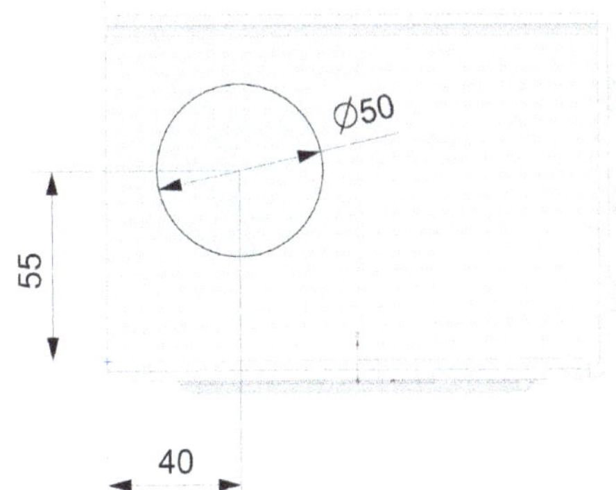

4. Click **Finish** on the ribbon.
5. Set **Depth** to 10.
6. Set **Side Angle** to 5.
7. Select **Side Walls > Material Outside**.
8. Expand the **Settings** section and check the **Blend Drawn Cutout Edges** option.
9. Uncheck the **Blend Section Corners** option.
10. Set **Die Radius** to 3.
11. Click **OK** to add the drawn cutout.

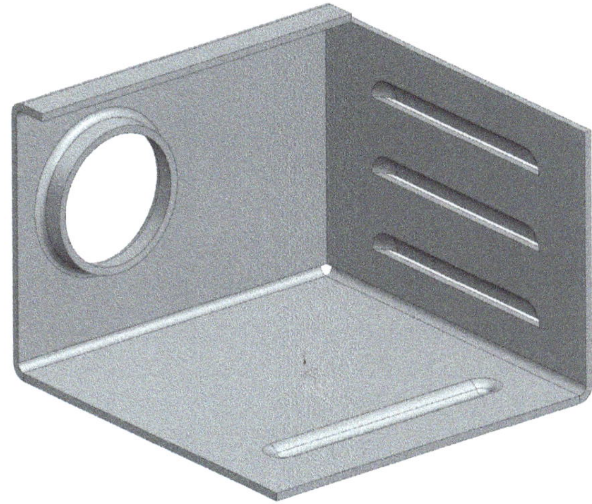

Adding Gussets

1. To add gussets, click **Home > Punch > More > Gusset** on the ribbon.
2. On the **Gusset** dialog, select **Type > Automatic Profile**.
3. Click on the bent face of the contour flange.
4. Under the **Location** section, select **XC-ZC Plane** from the drop-down.

5. Under the **Shape** section, set **Depth** to 12.
6. Select **Form > Round**.
7. Set **Width** to 10.
8. Set **Side Angle** to 2.
9. Set **Die Radius** to 2.
10. Click **OK** to add gussets.

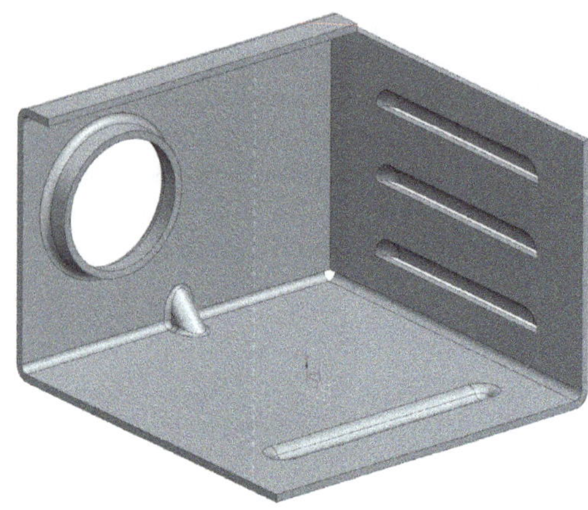

Constructing the Mirror Feature

1. To construct the mirror feature, click **Menu > Insert > Associative Copy > Mirror Feature** on the Top Border Bar.
2. Under the **Part Navigator**, press the Ctrl key, and then select the contour flange, closed corner, bead feature, and gusset.

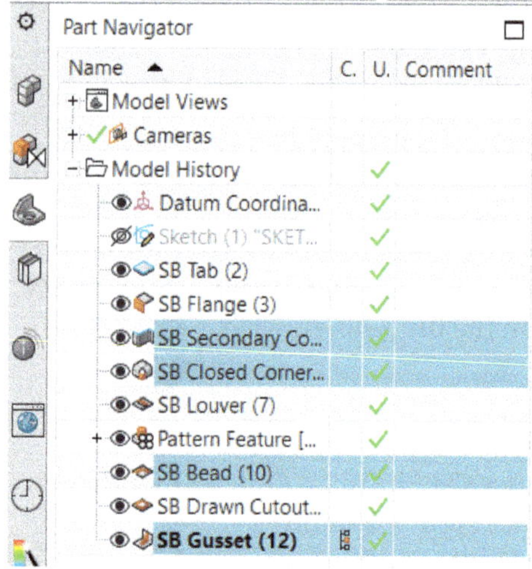

3. Under the **Mirror Plane** section, click **Select Plane.**
4. Select the YZ plane.

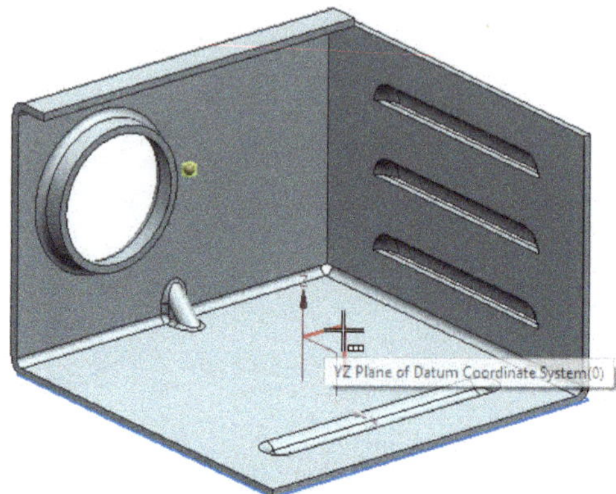

5. Click **OK** to construct the mirror feature.

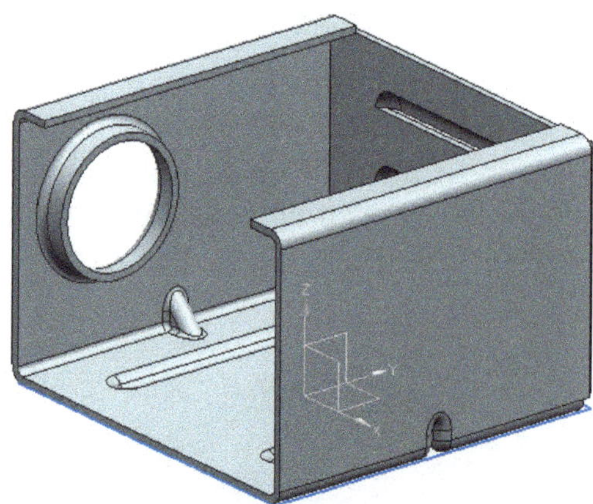

Making the Flat Pattern

1. To make the flat pattern, click **Home > Flat Pattern > Flat Pattern** on the ribbon.
2. Click on the top face of the tab feature.

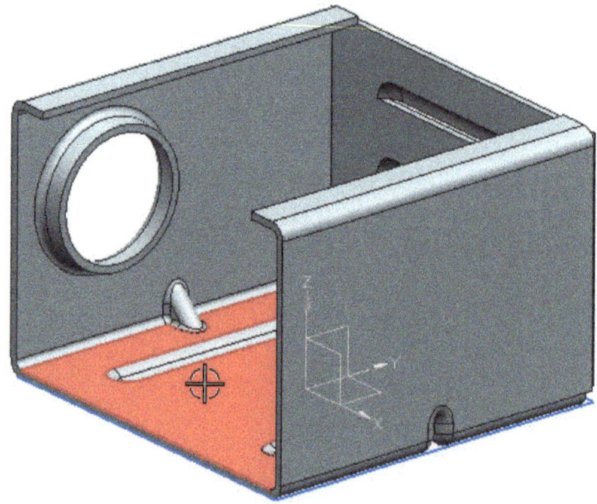

3. Select **Orientation Method > Default** from the **Orientation** section.
4. Click **OK** to make the flat pattern.
5. On the **Sheet Metal** message, click **OK.**
6. To view the flat pattern, click **Menu > View > Layout > New** on the Top Border Bar.
7. On the **New Layout** dialog, select FLAT-

PATTERN#1 and click **OK**.

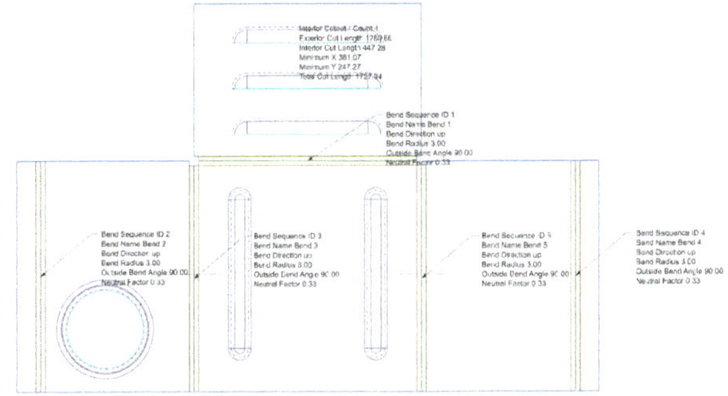

8. To view the 3D model, click **Menu > View > Layout > New** on the Top Border Bar.
9. On the **New Layout** dialog, select **Isometric** and click **OK**.

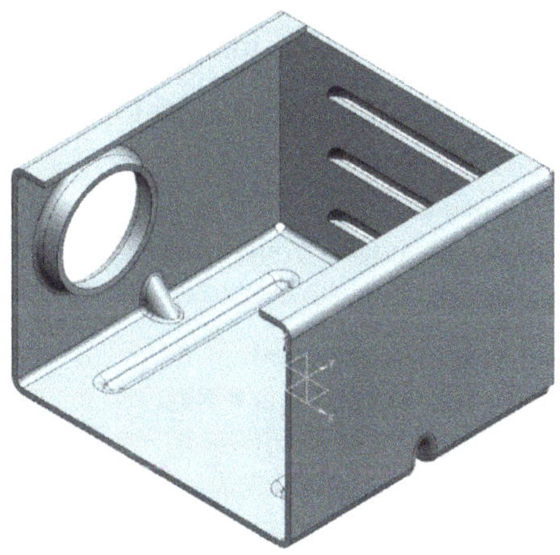

10. Save and close the file.

TUTORIAL 2

In this tutorial, you will apply corner relief to 3 Bend corner.

1. Download and open the Tutorial_2 part file from the companion website.
2. On the ribbon, click **Home** > **Corners** > **More** gallery > **Three Bend Corner**.

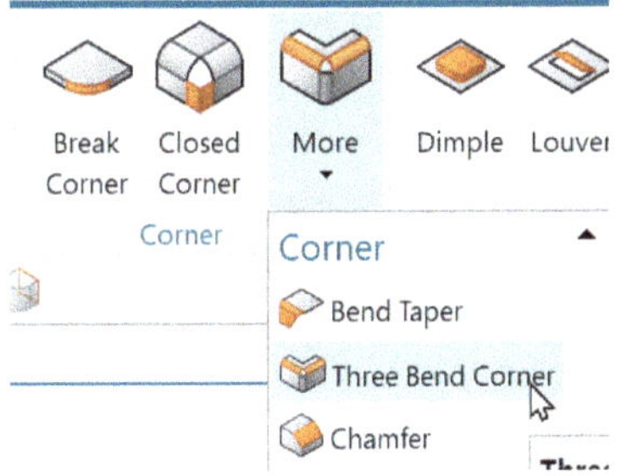

3. Select the two bend faces adjacent to the corner, as shown.

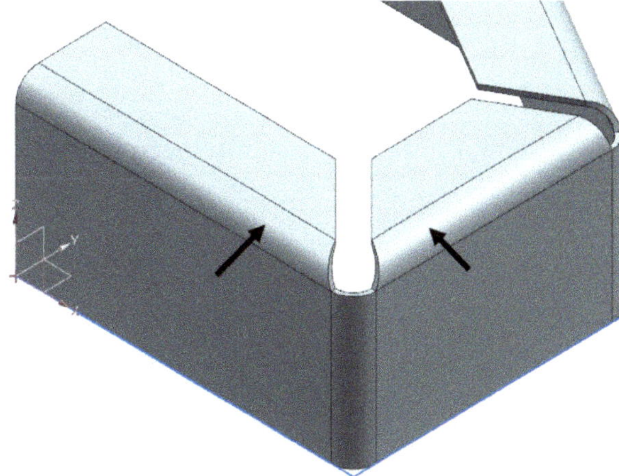

4. On the Three Bend Corner dialog, under the **Corner Properties** section, select **Treatment > Circular Cutout** .
5. Uncheck the **Miter Corner** option.
6. Type 10 in the **Diameter** box available in the **Relief Properties** section.
7. Click **OK** on the **Three Bend Corner** dialog.

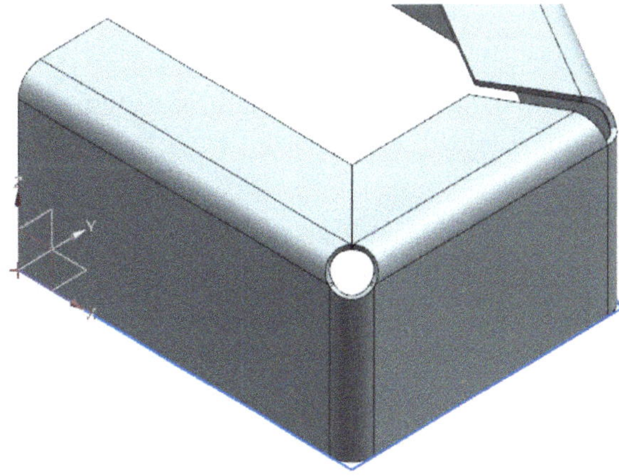

TUTORIAL 3

In this tutorial, you will create a multi-body sheet metal part.

1. Start a new NX Sheet metal part file.
2. On the ribbon, click **File** tab > **Preferences** > **Sheet Metal**.
3. Leave the default settings on the **Sheet Metal Preferences** dialog, and then click **OK.**
4. On the ribbon, click **Home > Base > Tab**.
5. Click on the XY plane.
6. Create a rectangle and add dimensions to it, as shown.

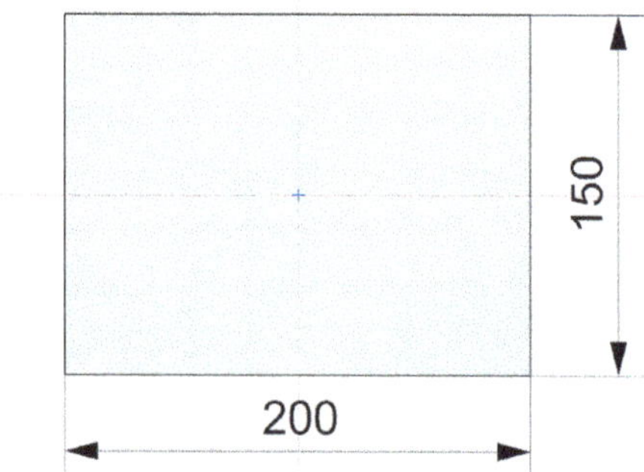

7. Click **OK**.

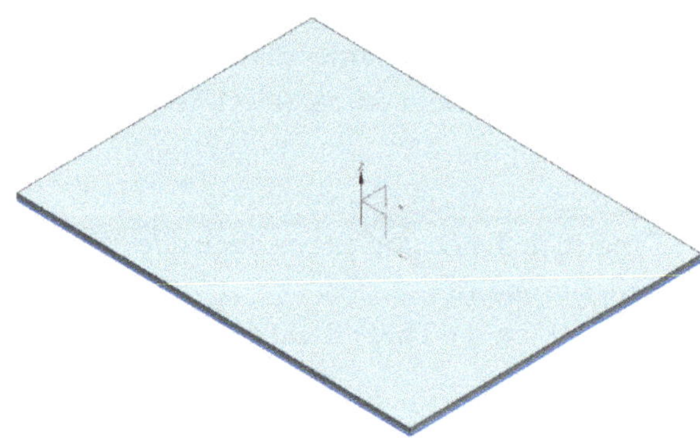

8. Create flanges of 40 mm length, as shown.

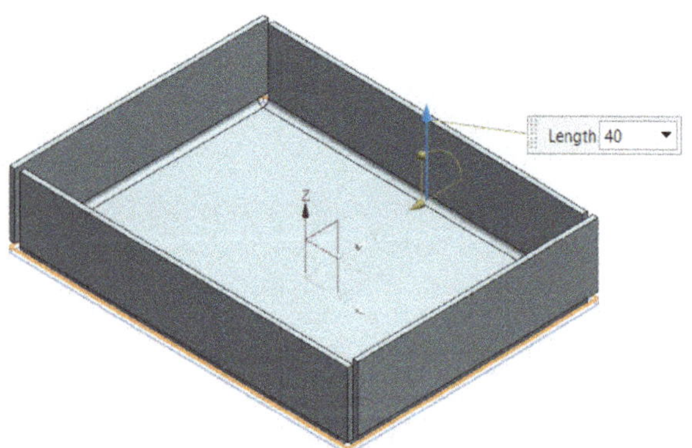

9. On the ribbon, click **Home** tab > **Corner** group > **Closed Corner** .
10. On the **Closed Corner** dialog, select **Type > Close and Relief**.
11. Select the two bends forming a corner, as shown.

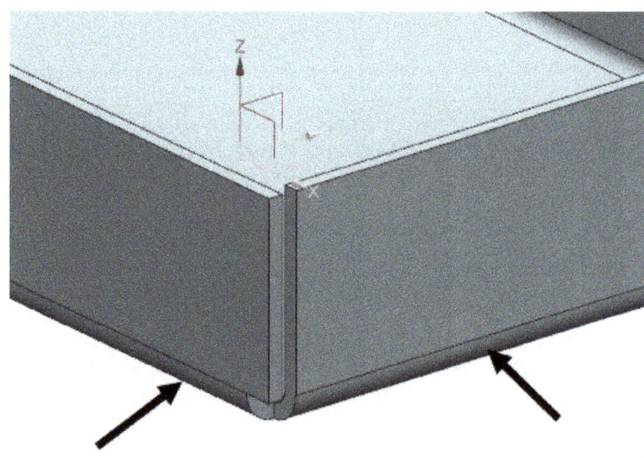

12. On the **Closed Corner** dialog, under the **Corner Properties** section, select **Treatment > Open**.
13. Select **Overlap > None.**
14. Click **OK** to close the corner and apply the relief.
15. Likewise, apply the corner relief to the remaining corners.
16. Activate the **Tab** command.
17. On the **Tab** dialog, select **Type > Base.**
18. Click on the outer face of the flange.

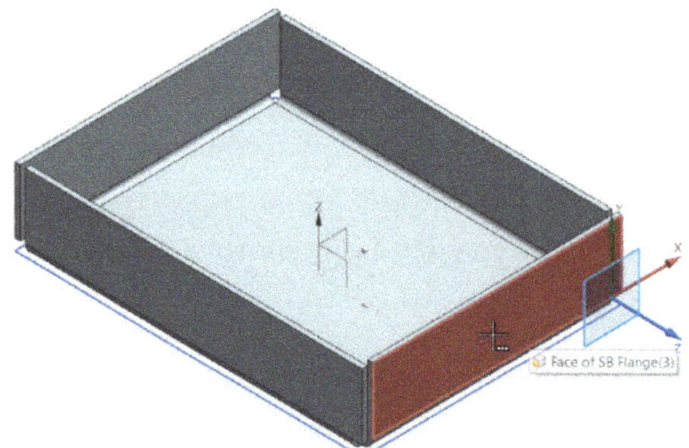

19. Create a rectangle, as shown.

20. Press Esc to deactivate the **Rectangle** command.
21. On the Top Bordar Bar, select **Selection Scope > Within Work Park Only**.
22. Select the bottom edge of the bend.
23. Select the bottom horizontal line of the rectangle.
24. Click the **Collinear** icon the Sketch Scene Bar; the line is made collinear with the horizontal edge of the bend.

25. Likewise, make the vertical line collinear with the side edges, as shown.

26. Add dimension to the vertical line, as shown.

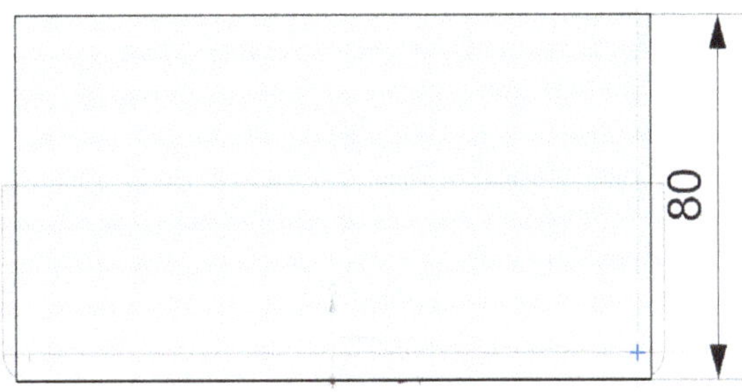

27. Click **Finish** on the ribbon.
28. Click **OK**; a separate tab feature is created.

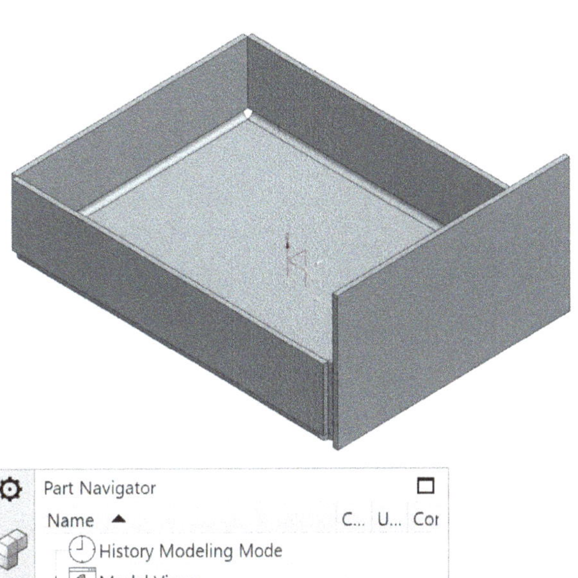

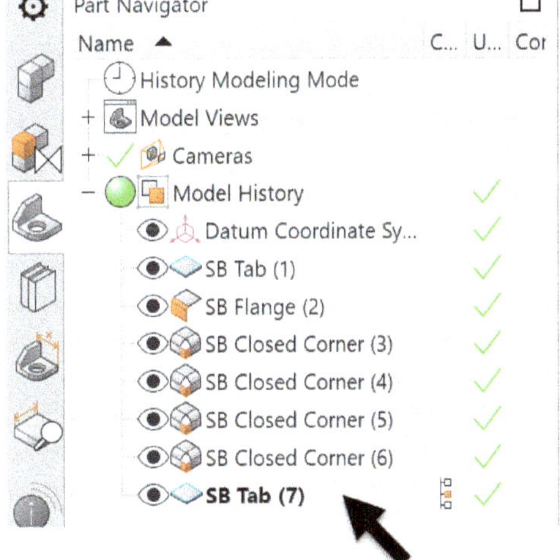

29. Click on the Z-axis of the triad located at the bottom left corner of the graphics window.
30. Type **180** in the **Angle** box, and then press Enter; the orientation of the model is changed.

31. Activate the **Tab** tool.
32. On the **Tab** dialog, select **Type > Base.**
33. Click on the edge flange face.

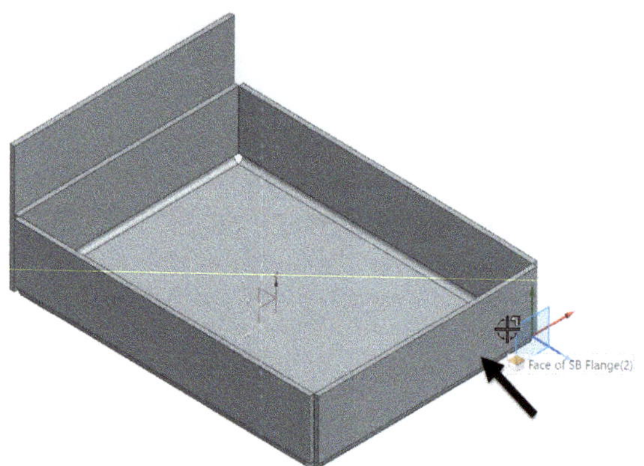

34. Activate the **Rectangle** tool.
35. On the Top Bordar Bar, select **Selection Scope > Within Work Park Only.**
36. Click on the first and second corners, as shown.

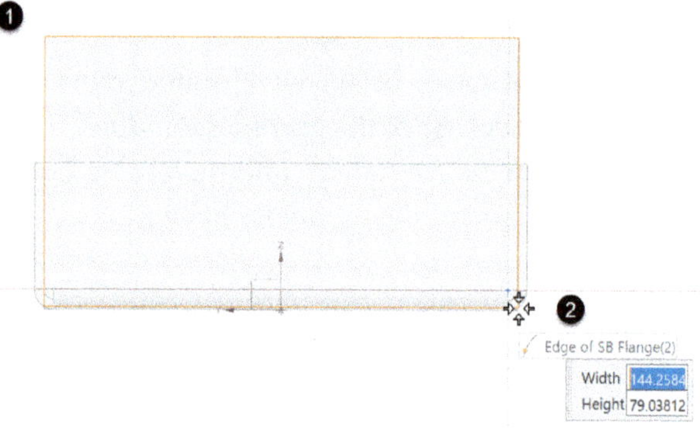

37. Click **Finish** on the ribbon.
38. Click **OK.**

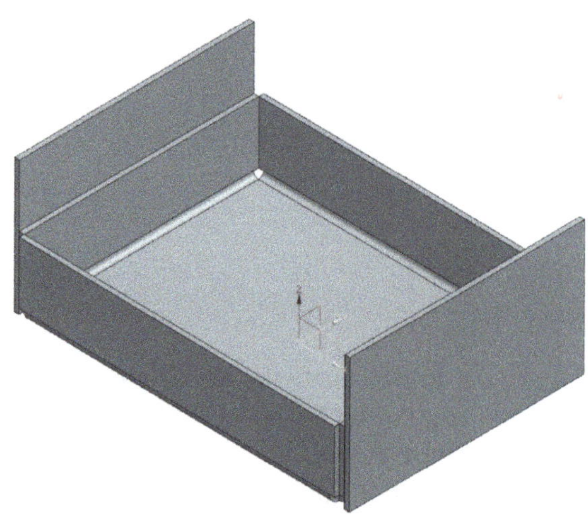

39. On the ribbon, click **Home > Bend > More gallery > Bridge Bend.**

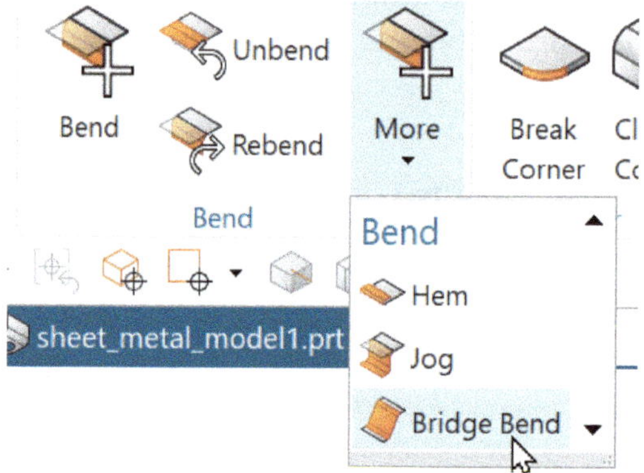

40. On the **Bridge Blend** dialog, select **Type > Z or U Transition.**
41. On the **Bridge Blend** dialog, under the **Width** section, select **Width Option > Full Both Edges.**
42. Click on the edge of the third sheet metal body, as shown.

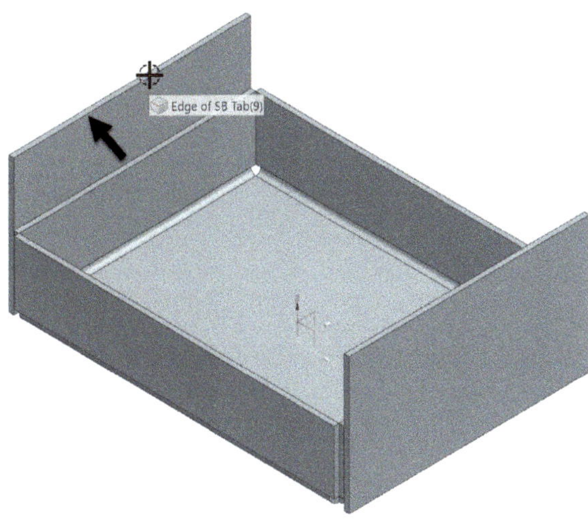

43. Select the edge of the second tab feature, as shown.

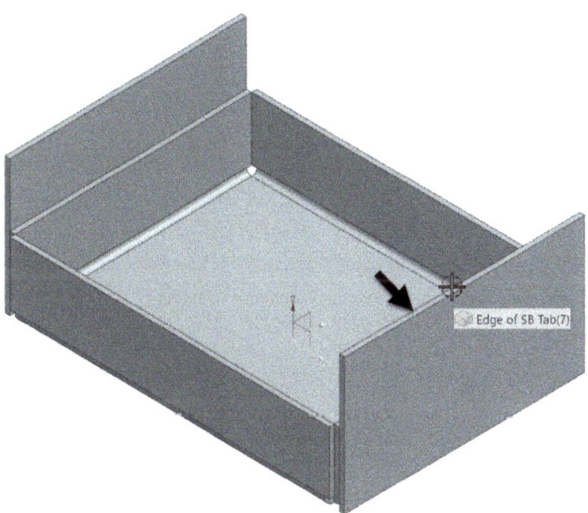

44. Click **OK** on the dialog.

45. Activate the **Flange** tool.
46. Click on the edge of the previously created edge flange, as shown.

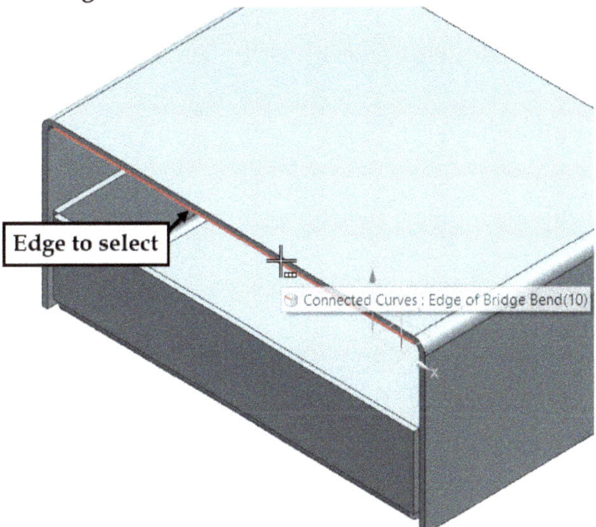

47. On the **Flange** dialog, select **Width Option > Full**.
48. Select **Length Reference > Web**.
49. Select **Inset > Bend Outside**.
50. Type **80** in the **Length** box.
51. Select the edge on the other side of the bridge
52. Expand the **Relief** section, and then select **Corner Relief > Bend/Face Chain**.
53. Click **OK**.

Chapter 9: Top-Down Assembly

In this chapter, you will learn to

- Create a top-down assembly
- Insert fasteners
- Create Sequences
- Create Deformable Parts and assemble them

TUTORIAL 1

In this tutorial, you will create the model shown in the figure. You use the top-down assembly approach to create this model.

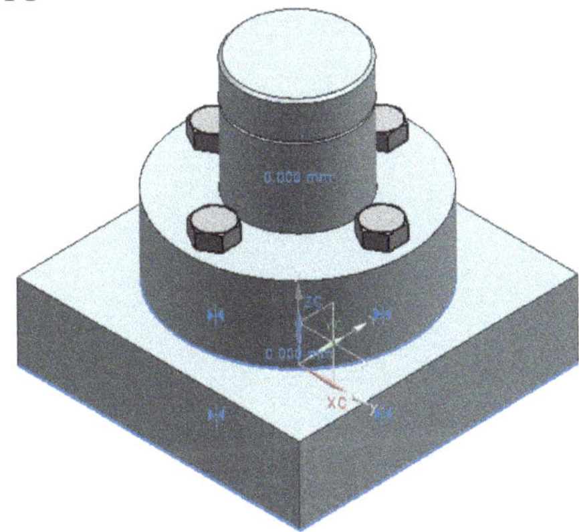

Creating a New Assembly File

1. Click the **New** icon on the Quick Access Toolbar, select the **Assembly** template, and click the **Browse** icon located next to the **Name** box.
2. Create a new folder and open it.
3. Type Tutorial 1 in the **File Name** box.
4. Click **OK** twice.
5. Click **Cancel** on the **Assemble** dialog.

Creating a component in the Assembly

In a top-down assembly approach, you create components of an assembly directly in the assembly by using the **Create New** tool.

1. On the ribbon, click **Assemblies > Base > New Component**.
2. Click **OK** on the **Create New Component** dialog.
3. Click the **Assembly Navigator** tab on the **Resource Bar**.
4. Double-click on the **model1** component. The part mode is activated.

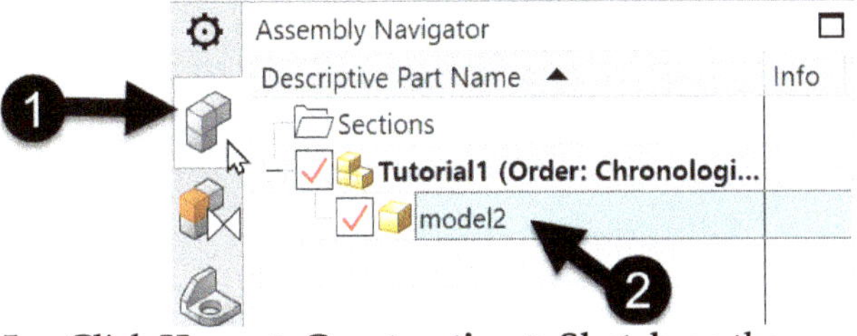

5. Click **Home > Construction > Sketch** on the ribbon.
6. Select **Sketch Type > On Plane** from the **Create Sketch** dialog.
7. Select the Top plane from Datum Coordinate System and click **OK**.
8. Create the sketch, as shown below.

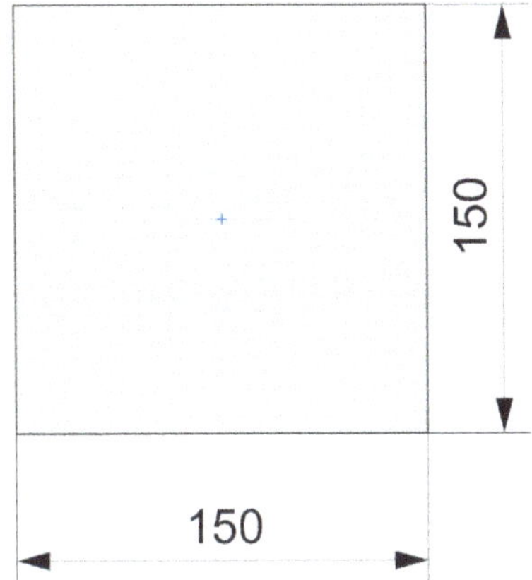

9. Click **Finish** on the **Sketch** group.
10. Click **Home > Base > Extrude** on the Ribbon and extrude the sketch up to 40 mm.

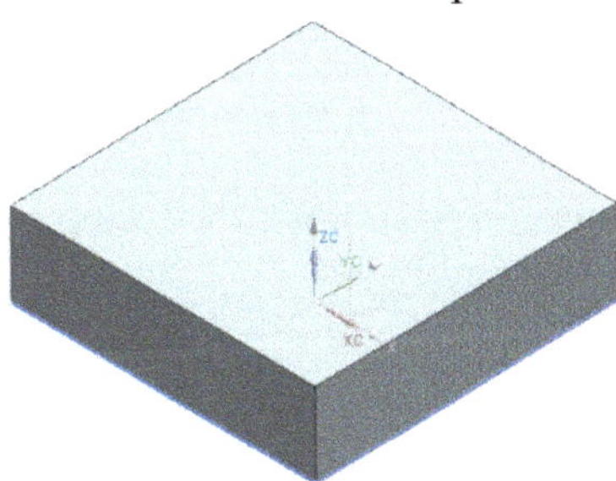

11. Create a cylinder of 50 mm diameter and 95 mm length on the top face.

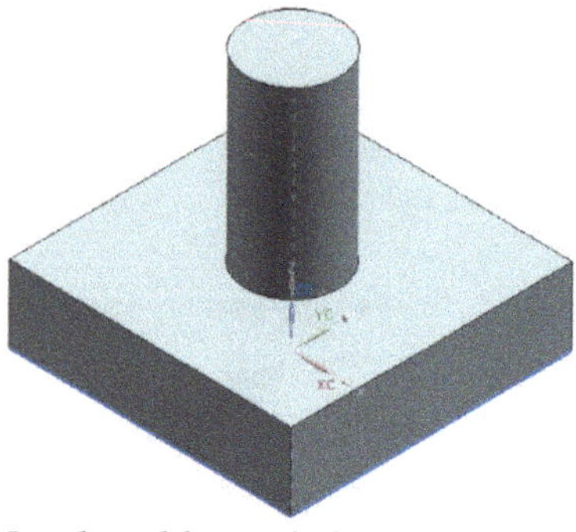

12. On the ribbon, click **Home > Base > Hole.**
13. On the **Hole** dialog, select **Type > Counterbored.**
14. In the **Form and Dimensions** section, set the parameters, as shown.

    Hole Size: Custom
    Hole Diameter: 25
    C-Bore Diameter: 30
    C-Bore Depth: 12

15. Select **Depth Limit > Through Body** from the **Limit** section.
16. Select the center point of the top circular edge.
17. Click **OK.**

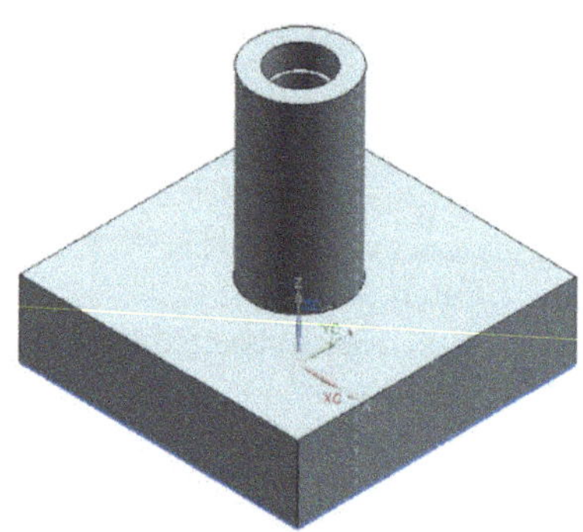

18. On the ribbon, click the **Assemblies > Context > More > Work on Assembly.**

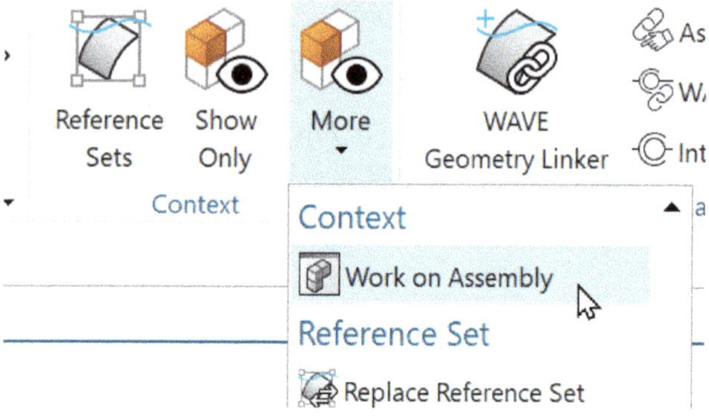

Creating the Second Component of the Assembly

1. On the ribbon, click **Assemblies > Base > New Component** .
2. Click **OK** on the **New Component** dialog.
3. In the Assembly Navigator, double-click on the second part under the assembly to activate the **Work part** mode.

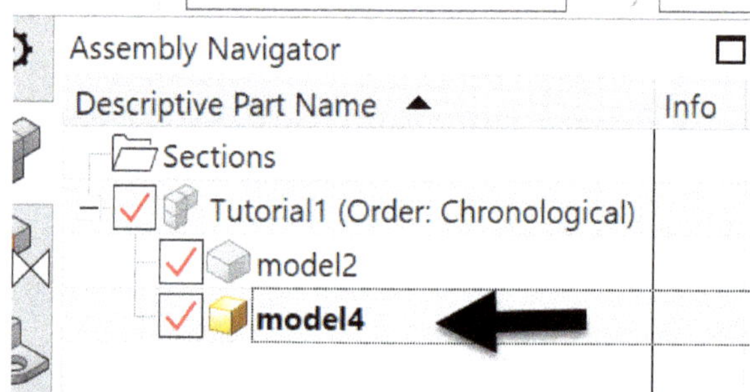

4. Click **Home > Construction > Sketch** on the Ribbon.
5. On the Top Border Bar, set the **Selection Scope** to **Entire Assembly.**
6. Select the top face of the Base.

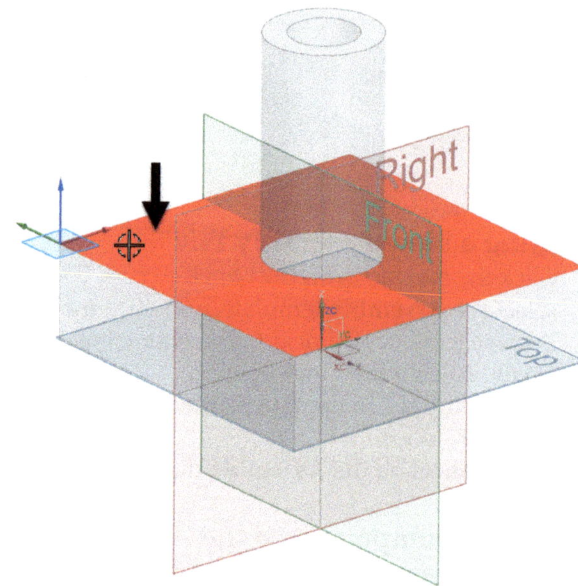

7. Click **OK.**
8. On the Top Border Bar, click the down-arrow located at the right side, and then select **Selection group > Create Interpart Link.**

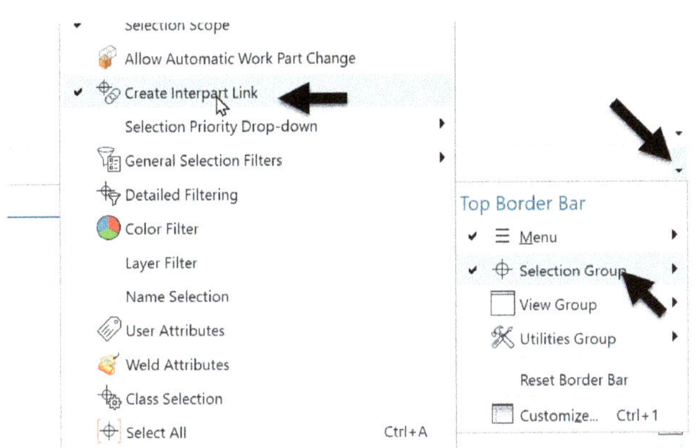

9. On the ribbon, click **Home > Include > More > Project Curve** .
10. Click the **Create Interpart Link** icon on the Top Border Bar.

11. Select the circular edge of the Base.

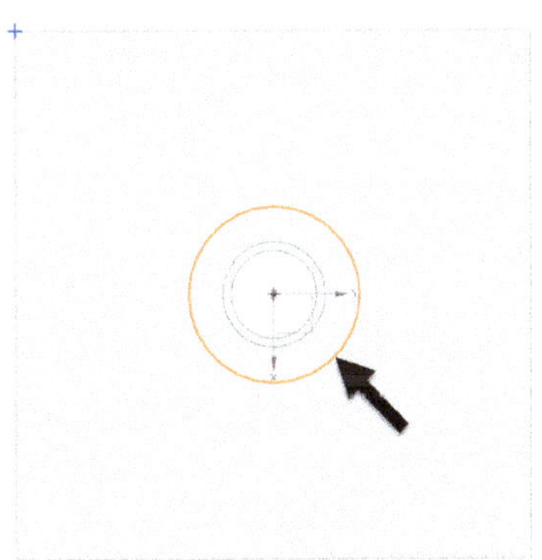

12. Click **OK** on the **Interpart Copy** message box.
13. Click **OK.**
14. Draw a circle of 120 mm in diameter.

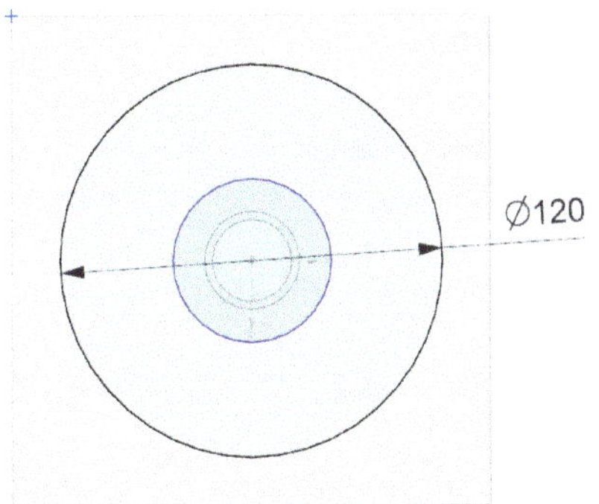

15. Click **Task > Finish Sketch.**
16. Activate the **Extrude** tool and extrude the sketch up to 40.

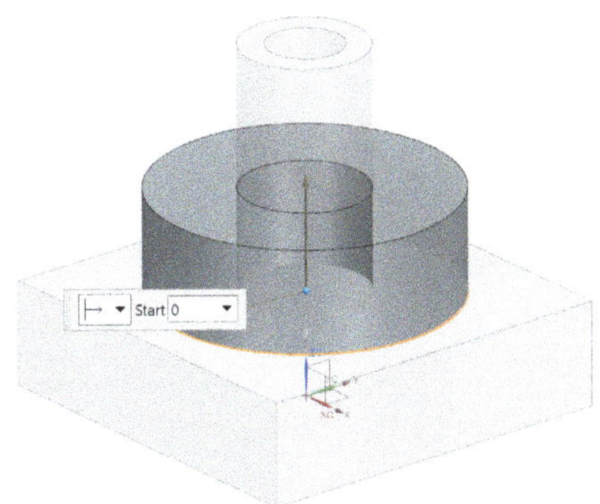

17. In the **Assembly Navigator**, double-click on **Tutorial 1** to switch to the assembly mode.

Creating the third Component of the Assembly

1. On the ribbon, click **Assemblies > Base > New Component** .
2. Click **OK** on the **New Component** dialog.
3. In the **Assembly Navigator**, right click on the third part under the assembly and select **Make Work Part.**

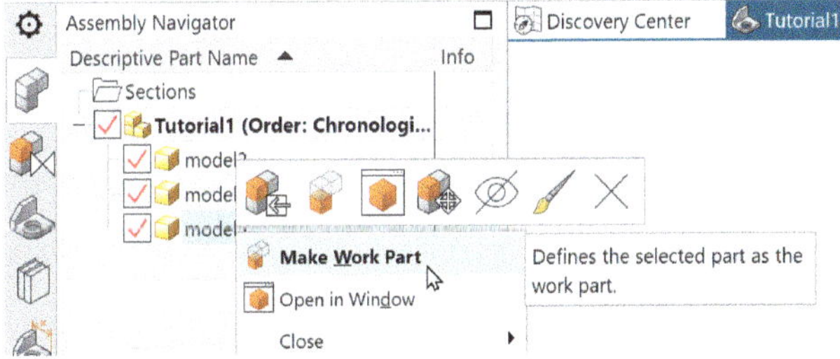

4. On the ribbon, click **Home > Construction > Sketch.**
5. Select the Front Plane from the Datum Coordinate System.
6. Click the **Create Interpart Link** icon on the Top Border Bar.
7. On the ribbon, click **Home > Include > More > Intersection Curve** .
8. On the Top Border Bar, set the **Selection Scope** to **Entire Assembly.**
9. Rotate the view and select the faces, as shown.

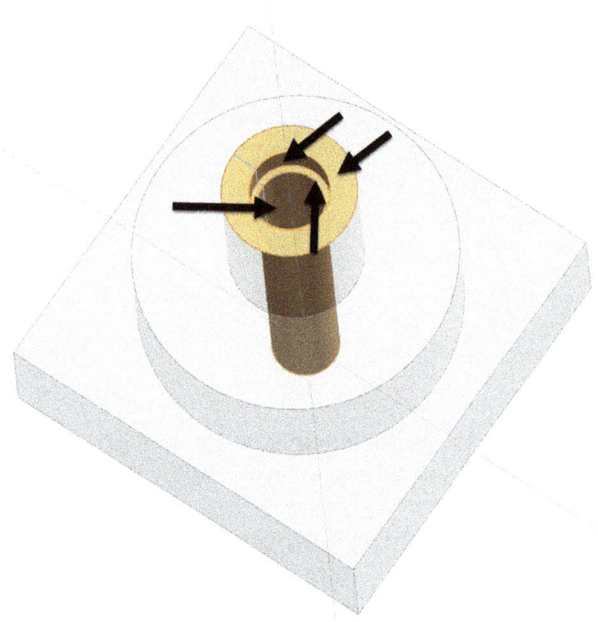

10. Click **OK**.
11. Right click and select **Orient View to Sketch**.
12. Draw the other lines, as shown.

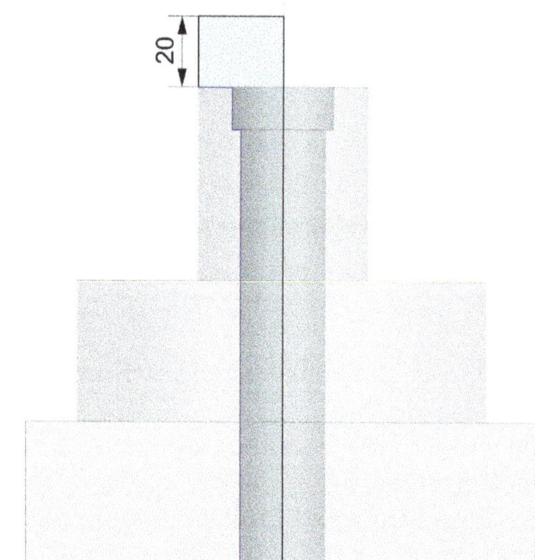

13. Right-click and select **Finish Sketch**.
14. Activate the **Revolve** tool and revolve the sketch.

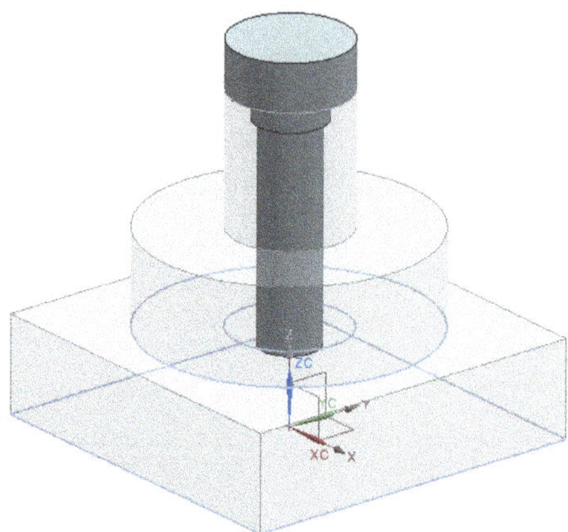

15. Activate the **Chamfer** tool and chamfer the edges, as shown in the figure.

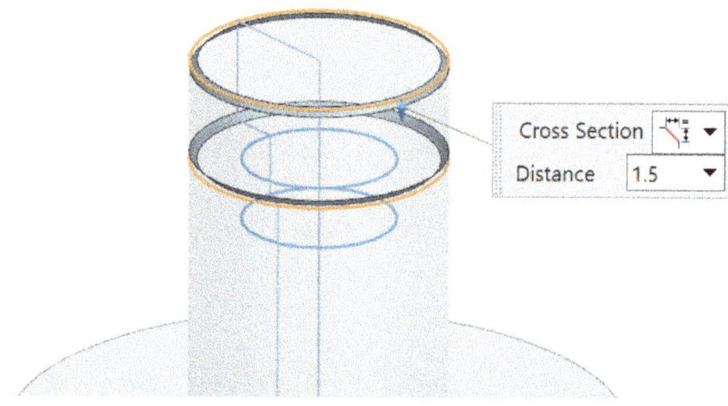

16. Activate the **Edge Blend** tool and round the edges, as shown in the figure.

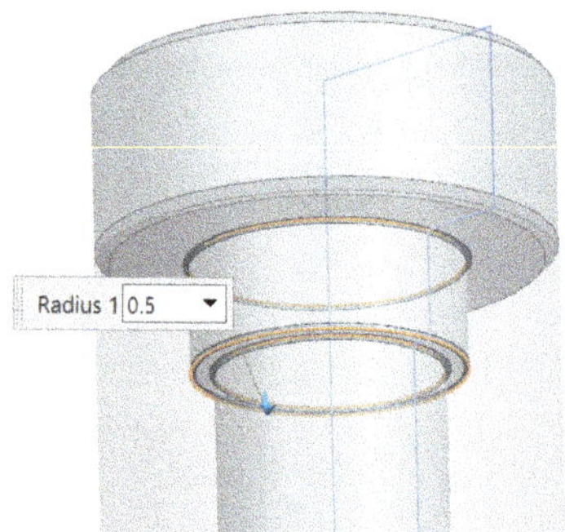

17. On the ribbon, click **Home > Assemblies > Work on Assembly**.

Editing the Linked Parts

1. Right click on the Base and select the **Make Work Part**.
2. Select the circular face of the Base.
3. Click **Edit with Rollback** on the Shortcuts toolbar.
4. Type 80 in the **End** box attached to the extrude feature.
5. On the **Extrude** dialog, click the **Sketch Section** icon in the **Section** section.

6. Change the diameter of the circle to **60** and click Finish on the ribbon.
7. Click **OK** on the **Extrude** dialog.
8. Activate the Assembly mode and notice that the linked parts are also modified.

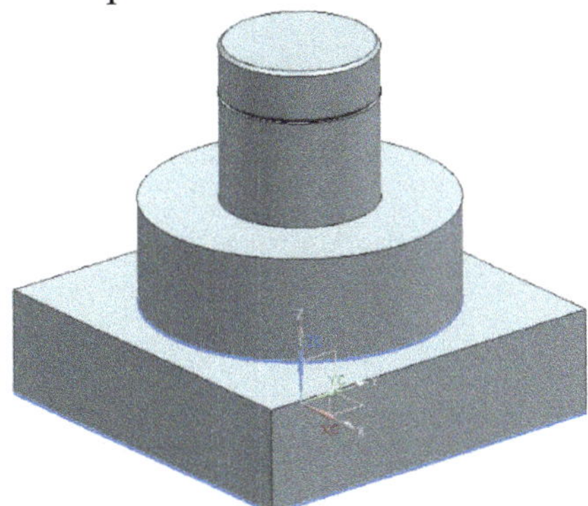

9. On the ribbon, click **Assemblies > Interpart Links > More > Interpart Link Browser**. The **Interpart Links Browser** dialog has two sections: **Parts** and **Interpart Links in Selected Parts.**

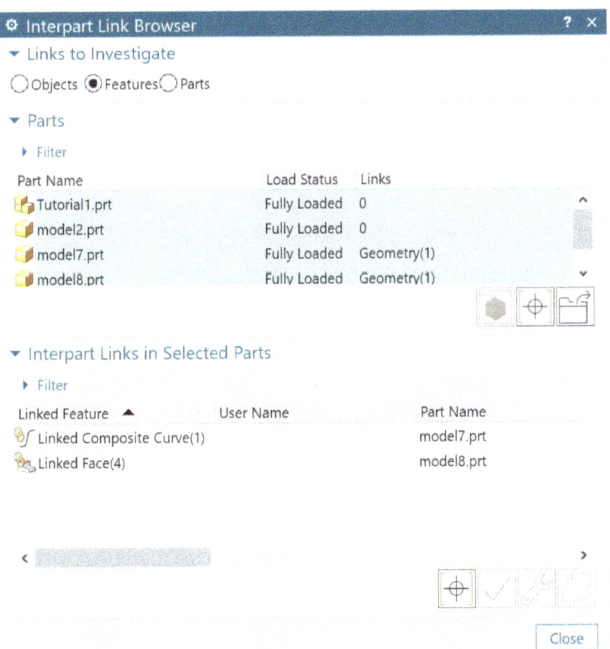

You can edit a link by selecting it and clicking the **Edit** icon. You can also use the **Break Link** icon to remove the link.

10. Close the **Interpart Link Browser** dialog.

Creating Hole Series

A hole series is created through different parts of the assembly.

1. On the ribbon, click **Home > Base > Hole.**
2. Click the **Sketch Section** icon in the **Position** section.
3. Select the top face of the Flange.
4. Click **OK.**
5. Place a point and add dimensions to it, as shown.

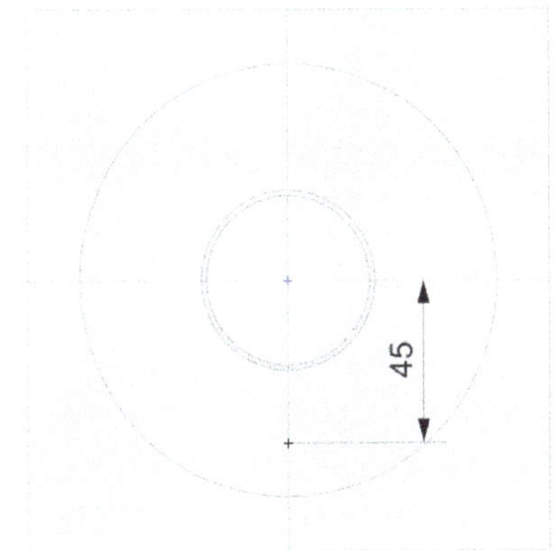

6. Click **Finish.**
7. Select **Type > Hole Series.**

Under the **Specification** section, notice the three tabs: Start, Middle, and End. They are used to set the hole parameters for the three bodies through which the hole passes. For this example, you are required to set the Start and End parameters only.

8. Under the **Specification** section of the **Hole** dialog, click the **Start** tab and set the parameters, as shown.

Form: Simple
Screw Type: General Screw Clearance
Screw Size: M12
Fit: Normal (H13)

9. Click the **End** tab and set the parameters, as shown.

Form: Threaded
Depth Type: Full
Handedness: Right Handed
Depth Limit: Through Body

10. Click **OK.**
11. Likewise, create three more series holes.

Adding Fasteners to the assembly

1. On the ribbon, click **Tools > Reuse Library > Fastener Assembly**.
2. On the **Fastener Assembly** dialog, select **Type >Hole.**
3. Select any one of the holes.
4. Click the **Add Fastener Assembly** icon.
5. Set the **Configuration Name** to **AM-Hex Bolt/Stacks.**
6. Under the **Fastener Configuration** section, click the **Remove** icon next to **Plain Washer, Regular, AM** under **Top Stacks.**

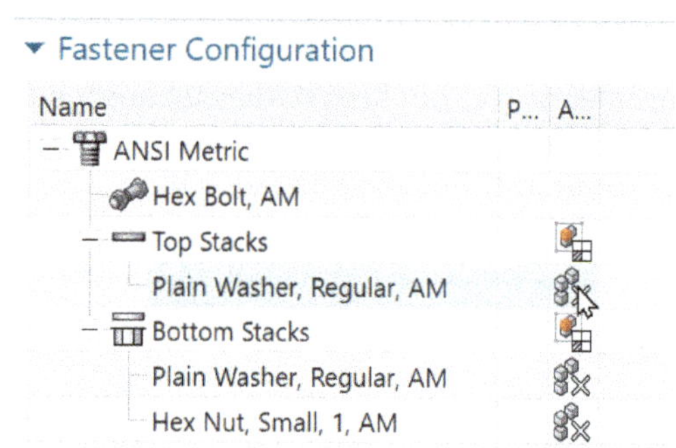

7. Click **OK.**
8. On the **Configuration** section, click the **Properties** icon next to **Hex Bolt, AM.**
9. On the **Edit Reusable Component** dialog, set the **(L) Length** value to **100.** Also, notice the parameters of the hex bolt in the **Details** section. They are read-only.
10. Click **OK.**
11. Expand the **Settings** section and check the **Create Constraints Automatically** option.
12. In the **Configuration** section, right click on **AM-Hex Bolt Stacks** and select **Save Configuration.**

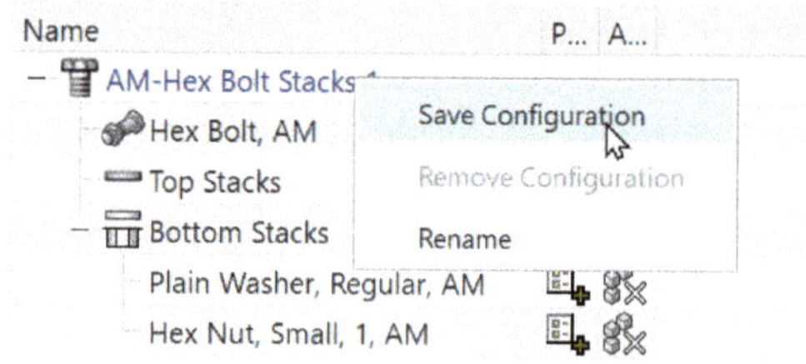

13. Type **Fastener 1** in the **Name** box and click **OK.**
14. Click **OK** to add the fastener assembly.

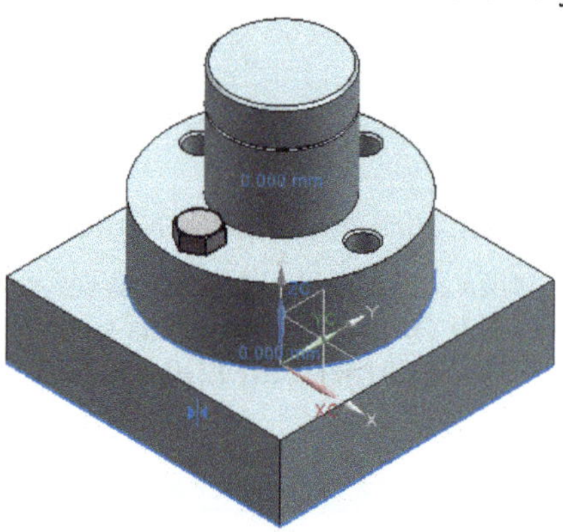

15. Likewise, create add fasteners to other holes.

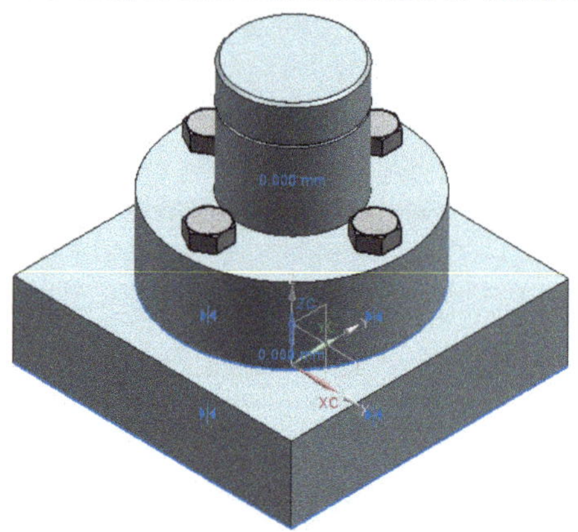

16. Click the **Save** icon on the Quick Access Toolbar.
17. On the **Named Parts** dialog, select the first part from the **Parts to Name** list.
18. Type **Base** in the **Name** box.
19. Select the second part from the **Parts to Name** List.
20. Type **Spacer** in the **Name** box.
21. Likewise, name the third part as **Shoulder Screw.**
22. Click **OK.**
23. Close the assembly.

TUTORIAL 2

In this tutorial, you create a sequence of the assembly.

1. Download the Tutorial 2 files of Chapter 9.
2. Open the Tutorial_2 assembly file.

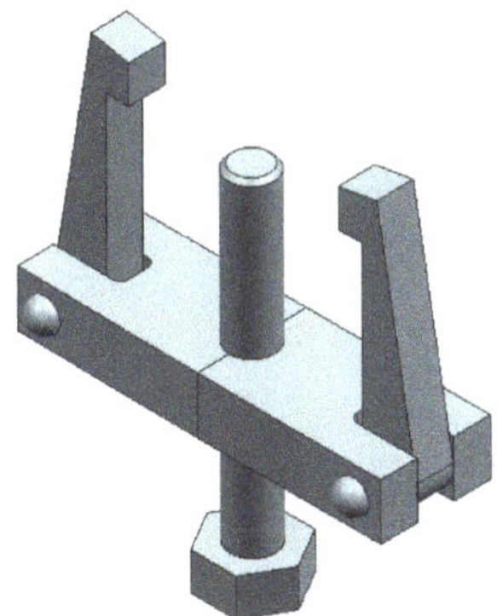

3. On the ribbon, click **Assemblies > Sequence > Sequence** .
4. On the ribbon, click **Home > Assembly Sequence > New** .
5. On the Resource Bar, click the **Sequence Navigator** tab and select **Sequence_1**.
6. Expand the **Details** section of the **Sequence Navigator** and change the **Name** to Hub Puller.
7. In the **Details** section, double-click in the **Value** column of the **Display Split Screen** row. The graphics window is split into two parts.
8. Drag a selection box around the assembly displayed on the right side.
9. On the ribbon, click **Home > Sequence Steps > Disassemble** . The disassemble events are displayed under the **Preassembled** folder of the **Sequence Navigator**.

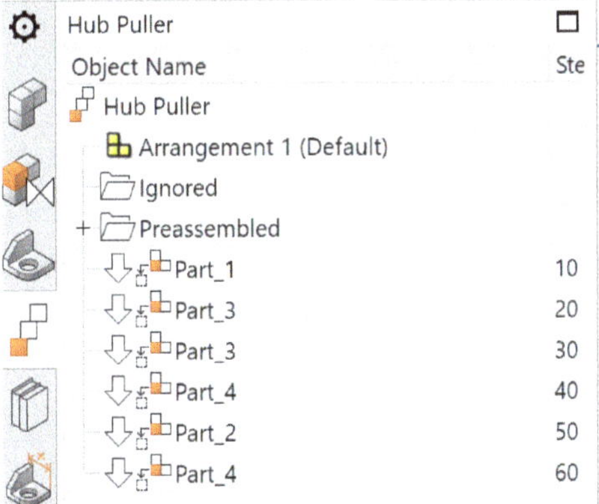

10. On the ribbon, click **Home > Playback > Play Backwards** . Notice that the parts are assembled back in a random sequence.
11. In the **Sequence Navigator**, press the Ctrl key and select all the events under the **Preassembled** folder.
12. Right click and select **Delete**.
13. Expand the **Preassembled** folder.
14. Press and hold the Ctrl key, and then select the two instances of Part_4.
15. Click the **Disassemble Together** icon on the ribbon.
16. Select the **Sequence Group 1** from the **Sequence Navigator** and change its Name to Pins.
17. Select the Part_3 and click the **Disassemble** icon on the ribbon.
18. Likewise, disassemble the other instance of Part_3, Part_2, and Part_1.
19. On the ribbon, click the **Record Camera Position** icon.
20. In the **Sequence Navigator**, select the **Pins** event and change the **Total Duration** value in the **Details** section to 2.
21. Likewise, change the **Total Duration** values of other events to 2.
22. On the **Playback** group of the ribbon, change the **Playback Speed** to **10**.
23. On the **Playback** group, click the **Export to Movie** icon.
24. Type **Hub Puller assembly** in the **File name** box and **OK**. The movie of the assembly sequence is recorded.
25. Click **OK** on the **Export to Movie** message.
26. Click **Finish**.
27. Open and play the video.
28. Close all the parts.

TUTORIAL 3

In this tutorial, you create a deformable part and add it to an assembly.

Creating the Deformable Part

1. Download the Tutorial 3 files of Chapter 9.
2. Open the Deformable_part.prt file.

3. On the Top Border Bar, click **Menu > Tools > Define Deformable Part**.
4. Leave the default **Name** value and click **Next**.
5. Press and hold the Ctrl key, and then select all the features from the **Features in Part** list.
6. Click **Add Feature**.
7. Click **Next**.
8. Select **Pitch = 15** from the **Available Expressions** list and click **Add Expression**.
9. Type **Pitch** in the box below the **Deformable Input Expressions** list.
10. Set the **Expression Rules** to **By Number Range**.
11. Type 8 and 15 in the **Minimum** and **Maximum** boxes.
12. Click **Next** and **Finish**.
13. Save and close the file.

Adding the Deformable part to an Assembly

1. Open the Tutorial 3 assembly file.

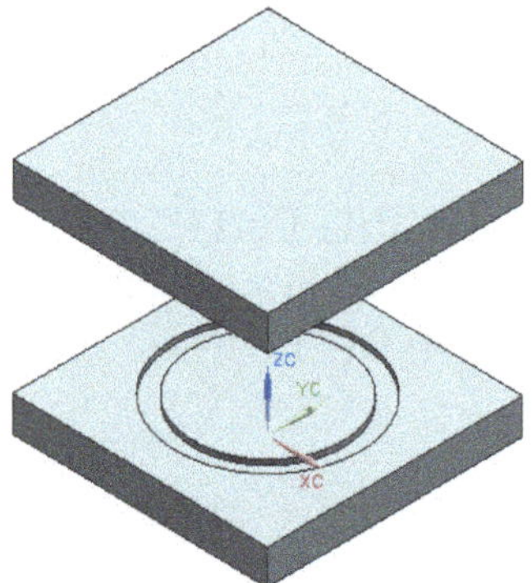

2. On the ribbon, click **Assemblies > Base > Add Component**.
3. Click the **Open** icon on the **Add Component** dialog.
4. Go to the location of the Deformable_part.prt file and double-click on it.
5. Set **Placement** to **Constrain**.
6. Under the **Settings** section, select **Reference set > Entire Part**.
7. Under the **Placement** section, select **Constraint Type > Touch Align**.
8. Under the **Geometry to Constrain** section, select **Orientation > Touch**.
9. Select the flat bottom face of the deformable part.

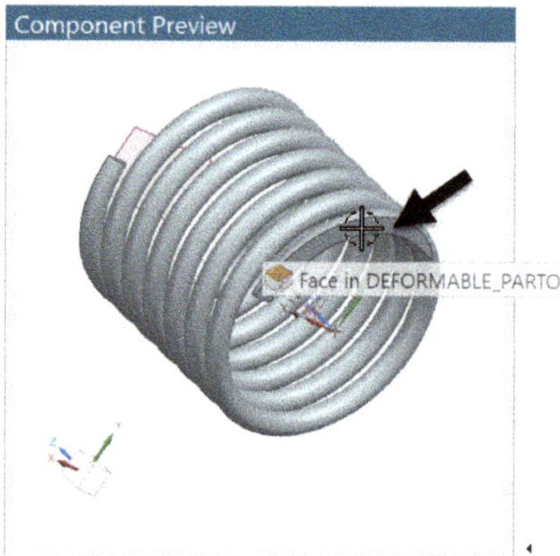

10. Select the flat face of the plate, as shown.

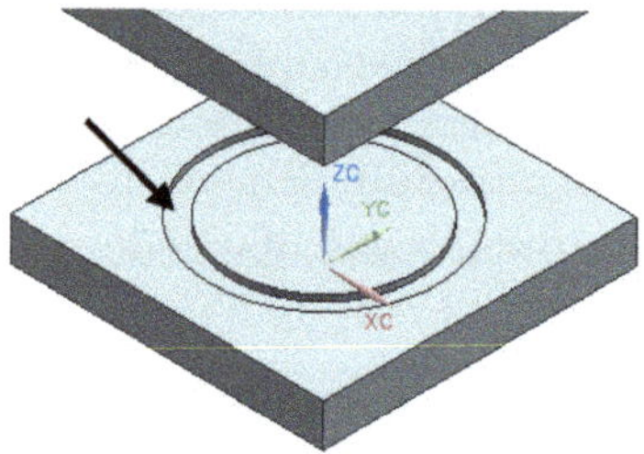

11. Select the flat top face of the deformable part.

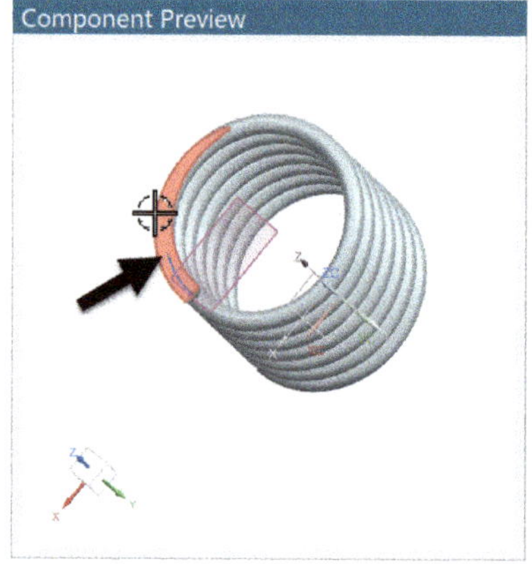

12. Select the flat face of the upper plate, as shown.

13. Under the **Geometry to Constrain** section, select **Orientation > Infer Center/Axis**.
14. Select the Z-axis of the deformable part.

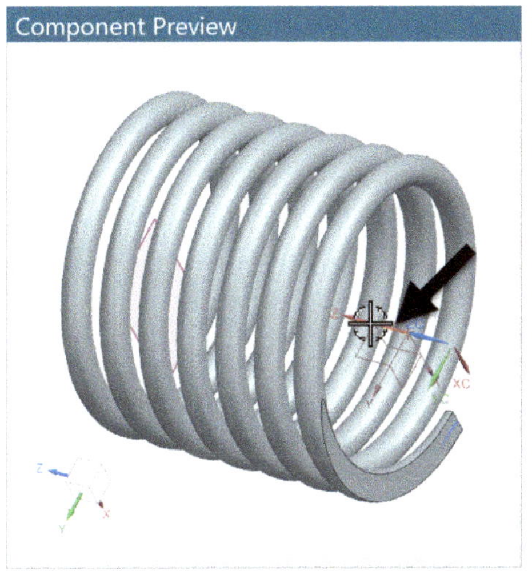

15. Select the select circular edge of the plate.

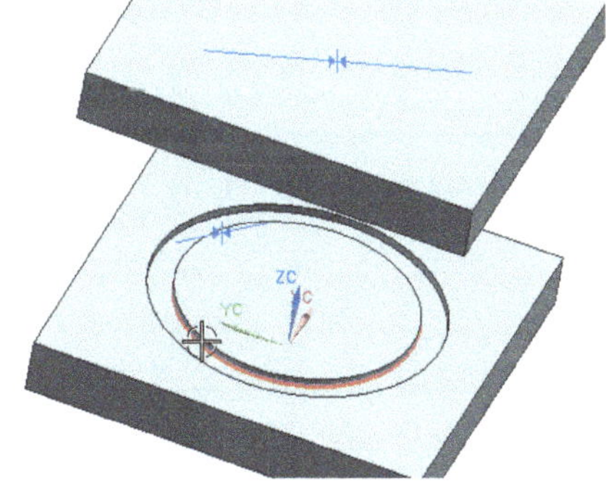

16. Click **OK**.
17. Change the **Pitch** value on the **Deformable_part** dialog to 10 by dragging the slider.
18. Click **OK**.

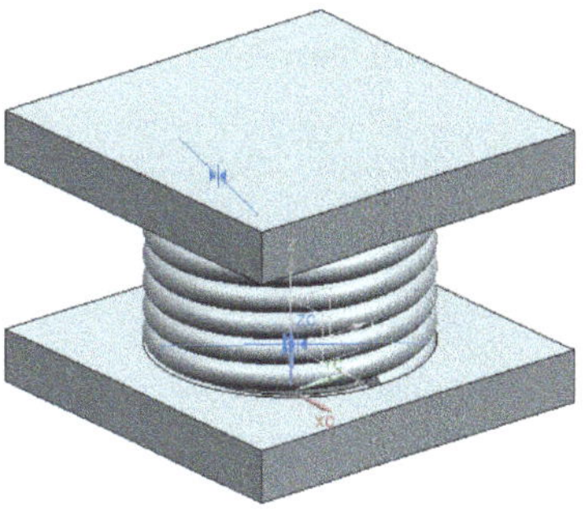

19. On the Resource Bar, click the **Part Navigator** tab.
20. Right click on the **Deformable_part** feature and select **Edit Parameters**.
21. Drag the slider to change the pitch value to **15**.
22. Click **OK**. The assembly is updated.

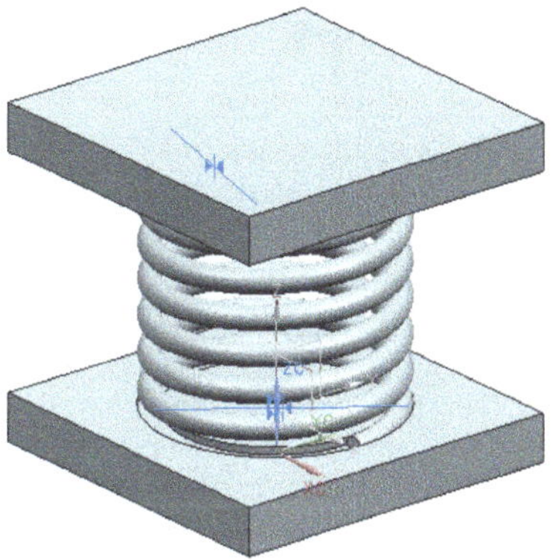

23. Save and close the files.

In this chapter, you will learn to

- Create Centerlines and Center Marks
- Edit Hatch Pattern
- Apply Dimensions
- Place Datum Feature
- Place Feature control frame
- Place Surface Finish symbol

TUTORIAL 1

In this tutorial, you create the drawing shown below.

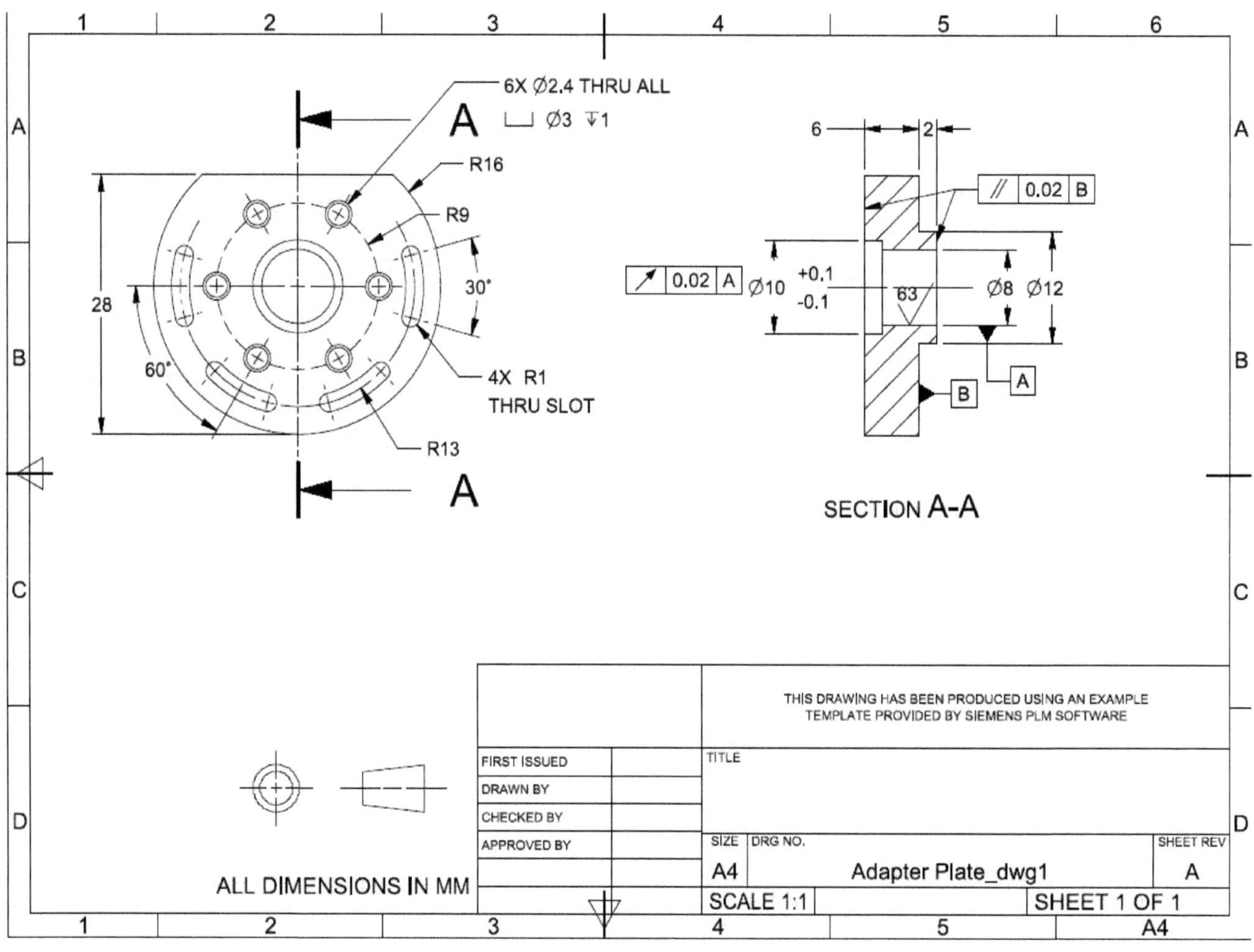

1. Download the Adapter Plate file of Chapter 10.
2. Start NX and click the **New** icon on the ribbon.
3. Click the **Drawing** tab, select **Relationship > Reference Existing Part**.
4. Select the A4 template.
5. Click the **Browse** icon under the **Part to create a drawing of** section.
6. Click **Open** on the **Select master part**.
7. Go to the location of the Adapter Plate file and double-click on it.
8. Click **OK** on the **Select master part** and **New** dialogs.
9. Type your values on the **Populate Title Block** dialog and click **Close**.

Creating a View with Center Marks

1. On the Top Border Bar, click **Menu > Insert > View > View Creation Wizard.**

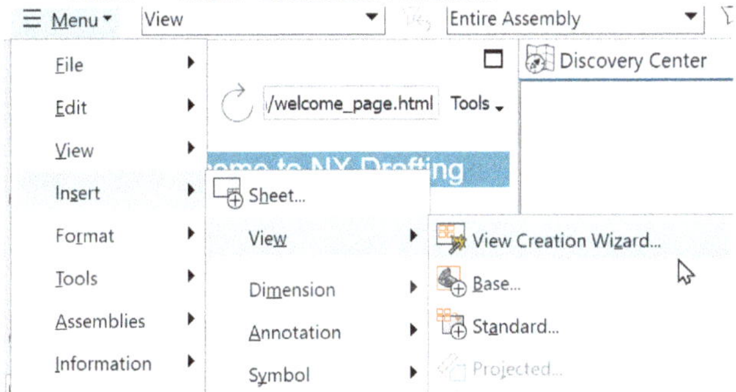

2. Click the **Reset** button on the **View Creation Wizard.**

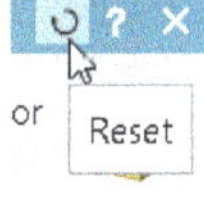

3. Click the **Next** button on the **View Creation Wizard.**
4. On the **Options** page, leave the **Show Centerlines** option selected.
5. Click **Next.**
6. Select **Front** view and click **Finish.**

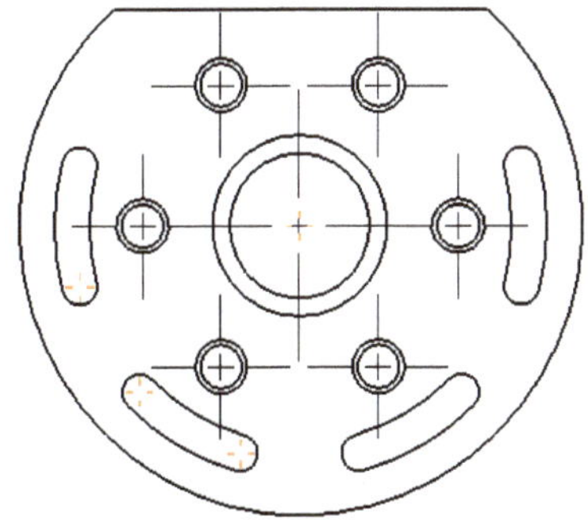

7. Select the view and press **Delete.**
8. On the ribbon, click **Home > View > Base View.**
9. On the **Base View** dialog, expand the **Settings** section and click the **Settings** icon.
10. On the **Settings** dialog, click **General** from the tree.
11. On the **General** page, uncheck the **Create with Centerlines** option and click **OK.**
12. Select **Model View to Use > Front.**
13. Set the **Scale** value to **2:1.**
14. Click on the drawing page, as shown.

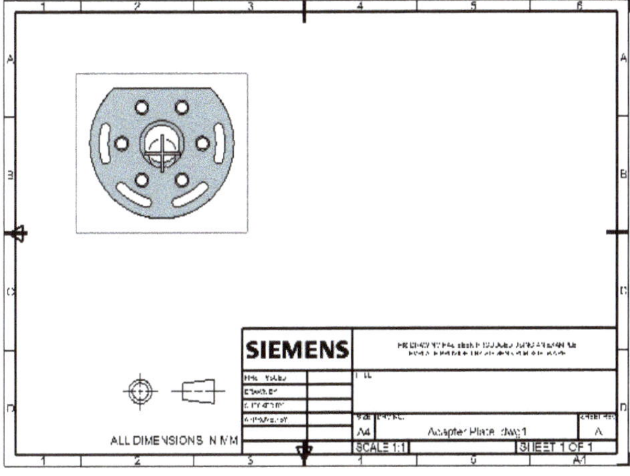

15. Close the **Projected View** dialog.
16. Click **Home > View > Section View** on the Ribbon.
17. Select the center point of the front view.
18. Place the section view on the right side.
19. Click **Close.**

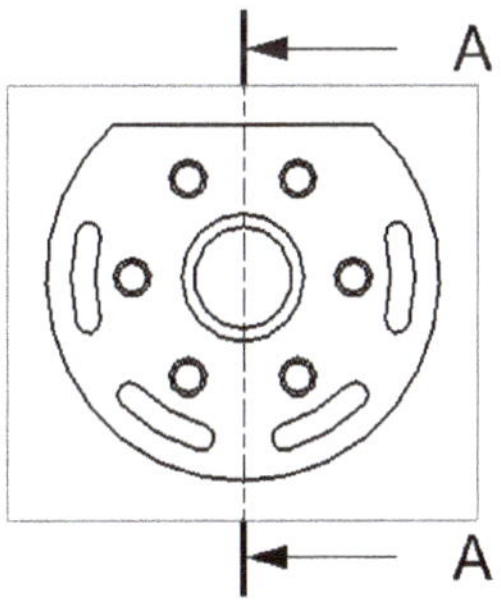

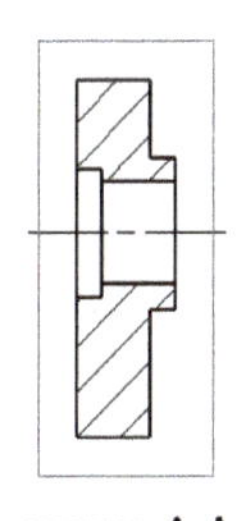

SECTION A-A

Creating Centerlines and Center Marks

1. Click **Home > Annotation > Center Mark > Bolt Circle Centerline** on the Ribbon.
2. On the **Bolt Circle Centerline** dialog, select **Type > Through 3 or More Points.**
3. Leave the **Full Circle** option checked.
4. Select the counterbore hole pattern.

5. Drag the arrow that appears on the centerline to change its Extension length.

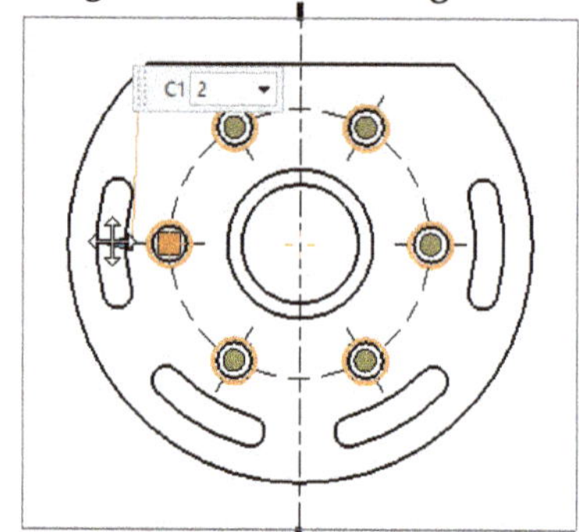

6. Click **OK**.
7. Click **Home > Annotation > Centerline drop-down> Circular Centerline** on the Ribbon.
8. On the **Circular Centerline** dialog, uncheck the **Full Circle** option.
9. Select the center points of the arcs, as shown.

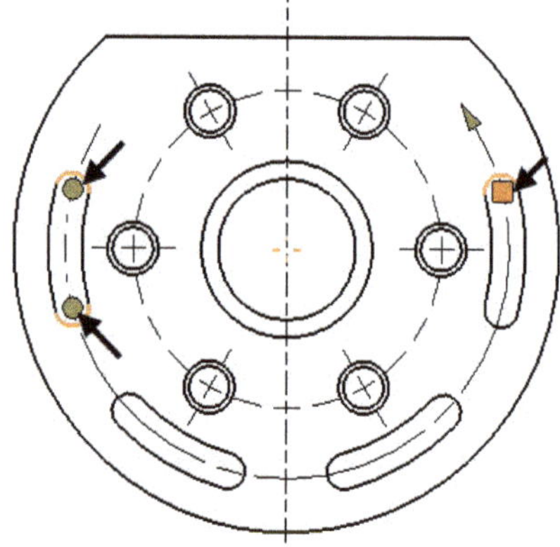

10. Click **OK**.
11. Click **Home > Annotation > Centerline** drop-down> **2D Centerline** on the Ribbon.
12. On the **2D Centerline** dialog, select **Type > By Points.**
13. On the **Snap Options** gallery, activate the **Control Point** and **Intersection** icons, and deactivate the **Arc Center** icon.

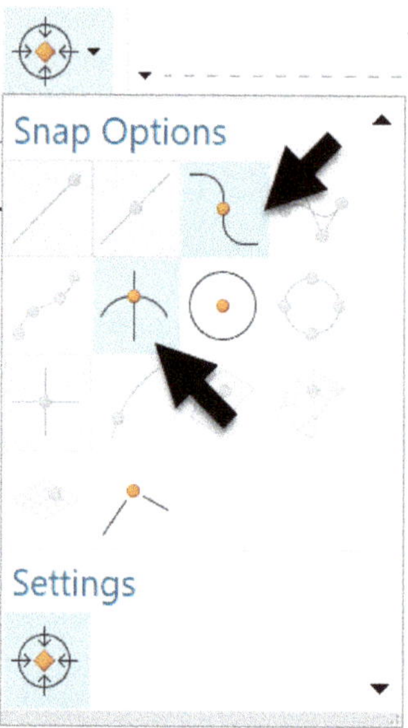

14. Select the points on the slot, as shown.

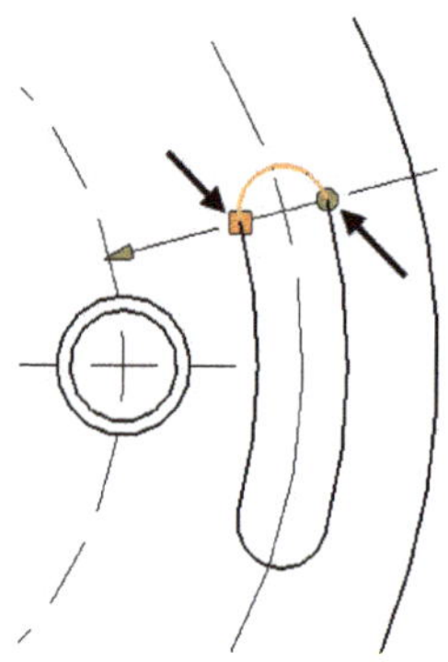

15. Drag the arrow to reduce the length of the centerline.

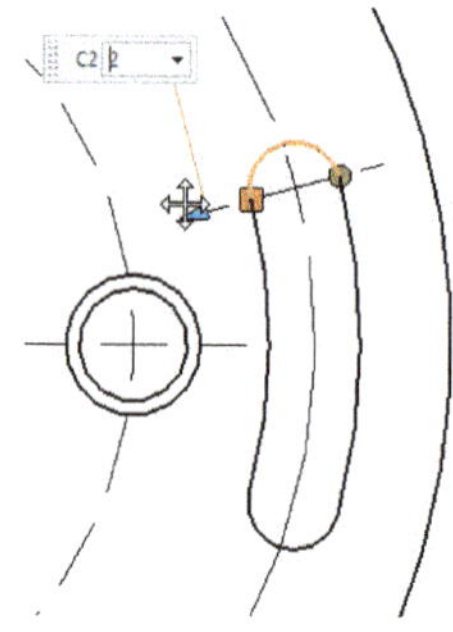

16. Click **Apply**.
17. Likewise, create centerlines on other slots, as shown.

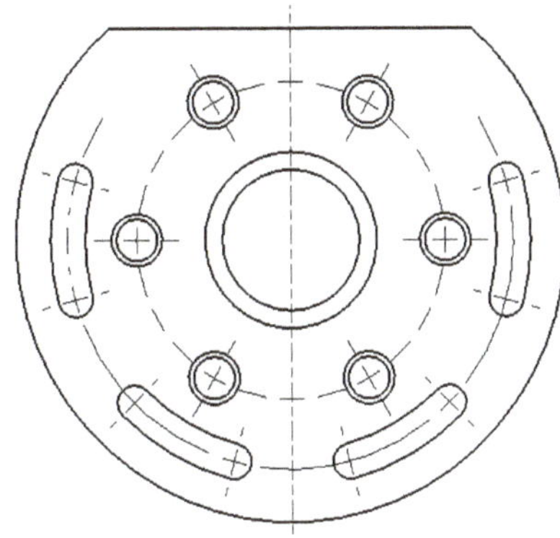

18. Click **Home > Annotation > Centerline drop-down> Automatic Centerline** on the Ribbon.
19. Select the front view and click **OK**; the remaining centerlines are created, as shown.

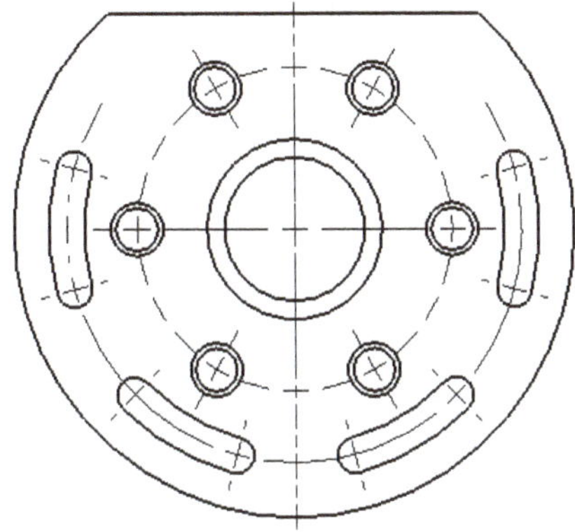

Editing the Hatch Pattern

1. Double-click on the hatch pattern of the section view. The **Crosshatch** dialog appears.
2. On the **Crosshatch** dialog, expand the **Settings** section and notice options to modify the hatch pattern.

You can select the required hatch pattern from the **Pattern** drop-down. You can adjust the distance, angle, color, width, boundary curve tolerance.

You can also select a different set of hatch patterns from the **Crosshatch Definition** drop-down.

3. Click **OK**.

Applying Dimensions

1. On the Top Border Bar, click **Menu > Tools > Drafting Standard**.
2. On the **Load Drafting Standard** dialog, select **Standard > ASME**.
3. Click **OK**.
4. Click **Home > Dimension > Rapid** on the Ribbon.
5. On the **Rapid Dimension** dialog, under the **Measurement** section, select **Method > Vertical**.
6. Select the horizontal edge and the outer arc of the front view.
7. Move the pointer toward the left and click.

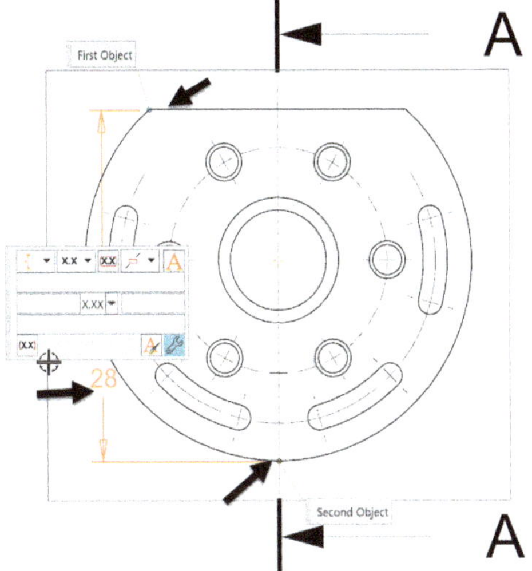

8. On the **Rapid Dimension** dialog, select **Method > Radial**.
9. Create radial dimensions by selecting the circular centerlines, outer arc, and slot arc.

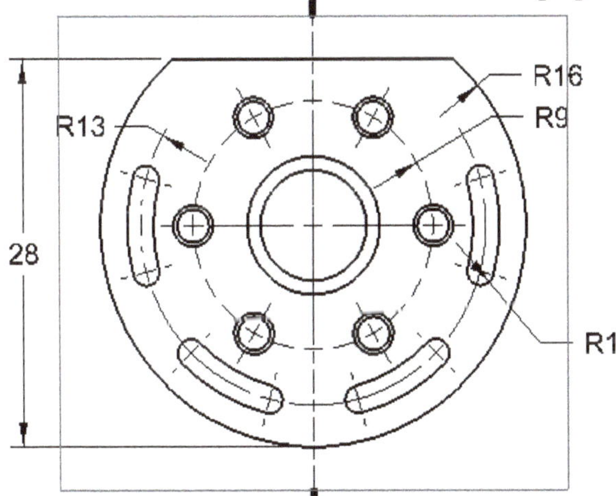

10. On the **Rapid Dimension** dialog, select **Method > Diametral**.
11. Select the counterbore hole and position the diameter dimension, as shown.

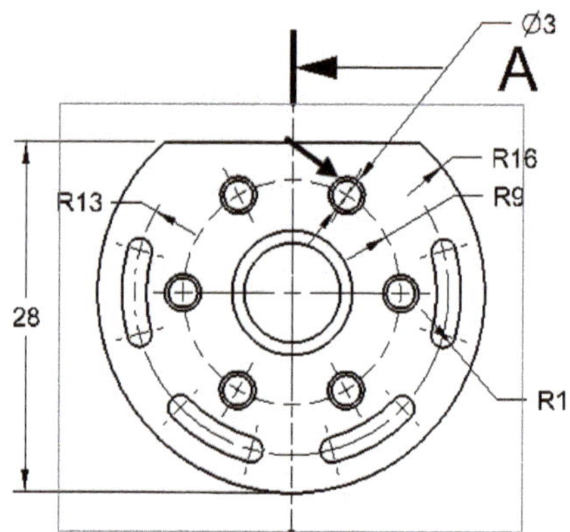

12. On the **Rapid Dimension** dialog, select **Method > Angular**.
13. Select the 2D centerlines of the slot and position the angular dimension, as shown.

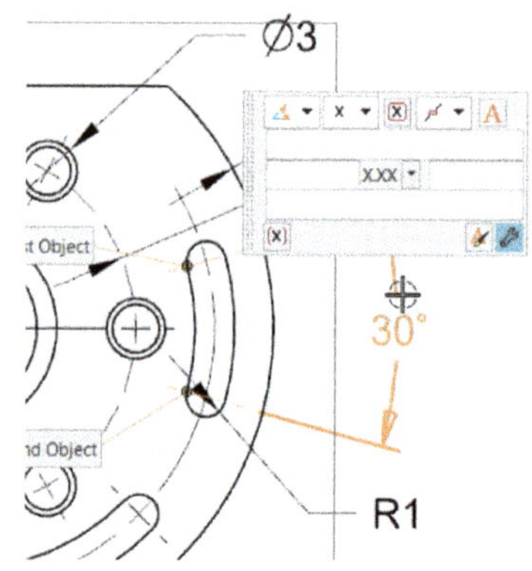

14. Likewise, create another angular dimension, as shown.

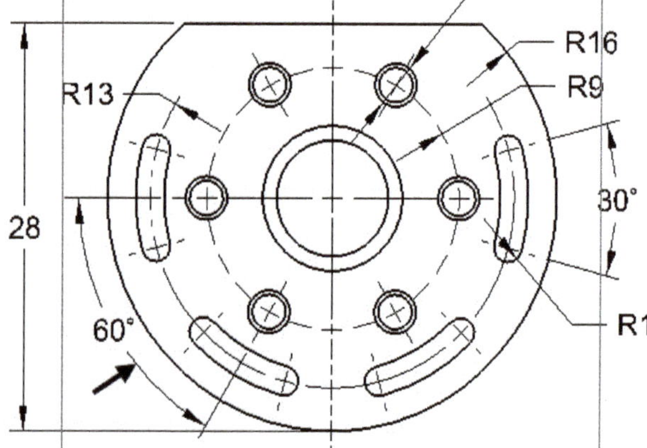

15. On the **Rapid Dimension** dialog, under the **Measurement** section, select **Method > Cylindrical**.
16. Zoom to the section view and select the endpoints, as shown.
17. Move the pointer right and position the dimension.

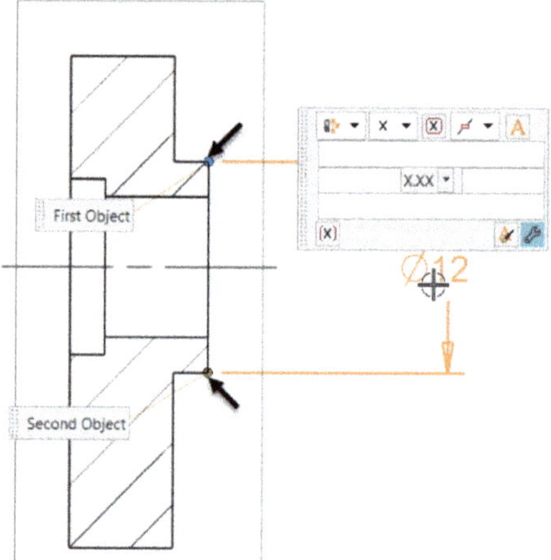

18. Select the horizontal edges of the hole and position the dimension, as shown.

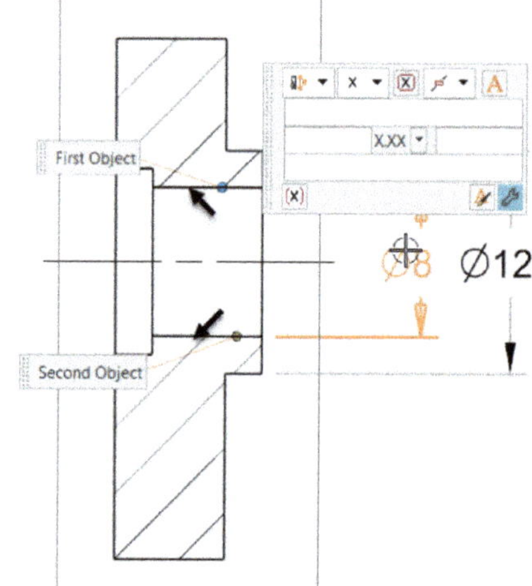

19. Create another cylindrical dimension for the counterbore hole.
20. Click **Home > Dimension > Linear Dimension** on the Ribbon.
21. Select the vertices of the section view, as shown.

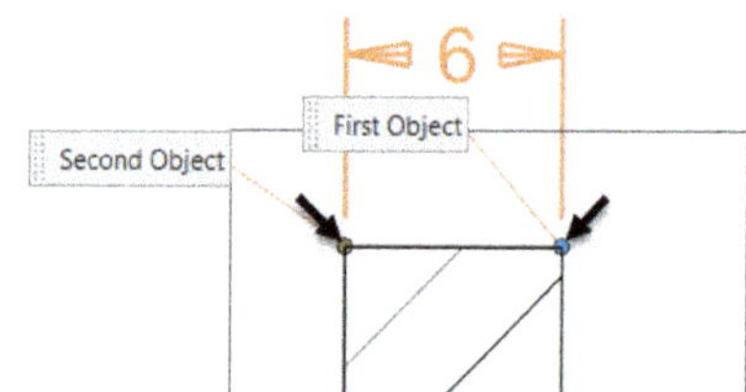

22. Move the pointer up and place the dimension.
23. On the **Linear Dimension** dialog, expand the **Dimension Set** section and select **Method > Chain**.
24. Select the vertex of the section view, as shown.

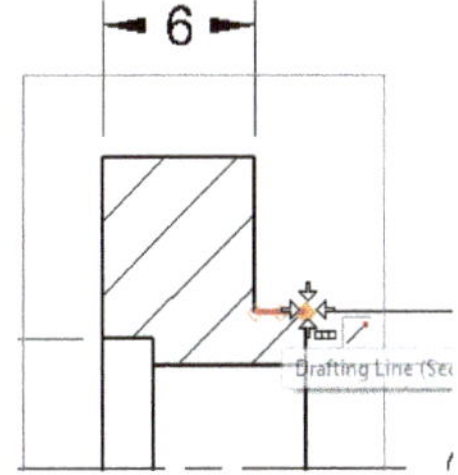

25. Click **Close** on the dialog.
26. Drag the dimension 6 toward left.

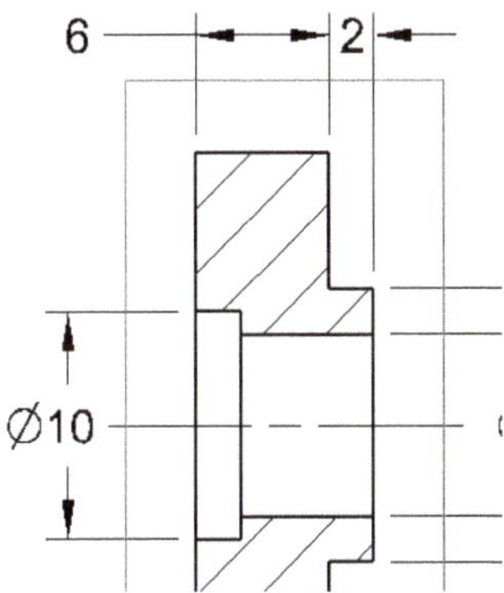

Attach Text to Dimensions

1. Zoom to the front view and double-click on diameter 3.
2. Click the **Arrows Out Diameter** on the palette.
3. Click the **Edit Appended Text** icon.
4. On the **Appended Text** dialog, select **Text Location > Above**.
5. Type 6X in the Text Input box and press the SPACEBAR.
6. On the ribbon, click **General > Insert > Symbol drop-down > Insert Diameter**.

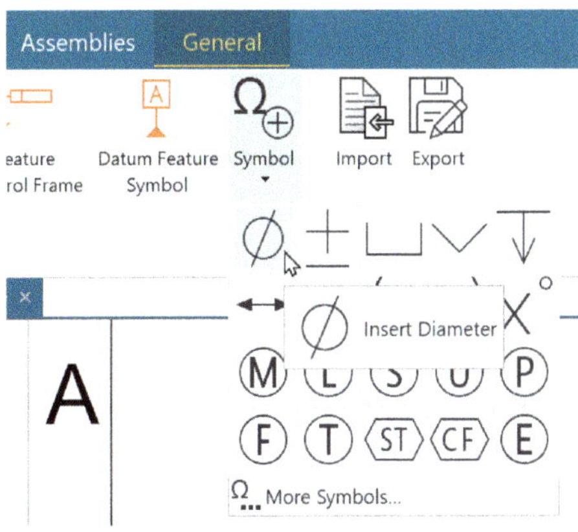

7. Type **2.4 THRU ALL.**

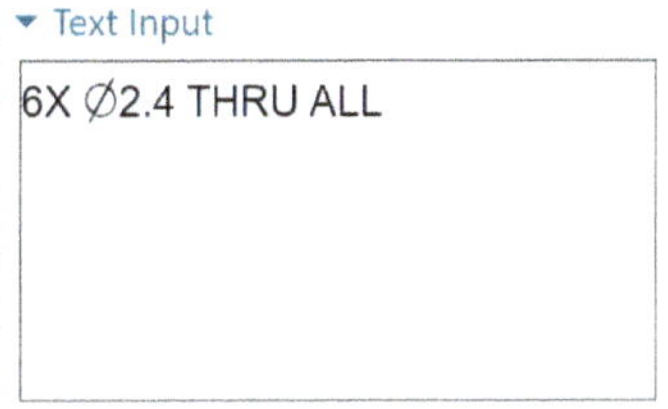

8. Select **Text Location > Before.**
9. On the ribbon, click **General > Insert > Symbol drop-down > Insert Counterbore.**

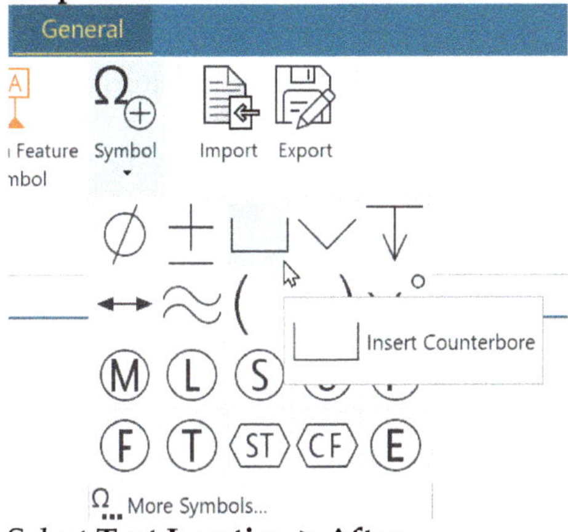

10. Select **Text Location > After.**
11. On the ribbon, click **General > Insert > Symbol drop-down > Insert Depth** .
12. Type **1** in the **Text Input** box.
13. Click **Close** on the dialog.
14. Drag the dimension, as shown.

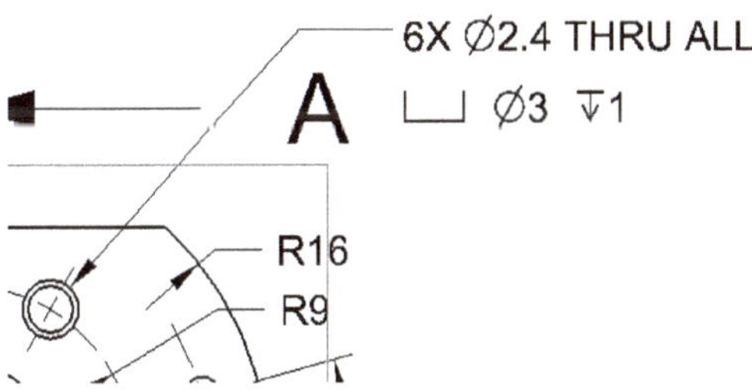

15. Likewise, attach text to the radius dimension of the slot.

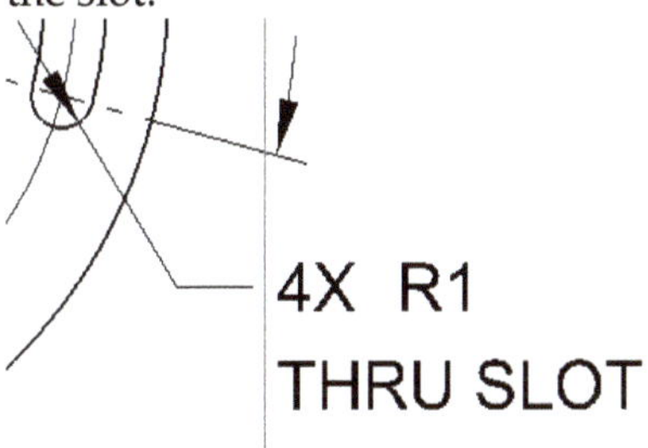

16. Double-click on the radius dimension.
17. Click on the square dot attached to the arrow.
18. Select the **Out** option from the handle.

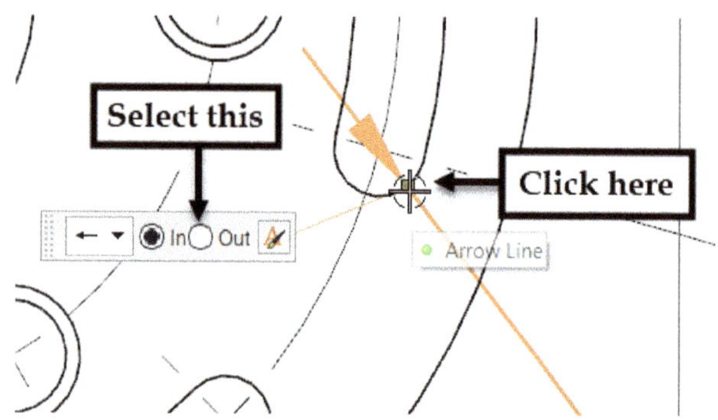

19. Likewise, change the arrow direction of the other radial dimensions.

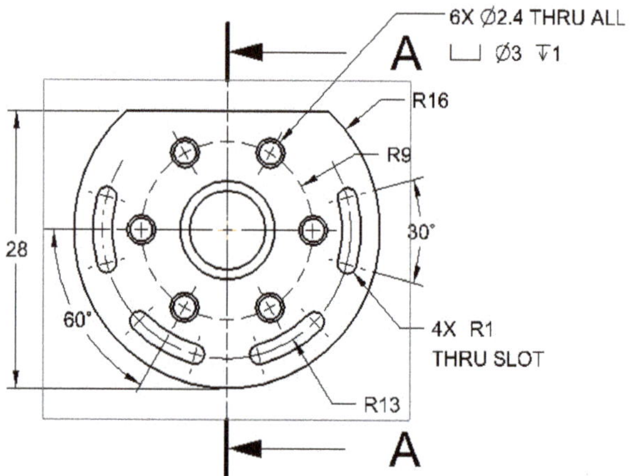

20. Double-click on the counterbore dimension of the section view.
21. On the palette, select **Bilateral Tolerance** from the Tolerance drop-down.
22. Type +0.1 and -0.1 in the tolerances boxes.

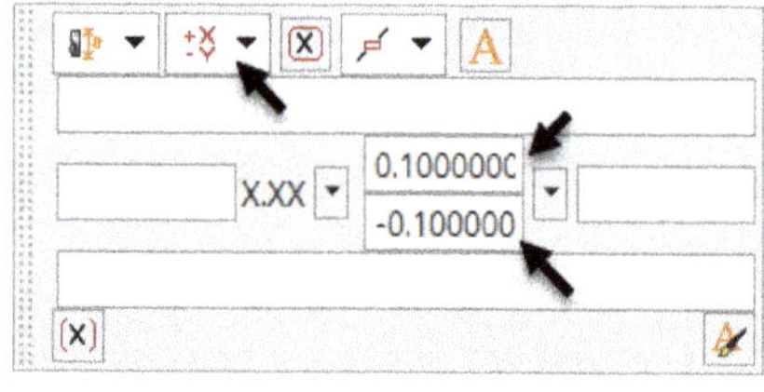

23. Click **Close**.

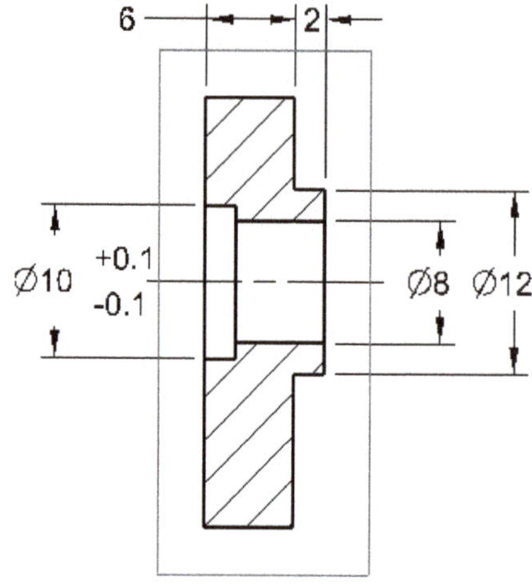

Placing the Datum Feature Symbol

1. Click **Home > Annotation > Datum Feature Symbol** on the Ribbon.
2. On the **Datum Feature Symbol** dialog, expand the **Leader** section and click **Select Terminating Object**.
3. Select the extension line of the dimension, as shown below.

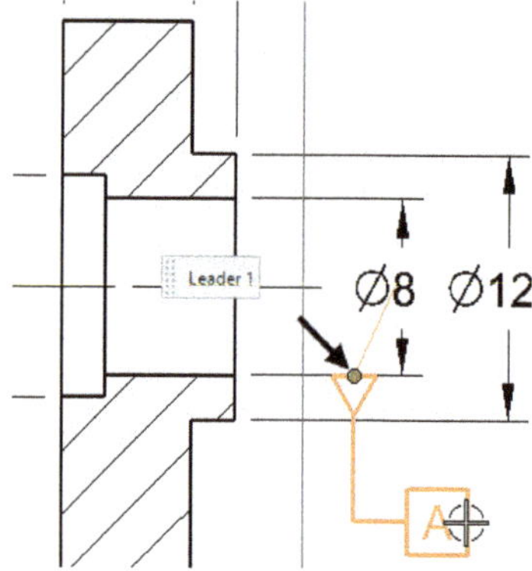

4. Move the cursor downward and click.
5. On the **Datum Feature Symbol** dialog, type **B** in the **Letter** box under the **Datum Identifier** section.
6. Click **Select Terminating Object** and select the vertical edge of the section view, as shown.
7. Move the pointer towards the right and click.
8. Click **Close**.

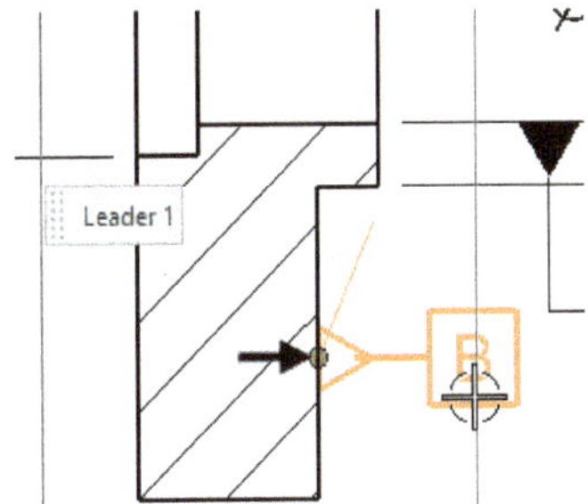

Placing the Feature Control Frame

1. Click **Home > Annotation > Feature Control Frame** on the Ribbon.
2. Place the pointer on the counterbore diameter dimension.
3. Click when a dashed rectangle appears.

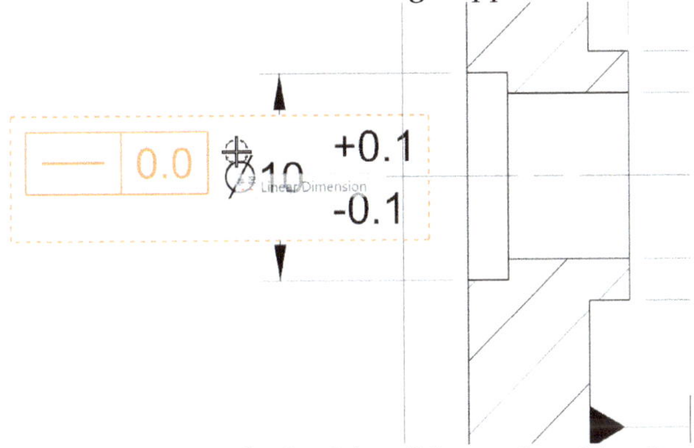

4. On the **General** tab of the ribbon, select **Circular Runout** from the **Characteristic** drop-down.

Characteris...

5. Type-in **0.02** in the **Tolerance** box of the **Tolerance** group.

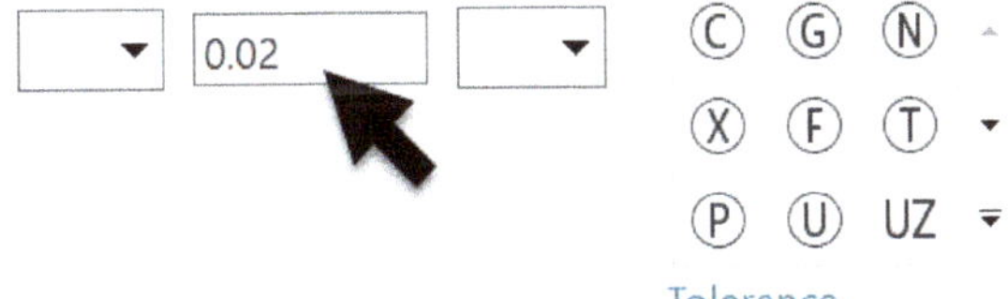

6. Select **A** from the **Primary** drop-down available on the **Datum Reference** group.

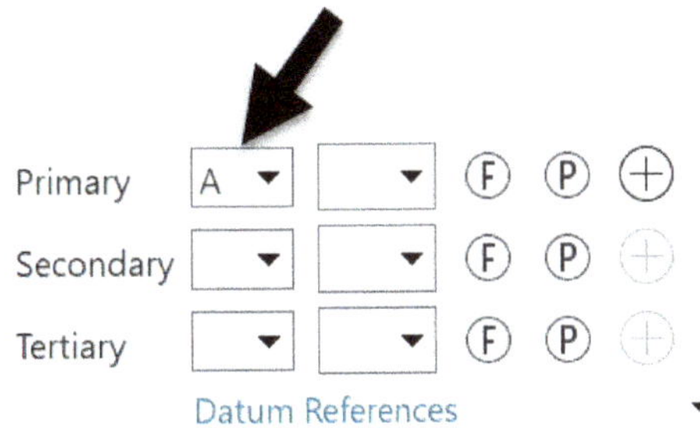

7. Click **Apply** on the dialog.
8. On the dialog,
9. Expand the Leader section, and click **Select Terminating Object**.
10. Select an edge parallel to the Datum B.
11. Click **Select Terminating Object** and select another edge which is parallel to the Datum B.

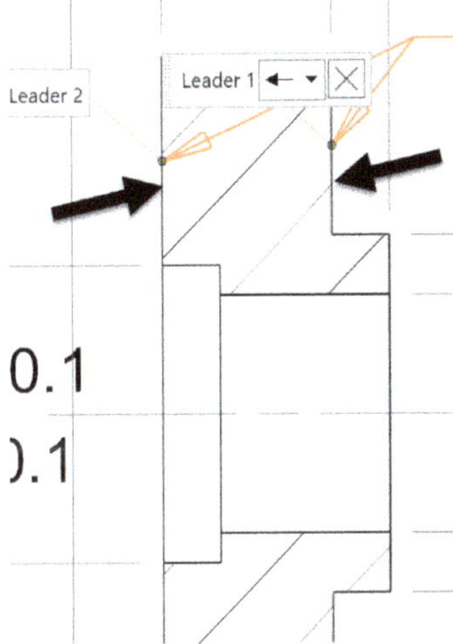

12. Move the pointer toward right and click.
13. On the **General** tab of the ribbon, select **Parallelism** from the **Characteristic** drop-down.

Characteris...

14. Type-in **0.02** in the **Tolerance** box.
15. Select **B** from the **Primary** drop-down available on the **Datum Reference** group.
16. Click **OK**.

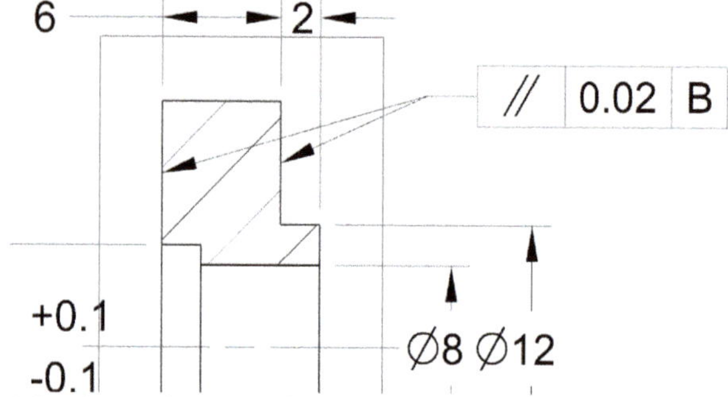

Placing the Surface Texture Symbols

1. Click **Home > Annotation > Surface Finish Symbol** on the Ribbon.
2. Set the **Roughness (a)** value to 63 on the dialog.
3. Click on the inner cylindrical face of the hole, as shown below.

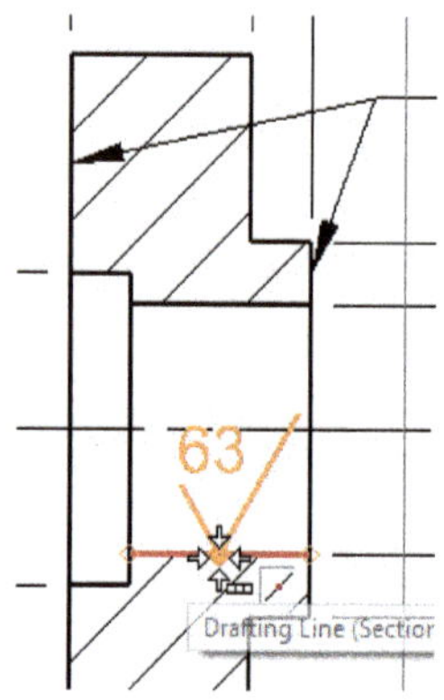

4. Click **Close**.
5. Save and close the file.

Chapter 11: Simulation Hands-on Tutorial

TUTORIAL 1

In this tutorial, you perform Finite Element Analysis on a part.

1. Download the Tutorial 1-part file of Chapter 11, and open it.

2. On the ribbon, click **Application > Simulation > Pre/Post** .
3. On the Simulation Navigator, select Tutorial 1.prt.
4. On the ribbon, click **Home > Context > New FEM and Simulation** .

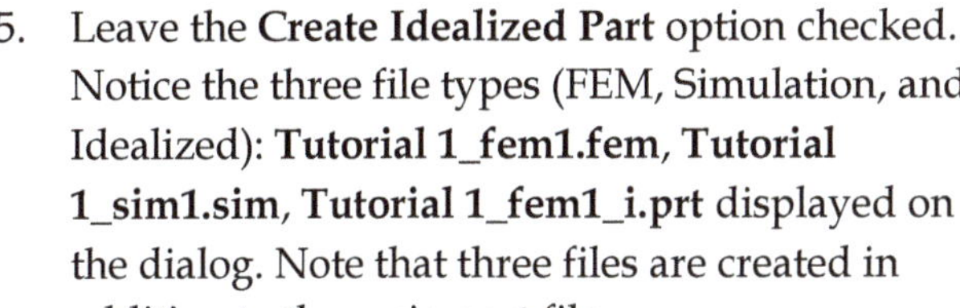

5. Leave the **Create Idealized Part** option checked. Notice the three file types (FEM, Simulation, and Idealized): **Tutorial 1_fem1.fem**, **Tutorial 1_sim1.sim**, **Tutorial 1_fem1_i.prt** displayed on the dialog. Note that three files are created in addition to the main part file.
6. Under the **Solver Environment** section, select **Solver > NX Design Simulation.**
7. Select **Analysis Type > Structural.**
8. Click **OK.**

On the **Simulation Navigator**, notice the **Status** of the Simulation and FEM files.

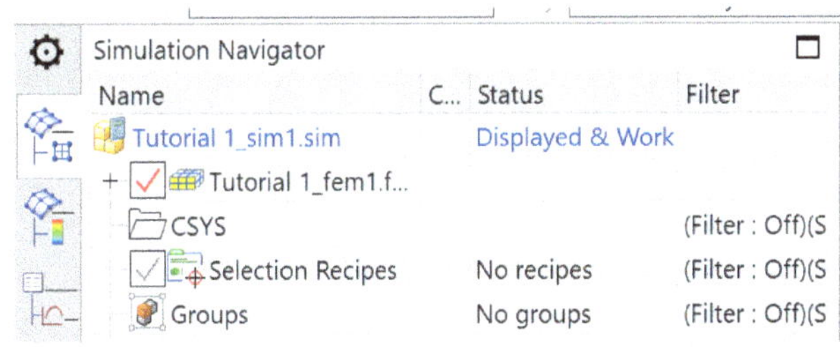

9. Expand the **Simulation File View** section, right click on **Tutorial 1_sim1**, and click **Save.** The simulation tools are displayed on the ribbon.

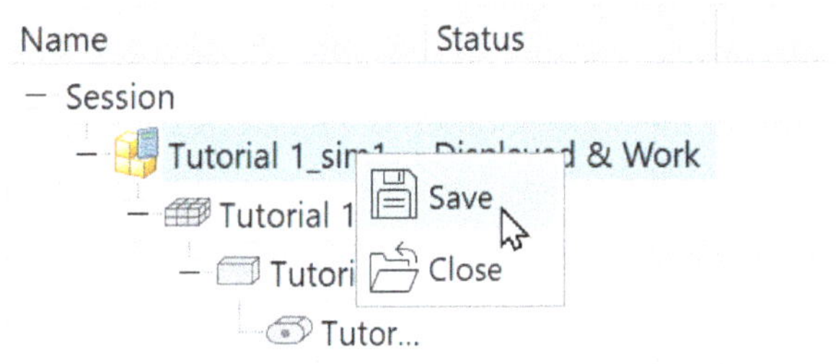

Preparing the Idealized Part

1. Hide the **Simulation File View** section.
2. On the ribbon, click **Home > Context > Change Displayed Part.**
3. On the **Change Displayed Part** dialog, select the Tutorial 1_fem1_i.prt.
4. Click **OK.**
5. Click **OK** on the **Idealized Part Warning** message box. Notice the Status of the idealized part.

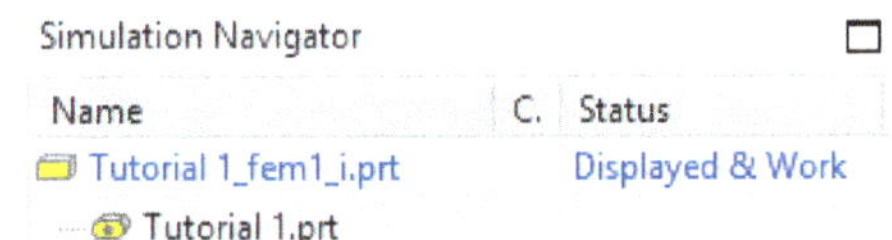

6. On the ribbon, click **Home > Start > Promote** .
7. Select the geometry from the graphics window and click **OK.** The program establishes an associative link between the idealized part and

the main part file.

Now, you need to prepare the idealized part by removing some features such as holes and blends.

8. On the ribbon, click **Home > Synchronous Modeling > Delete Face**.
9. On the **Delete Face** dialog, select **Type > Hole**, and uncheck the **Select Holes by Size** option.
10. Select the circular face of the counterbore, as shown.

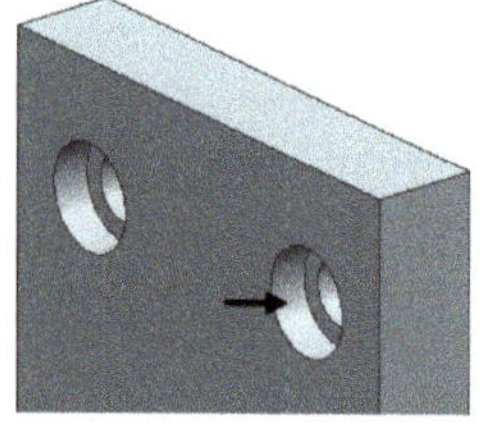

11. Select the other counterbore holes, as shown.

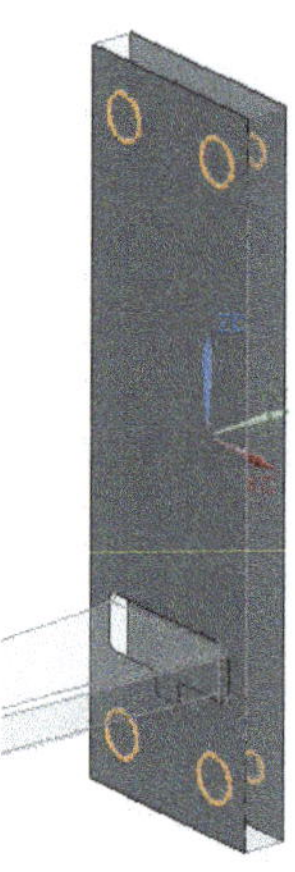

12. Click **Apply** to delete the counterbore holes.
13. On the **Delete Face** dialog, select **Type > Blend**.
14. Select the edge blends of the geometry and click **OK**.

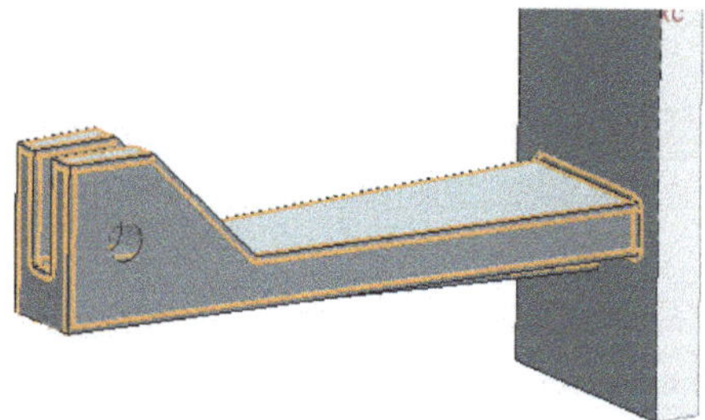

15. Click **Save** on the **Quick Access Toolbar**. Now, you need to switch to the FEM file.

Meshing the FEM file

1. On the ribbon, click **Home > Context > Change Displayed Part**.
2. Select **Tutorial 1 _fem1.fem** and click **OK**. The **Information** window appears showing the **CAE Polygon Update Log**.
3. Close the **Information** window. Also, notice the **Status** of the **Tutorial 1 _ fem1.fem** file on the Simulation Navigator.
4. On the ribbon, click **Home > Properties > Mesh Collector** .
5. On the **Mesh Collector** dialog, select **Element Family > 3D**.
6. Click the **Create Physical Properties** icon.
7. On the **PSOLID** dialog, type Cantilever in the **Name** box.
8. Click the **Choose Material** icon.
9. On the **Material List** dialog, select **Steel** from the **Material** section and click **OK**.
10. Click **OK** on the **PSOLID** and **Mesh Collector** dialogs.
11. On the ribbon, click **Home > Mesh > 3D Tetrahedral** .
12. Select the geometry from the graphics window.
13. On the **3D Tetrahedral Mesh** dialog, select **Type > CTETRA (10)**. You can also set the element type to **CTETRA (4)**.
14. Set the **Element Size** to **3**.
15. Expand the **Destination Collector** section, uncheck the **Automatic Creation** option, and make sure that the **Mesh Collector** is set to **Solid (1)**.
16. Click **OK** to generate the mesh.

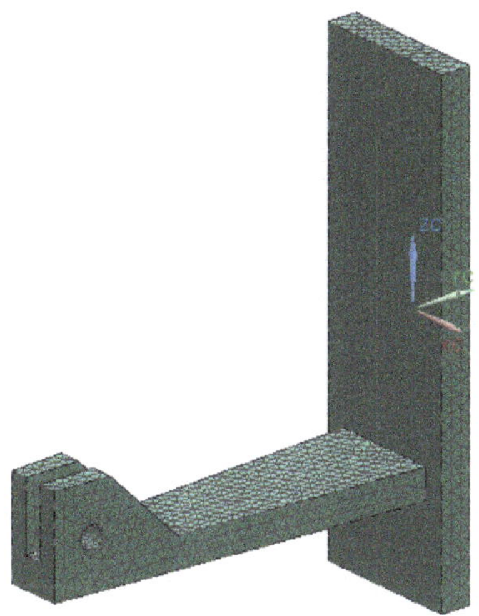

You can edit or remove the mesh from the Simulation Navigator.

17. Expand the **3D Collectors** node in the **Simulation Navigator** and notice the mesh properties.

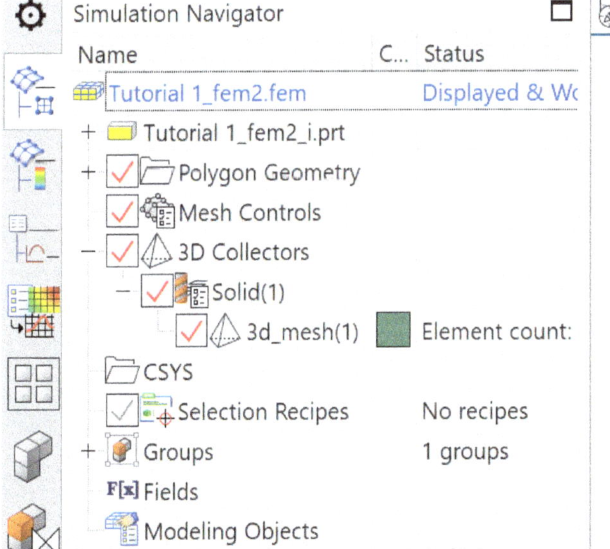

18. Click **Save** on the Quick Access Toolbar.

Applying Loads and Constraints to the Simulation file

1. On the ribbon, click **Home > Context > Change Displayed Part** .
2. Select **Tutorial 1 _sim1.sim** and click **OK**.
3. On the **Simulation Navigator**, expand the Tutorial 1_fem1 node and uncheck the **3D Collectors** node. The mesh is turned OFF.
4. On the ribbon, click **Home > Solution > Solution**.

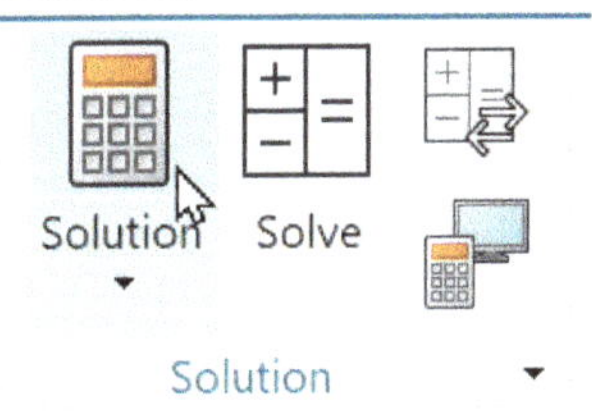

5. Click **Create Solution** on the **Solution** dialog.
6. On the **Solution** dialog, check the **Element Iterative Solver** option, and click **OK**.
7. On the ribbon, click **Home > Loads and Conditions > Load Type > Force**.

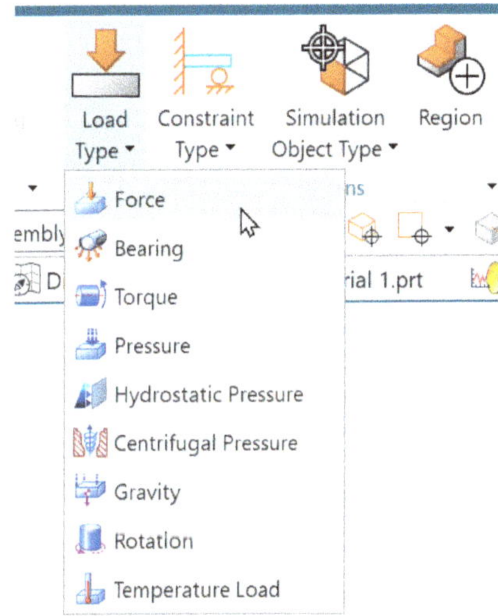

8. Select the holes, as shown.

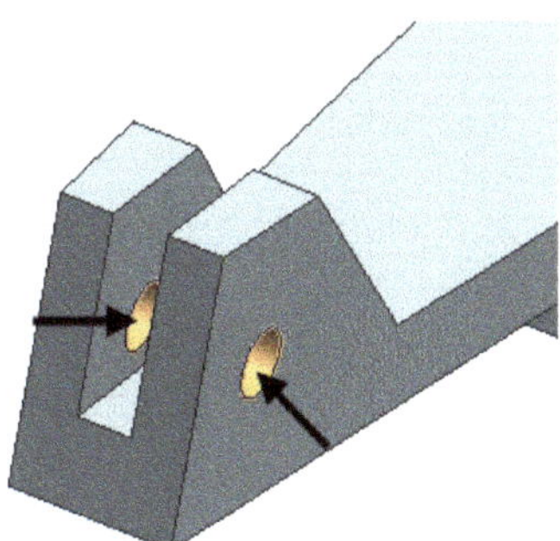

9. Under the **Magnitude** section, type **2000** in the **Force** box.
10. Under the **Direction** section, click **Specify Vector** and select the Z-axis from the triad.

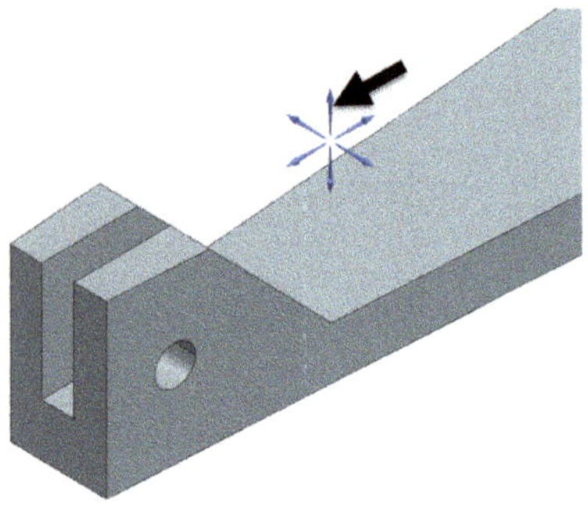

11. Click the **Reverse Direction** button.
12. Click **OK** to apply the Force load.
13. On the **Simulation Navigator**, expand the **Load Container** node, right click on **Force 1**, and select **Edit Display**.

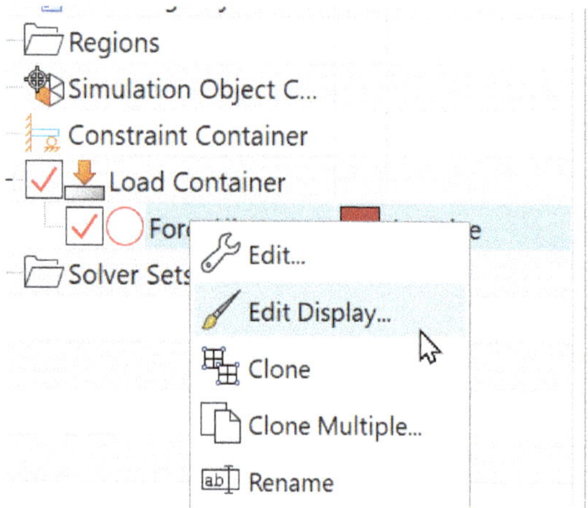

14. On the **Boundary Condition Display** dialog, drag the **Scale slider** to reduce the size of the load arrows.

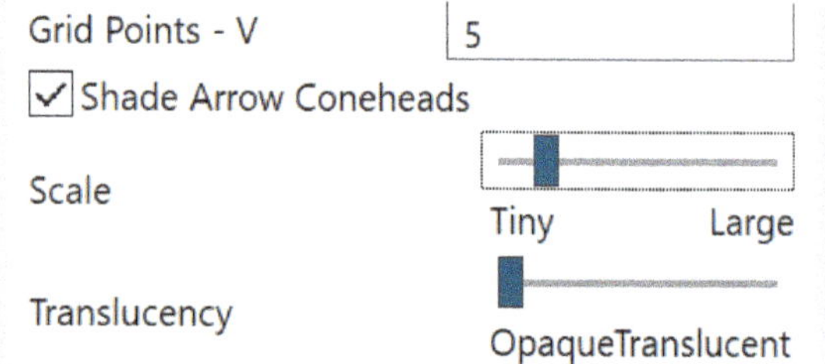

15. Click **OK**.
16. On the ribbon, click **Home > Loads and Conditions > Constraint Type > Fixed Constraint**.

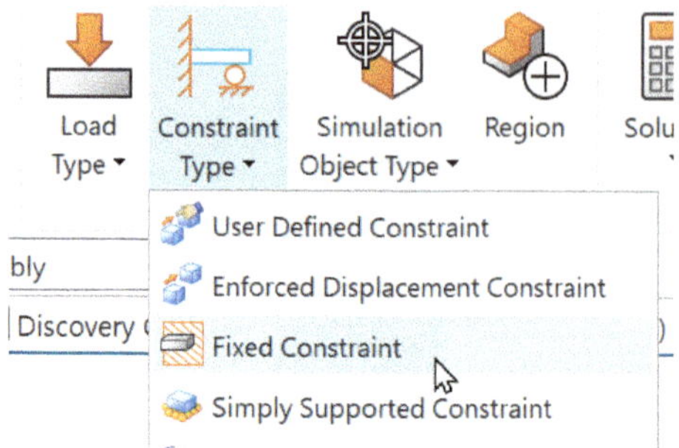

17. Select the back face of the geometry and click **OK**.

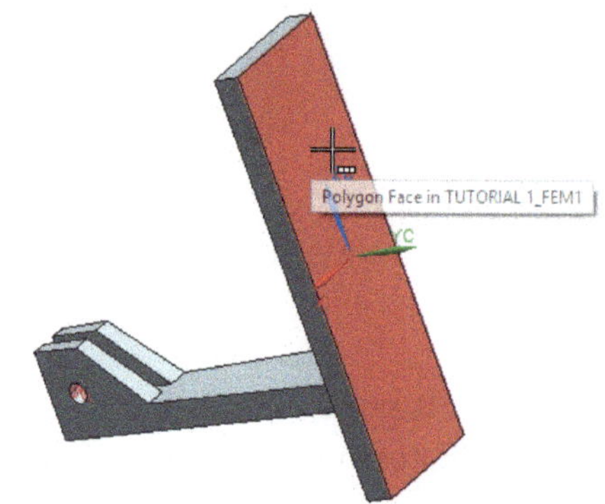

18. Click **Save** on the Quick Access Toolbar.

Simulating the Model

Now, you need to check whether the simulation model is setup properly.

1. On the ribbon, click **Home > Checks and Information > More > Model Setup**.

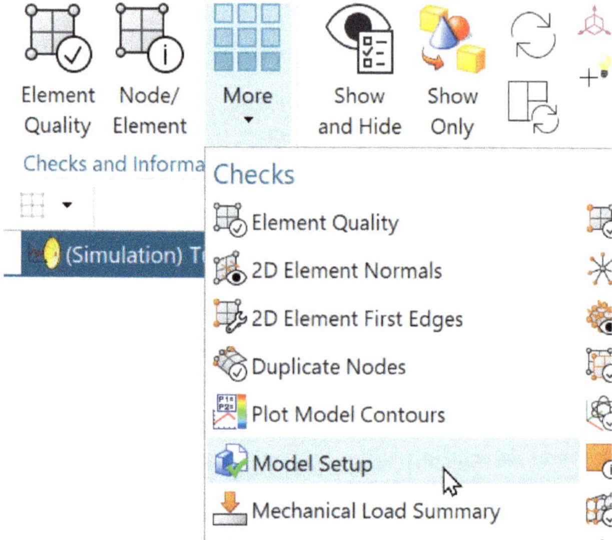

2. Leave all the options checked on the **Model Setup** dialog and click **OK**.

The program checks for any errors during the model setup and displays them in the **Information** window. Also, the Solution-Based Errors Summary displays the following information.

Solution-Based Errors Summary

Iterative Solver Option

More than 80 percent of the elements in this model are 3D elements.

It is therefore recommended that you turn ON the Element Iterative Solver in the "Edit Solution" dialog.

3. Close the **Information** window.
4. On the ribbon, click **Home > Solution > Solve** .
5. Click **OK** on the **Solve** dialog.
6. Close the **Information** window, **Solution Monitor**, and click **Cancel** on the **Analysis Job Monitor** dialog.
7. On the ribbon, click **Home > Context > Activate Meshing > Open Results**.

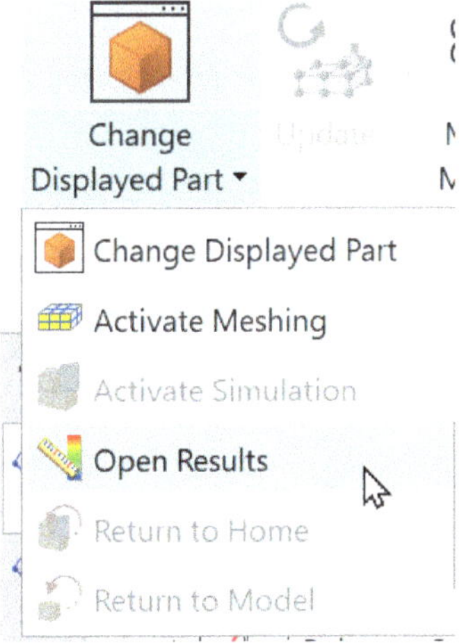

8. On the **Post Processing** Navigator, go to **Solution 1 > Structural** > **Stress - Element-Nodal**.
9. Double-click on **Von-Mises**. The result will appear.

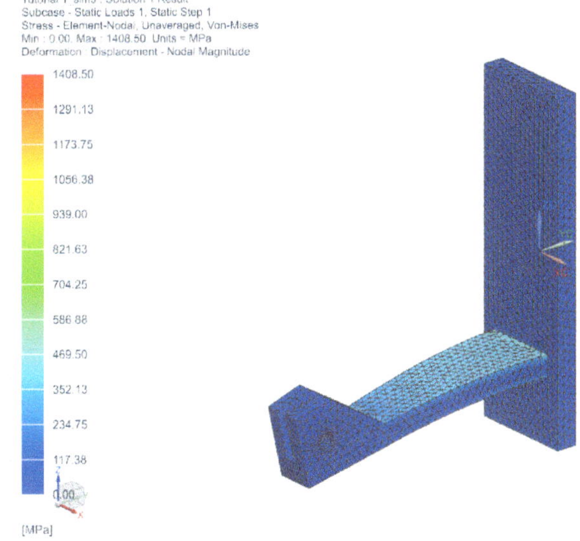

10. On the ribbon, click **Results > Animation > Play** . The model is simulated in the graphics window.
11. Click **Stop** on the **Animation** group.
12. On the **Post Processing** Navigator, expand **Solution 1 > Structural** > **Displacement – Nodal**.
13. Double-click on **Z**. The result will appear.

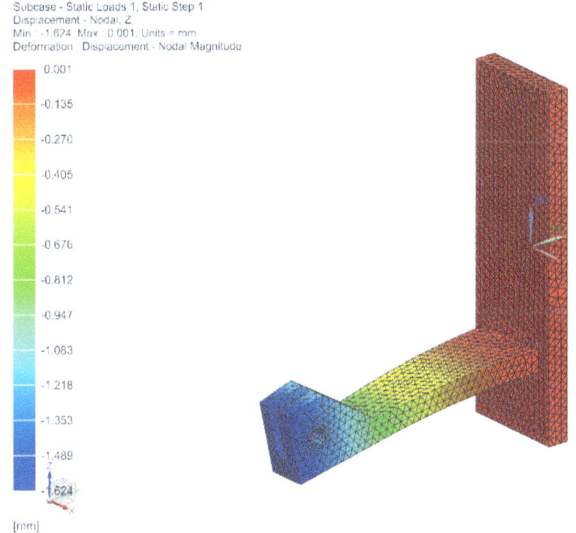

14. On the ribbon, click **Results > Context > Return to Home** .
15. Click **File > Close > All Parts**.
16. Click **Yes Save and Close**.

17. Click **Yes**.

Chapter 12: Product and Manufacturing Information

Providing dimensions and annotation in 2D drawings is a common and well-known method. However, you can provide product and manufacturing information to 3D models, as well. The PMI tools help you to add this information to 3D models based on universal standards such as ASME Y14.5 - 2009 and ISO 1101: 1983.

In this chapter, you will learn to use **PMI** tools to add GD&T information to parts. The **PMI** tools are available on the **PMI** tab of the ribbon. If the **PMI** tab is not displayed by default, you can add it to the ribbon. Click the **Application** tab on the ribbon, and then click the **PMI** icon on the **Design** group.

TUTORIAL 1

In this tutorial, you will add PMI dimensions and annotations to the part model.

1. Download the Tutorial 1 part file from the companion website.
2. Open the Tutorial 1 part file.
3. On the ribbon, **Application > Document > Toolbox > PMI.**

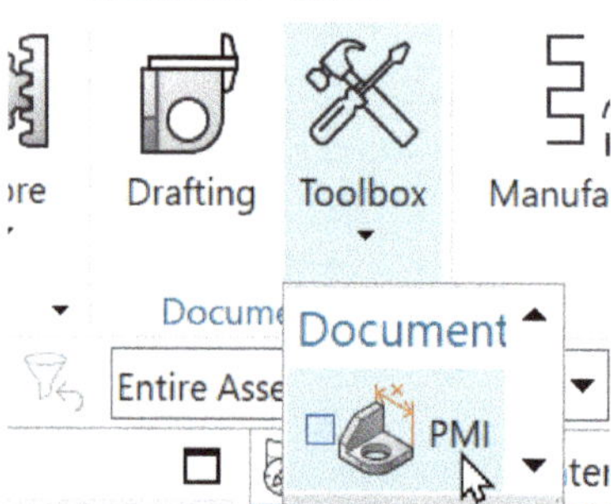

4. On the ribbon, click **PMI > Annotation > Datum Feature Symbol** .
5. On the **Datum Feature Symbol** dialog, type **A** in the **Letter** box under the **Datum Identifier** section.
6. Select the alternate plane from the graphics window, as shown.

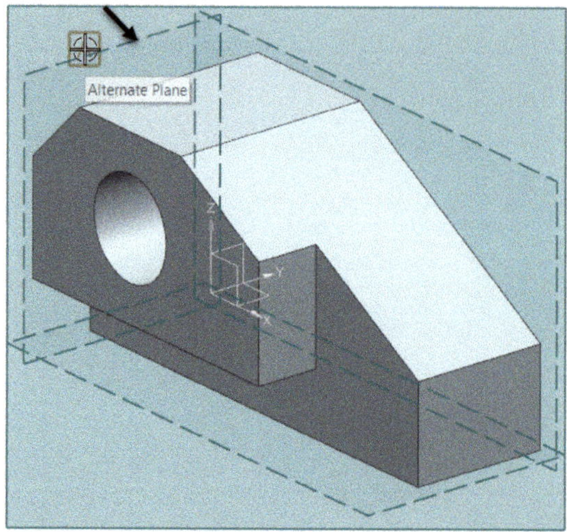

7. Expand the **Leader** section, and then click **Select Terminating Object.**
8. Select the front face of the geometry.
9. Move the pointer and click to position the datum.

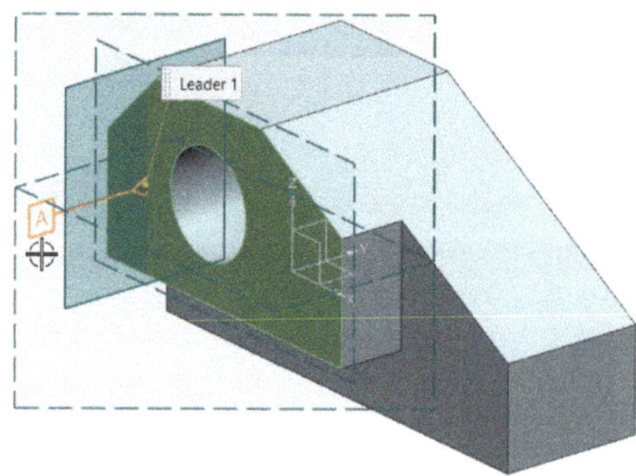

10. Select the alternate plane from the graphics window, as shown.

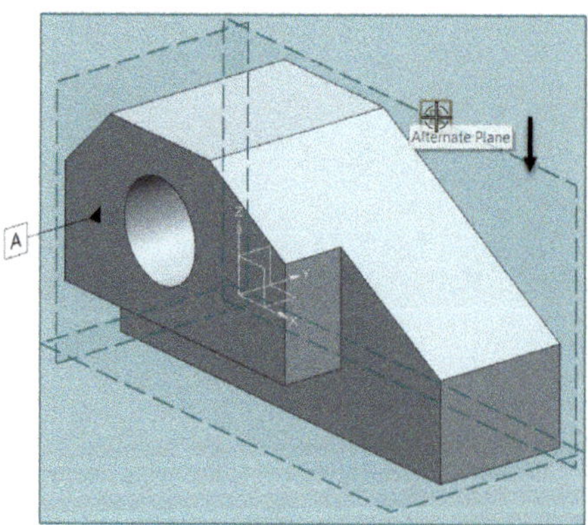

11. Click **Leader > Select Terminating Object.**
12. Select the top face of the model.

13. Move the pointer upward, and click to position the **B** datum.

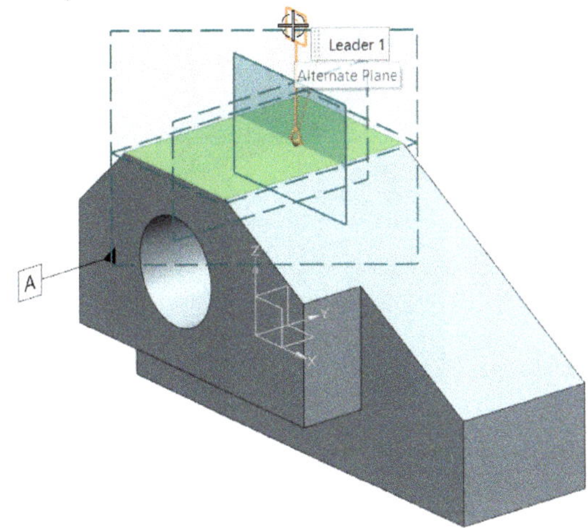

14. Select the alternate plane from the graphics window, as shown.

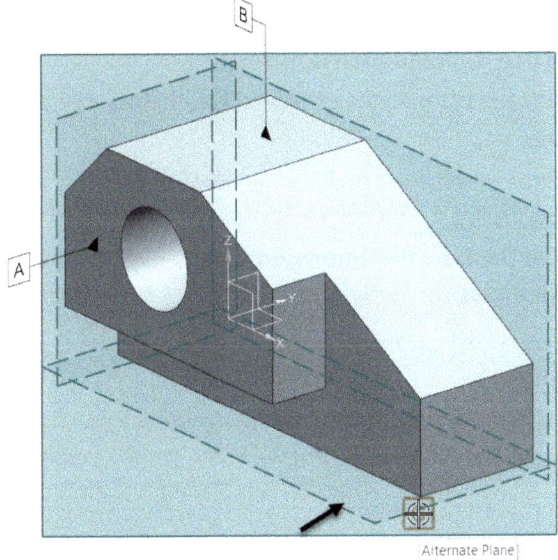

15. Click **Leader > Select Terminating Object**.
16. Select the right face of the model.
17. Move the pointer toward the right and click to position the C datum.

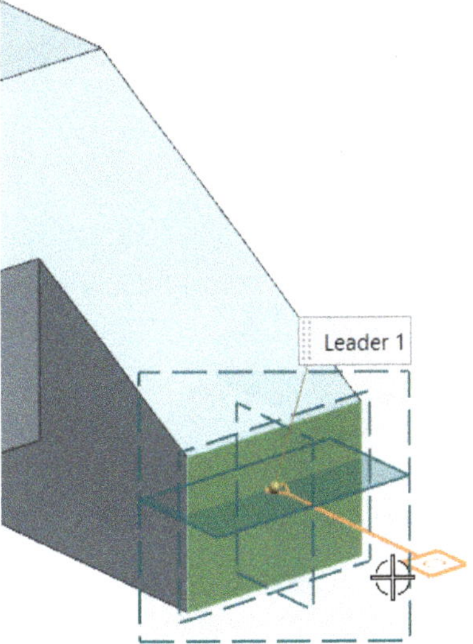

18. Click **Close** on the **Datum Feature Symbol** dialog.
19. Click the **MBD** tab on the Navigator.
20. In the MBD Navigator, expand the **Annotation** node.

Notice the three plane features in the **Annotation** tree.

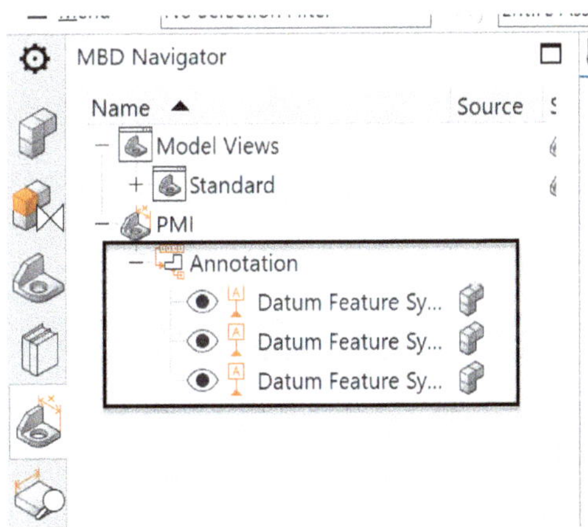

You can click and drag the datum feature symbol.

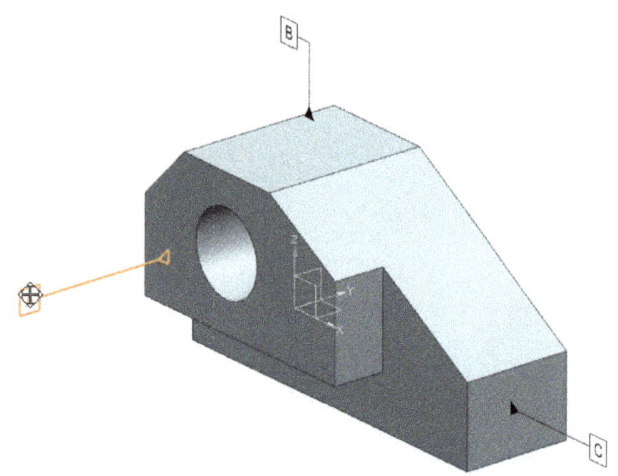

Adding Hole and Thread Callout

1. On the **File** tab of the ribbon, click **Preferences > PMI**.
2. On the **PMI Preferences** dialog, expand the **Dimension** node, and then select **Tolerance**.
3. On the **Tolerance** page, under the **Type and Values** section, select **Type > Equal Bilateral Tolerance** ±X .
4. Type **2** in the **Decimal Places** box.
5. Type **0.25** and **-0.25** in the **Upper Limit** and **Lower Limit** boxes, respectively.
6. Expand the **Text** node, and then select **Units**.

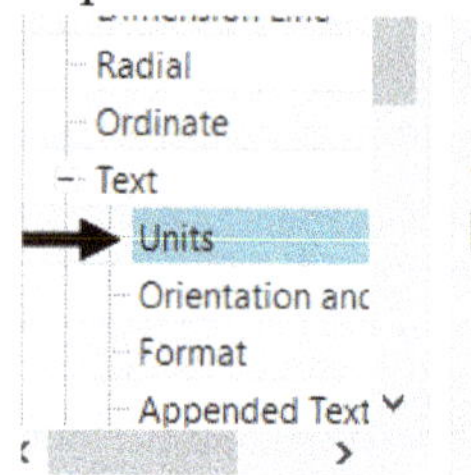

7. On the **Units** page, select **Decimal Delimiter > Period.**
8. Click **OK** on the **PMI Preferences** dialog.
9. On the ribbon, click **PMI > Dimension > Hole and Thread Callout** .
10. On the **Hole and Thread Callout** dialog, select **Type > Radial**.
11. Select the hole and place the dimension, as shown.

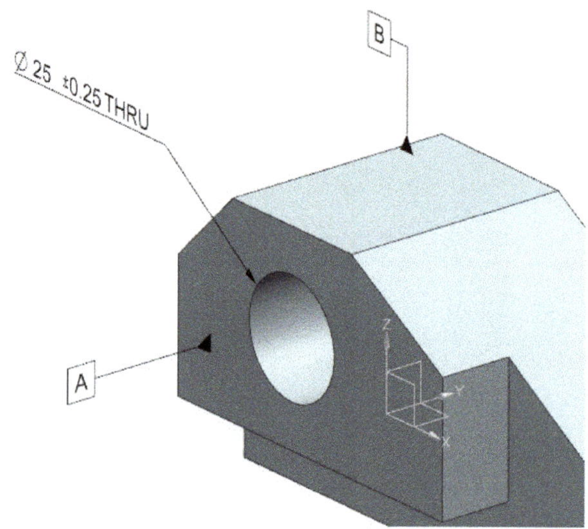

12. Click **Close** on the **Hole and Thread Callout** dialog.

Adding Linear Dimensions

1. On the ribbon, click **PMI > Dimension > Linear** .
2. Select the lower horizontal edge of the geometry.
3. On the **Linear Dimension** dialog, expand the **Orientation** section, and then click the **Alternate Plane** button.
4. Move the pointer downward and click to position the dimension.

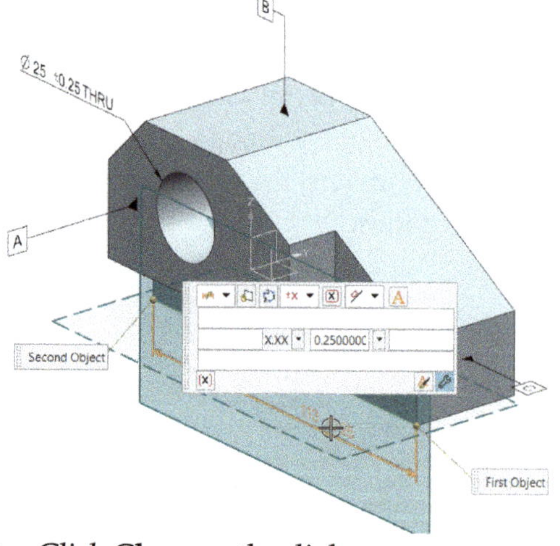

5. Click **Close** on the dialog.

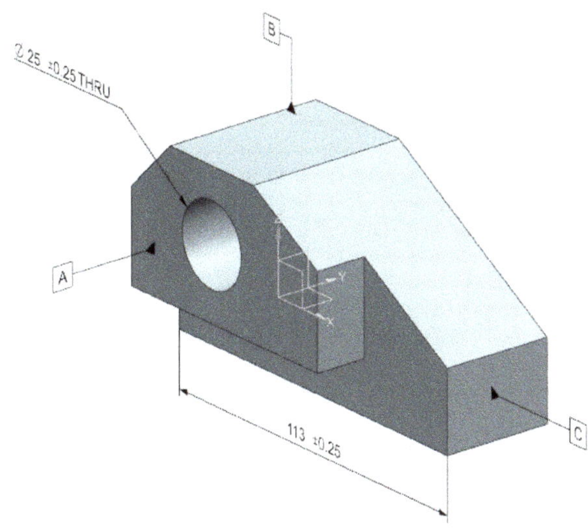

Adding Chamfer Dimensions

1. On the ribbon, click **PMI > Dimension > Chamfer** .
2. Rotate the model and click on the chamfer.
3. Click on the top face of the model to define the reference face of the chamfer (the face from which the chamfer angle is measured).
4. On the Dimension palette, select the **Leader Perpendicular to Chamfer** option from the drop-down available at the bottom.

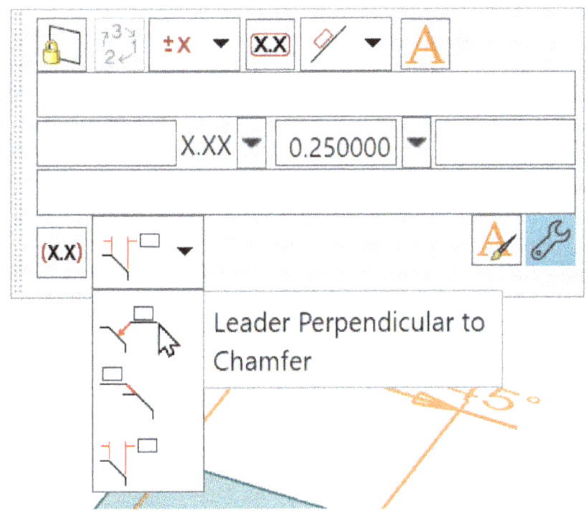

5. Move the pointer and click to position the chamfer dimension.
6. Click **Close** on the **Chamfer Dimension** dialog.

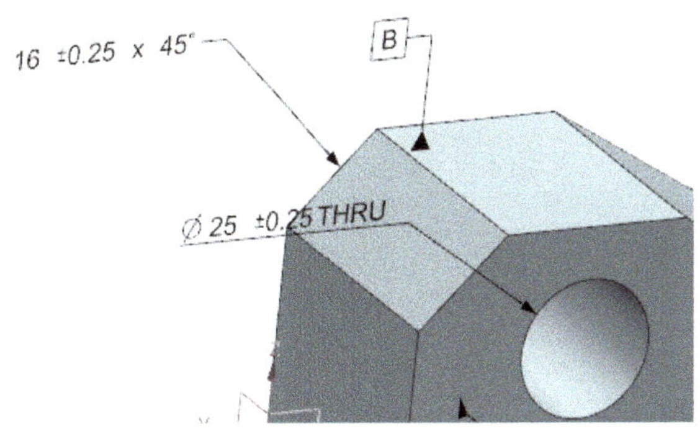

Adding Angular Dimensions

1. On the ribbon, click **PMI > Dimension > Angular** .
2. On the **Angular Dimension** dialog, select **Selection Mode > Objects.**
3. Select the angled and horizontal faces, as shown.
4. Move the pointer toward the right, and then click to place the angular dimension.

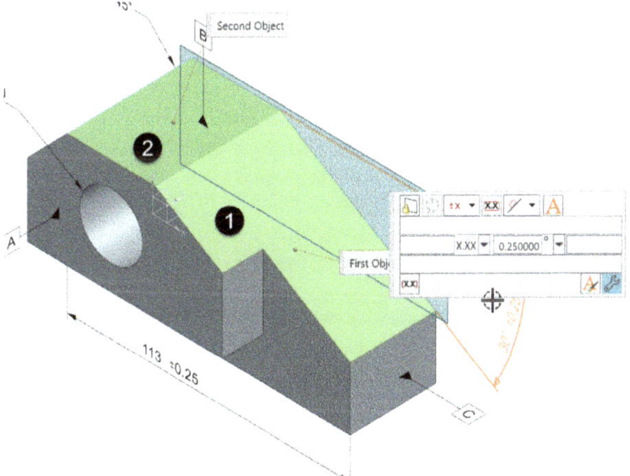

5. Click **Close** on the **Angular Dimensions** dialog.

Using the Rapid command

1. On the ribbon, click **PMI > Dimension > Rapid**

   .
2. Click the **Reset** icon on the **Rapid Dimension** dialog.
3. Click on the two faces of the model, as shown.

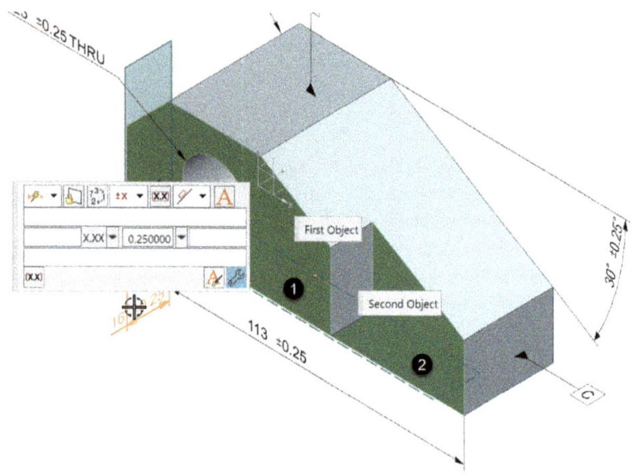

4. On the **Rapid Dimension** dialog, expand the **Orientation** section, and then click the **Alternate Plane** button.
5. Move the pointer downward and click to position the dimension, as shown.

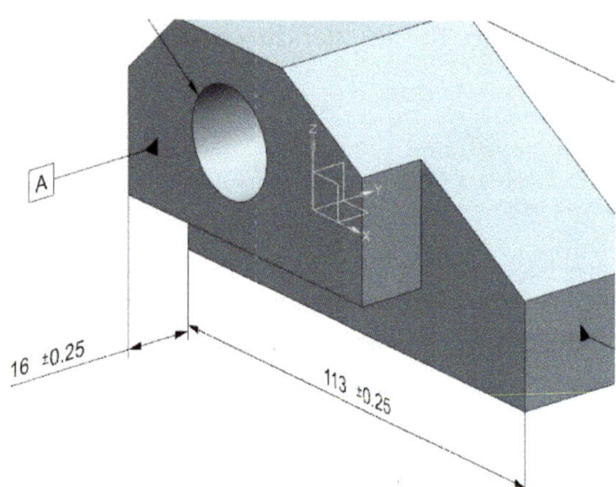

Adding Thickness Dimensions

1. On the ribbon, click **PMI > Dimension> Thickness** .
2. On the **Thickness Dimension** dialog, click the **Reset** icon.
3. Select the two edges of the model, as shown.

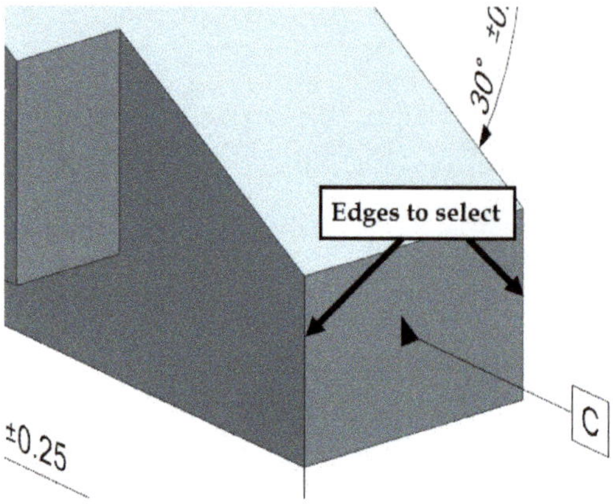

4. On the **Thickness Dimension** dialog, select **Origin** > **Orientation > Specify Plane.**
5. Select the face of the model, as shown; the dimension is placed on the orientation plane.

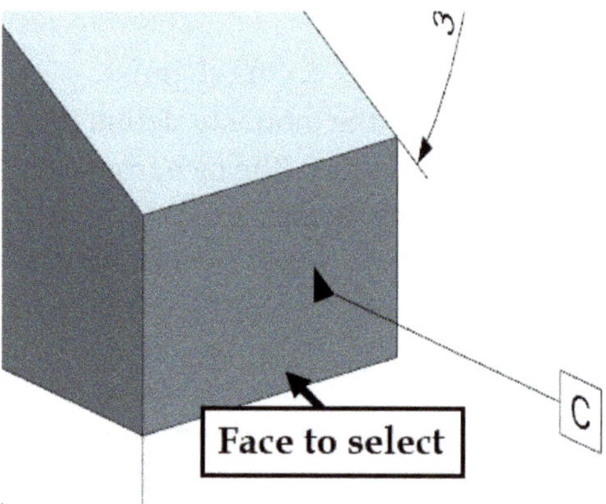

6. Move the pointer downward and click to position the dimension.

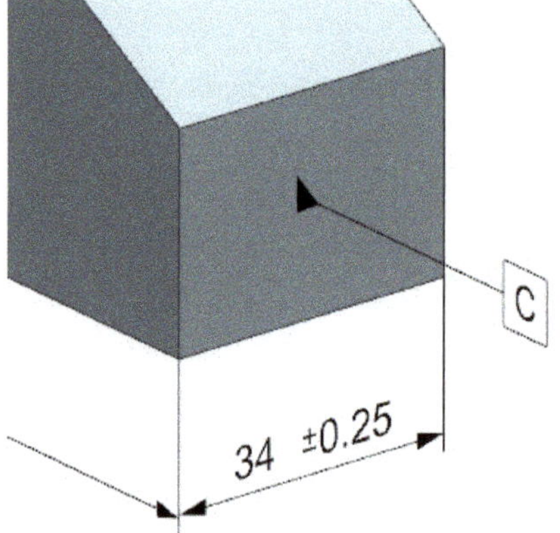

Adding Feature Control Frame

1. On the ribbon, click **PMI > Annotation > Feature Control Frame** .

2. On the **Feature Control Frame** dialog, click the **Reset** icon.
3. In the graphics window, place the pointer on the bottom edge of the radial dimension of the hole, as shown; the **Feature Control Frame** snaps to the dimension, and a dashed box appears.

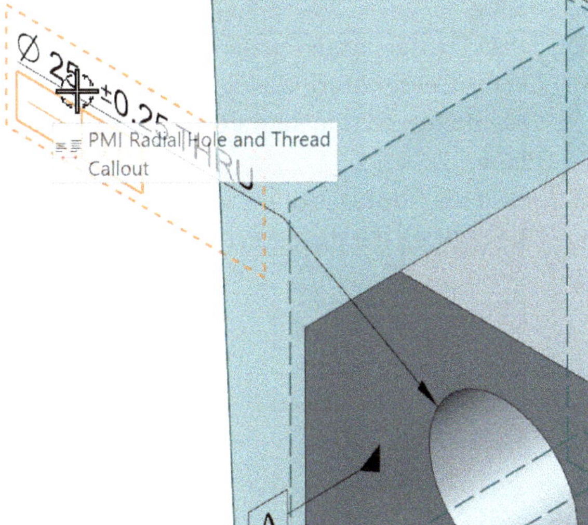

4. Click to place the **Feature Control Frame**.

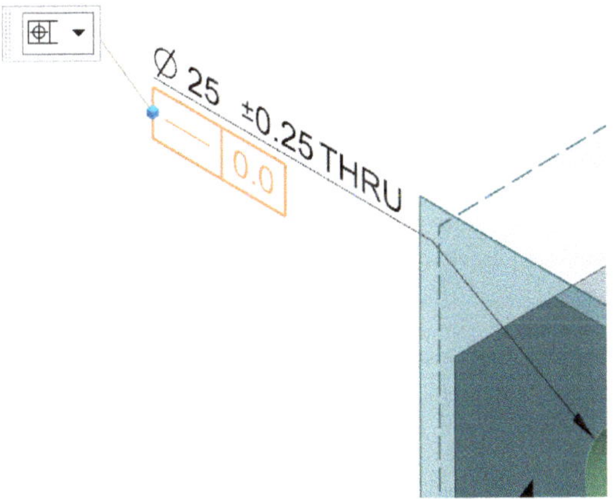

5. On the **General** tab of the ribbon, select **Characteristic > Position**.

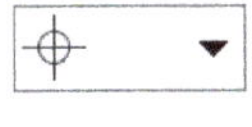

Characteris...

6. In the **Tolerance** group, set the values, as shown.

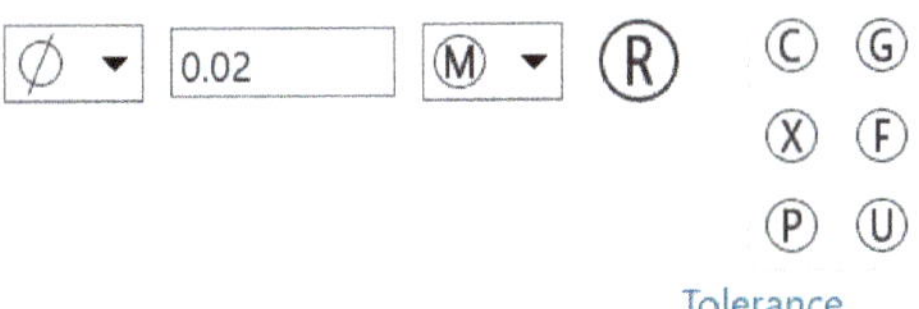

Tolerance

7. On the **Datum Reference** group, select **A** from the **Primary** drop-down.
8. Likewise, select **B** and **C** from the **Secondary** and **Tertiary** drop-down, respectively.
9. Expand the **Secondary Datum Reference**
10. Click **OK** on the dialog.
11. Activate the **Feature Control Frame** command.
12. Click the **Reset** icon on the **Feature Control Frame** dialog.
13. Select **Origin > Orientation > Specify Plane.**
14. Select the front face of the model.
15. Click **Leader > Select Terminating Object.**
16. On the **Snap Options** gallery, click the **Point on Face** icon.

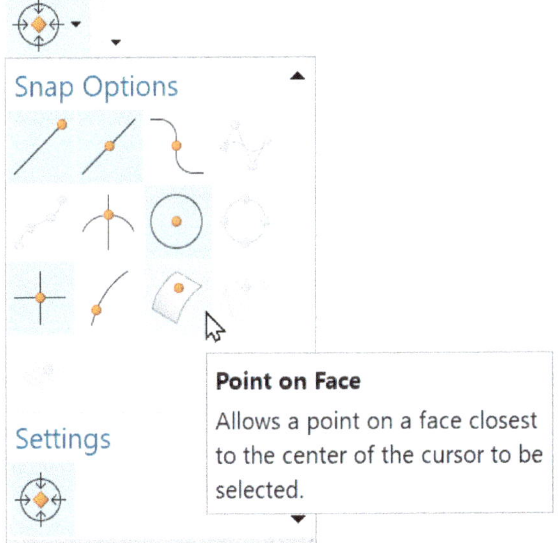

17. Click on the front face of the model.
18. Move the pointer and click to specify the location of the Feature Control Frame.

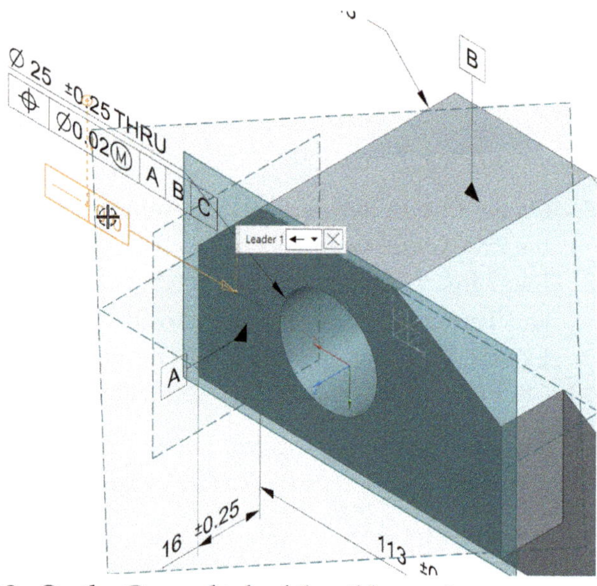

19. On the **General** tab of the ribbon, select **Characteristic > Flatness**.

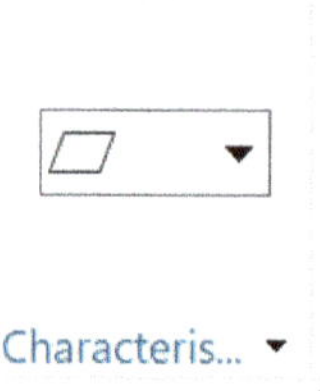

20. In the **Tolerance** group, set the values, as shown.

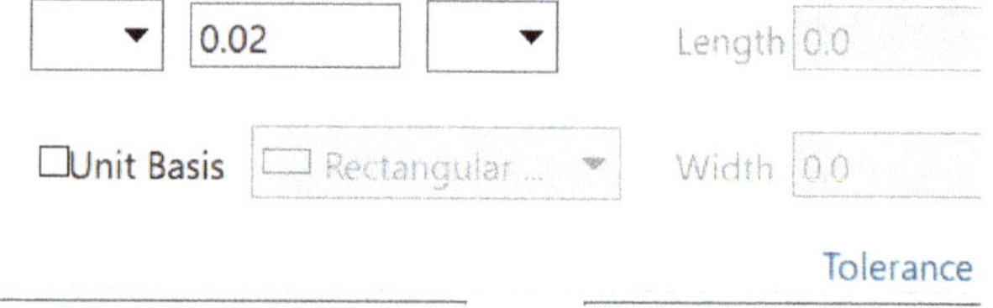

21. Click **OK** on the dialog.
22. Add two feature control frames to the faces, as shown.

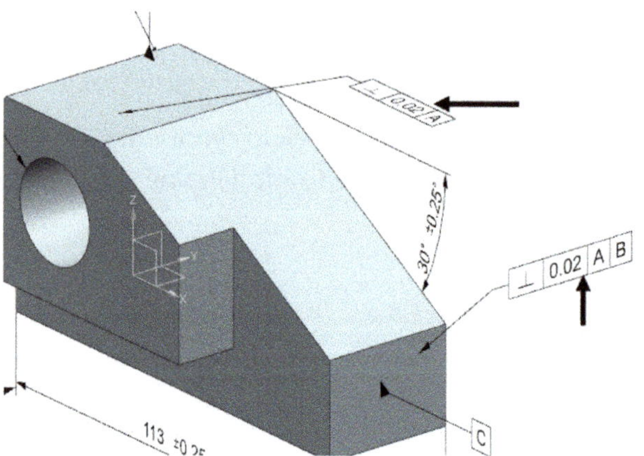

Adding centermarks

1. On the ribbon, click **PMI > Supplemental Geometry > Center Mark** .
2. Click the **Reset** icon on the **Center Mark** dialog.
3. Select the hole from the model.
4. On the **Center Mark** dialog, expand the **Orientation** section, and then click **Specify Plane**.
5. Select the front face of the model.
6. Click **OK** on the dialog to create the center mark.

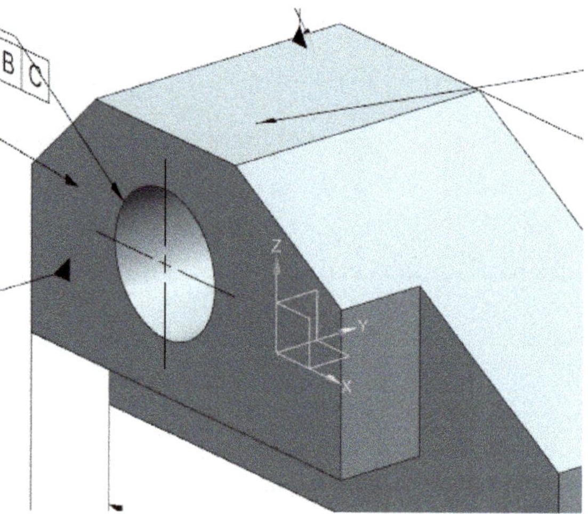

7. Add remaining dimensions to the part.

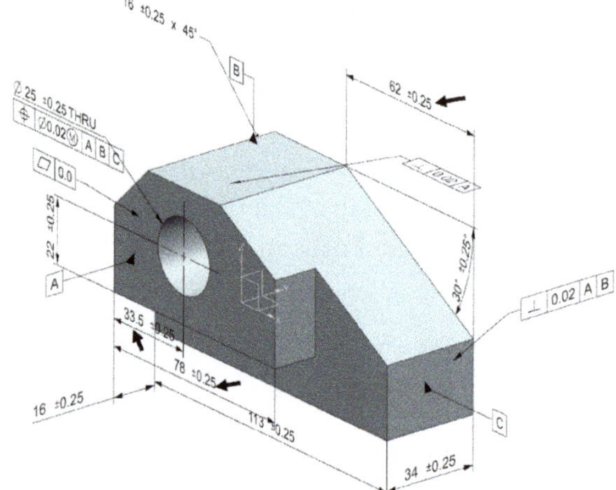

8. Save and close the file.

TUTORIAL 2 (Using the PMI data in drawings)

1. Open the Tutorial 1 part file.
2. On the ribbon, click **File** tab > **New**.
3. Click the **Drawing** tab on the **New** dialog.
4. Select **A3 - Size** from the **Templates** section, and then click **OK**.
5. Click **Close** on the **Populate Title Block** dialog.
6. On the Top Border Bar, click **Menu > Insert > View > View Creation Wizard**.
7. On the **View Creation Wizard,** click the **Inherit PMI** option located on the left side.
8. On the **Inherit PMI** page, select **Aligned to Drawing (Entire Part)**.
9. Check the **Inherit PMI onto Drawing** option.
10. Click **Next**.
11. On the **Orientation** page, select **Front** from the **Model Views** list.
12. Click **Next**.
13. On the **Layout** page, select the **Top** and **Right** views.

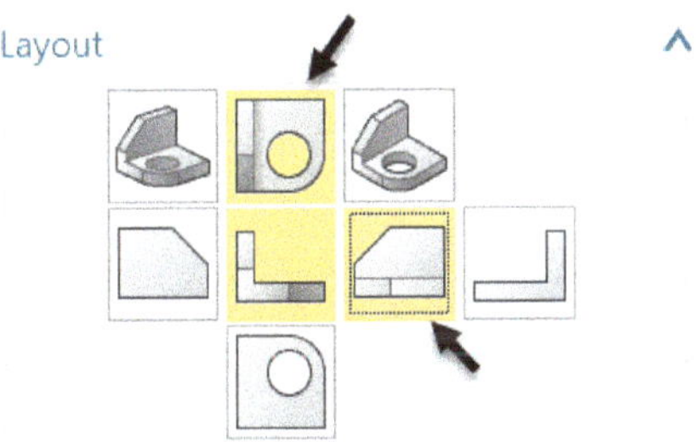

14. Under the **Placement** section, select **Option > Manual**.
15. Move the pointer and click it at the location, as shown.

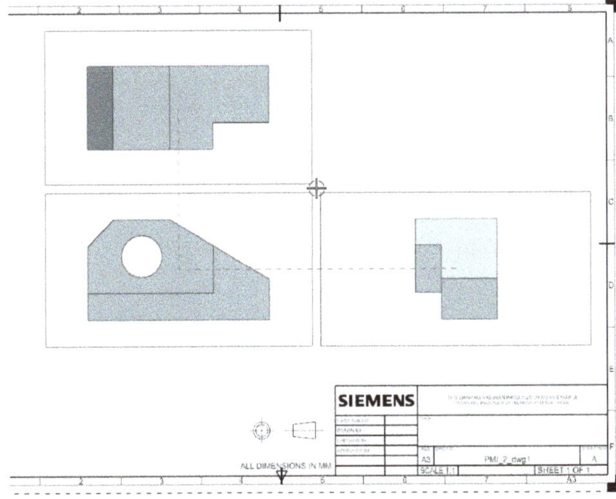

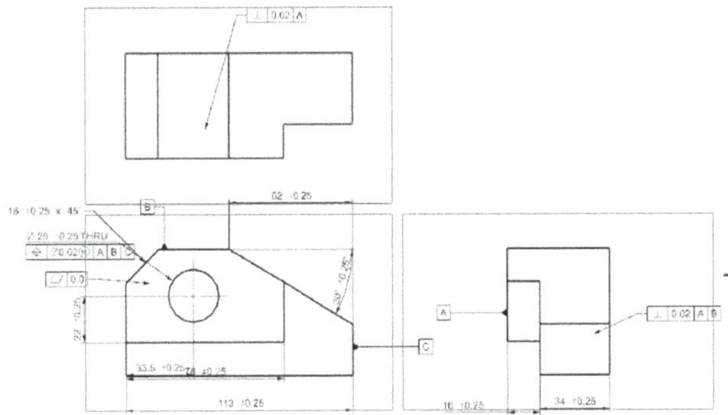

16. Adjust the dimensions by dragging them.

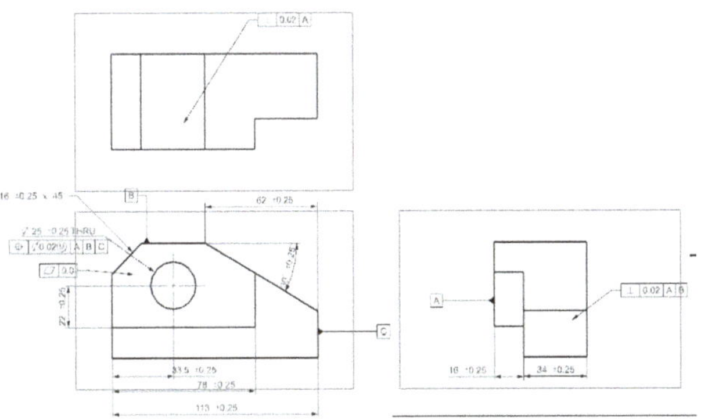

17. Save and close the drawing file.

Chapter 13: Visualization and Rendering

In this chapter, you will:

- Add Materials to the model
- Apply Backgrounds and Scenes to the model
- Render Images
- Add Cameras and Lights
- Add Decals

TUTORIAL 1 (Working in the True Shading environment)

1. Download the Visualization and Rendering part files from the Companion website and open the Tutorial 1 file.

2. On the ribbon, click **View** tab > **Display** drop-down >**True Shading**.

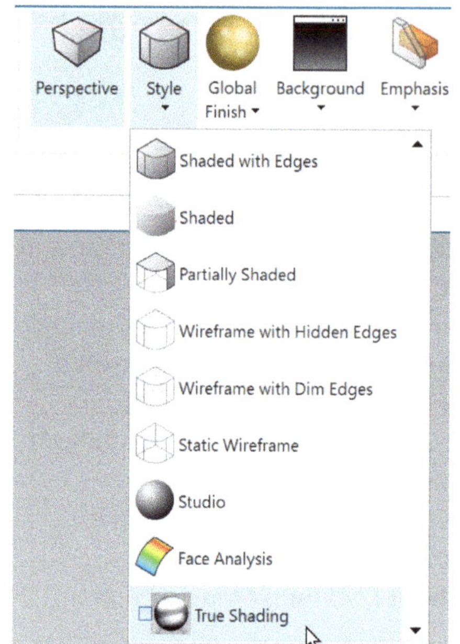

3. On the ribbon, click the down arrow on the **True Shading Setup** panel, and then select the **Object Materials Gallery** drop-down option; the **Object Materials** gallery is displayed on the **True Shading Setup** panel.

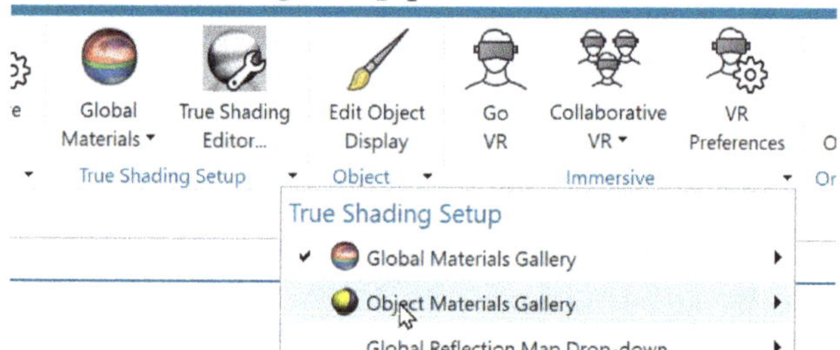

4. On the Top Border Bar, select **Type Filter > Face**.

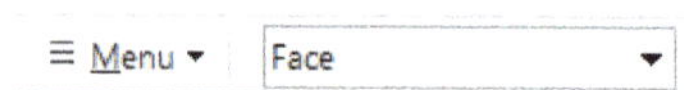

5. Click on the flat face and edge fillet of the model, as shown.

6. On the ribbon, click **View** tab > **True Shading Setup** > **Object Materials** gallery > **White Glossy Plastic**.

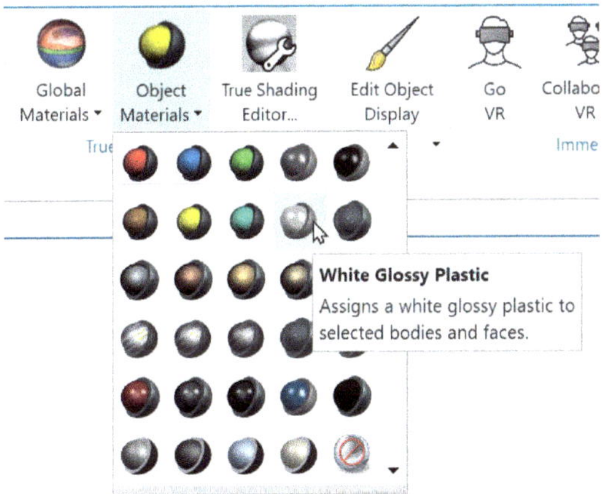

7. Click on the edge fillet, as shown.

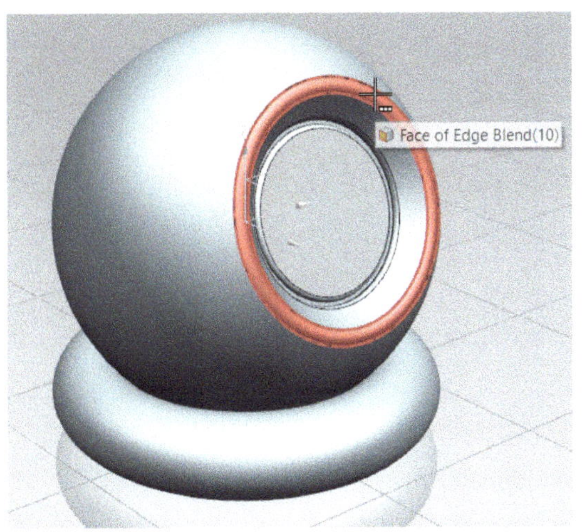

8. Select **White Glossy Plastic** from the **Object Materials** gallery.

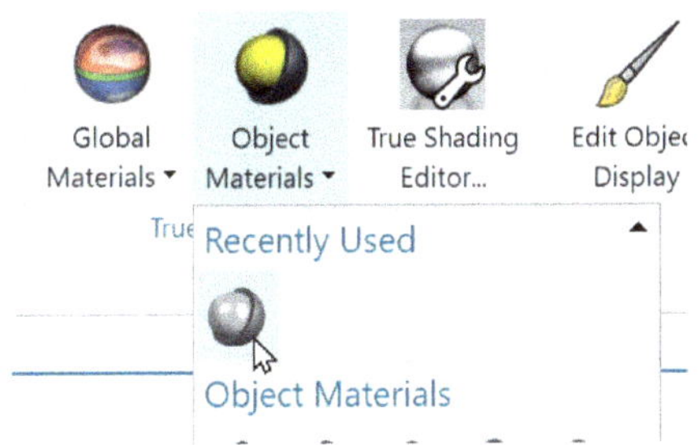

9. Select the faces of the model, as shown.

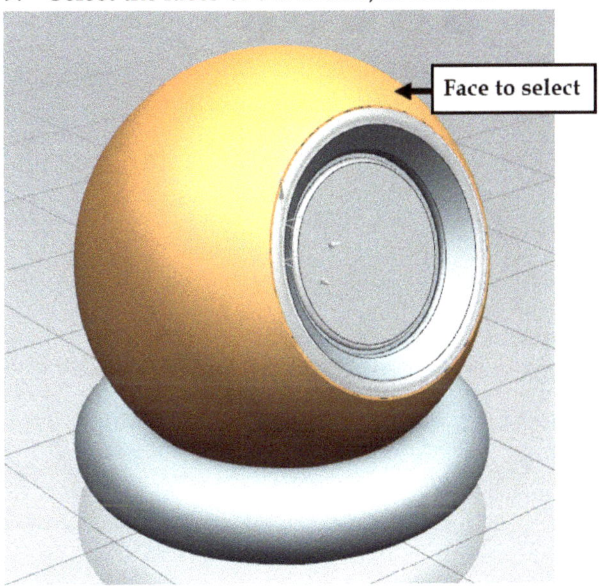

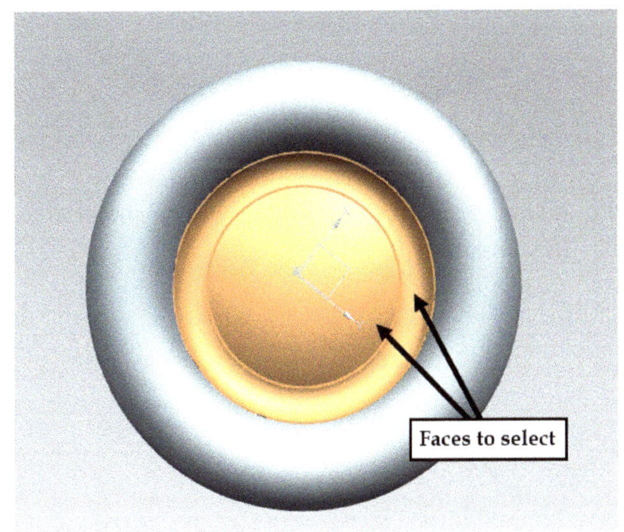

10. On the ribbon, click **View tab > True Shading Setup > Object Materials** gallery **> Red Glossy Plastic.**

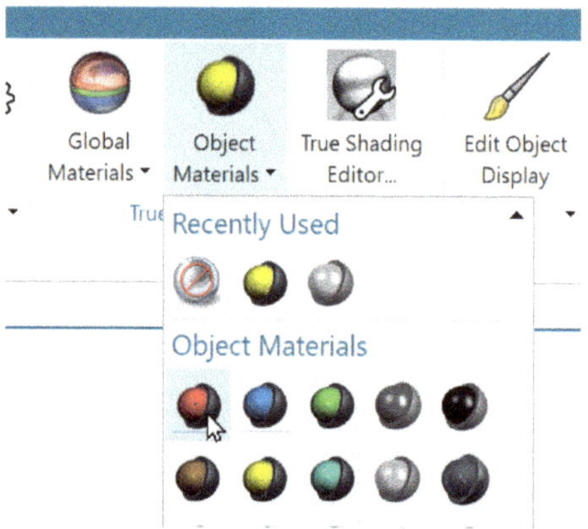

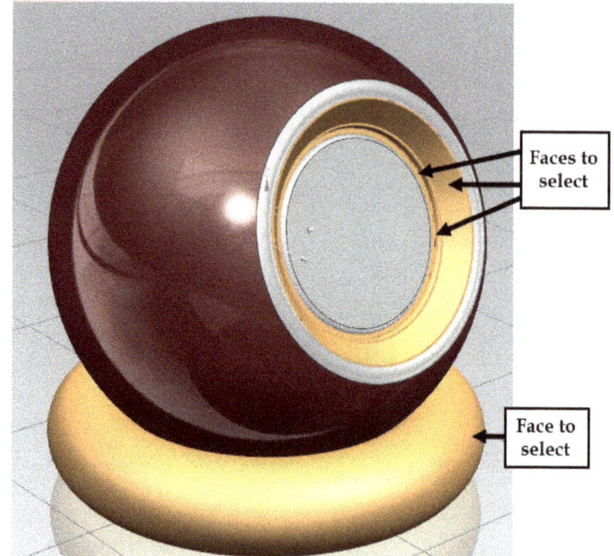

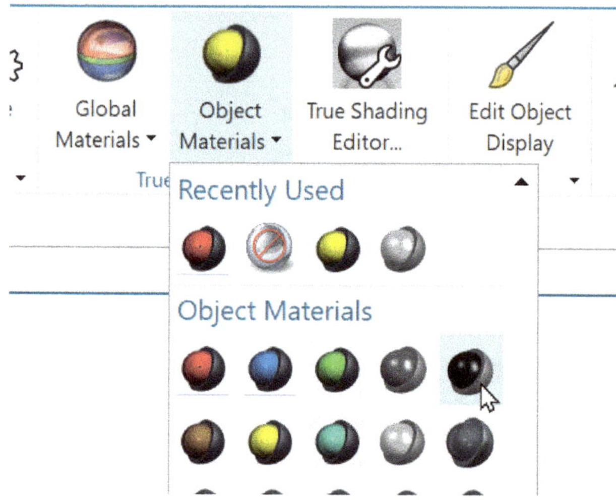

11. Likewise, apply **Black Glossy Plastic** material to the remaining faces

12. On the ribbon, click the down arrow available on the **True Shading Setup** panel of the **View** tab.
13. Select the **Background** drop-down option; the Background drop-down is displayed on the **True Shading Setup** panel.

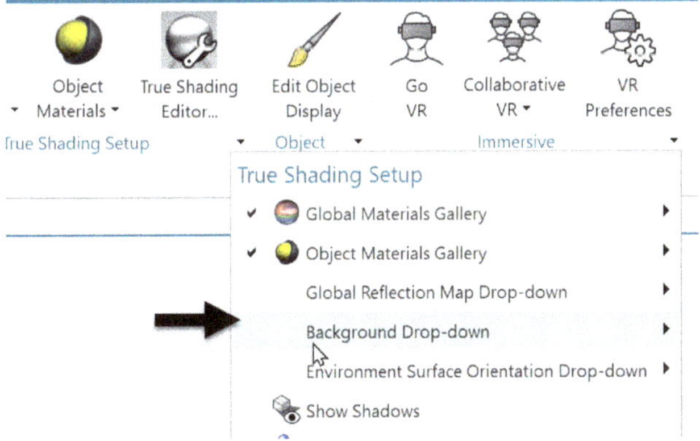

14. On the ribbon, click **View** tab > **True Shading Setup** > **Background** drop-down > **Inherit Shaded Background**.

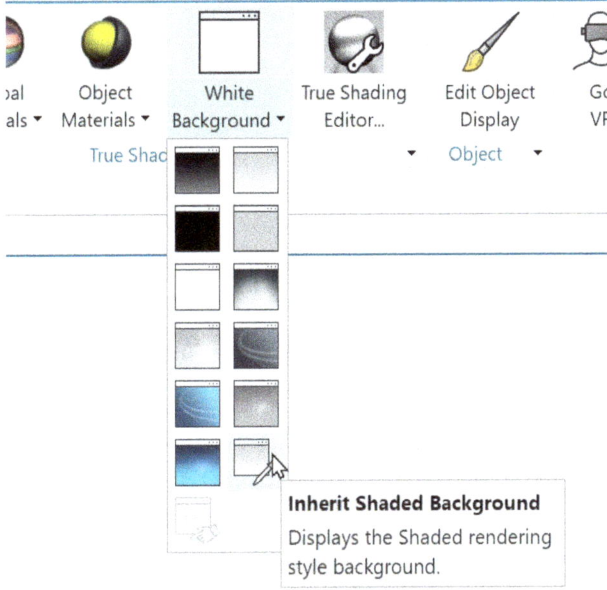

15. On the ribbon, click **View** tab > **True Shading Setup** > **True Shading Editor**; the **True Shading Editor** dialog pops up on the screen.

In this dialog, you set all the options related to the True Shading environment. The **Global Reflections** section has options to display the material with different reflections.

The **Floor** section has the options to modify the environment surface. The **Orientation** drop-down has the options to change the orientation of the environment surface to **Bottom**, **Back**, or **Bottom Fixed**.

The **Bottom** option displays a floating environment surface at the bottom. When you rotate the model, the environment surface changes its orientation along with the model.

The **Back** option displays the shadow of the model on a fixed back plane.

The **Bottom Fixed** option displays the shadow and reflection of the model on a fixed bottom plane.

The **Specify Plane** option helps you to change the orientation of the environment surface by creating a new plane.

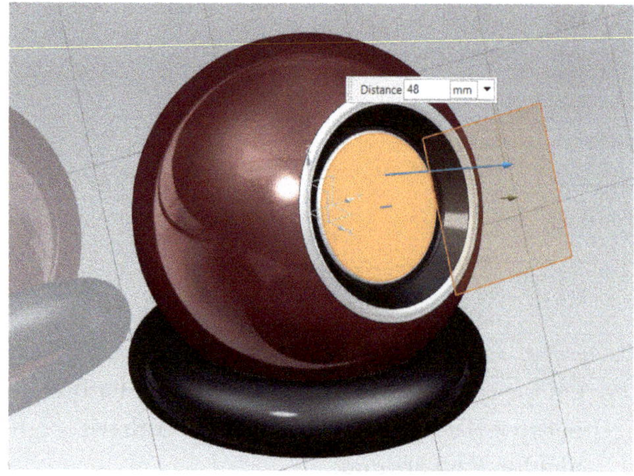

The **Offset** slider helps you to offset the environment surface.

16. On the **True Shading Editor** dialog, under the **Background** section, select **Background Type > White**.
17. Expand the **Lights** section, and then drag the **Brightness** slider to change the brightness of the lights.

The **Active Scene Lights** drop-down has five different settings.

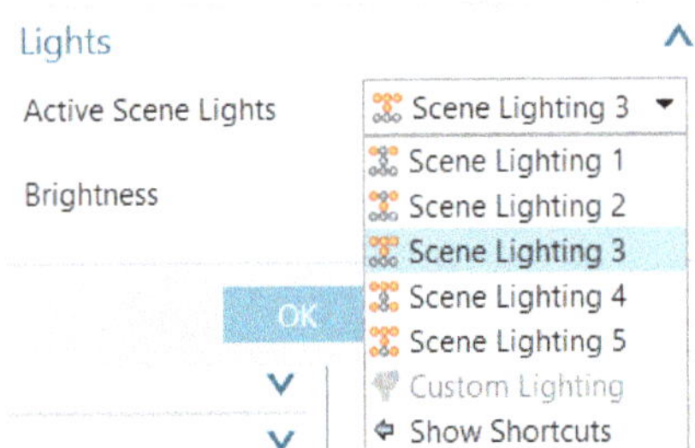

18. Click **OK** on the dialog.
19. Save and close the part file.

Tutorial 2 (Assigning Visual materials)

1. Download the Visualization and Rendering part files from the Companion website and open the Tutorial 2 file.
2. On the ribbon, click **Render** tab > **Setup > Assign Visual Materials** .
3. On the Top Border Bar, select the **Type Filter > Solid Body**.

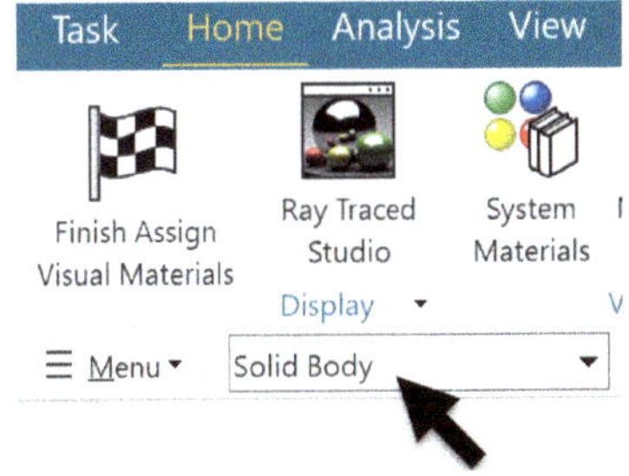

4. On the ribbon, click **Home > Visual Material > System Materials** ; the **System Studio Materials** tab of the **Resource Bar** appears.
5. Click on the model geometry.
6. On the **System Studio Materials** tab, click **Metal > Silver**.

The selected material is added to the whole part.

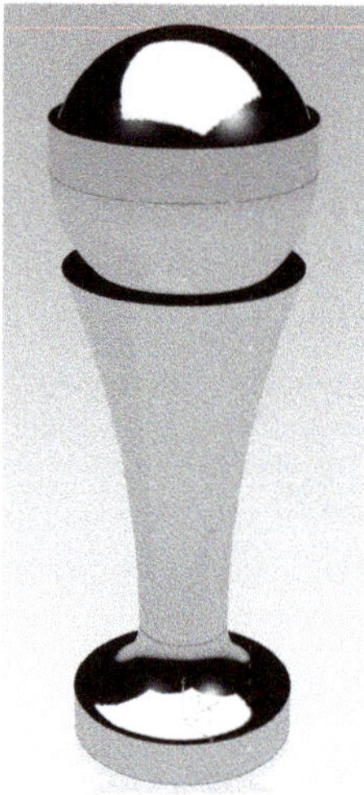

7. Click the **Materials in Part** icon on the **Visual Material** panel of the **Home** tab.

Also, notice the **Silver** material on the **Studio Materials in Part** tab of the **Resource Bar**.

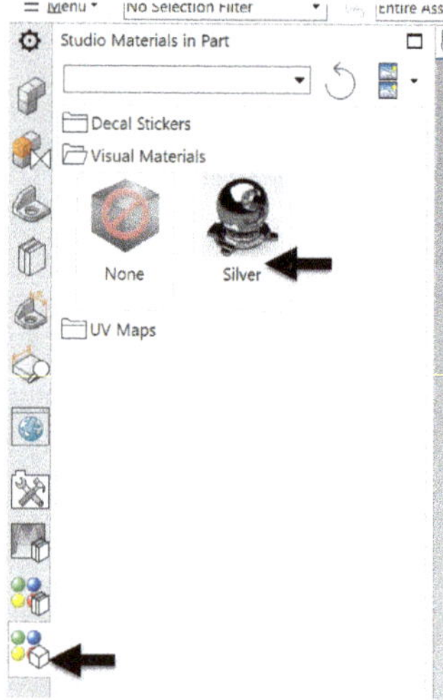

8. On the Top Border Bar, click **Type Filter > Face.**
9. Click on the faces of the model, as shown.

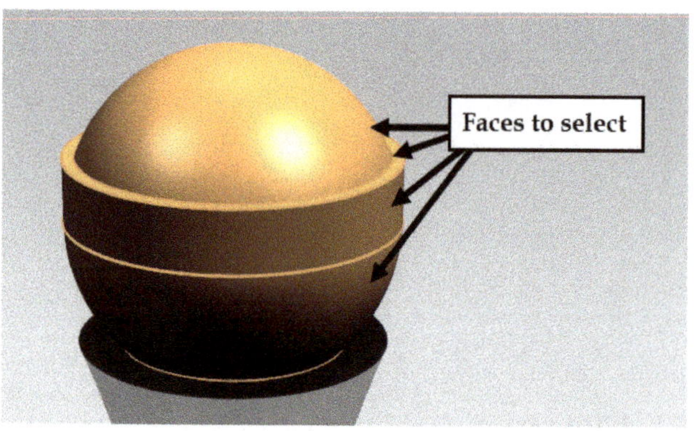

10. On the **System Studio Materials** tab, click **Metal > Gold**.

11. Click the **Studio Materials in Part** tab on the Resource Bar.
12. Click the right mouse button on the **Gold** material, and then select **Edit**.

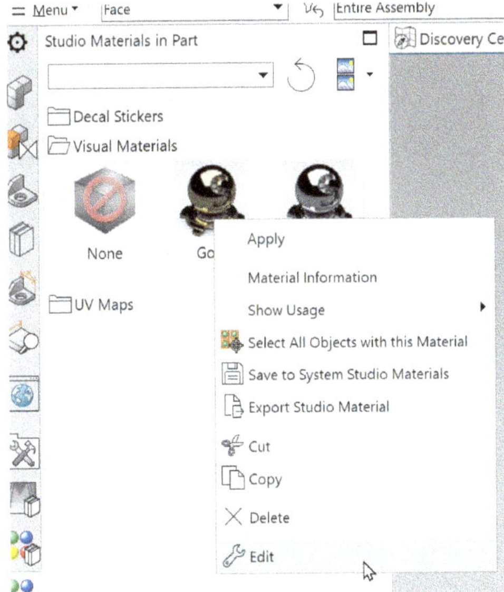

13. Select **Parameters > Finish** in the tree view.
14. Under the **Reflectance** section, drag the **Roughness** dragger to change the roughness value.

Place the pointer on the **Roughness** option and notice the illustration. It shows the level of smoothness from the value that enter in the **Value** box.

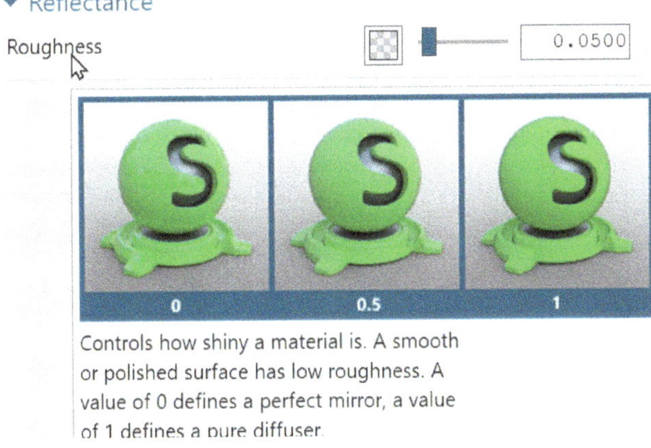

15. Click **OK**.
16. Click **Finish Assign Visual Materials** on the ribbon.
17. Save and close the part file.

Tutorial 3 (Scenes)

After adding materials, a Scene is an essential part of the rendering process. Material is added to the geometry, whereas a Scene is added to the NX environment. A Scene creates a realistic environment in which the model is placed. For example, you can add a road scene to a car model.

1. Open the Tutorial 3 file.

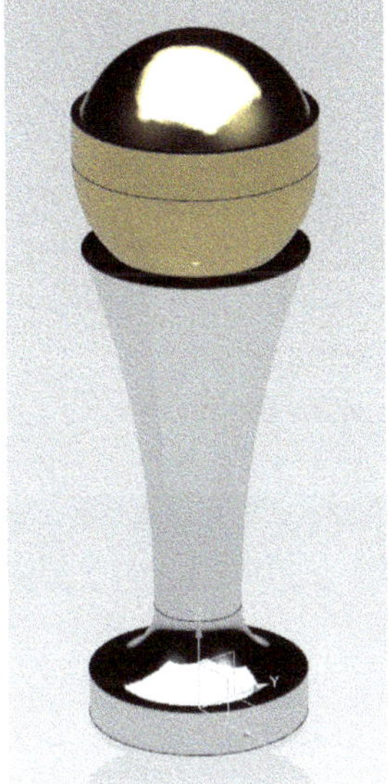

2. Right-click and select **Orient View** Drop-down > **Trimetric**.
3. On the Resource Bar, click the **System Scenes** tab.
4. On the **System Scenes** tab, notice the three folders: **Indoor**, **Outdoor**, and **Studio**.
5. Click on the **Indoor** folder and notice the thumbnails displayed in the Resource Bar.

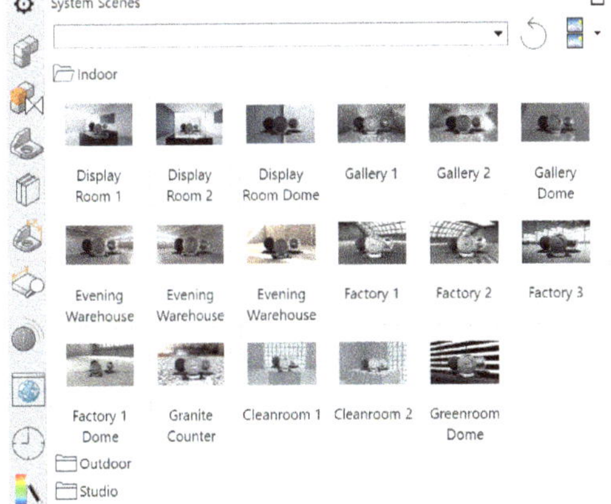

6. Double click on the **Display Room 1** scene in the Resource Bar.
7. Click the middle mouse button and drag the mouse. Notice that the background remains static.

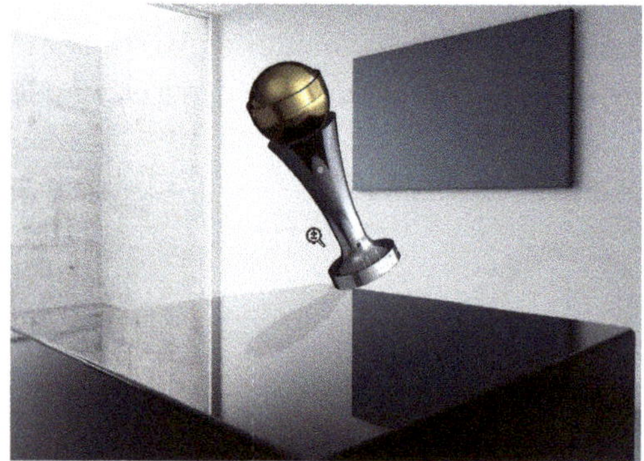

8. Select the **Factory 1 Dome** scene.
9. Rotate the model and notice that the environment rotates along with the model.

10. Likewise, examine the **Outdoor** and **Studio** folders.

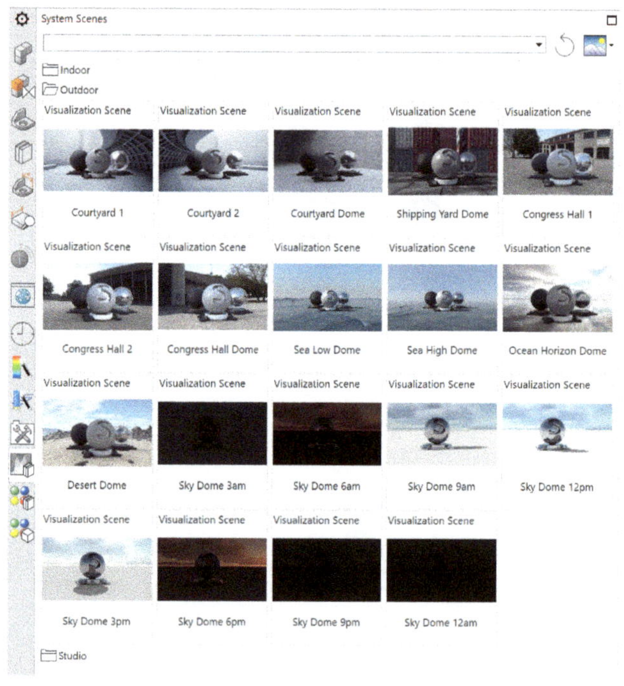

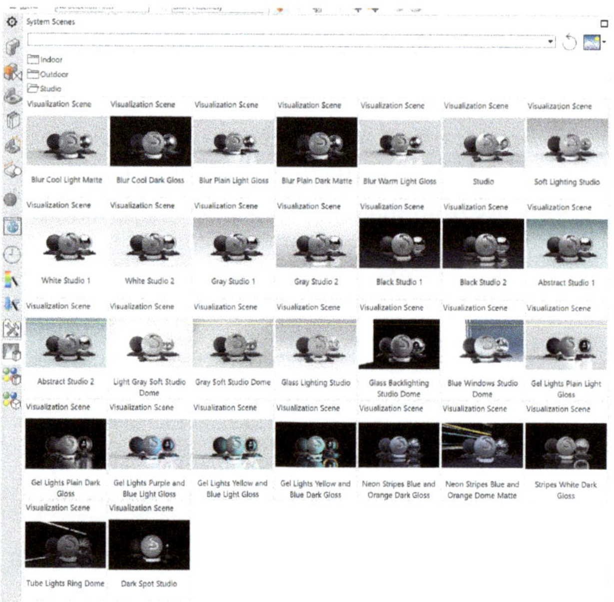

11. Close the file without saving it.

Customizing a Scene

1. Open the Tutorial 2 part file.
2. On the ribbon, click **Render > Studio Setup > Scene Preferences**.

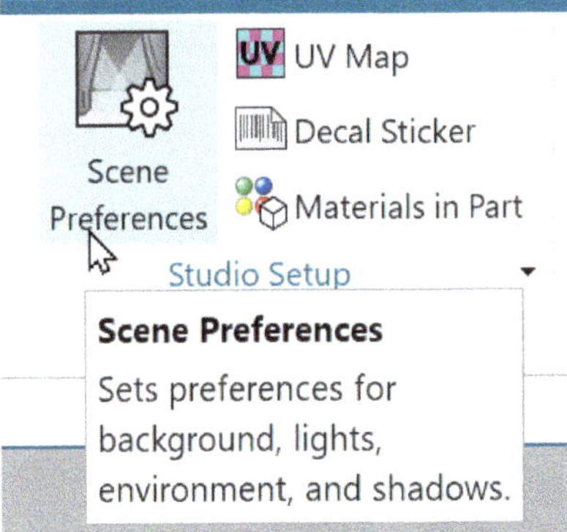

3. On the **Scene Preferences** dialog, click the **Background** option on the tree view.
4. Select the **2D Background** from the **Settings** section.
5. Select **Type > Image File.**
6. Click the **Choose from Image Palette** icon.
7. On the **Environment Image Palette** dialog, click the **Indoor** tab.
8. Select the third image from the top.

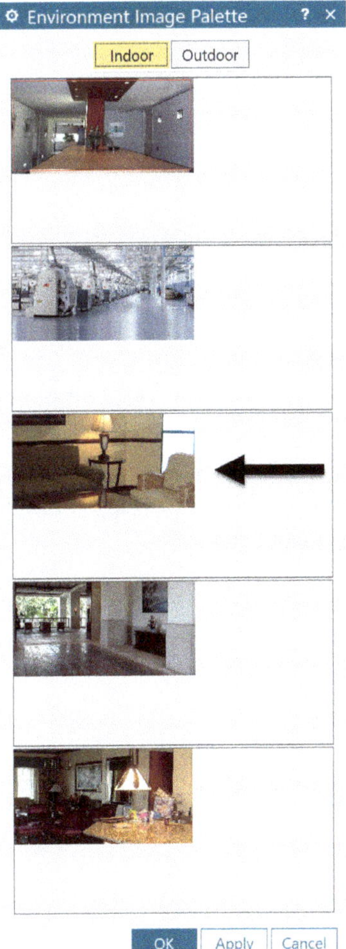

9. Click **OK**.

10. Click the **Lights** option in the tree view and click **Specify Orientation**.
11. Right-click and select the **Orient View** drop-down **> Top**.
12. Click and drag the Angle handle of the Dynamic Coordinate System such that the Light Direction points to the model.

13. Use the **Zoom**, **Pan**, **Fit**, **Orient View**, and **Rotate** tools to fit the model in the background image.

14. Drag the **Intensity** slider to adjust the light intensity.
15. Select **Soft edged** option from the **Advance Studio Shadow Type** drop-down.
16. Click **OK**.
17. Save and close the part file.

Tutorial 4

1. Open the Tutorial 4 file.

2. On the ribbon, click **Render > Setup > Assign Visual Materials.**
3. On the Resource Bar, click the **System Studio Materials** tab.
4. On the **System Studio Materials** tab, click the **Metal** folder.
5. Select the solid body from the graphics window.
6. Click **Wheel Aluminum** under the **Automotive** folder.

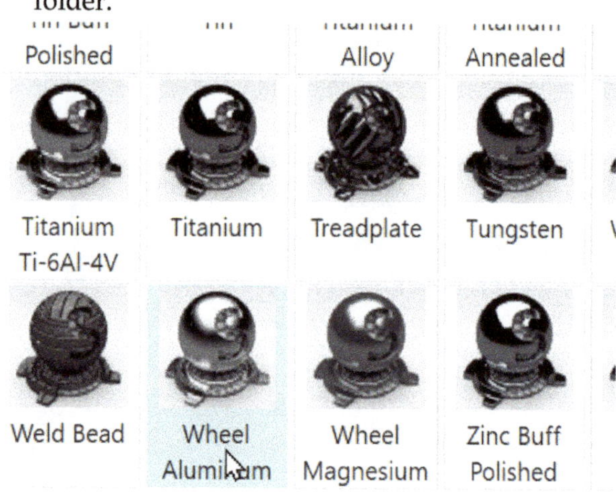

7. On the Resource Bar, click the **System Scenes** tab.
8. Click the **Studio** folder and select the **White Studio 2.**

Creating Cameras

1. On the Resource Bar, click the **Part Navigator** tab.
2. Press and hold the Shift key and select all the points and lines available in the Part Navigator.
3. Right click and select **Show.**

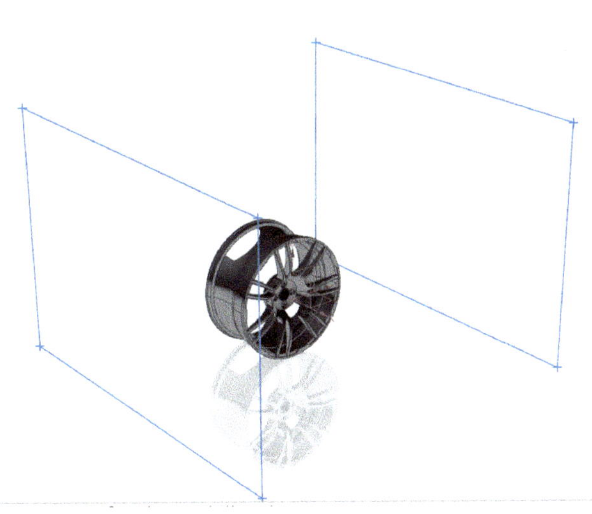

4. On the Top Border Bar, click **Orient View** drop-down > **Trimetric**.
5. In the Part Navigator, click the right mouse button on the **Cameras** node, and then select **Create**.

The **Camera** dialog appears. Also, the **Rendering Style** of the model changes to **Static Wireframe**. The resultant view is displayed in the upper right corner of the graphics window.

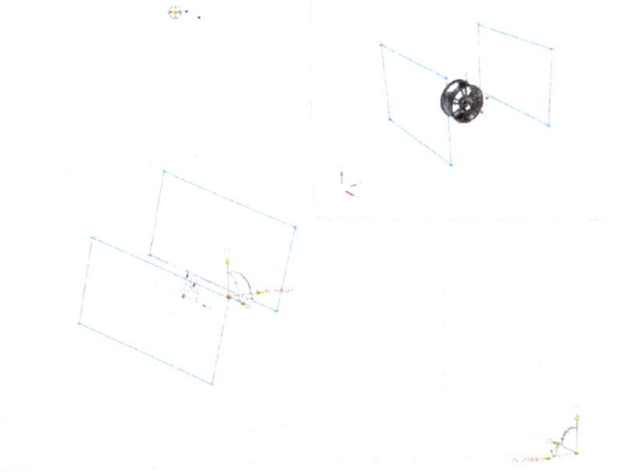

6. Right click in the graphics window, and then select **Orient View > Isometric**.

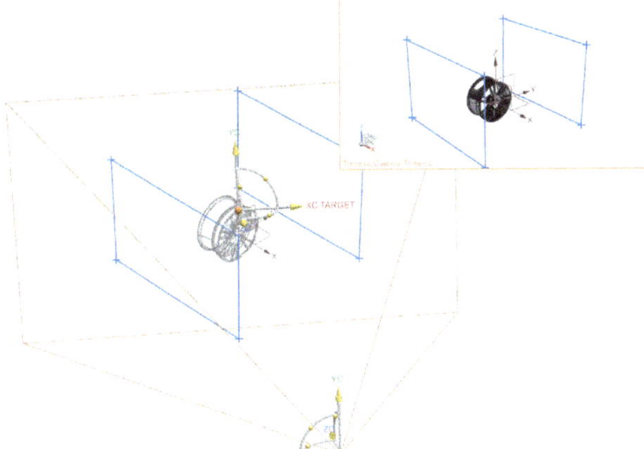

7. On the **Camera** dialog, select **Type > Perspective**.
8. Type **Position1** in the **Camera Name** box under the **Name** section.
9. Click on the origin point of the camera, and then drag. Notice that the target point of the camera is fixed.

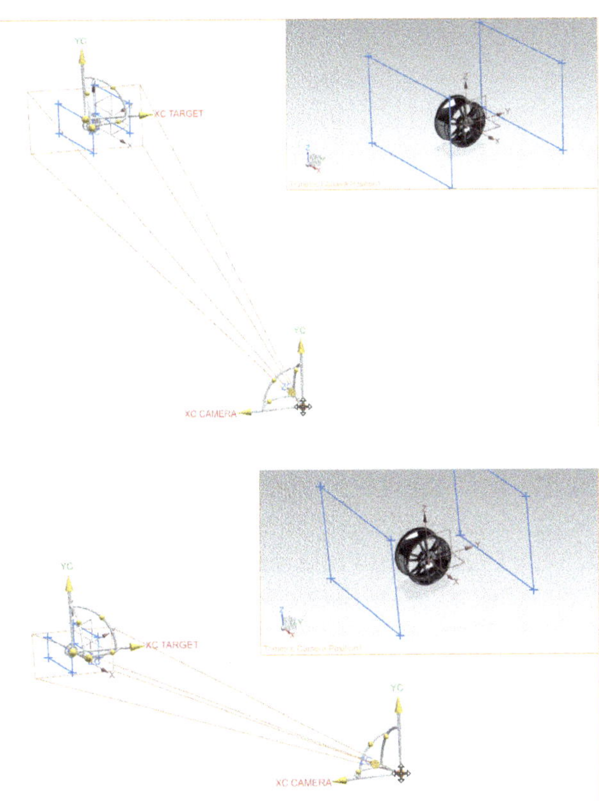

10. Check the **Move Origin with Camera** option in the **Target** section.
11. Now, click and drag the camera. Notice that the target point moves along with the camera.

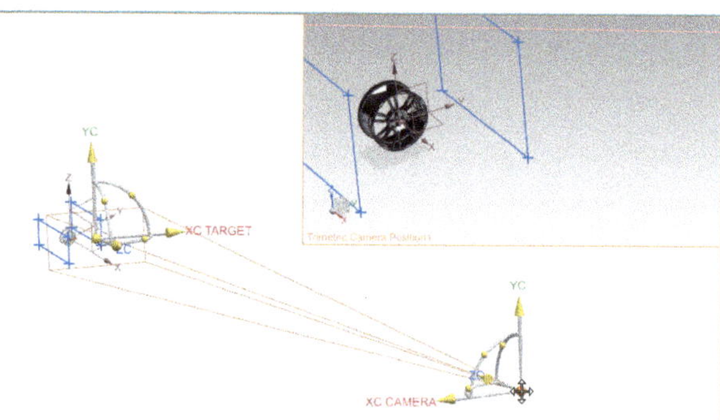

12. Likewise, click and drag the target position of the camera. Notice that the camera position is fixed. You can unlock the camera position by checking the **Move Origin with Target** option in the **Camera** section.

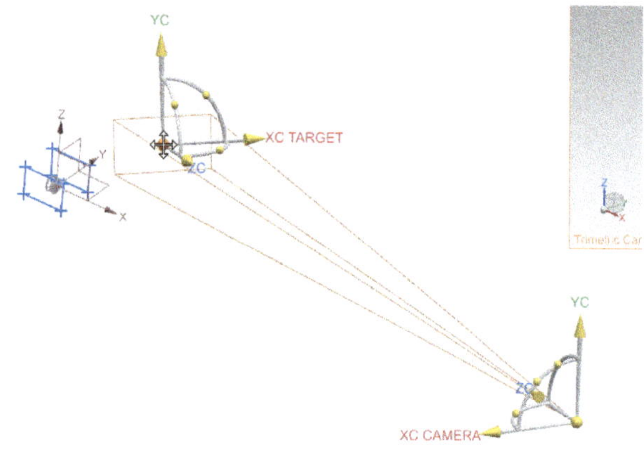

13. Click the **Point Dialog** icon in the **Target** section.
14. On the **Point** dialog, under the **Output Coordinates** section, select **Reference > WCS**.
15. Click the **Reset** icon on the **Point** dialog; the X, Y, Z values of the point are set to 0,0,0.
16. Click **OK** on the **Point** dialog.
17. Uncheck the **Move Origin with Camera** and **Move Origin with Target** options.
18. Click the **Specify Orientation** option in the **Camera** section.
19. Select the point from the graphics window, as shown.

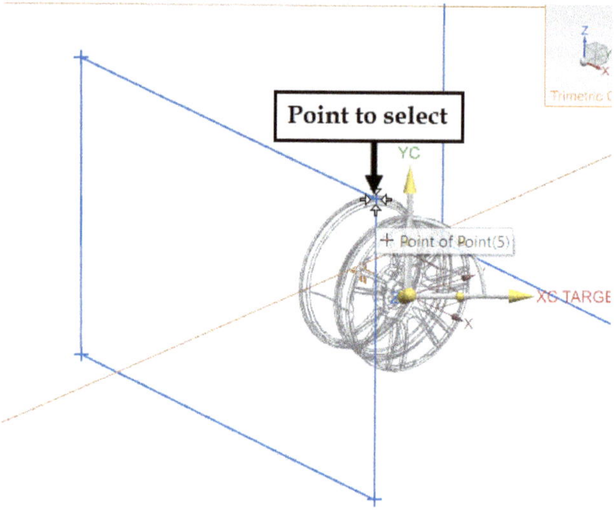

The view is updated in the window displayed at the upper right corner.

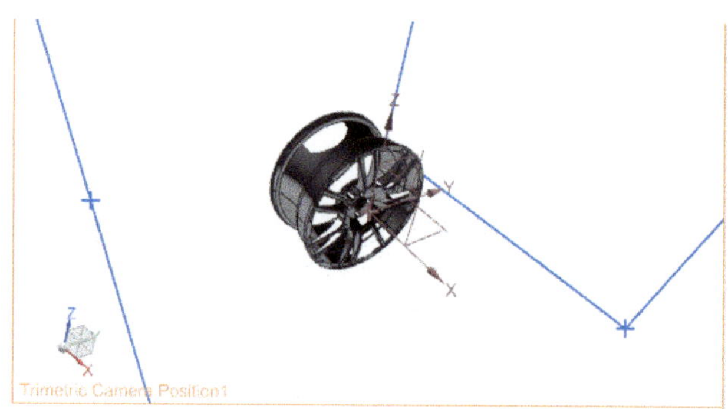

20. Expand the **Custom Zoom** section and the type 0.14 in the **Magnification** box.
21. Click **OK** on the **Camera** dialog.

In the **Part Navigator** tab, expand the **Cameras** node and notice that the **Position1** camera view is added to the list.

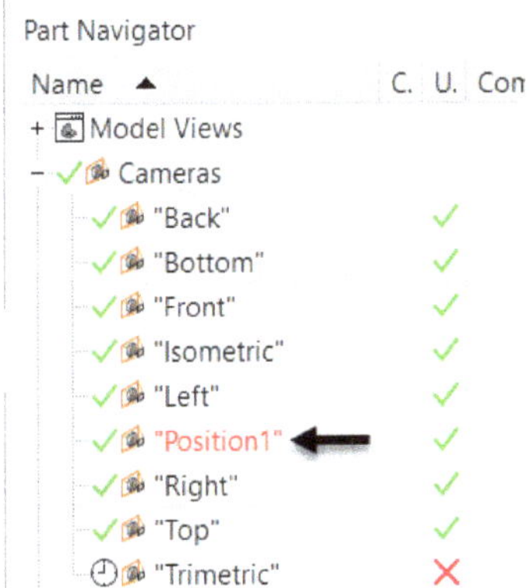

22. Likewise, create two more camera views at the positions, as shown.

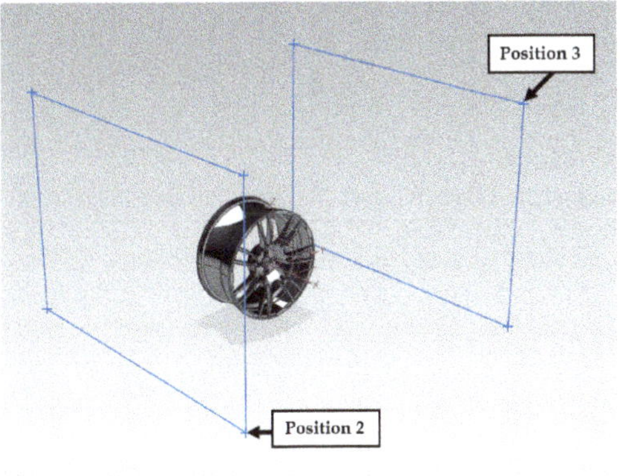

Position 2

Position 3

Rendering in Ray Traced Studio

1. In the Part Navigator, expand the **Cameras** node.
2. Double-click on the **Position2** camera to activate it.
3. On the ribbon, click **Render >Display > Ray Traced Studio**; the **Ray Traced Studio** window appears.
4. Click the **Pause** button at the upper left corner to pause the rendering.
5. Click the **Ray Traced Studio Preferences** icon.
6. On the **Ray Traced Studio** dialog, under the **Dynamic Render** section, select **Render Mode > Photoreal**.
7. Set the **File Save Format** to **JPEG**.
8. Set the **Units** to **Pixels**.
9. Set the **Size** to **Use Defined**.
10. Set the **Orientation** to **Landscape**.
11. Leave the other default options and click **OK**.
12. On the **Ray Traced Studio** window, click the **Start/Resume** icon. Notice the preview of the rendering.

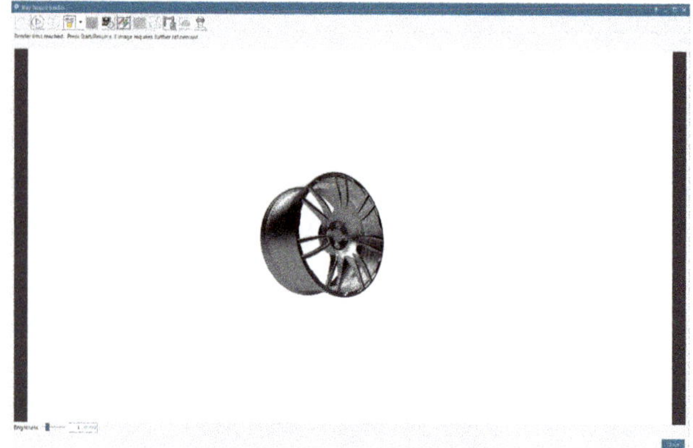

13. Click and drag the **Brightness** slider to change the brightness of the rendered image.
14. Zoom in or out using the mouse scroll wheel. Notice that the rendering starts from the beginning.
15. Double-click on the **Positon2** camera in the Part Navigator.
16. On the **Ray Traced Studio** window, click the **Start Static Image** icon. This option renders a high-quality image at the current camera position. The rendering will continue even if you change the orientation or camera position in the graphics window.
17. Wait until the image is rendered.
18. Click the **Save Image** icon to save the image.
19. On the **Save Image** dialog, click the **Browse** icon and specify the location of the image file.
20. Click **OK** on the **Save Image** dialog.
21. Close the **Ray Traced Studio** window.

22. Save and close the part file.

Tutorial 5

Lights are essential in rendering a photorealistic image. They can enhance the image to look more realistic by highlighting some portions and creating shadows. You can access the lights on the **Scene Preferences** and **Advanced Lights** dialogs.

Working with Scene Preferences dialog

1. Open the Tutorial 5 file.
2. On the ribbon, click **View > Display > More > Scene Preferences.**
3. On the **Scene Preferences** dialog, click the **Lights** option in the tree view.
4. Drag the **Scene Dimmer** dragger to make the scene lighter or darker.

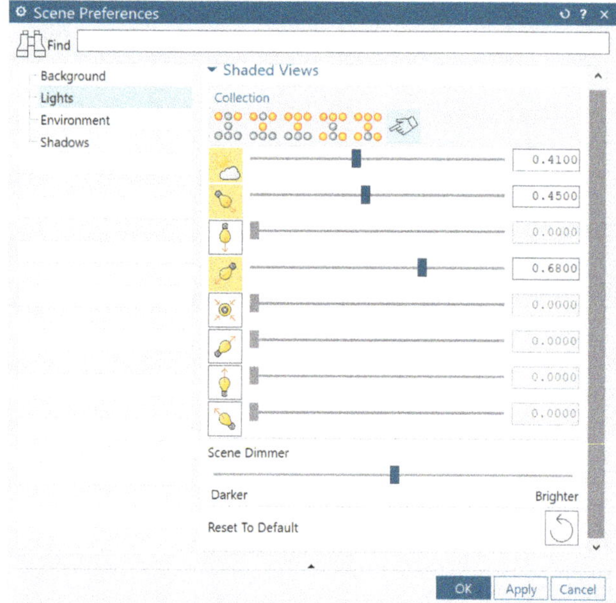

5. On the **Scene Preference** dialog, click the **Reset to Default** button. Notice that **Light Collection 4** is activated.

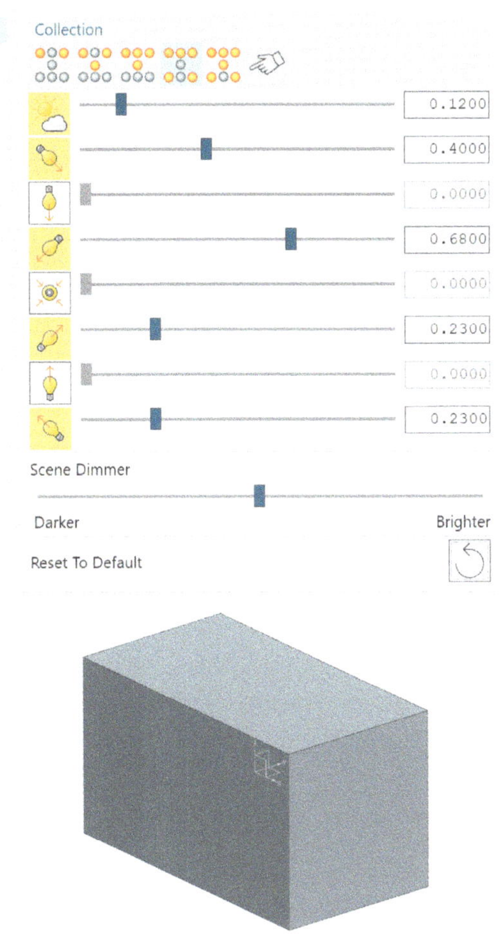

6. Drag the sliders of the lights to change their intensity.
7. Click **OK** on the dialog to apply the changes.

Tutorial 6 (Working with directional Lights)

NX adds directional lights to the model automatically. It is used to highlight a portion of the geometry and display shadows. You can add, delete, move, or adjust a directional light.

1. Open the Tutorial 6 file.

2. On the Top Border Bar, click **Menu > View > Visualization > Advanced Lights** .
3. On the **Advanced Lights** dialog, click the **Scene Ambient** icon in the **On** section. The ambient light falls on the model from all directions.
4. Click the **Turn Light OFF** icon.

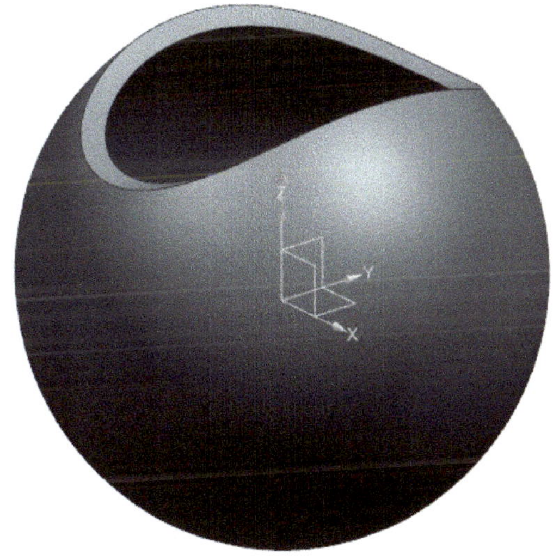

5. Likewise, turn OFF the **Scene Left Top** and **Scene Right Top** lights on the **Advanced Lights** dialog.

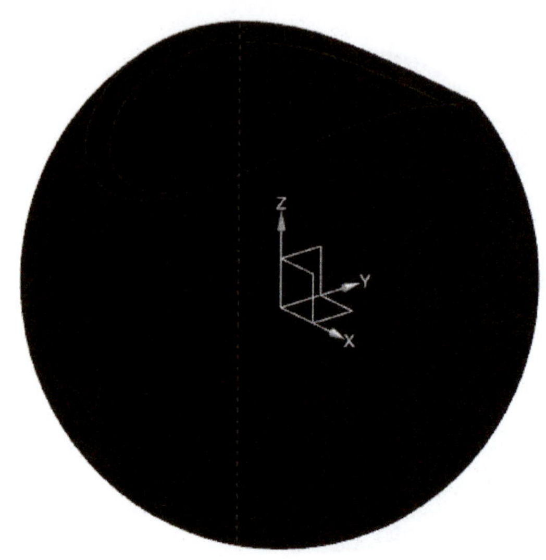

Note that the directional lights are also turned ON or OFF based on the type of scene.

6. Click **Cancel** on the **Advanced Lights** dialog.
7. On the **System Scenes** tab of Resource Bar, select the **Studio** folder, and then select the **White Studio 1** scene.
8. On the ribbon, click **Studio Setup > More > Advanced Lights.**
9. On the **Advanced Lights** dialog, under the **Orient Light** section, select **Show > All Lights.** Notice two directional lights related to the selected scene.

10. Select the **Scene Front** light from the **Off** section.
11. Click the **Turn light ON** icon.

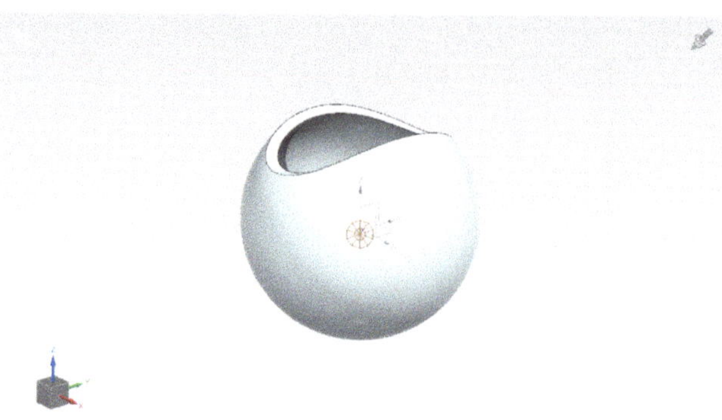

12. Select the **Scene Front** light from the **On** section.
13. On the **Advanced Lights** dialog, under the **Basic Settings** section, click the **Color** swatch.
14. On the **Color** dialog, select the red color, and then click **OK.**
15. Drag the **Intensity** slider to 1.0 position.
16. Press and hold the middle mouse button, and drag the mouse; the model view rotates. Notice that the **Scene Front** light also rotates along with the model.

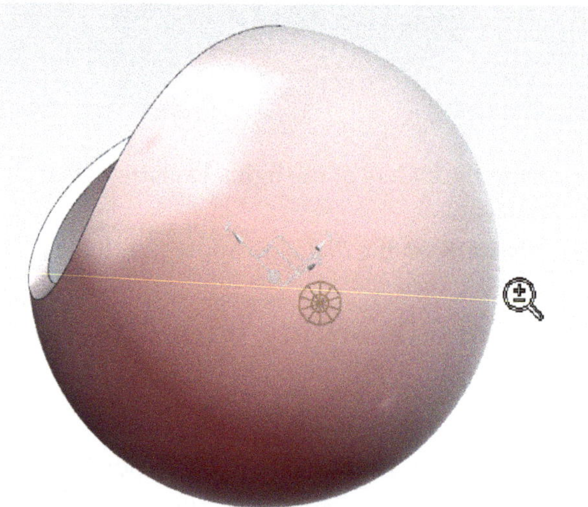

17. Click **OK** on the **Advanced Lights** dialog.
18. On the ribbon, click **Studio Setup > Scene Preferences.**
19. On the **Scene Preferences** dialog, click the **Environment** tab.
20. Under the **Advanced Studio Settings** section, check the **Use with Real Time Image-based Lighting** option.
21. Click **OK.**

22. On the ribbon, click **Home > Display > Ray Traced Studio**. Notice that the image is rendered with the **Scene Front** light.

23. Close the **Ray Traced Studio** window.
24. Close the part file without saving it.

TUTORIAL 7 (Decal Sticker)

NX allows you to add images such as logos to your model by using the **Decal Sticker** command. Adding decals makes the rendered model look more realistic.

Adding a Decal sticker and embossing it

1. Open the Tutorial 7 part file.
2. Download the decal_sticker.jpg from the companion website.
3. On the ribbon, click **Render > Studio Setup > Decal Sticker** .
4. On the **Decal Sticker** dialog, under the **Image** section, click the **Choose Image File** icon.
5. Go to the location of the decal_sticker.jpg file and double-click on it.
6. On the **Decal Sticker** dialog, under the Image section, check the **Preview** option.
7. Under the **Target** section, click **Select Face or Body**, and then click on the face, as shown.

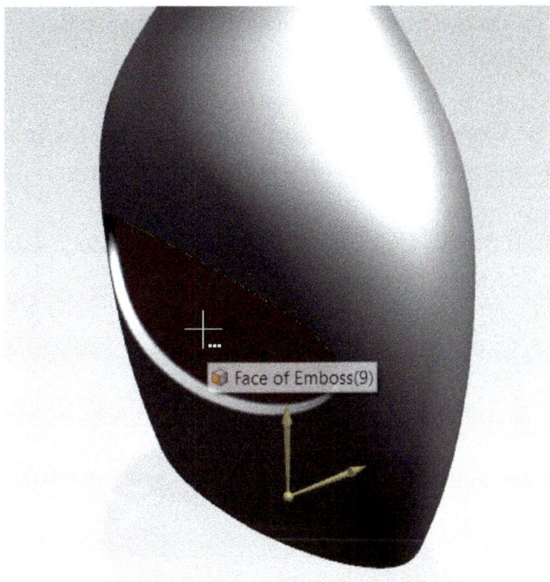

8. Right click in the graphics window and select **Orient View > Front**.
9. On the **Decal Sticker** dialog, under the **Mapping** section, select **Anchor Type > Middle Center**.
10. Click the **Specify Orientation** option, and then select **Point on Face** from the **Snap Options** gallery.
11. Click on the approximate center of the embossed face.

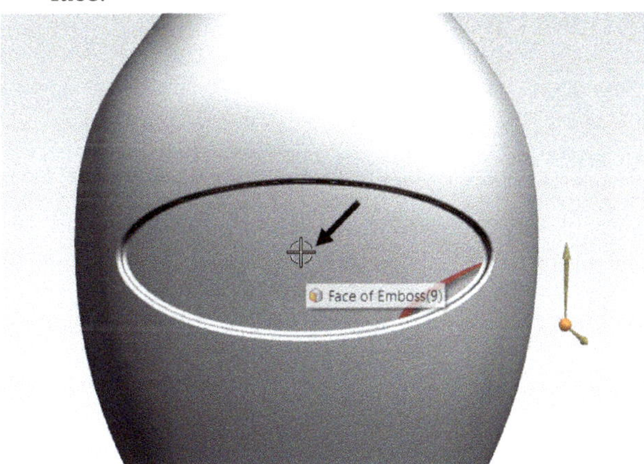

12. Under the **Size** section, select **Scaling Method > User Defined**.

You can also select the **Image Size** option from the **Scaling Method**.

The **Image Size** option scales the image to its original size.

The **User-Defined** option is used to scale the image by specifying the **Width** and **Height** values.

13. Use the scale handles to increase or decrease the size of the image.

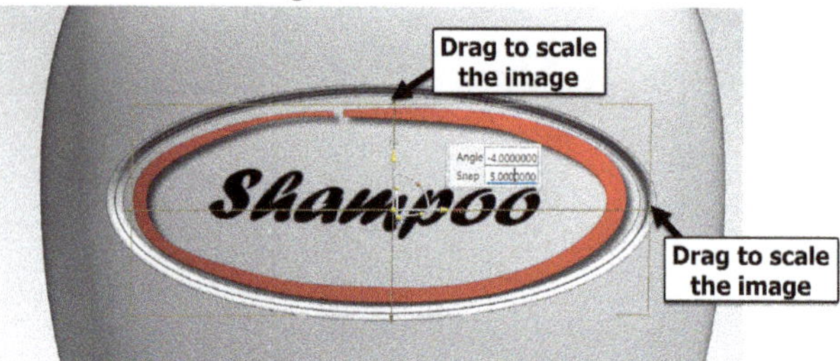

14. Check the **Lock Aspect Ratio** option, if you want to lock the aspect ratio of the image.
15. Use the handles of the Dynamic CSYS to move and rotate the image.
16. On the **Decal Sticker** dialog, under the **Settings** section, select Transparency > Pixel Color.
17. Set the **Pixel Color Tolerance** value to **50**; the edges of the image are refined.
18. Select **Reflectivity > Plastic**.
19. Check the **Bump** option.
20. Set the **Strength** value to 0.2
21. Click **OK**.

22. Save and close the file.

Index